Freedom of Religion at Stake

CHURCH OF SWEDEN
Research Series

Church of Sweden Research Series (CSRS) is interdisciplinary and peer-reviewed. The series publishes research that engages in topics and themes in the intersection between church, academy, and society.

Editor of the CSRS: Jonas Ideström

Freedom of Religion at Stake

Competing Claims among
Faith Traditions, States, and Persons

DION A. FORSTER,
ELISABETH GERLE,
and
GÖRAN GUNNER,
editors

PICKWICK *Publications* · Eugene, Oregon

FREEDOM OF RELIGION AT STAKE
Competing Claims among Faith Traditions, States, and Persons

Church of Sweden Research Series 18

Pickwick Publications
An Imprint of Wipf and Stock Publishers
199 W. 8th Ave., Suite 3
Eugene, OR 97401

www.wipfandstock.com

PAPERBACK ISBN: 978-1-5326-6056-6
HARDCOVER ISBN: 978-1-5326-6057-3
EBOOK ISBN: 978-1-5326-6058-0

Cataloguing-in-Publication data:

Names: Fortster, Dion, editor | Gerle, Elisabeth, editor. | Gunner, Göran, editor.

Title: Freedom of religion at stake : competing claims among faith traditions, states, and persons / edited by Dion Forster, Elisabeth Gerle, and Göran Gunner.

Description: Eugene, OR: Pickwick Publications, 2019 | Series: Church of Sweden Research Series 18 | Includes bibliographical references.

Identifiers: ISBN 978-1-5326-6056-6 (paperback) | ISBN 978-1-5326-6057-3 (hardcover) | ISBN 978-1-5326-6058-0 (ebook)

Subjects: LCSH: Freedom of religion. | Religion and politics. | Church and state. | Religious tolerance.

Classification: BL65.P7 F74 2019 (print) | BL65.P7 (ebook)

Manufactured in the U.S.A.   OCTOBER 30, 2019

Contents

List of Tables and Figures

List of Abbreviations

AIC	African Independent Churches
ANC	African National Congress
ATR	African Traditional Religion
CEC	Conference of European Churches
CoE	Council of Europe
CRC	Convention of the Rights of the Child
CRL	Comission for the Promotion and Protection of the Rights of Cultural, Religious, and Linguistic Communities
DCMI	Dominion Chapel Ministries International
ECHR	European Convention on Human Rights
ECtHR	European Court of Human Rights
EKD	Evangelical Church in Germany
EU	European Union
FGM	Female Genital Mutilation
GDP	Gross Domestic Product
HBTQIA	Homosexual, bisexual, trans, queer, intersex, a-sexual
ICCPR	International Covenant on Civil and Political Rights
LGBTIQ+	Lesbian, gay, bisexual, transsexual, intersex, queer, asexual, and gender-nonconforming

MCSA	Methodist Church of Southern Africa
NGO	Non-Governmental Organization
NP	South African National Party
OGOD	Organisasie vir Godsdienste-Onderrig en Demokrasie
OLS	Ordinary Least Squares
OSCE	Organization for Security and Co-operation in Europe
SACC	South African Council of Churches
SACRRF	South African Charter of Religious Rights and Freedoms
SALRC	South African Law Reform Commission
SDA	Seventh Day Adventists
STIAS	Stellenbosch Institute for Advanced Study
SWEM	Soul Winners Evangelistic Ministry
TRC	Truth and Reconciliation
UDHR	Universal Declaration of Human Rights
UN	United Nations
WVS	World Values Survey

Structure of the Book and Contributors

This book—*Freedom of Religion at Stake: Competing Claims among Faith Traditions, States, and Persons*—is divided into four parts. PART I: Religious freedom in different settings; PART II: Perspectives from Kenya; PART III: Perspectives from South Africa; and PART IV: Perspectives from Europe.

The contributors to the book are:

Dion Forster, Professor of Public Theology and Ethics and Director of the Beyers Naudé Centre for Public Theology, Stellenbosch University, South Africa.

Elisabeth Gerle, Professor of Ethics at Lund University, Sweden.

Göran Gunner, Associate Professor at University College Stockholm, Sweden.

Newton Kahumbi Maina, Dr. at the Department of Philosophy and Religious Studies, Kenyatta University, Kenya.

Elizabeta Kitanovic, Dr. and Executive Secretary for Human Rights at the Conference of European Churches, Brussels, Belgium.

Maria Klasson Sundin, Dr. and Chaplain for the Bishop in the Diocese of Luleå, Church of Sweden.

Hennie Kotzé, Professor and Research Associate at the Centre for International and Comparative Politics, Stellenbosch University, South Africa.

Keith Matthee, Senior Counsel and former Judge in the High Courts of Mthatha, Grahamstown, Port Elizabeth, East London, Cape Town, and South Gauteng, South Africa.

Nokuzola Mndende, Dr. and Director of Icamagu Heritage Institute, Idutywa, Eastern Cape, Research Associate, Faculty of Theology, University of the Free State, South Africa.

Selina Palm, Dr. and Researcher at the Unit for Religion and Development Research at Stellenbosch University, South Africa.

Damaris Seleina Parsitau, Dr. and Senior Lecturer of Religion and Gender Studies at Egerton University Kenya, and Research Associate at Harvard Divinity School, USA.

Peter Petkoff, Dr. and Director of Religion, Law and International relations Program, Regent's Park College, Oxford, UK.

Mary-Anne Plaatjies-Van Huffel, Professor of Systematic Theology and Ecclesiology at Stellenbosch University, South Africa.

Fatima Seedat, Dr. and Senior Lecturer in Gender Studies at the University of Cape Town, South Africa.

Charlene van der Walt, Associate Professor in Biblical Studies, Gender Studies, and Religion at University KwaZulu-Natal, South Africa.

Freedom of Religion at Stake: An Introduction

ELISABETH GERLE, GÖRAN GUNNER,
AND DION FORSTER

What should the relationship be between freedom of religion and other human rights? The answers to this question are contested and varied. There does seem to be consensus that freedom of religion or belief ought to be protected by the states as well as by regional and global conventions and institutions. However, as we shall see, there are a variety of interpretations around the world of what this means. One could account for these variations by asking a few pertinent questions. What is the role of religion or belief in a particular society? Answers to this question vary significantly between states in Africa and Europe, for example. Moreover, is the term "religion" only used for the other? What about the relationships between various religions in a society? Should faith traditions in a minority position be protected against majority claims? What is the responsibility of the religious communities? What is the responsibility of the state in this regard? Yet, when does the state risk overstepping its boundaries in the delicate balance between freedom of religion and human rights?

Of course, one could ask a myriad more questions on this complex and fascinating topic. What is clear is that there is often some tension between the particular and the universal. Those who work in the field of freedom of religion often need to manage competing truth claims and world views in ways that maintain the respect and the integrity of diverse communities.

As a result, studies on freedom of religion, such as this one, often spend some time considering the complexity of relationships that exist in societies. A necessary starting point is to consider the relationships that faith communities, and individuals with faith convictions, have with the state. Yet, there are other relationships that also need to be studied and engaged, such as the relationships between faith communities in society. This is, however, somewhat complicated when one comes to recognise that faith traditions are not homogenous in and of themselves. Different hermeneutical perspectives operate, not only between faith traditions but also within such traditions. While some form their beliefs through literalist readings of ancient scriptures, others argue that texts are always to be read and interpreted in relation to their contexts of origin and development. This frequently involves commuting one's understanding between current contextual concerns and the particular social and historical contexts within which the sacred texts and religious convictions of a faith community originated. Such complexity can lead to misunderstanding, and even conflict, between faith communities, or within faith communities. Religion can become a site of struggle in relation to human rights and freedoms. Examples of this are issues related to religion and gender roles, or religious engagements on reproductive rights, or religion and the rights of sexual minorities. These are just a few examples of issues, which are central in most people's lives that have become hot topics within many faith traditions. In such instances one can see why, and how, considerations related to the nature and scope of freedom of religion and human rights within faith traditions, between different faith traditions, or between faith traditions and the state, come to the fore. A basic question arises: how can freedom of religion protect the dignity of every human being and safeguard the well-being of creation?

This volume seeks to unpack and wrestle with some of these challenges. In order to do so we therefore invited scholars from different contexts in Africa and Europe to write about freedom of religion from various angles. We first met at a small symposium in April 2017 that was sponsored by Church of Sweden. The symposium was co-hosted by the Stellenbosch Institute for Advanced Study (STIAS), and the Beyers Naudé Centre for Public Theology in the Faculty of Theology at Stellenbosch University.[1]

The book begins with an extremely fascinating comparison of "religiosity" in Sweden and South Africa. In this chapter, Hennie Kotzé, bases his

---

1. Wallenberg Research Centre at Stellenbosch University, Stellenbosch 7600 South Africa.

analysis of the two contexts upon data from the World Values Survey. His analysis helps us to understand some of the subtleties of the construction of belief, values, and the operational aspects of religions in both contexts. Kotzé's hypothesis is that secularisation and religiosity can be understood in relation to "existential security" on the one hand, "cultural traditional" axioms on the other. This may help us to understand why religion is so important in South Africa, and some of the other African contexts that are reflected upon in this book. Moreover, it also offers very helpful insights into the varying roles that religion and the religious play in relation to social and political factors in Europe and Africa.

In many parts of Europe religious freedom has developed in relation to a normative discourse focusing on tolerance and pluralism. However, as Göran Gunner points out in his chapter, many European countries seem to give states the right to decide what tolerance and pluralism entails within their context. References to culture and heritage are often used to permit privileges for a specific faith tradition, sometimes in conflict with international conventions on the freedom of religion or belief. How does one understand and critically engage such particularity in relation to more universal values? Moreover, are these values sufficient to safeguard the rights and dignity of minority religious traditions? Peter Petkoff considers an added layer of complexity that emerges when one brings the views of various nations and states into conversation with one another. He offers some helpful, technical, analyses of the tensions that exist between human rights declarations on freedom of religion, and the rights of states to seek protection against external forces. Limitations on religious freedoms are generally aimed at maintaining social cohesion, and, in cases like the United Kingdom and Greece, the constitutional status of the majority faith traditions. The result is, however, that undermining a dominant faith tradition is often conceived as an attack on the constitutional cohesion of society and can even be considered an act of borderline treason.

The recent emergence of nationalist agendas in some countries has acted to protect the religion of the majority as part of their cultural identity, whether it is a state supported faith or not. Peter Petkoff holds that "with nationalist movements effectively ruling a substantial part of New and Old Europe, new religious policies quickly eradicate the achievements of the past 20 years, aligning these religious policies to a greater extent with Moscow and with Ankara rather than with Brussels or Strasbourg."

In other parts of Europe religion is seen as something belonging to the past (at best) or as the superstitions of simpletons (at worst). In such instances it is held that religion would increasingly disappear as the consequences of modernity unfold. Faith and a shared world view as a common horizon have thus been relativised. One reaction to these sentiments is that notions such as religion, or world religions, have often been combined with defending a Christian homogenous West. As Elisabeth Gerle points out in her chapter, this has even been combined with a perspective that sees religion as something for the other, for the exotic, non-Modern. This has significant social and political consequences for religious communities.

In her chapter she draws on scholars such as Tumoko Masuzawa, who claims that notions such as pluralism and world religions went hand in hand with the early secularisation theories predicting that the role of religion would become less important and more private. A common (self) description was to portray Europe as an exception. First in terms of being Christian in a Modern, "enlightened way," and later understood as a region where religious faith and practices were seen as vanishing, basically belonging to the past. Grace Davis coined the expression, "belonging but not believing" and "believing but not belonging" in relation to traditional European national churches.[2]

In what is often called a post-secular era, secularisation theorists have admitted that their predictions were wrong. Religion has not disappeared or become entirely private. Quite the opposite, religion is currently more visible in the public sphere than in recent decades. The polarisation between those who want to understand freedom of religion as freedom not to be disturbed by religious practices and those, who claim their right to profess their religion as persons and as groups, private as well as public, has grown. A secularist agenda, that wants to rid society of religion in the public sphere altogether, is encountering, and may also be reinforced by, the presence of religious expressions in public.

In many African countries Modernity brought, Biblicist, evangelical, patriarchal, religious interpretations to the fore. Mainline churches saw themselves competing with prosperity churches and "faith healers." Moreover, there is increasing tension between faith traditions, such as Christianity and Islam, in many African countries. The relationship between Christianity and Islam in Kenya offers a clear contemporary example of such interreligious competition. Newton Kahumbi Maina's reflection on this context, claims, this "ultimately heightens tensions and endangers freedom of religion in the country." Acts of terror committed in the name of Islam has not made things easier. He shares some of the background related to the first acts of terrorism attributed to radicalism and extremism. One was the bombing of USA embassy in Nairobi on August 7, 1998, by alleged Al-Qaida terrorists, which killed 216 people. Terror attacks then intensified

2. Davis, *Europe.*

when the Kenyan Defence Forces entered Somalia in 2011 to flush out Al-Shabaab. Mania claims that such terror attacks, and the responses to them, have had significant implications for the freedom of religion in the country. Some Christians do not feel secure to practise their religion freely because they fear being attacked. Totalising claims, which most world views hold, have not disappeared. They have, however, had to accommodate themselves to a reality with competing claims. In a time when acts of terror are playing out in various places around the world, totalising claims that may have very little to do with religion are nevertheless being connected with certain faith traditions. This is a grave concern for the rights and freedoms of religious persons and faith-communities.

Religion has always played an important role in society. Its pervasive presence has often shaped shared world views. As a result, it is often almost impossible to differentiate between culture and religion. In post-colonial Africa, African traditional religion has reemerged with new visibility challenging a Christian hegemony that is considered to be connected with the ideals of colonialism. Yet, an asymmetry remains due to the subtle and pervasive entrenchment of colonial values and beliefs that have been knowingly, and unknowingly, incorporated into the contemporary African social imaginary. Nokuzola Mndende asks in her chapter if there really is freedom of religion in South Africa? She claims,

> The fact of the matter is that the religion of the wealthy, who are able to attract the needs of the underprivileged, always dictates how freedom of religion should be defined and upon which guidelines it should be based. As religious equality can never be reached within one country because of inherent inequalities, it is doubtful that there could be equality of religions in any state where there are inequalities amongst religious groupings.

She invites us to critically re-assess the relationship between religion and the dominance of economic and political forces in society, which are themselves products of Western and colonial values. How does one appreciate the value of African traditional religion in a society in which Western political and economic systems dominate the aspirations of citizens? Mndende helps us to consider the complex interplay between dominating world views (which are not primarily religious) and their impact on shaping of religious values and beliefs.

Religious freedom and religious pluralism, with an emphasis on tolerance and co-existence is thus under pressure. Pre-Modern, Modern, Late, or Post-Modern, interpretations of religious freedom are evidenced around the globe.

Furthermore, if religious pluralism as a phenomenon has had a tendency to think of religions and faith traditions as homogenous entities, late modernity, or post modernity, has brought to the fore a new awareness of contradictory interpretations. Women and lesbian, gay, bisexual, transsexual, intersex, queer, asexual, and gender-nonconforming, i.e., LGBTIQA+ persons have made explicit hermeneutical challenges in many traditional faith communities. They are challenging their own traditions pointing out that the Bible and the Quran can be read and interpreted in a variety of different ways. Issues of representation emerge as a consequence. Who has the authority, and the power, to decide which interpretation is right? Religious freedom is, therefore, no longer only an issue between states and different faith communities, or between various religions or traditions, rather it is something that cuts through every tradition.

Religious pluralism pursued in relation to the state, both in Africa and in Europe, thus encounters new tensions with the rights of the individual. Women with a feminist perspective, as well as LGBTIQA+ movements have shown that no faith tradition is homogenous. Rather all faith traditions are diverse in nature. Fatima Seedat, critically considers the constitutionally guaranteed right to freedom of religion in terms of unrepresented segments of religious communities. In her chapter she highlights how the South African state has failed to uphold the rights of women and people with queer sexualities in Muslim communities in South Africa. The result is that the state inadvertently sanctions abuse through its policies and legislation. The state claims that it does not wish to interfere, or unnecessarily intervene, in the internal functioning of religious communities. Yet, this distance has meant that oppressive social and religious practices are allowed to proliferate and minorities have become vulnerable to state condoned religious abuses.

Dion Forster's chapter highlights this tension further. When should the state "step in" to protect the rights and safety of its citizens from religious abuse? Under what conditions is it acceptable for the state to curtail religious freedoms to safeguard human rights? These are complex questions for which there are no easy answers. Forster relates how the state abused its power during apartheid to curtail the rights of religious movements and persons who took a "prophetic stand" to oppose to the dehumanising policies of the state. The apartheid state claimed it was doing this to protect its citizens from the evils of communism. Faith movements were banned and religious leaders were arrested and detained. Some thirty years later, in the democratic South Africa, the state is once again wanting to assert its right to curtail religious freedom. In this instance it also claims to want to do so to protect the rights of its citizens against abusive religious practices. The incident that precipitated the state's decision to curtail religious freedom, was when a religious leader used a deadly insecticide (called "Doom") to "heal" believers from sickness and sin during a Church service. How should the state, and religious communities, deal with "prophetic witness" and the "prophets of Doom"?

The role of states, religions, constitutions and political leaders are, therefore, again at the center of many discussions in Africa as well as in Europe. The conventional idea of European individualism and African collectivism is being challenged in the light of more textured and nuanced views of individual and social identity. Modernity has many faces. Religious freedom can be seen as a fundamental human right, connected to the freedoms of association and expression. Collective rights for religious groups and organisations are often heard as an argument in relation to states not to interfere in internal affairs of, for instance, a Church.

However, as Charlene van der Walt shows in her chapter, it easily becomes a matter of choice whether the Constitution is supposed to protect the rights of the individual or those of the group. LGBTIQA+ persons have, according to the South African Constitution, the right and freedoms to flourish. Van der Walt shows that these constitutional sentiments are not always shared by the decisionmakers in faith bodies. So, who decides what is permissible, and what rights are to be supported and upheld? Whose authority serves to guide society in such instances?

Charlene van der Walt describes this in her chapter as

> the gap between the freedom of religion and the rights and liberties of LGBTIQA+ people as guaranteed by the South African Constitution.

The primary case study on this gap forms the springboard into reflecting on a number of other, maybe more subtle gaps such as the

> gap between the rule of law and the lived experience of people affected by the law, the gap between our own embodied understanding of personal experiences of exclusion and the capacity to extend that knowledge to the liberation struggle of others, the gap between the letter of the law and the heart of the law and the gap between the Bible reader and text of the Bible. All these implied gaps call for the development of hermeneutical skills that enable accountability, empathy, and responsibility.

The tension that exists between what is seen as cultural rights or religious rights, the religious freedom, is dealt with in many chapters from various angles. Keith Matthee, considers this tension from the perspective of a lawyer. Matthee challenges the view of a so-called "normative ethical" value system that serves as a subtle, yet powerful, informant in legal rulings on issues of religious concern. Matthee argues that the law is not hermeneutically neutral and that traditional Christian communities have been marginalised since they have abdicated their responsibility to robustly challenge laws and rulings that may conflict with their religious beliefs. He questions whether there is a "mutually respectful co-existence between the secular and the sacred"? Following this line of reasoning he concludes that it is not the task of the Court to force the one into the sphere the other. Instead, Matthee suggests a "constitutionally permitted free space." In his view the Constitution is not a source of ethical guidance, something many others would argue that it is. Writing as a lawyer, he is advocating a world view with clear borders between faith communities and a society. For theologians emphasizing that God is the creator of all, even secular insights may very well reflect divine, righteous sentiments. His critique against Constitutional Court Judges 'acting' as if the Constitution of South Africa has a normative ethical value system, is a highly sensitive issue in South Africa where many claim the necessity to challenge female submission upheld in the name of God, or rather, in the name of a special Biblical hermeneutics. If such a hermeneutic allows violent punishment of women in the name of male hierarchy, it may also be important to challenge private spaces.

As South Africa is a country with very high rates of violence against women, to argue in favour of a "constitutionally permitted free space," is therefore a controversial argument, as the Constitution is supposed to protect human dignity. One of the issues has to do with women and their role not only in private spheres but in society at large. This tension is more intense the closer it gets to privacy and autonomy, as Seedat's chapter points out.

Many European countries also seem to operate with a previously mentioned dichotomy between belief and practice as well as "an assumption that 'private' belief cannot be allowed to intrude into the world of 'public' practices and legislation."[3] Such a perspective seems to "grant unconditional freedom to the rights of conscience." However, it seems "unable to adjudicate on how, or even whether, that might be translated into action." Hence, judicial decisions "remain resolutely agnostic." As Elaine Graham claims, this is most acute "in cases where religious convictions conflicts with issues of sexual discrimination."[4]

3. Graham, *Between a Rock*, 27.
4. Graham, *Between a Rock*, 28.

What is described as a neutral position and as a "mutual coexistence between the secular and the sacred" can also be described with what Selina Palm labels using the right to freedom of religion as a protection against other human rights in her chapter. As the notion "religion" is not easy to define, so too are notions such as "secular" and "sacred" constantly re-negotiated and understood in a new light in relation to where the line between private and public, church and society, is drawn.

Palm also enters into this debate as she highlights the paradoxical nature of human rights "talk" between the state and religious communities. She does so by offering a critical historical overview of the relationship between human rights discourses and religious freedom in South Africa. Palm uses historical examples to illustrate that the situation is far too complex to simply allow autonomy for religious groups to function independently of the state, or alternatively, to simply allows the state to decide on the rights and freedoms accorded to religions. Palm suggests that what is needed is the cultivation of a culture of human rights that cuts across both the state and the religious. This necessitates a strong, actively engaged, civil society that hold both the state, and religions, to account for their values and actions.

Religious communities differ in their attitude and active support for human rights. One European body prioritising work on human rights and freedom of religion or belief is the Conference of European Churches. Elizabeta Kitanovic illustrates in her chapter tensions between states and religious communities in the European setting and concludes that

> work on human rights, including freedom of religion or belief, is needed in Europe since the region faces growing tensions including nationalistic intolerance and extremism.

This debate also relates to differences in as well as in relation to cultural circumstances and the presence of new voices in debates on religious freedom. As we have already seen, in this volume voices from different authors sometimes disagree with one another in what we hope is a fruitful discussion.

Damaris Seleina Parsitau shows in her analysis of Pentecostal mission in rural Maasai communities in Kenya, how Pentecostal beliefs, teachings, and practices have had many liberating consequences for women transforming cultures and traditions of conservative Maasai people that have resisted modernity for a very long time. It is difficult to predict the consequences of such social, historical and religious changes going forward.

Hence, we need to hold such views in tension with the various contributions of persons such as the chapters of Fatima Seedat and Charlene van der Walt. For example, what Seedat shows is that the state is not objective and neutral when it acts to protect a traditional dogmatic interpretation of where women are allowed to pray, or not, in a Muslim outdoor prayer gathering.

Issues around women are not only related to autonomy and privacy. If the South African Constitution is to be seen as "the legal and moral framework" within which South Africans have agreed to live, there are many areas of tension. If women and LGBTIQA+ people illustrate the complexities of religious freedoms, so does the universal rights of the child.

The best interest for the child is, according to Maria Klasson Sundin's analysis, supposed to be decided by at least four different actors; the child her or himself, parents, the group that offers an environment of language, cultural practices and traditions, and, finally the state. Again, this chapter illustrates the complex intersections between beliefs, values, rights, and who has the ultimate right to make decisions on behalf of others. Klasson Sundin's chapter offers an insightful analysis of the complexity of freedom of religion in schools. This is a topic that is also picked up, and critically engaged, by Mary-Anne Plaatjies-Van Huffel in her chapter. Plaatjies-Van Huffel adds an added layer of texture to these discussions when she introduces the rights of 'private' (charter) schools that are specifically established by religious communities to safeguard and propagate their beliefs and values for their children. Klasson Sundin and Plaatjies-Van Huffel offer some insights into the tensions that exist between the state's responsibility for protecting its citizens against abuse and ideological manipulation, and the rights of religious communities to operate according to their beliefs and values.

All of the issues mentioned above show that there is very little social consensus that would allow us to "determine what constitutes a legitimate sphere of inner religious belief or lawful manifestation of the belief."[5] States that want to stress national unity, and leaders of faith traditions that want to manifest collective values, are bound to meet dissidents and individual voices with differing or conflicting claims. This tension between the individual and the collective is not a difference between Africa and Europe but seems to be part of what can be described as *Freedom of Religion at Stake*.

BIBLIOGRAPHY

Graham, Elaine. *Between a Rock and a Hard Place: Public Theology in a Post-Secular Age*. London: SCM, 2013.
Davie, Grace. *Europe, the Exceptional Case: Parameters of Faith in the Modern World*. London: Darton Longman & Todd, 2002.

5. Graham, *Between a Rock*, 28.

Part I

Freedom of Religion in Different Settings

1

Religiosity in South Africa and Sweden

A Comparison

Hennie Kotzé

Many influential social thinkers in the nineteenth century—such as Auguste Comte, Herbert Spencer, Emile Durkheim, Max Weber, and Karl Marx—predicted that religion would slowly weaken and that its importance in many people's lives would disappear. As Norris and Inglehart pointed out: "The death of religion was the conventional wisdom in the social sciences during most of the twentieth century."[1] In this period, levels of secularization—that is "a systematic erosion of religious practices, values, and beliefs"—will rise and religiosity will fade away in the face of industrialization.

Furthermore, as Norris and Inglehart noted, with the prediction of the "death of religion" and, later in the twentieth century, the growing support for theories of secularization, it was always difficult to provide watertight explanations for the fading of religion. However, as it turned out, the prediction of its demise was premature. More recently, as societies become more industrialized, "demand side" theories, which stressed the gradual dwindling of religious beliefs and habits, became acceptable in certain circles as explanations for the erosion of religiosity. On the other hand "supply side,"

1. Norris and Inglehart, *Sacred and Secular*, 3.

or top-down theories, stress that there will always be a demand for religion; thus, "If you build a church, people will follow."[2]

Norris and Inglehart's book, *Sacred and Secular*, in which they make extensive use of the research on changing values on a global level, forms the basis for this chapter's comparison of levels of religiosity between Sweden and South Africa. They stress that their alternative theory of secularization based on conditions of existential security, is to a certain extent based on the demand-side theoretical perspective.

One of the most important arguments explaining this misreading of religious decline as presented in secularization was that most research in the past generally emphasized trends in church attendance by Protestants and Catholics in Europe. In fact, most surveys in post-industrialised nations indicated a steady decline in church attendance. This meant that the cross-cultural element in most of the reported research on the decline of religion was missing. Too many countries, especially those in the developing world were not initially included in the reported research. It is now clear that it would be a mistake to use, for instance, Western Europe to generalise for the whole world, while traditional religious views comprise maybe the largest percentage of the world's population. One, therefore, not only needs to consider these differences but should also include these populations in your research.

Norris and Inglehart, in examining trends in secularization, suggested that the importance of religiosity "persists most strongly among vulnerable populations, especially those living in poorer nations, facing personal survival-threatening risks."[3] For them, an indication of the level of secularization in rich nations relates to their values and behavior concerning religion. Their version of secularization theory, based on existential security, rests on two axioms: (1) the security axiom, and (2) the cultural traditions axiom.

The two values case studies I used in this chapter to compare the level of religiosity, are Sweden and South Africa, while the analysis is based on the "vulnerability" theory of Norris and Inglehart. It firstly illustrates the differences in levels of poverty between the citizens of the two countries and then examines the differences in the values and behavior concerning religion in the two countries. I employ a "most different system" research design to the greatest amount of differences in levels of religiosity between the two nations. It is in the main thus, mainly a descriptive analysis.

To begin with, I will compare the level of vulnerability in terms of the two countries' levels of modernization and human security. I will indicate

2. Norris and Inglehart, *Sacred and Secular*, 7.
3. Norris and Inglehart, *Sacred and Secular*, 4.

how these two countries differ in their respective levels of development—socially and economically. In line with Norris and Inglehart's thesis, the expectation would be that there would be substantial differences in the level of religiosity due to different levels of development in the two countries. Secondly, I will discuss the state structures, including their constitutions. Finally, using the cultural traditions axiom I will indicate the differences in their level of religiosity by comparing three core dimensions of religiosity; namely, religious participation, religious values and religious beliefs. The latter comparison is based on the 2013 dataset of World Values Survey (WVS) in the countries.

LEVELS OF VULNERABILITY AND STATE STRUCTURES

South Africa and Sweden are two vastly different countries with regards to size and development. South Africa is more than twice the size of Sweden. South Africa is 1.2 million square kilometres whilst Sweden consists of only 450,000 square kilometres, which is roughly a third the size of South Africa. Sweden, on the other hand, has only about one sixth the population (10 million) of South Africa's 56 million inhabitants. South Africa also has a multitude of ethnic groups who are acknowledged in the Constitution by language, which recognizes 11 official languages. On the other hand, Sweden is fairly homogeneous, with just over one million of the population born outside Sweden.[4]

Concerning the level of development, the differences between the two countries are even starker. In 2013, the GDP per capita in Sweden was 10 times that of South Africa—$60,000 compared to the $6,600. The Gini coefficient of the two countries also differ hugely, indicating the skewed distribution of income in South Africa. Different data sets, time periods, and variables used to measure South Africa's Gini coefficient indicate a range from 0.63 to 0.69, depending on the variables used.[5] According to World Bank statistics, Sweden has a Gini coefficient of 0.25.

South Africa's Gini coefficient is consistently one of the highest in the world, meaning it is a country with a very high level of inequality. This could mostly be ascribed to the colonial inheritance of white minority dominance and subsequent apartheid policies. An important element in this high level

---

4. For more detail on Swedish and South African demographics and political development, see, amongst others, World Population Review, "Sweden Population"; "South African Population." See also the Wikipedia overviews of these two countries.

5. The Gini coefficient is the measure of income inequality, ranging from zero to one. In a perfectly equal society, a value of zero is allocated and 1.00 represents absolute inequality.

of inequality is also the consistently high levels of unemployment (between 25–30 percent) in South Africa over the last two decades, whereas over a 30-year period, unemployment in Sweden averages just less than 6 percent.

Taking another measurement of inequality into account, the World Bank's figures that are reflected in the Human Development Index (a composite index measuring longevity, knowledge and standard of living) also reflect this very apparent gap between the two countries. Sweden falls into the "very high" category of states, 12th of all countries in the world, whereas South Africa falls into the "medium" category, 118th from the top. Tracking the movement in the index from 1980 to 2013, Sweden moved from 0.776 to 0.898 and South Africa from 0.569 to 0.650.[6]

Such severe inequalities at such high levels in South Africa result in massive negative impacts on human development; reduces financial investments; and leads to poor basic services with regards to most public goods. Some groups, especially the lower classes, feel discriminated against. This eventually culminates in political instability with high levels of protest potential.

Although both countries are multi-party democracies, Sweden has a much longer democratic trajectory, starting in 1766 and the instrument of government forming in 1809, which resulted in guarantees such as freedom of religion and freedom of the press. Universal suffrage in Sweden dates back to 1919, when women were allowed to vote at municipal level. The country is best described "as a modern neo-liberal welfare state." In comparison, it was only after a long struggle against apartheid that South Africa legislated a multi-party democracy in 1994. The Constitution was initiated and the negotiated settlement, mostly by the elite, delivered a constitution in 1996 that grants equal rights to life, equality, freedom, and dignity to all citizens. South Africa, thus, is a young democracy struggling to consolidate its democratisation process.

The materialist/post-materialist continuum illustrates another dimension of the perception of vulnerability of South Africans. Arguably, one of the best-known theories of value change (including religious values) is that of Inglehart in his book, *The Silent Revolution*.[7] For Inglehart the "silent revolution" is a slow change from materialist to post-materialist values—from physical survival and safety to placing much more emphasis on

---

6. For these statistics on Sweden and South Africa, see UNDP, "Table 1." For Gini placements and other indicators, see World Bank, "World Development Indicators."

7. Ingelhart, *Silent Revolution*.

post-materialist values, which express especially quality of life issues and self-expression.[8]

With the obvious vulnerability of a large part of the South African population in mind, I added in the South African wave of the World Values Survey (2001) the following items: "Providing shelter for all People"; "Providing clean water for all people"; "Making sure that everyone is adequately clothed"; "Making sure that everyone can go to school"; "Providing land for all people"; and "Providing everyone with enough food to eat." I regarded these factors as "measuring" pre-materialist values compared to the other twelve statements measuring materialism and post-materialism.

The inclusion of the six extra items by the principle investigator of the 1995 WVS in South Africa, which allows for the adding of the so-called pre-materialist dimension can be justified on the grounds of "the complexity and diversity of the South African population as far as values are concerned and the extent that poverty is affecting value orientations."[9] (Unfortunately, this measurement was not included in the Swedish WVS of 1995.)

The inadequacy of a dimension without a pre-materialist index does not, however, simply rest with the fact that some fundamental needs are not represented by the existing items, but that certain post-materialist items are wrongly interpreted to express certain pre-materialist or materialist needs, thereby skewing the results towards increased post-materialism, when this is not the case. One example of this is the item regarding "giving people more say in their work and in their community," which can be wrongly interpreted as pertaining to the employment situation and could in fact be focusing on such materialist needs as greater job security. The questionnaires for 1995 and 2001 have also replaced the item regarding "maintaining a stable economy" with one pertaining to employment levels, possibly due to increasing levels of unemployment having already proved themselves a potential problem to the principal investigators of the 1995 version of the WVS.[10]

More than 10 percent of the South African respondents in the 2001 survey fell in the pre-materialist category and another 6 percent on the lower end of materialism index. Confirming the vulnerable position of a large section of the South African population.[11]

---

8. Ingelhart is also regarded as the "father" of the World Values Survey, which he started in 1980—amongst other projects—to validate his value change theories.

9. Lategan, "Extending," 410.

10. See section above as regarding the magnitude of unemployment as a national problem.

11. Kotzé and Lombard, "Revising," 420.

Against this background, and concentrating on some aspects of the vulnerability theory, my expectation is that we would find substantially higher levels of religiosity in South Africa compared to Sweden if we use the same measurement instrument—in this case, the World Values Survey, which was conducted in the same year, 2013—in both countries.[12]

OPERATIONALIZATION OF RELIGIOSITY

Before describing how I measured religiosity, I need to clarify two issues. First, how much religious freedom is there in the respective states, and how we measure values that indicate the level of religiosity in the two countries.

With regards to the issue of religious freedom, we know that the constitutions of both countries guarantee freedom of religion. In Sweden, the state and church were officially separated in 2000. Faith communities may apply to become a religious community eligible for state funding and, qualified beside Church of Sweden (Lutheran) are the Free Churches (7), Eastern Orthodox and Oriental (15), Lutheran Churches (8), Islamic Organizations (7), and other faith communities (Anglican, Alevi, Catholic, Mandean Sabian, Buddhist, and Jewish).[13] Contrastingly, none of the denominations in South Africa are supported by the state.[14]

Regarding the second issue, the concept of *values* will prove a pivotal component of this discussion and hence requires careful conceptualisation. Therefore, for the purposes of this study, the essence of values is implied in the three preconditions of values offered by Jan Van Deth and Elinor Scarbrough, namely that "they cannot be directly observed; they engage moral considerations and are conceptions of the desirable."[15] These values therefore serve as criteria for judgment, preference and choice; although these value systems are often not explicitly identifiable.[16] Despite the fact that values can be conceptualised in much broader terms, this chapter is premised on the definition of values "as the patterns of choice in the sets of goals of a specified population, which can become indirectly evident through social observation."[17] We employed the same indicators as Norris and Inglehart to measure religiosity, namely "Religious Participation," "Religious Values," and "Religious Beliefs" also with the same items operationalizing each

12. For information on the data and questionnaires, see World Values Survey, "Welcome."

13. Myndigheten, "Faith Communities."

14. See Constitution of the Republic of South Africa ch. 2.

15. Van Deth and Scarbrough, *Impact of Values*, 28.

16. Rockeach, *Understanding Human Values*, 16.

17. Inglehart, *Silent Revolution*, 182.

concept.[18] The secularization process is understood to cause a decline in religious participation, as well as religious values and beliefs. Essentially, the cultural traditions axiom "assumes that the distinctive world views that were originally linked with religious traditions have shaped the cultures of each nation in an enduring fashion."[19] As Norris and Inglehart pointed out, "today these distinctive values are transmitted to citizens even if they never set foot in a church, temple or mosque."[20] Therefore, this element of culture could be measured by ascertaining the level of religiosity in a nation.

For a comparison of the levels of religiosity (and/or secularization) between Sweden and South Africa we used the World Values Survey that was conducted in both countries in 2013.

The general public data forms part of the WVS, with the sixth wave of the survey having been conducted in 2013 in both countries.[21] The WVS provides us with a valuable tool with which to analyse changing value patterns at the mass level. This increasingly prominent worldwide values research—and in particular the pioneering work carried out by Ronald Inglehart[22]—convincingly shows that changing value patterns have a strong impact on political and social developments within a country.

The WVS is conducted via face-to-face interviews in the language of preference of respondents. Probability samples are drawn, with all citizens 16 years and older having an equal chance of being selected. The samples are also stratified into homogenous sub-groups defined by various demographic attributes. Since the samples are weighted to the full population and within a statistical margin of error of less than 2 percent at 95 percent confidence level, they are representative of the adult population of a given country. Table 1 illustrates the sample size per country.

Country	Sample size (N)
South Africa	3531
Sweden	1003
TOTAL	4534

Table 1: Size of Mass WVS Samples (2013)[23]

18. Norris and Inglehart, *Sacred and Secular*, 41.

19. Norris and Inglehart, *Sacred and Secular*, 17.

20. Norris and Inglehart, *Sacred and Secular*, 17.

21. For information on the data and questionnaires, see World Values Survey, "Welcome."

22. Inglehart, *Silent Revolution*; Inglehart, *Cultural Shift*.

23. I thank my colleague Carlos Rivero (Valencia University) for his assistance with the data analysis. However, I take full responsibility for the interpretation of

In the analysis of levels of religiosity, I have incorporated a number of items that indicate (1) "Religious Participation"; (2) "Religious Values"; and, (3) "Religious Beliefs" based on those that Norris and Inglehart employed in their book *Sacred and Secular*. These variables clustered together in a factor analysis.

To establish whether a respondent belong to a religious community the following question was asked:

> Question: "Do you belong to a religious denomination? If yes, which one?"
>
> Response: "BELONG."

I also combined this with the statement in a cross tabulation: "Voluntary association or group membership."

> Question 25: "I'm going to read off a list of voluntary organizations, for each one, could you tell me whether you are an active member, an inactive member, or not a member of that type of organization: Church or religious organization."

Religion	South Africa[24]*				Sweden			
	Not a member	Inactive member	Active member	Belong	Belong	Not a member	Inactive member	Active member
None	52.2	21.6	6.5	18.1	33.8	54.6	6.4	2.9
Buddhist	0.4	0.3	0.4	0.4	0.1		0.2	
Hindu	1.7	1.8	1.8	1.7	0.2	0.3		
Independent African Church	10.1	13.6	21.2	17.4				

the data patterns.

24. According to the Report on International Religious Freedom: "African Independent Churches (AICs) are the largest group of Christian churches. Once regarded as Ethiopian churches, the majority is now referred to as either Zionist or Apostolic churches (with 6.9 and 5.9 million adherents, respectively). It is estimated that more than 10,000 AICs, with a membership of nearly 13 million exist in South Africa. The Zion Christian Church is the largest AIC. AICs serve more than half the population in the northern KwaZulu-Natal and Mpumalanga areas. There are at least 900 AICs in Soweto. Other Christian groups include Protestants (Methodist, Dutch Reformed, Anglican, Baptist, Congregational, Lutheran, and Presbyterian), Pentecostal/charismatic churches, and the Roman Catholic Church. Greek Orthodox, Scientology, and Seventh-day Adventist churches are also active. Please refer to Appendix C in the Country Reports on Human Rights Practices for the status of the government's acceptance of international legal standards" (US Dept. of State, "2010 Report").

Religion	South Africa[24]*				Sweden			
	Not a member	Inactive member	Active member	Belong	Belong	Not a member	Inactive member	Active member
Jehovah Witnesses	0.4	1.9	1.7	1.5				
Jew	0.2	0.5	0.2	0.3	0.1	0.1		
Muslim	0.9	1.8	1.6	1.5	2.4	2.5	1.8	5.9
Orthodox	0.2	0.4	0.3	0.3	0.8	0.6	0.9	2.9
Other (Not specific)	3.1	7.9	9.0	7.7	0.6	0.4		5.9
Pentecostal	0.6	2.7	3.1	2.5				
Protestant	9.0	16.1	15.2	14.3	1.2	1.0	1.4	1.5
Roman Catholic	10.5	17.6	17.5	16.3				
Evangelical/Apostolic Faith Mission	5.7	10.3	15.4	12.4				
African Traditional Religion	5.1	3.7	6.1	5.3				
Free church/Non-denominational church					2.5	0.1	1.8	30.9
The Church of Sweden					58.3	40.3	87.5	50.0

Table 2: Religion in South Africa and Sweden

There are interesting differences if one adds up the percentages in this table. My speculation is that belonging to a "religious denomination" was interpreted as belonging to a "church." However, in question 25 we asked about active/inactive membership in "church or religious organization," which is not strictly speaking the same type of institution. Thus, a poor operationalisation of membership may be responsible for the differences in percentages. The very high number of different "denominations" among the African population may also be linked to the previously mentioned "supply side" or top-down theories of religion.

Items in Indexes:

Religiosity

The items in measuring "Religiosity" *are* in the form of an Index:

1. V 152: *How important is God in your life?*—Options: Scale 1–10, from not at all important to very important (*Religious values*);

2. V 145: *Apart from weddings and funerals, about how often do you attend religious services these days?*—Options: More than once a week; Once a week; Once a month; Only on special holy days; Once a year; Less often; Never, practically never; Don't know/refuse (*Religious participation*);

3. V 53: *How much confidence to you have in churches?*—Options: A great deal; Quite a lot; Not very much; None at all (*Religious values*);

4. V 146: *How often to you pray to God outside religious services?*—Several times a day; Once a day; Several times a week; Only when attending religious services; Only on special holy days; Once a year; Less often; Practically never (*Religious participation*);

5. V 9: *How important is religion in your life?*—From a great deal to none at all (*Religious Values*).

Morality

Morality refers to an index I constructed using an introduction to a list of items, which read: "Using this scale, please tell me for each of the following actions whether you think it can "always be justified" (10), "never is justified" (1), or "something in between": Divorce; Abortion, Homosexuality? (Factor together in Sweden and South Africa). There were more items on the list, but these items using factor analysis (Principal component) gave me a grouping of variables indicating that they measure the same construction, in this case, we called the variable "morality." (The main function of factor analysis is to reduce many items to one construct—it may thus consist of many individual variables that we then combine to form an "index.")

	Religiosity	Morality	V152 How important is God in your life	V 145 How often do you attend religious services	V 53 Confidence: The Churches	V 146 How often do you pray	V 9 Important in life: Religion
South Africa	17.81	12.92	8.06	5.09	3.17	6.2	3.37
Sweden	10.4	24.32	3.65	2.06	2.43	2.57	2
			(1–10)	(1–7)	(1–4)	(1–8)	(1–4)

Table 3: Items in the Religiosity Index and the Morality Index[25]

In table 4 the answer to the following statement is reflected:

Question 147: "Independently of whether you attend religious services or not, would you say you are—?" (Religious Beliefs).

	South Africa	Sweden
A religious person	80%	32.4%
Not a religious person	18.2%	50.2%
An atheist	1.8%	17.4%

Table 4: Religious Person

In table 5 the Question was:

Question 149: "Do you believe in hell?" With response choice: Yes or NO (DK/Refused) (Religious Beliefs).

	South Africa	Sweden
Yes	46.1%	15.1%
No	53.9%	84.9%

Table 5: Believe in Hell

We also used a number of independent variables in a regression analysis. Regression analysis helps us to understand which independent variable (the one that causes change in the dependent variable—in this case, religiosity)

25. Variable named "rec"; means the variable has been recoded. Higher values indicate higher level of agreement (e.g., 1: nothing; 4: very much). Some variables have been recoded to allow all of them measure religiosity in the same way (higher values, indicate higher religiosity). In the morality index the maximum score could be 30 and lowest 3. What we have here is the average score on the three items combined.

is related to the dependent variable and how strong this influence is. Therefore, in a sense it may indicate a causal relationship between the independent variable and the dependent variable.

The statistical technique used is an Ordinary Least Squares (OLS) regression, with religiosity as the dependent variable, and determining which independent variable "explains" the level of religiosity the best. We selected the most important independent variables that may explain a high or low religiosity (the dependent variable). The following independent variables were included: gender, age, social trust, voluntary activism, life satisfaction, and left-right self-placement, level of education, political interest and diffuse support for democracy.

It should be noted that these are all variables in the survey that I included as independent variables in the analysis. The rationale for selecting these independent variables is derived from influential writers' analyses of social, political, and cultural variables that shaped the level of religiosity in a country.

	Model 1		Model 2		Model 3	
	Beta	S.E.	Beta	S.E.	Beta	S.E.
Constant	15.642***	.464	17.673***	1.132	13.365***	1.36
Morality	-.348***	.018	-.353***	.018	-.35***	0
Tolerance			-.058*	.018	-.039	.3
Age					.12***	.0
Upper class (1)					1.594	1.4
Middle class					.016	.3
Education					.038	.1
Gender					.133***	.2
Black (2)						
White						
Colored						
R	.348		.352		.395	
R2	.121		.124		.156	
Adj. R2	.12		.122		.151	

Table 6: Regression Analysis: Religiosity in Sweden[26]

26. Beta is the standardized regression coefficient (unstandardized for dummy variables—class). S.E. the standard error. * Significant at the .05 level; ** Significant at the, 005 level; and *** Significant at the, 000 level. (1) Reference: Lower class; (1): Reference: Indian (they have highest level of religiosity). Dependent variable: Religiosity.

What I found was that the level of religiosity in Sweden depends mainly on morality (12 percent variance). Tolerance also shows some, albeit minimal, effect on religiosity but less than morality. When socio-demographic variables are included, the percentage of explained variance barely increases by 3 percent. Gender and age are the only variables that show some effect but cultural variables still show a larger effect.

	Model 1		Model 2		Model 3	
	Beta	S.E.	Beta	S.E.	Beta	S.E.
Constant	18.892***	.106	17.894***	.348	15.592***	.582
Morality	-.21***	,004	-.212***	.004	-.207***	0
Tolerance			.053**	.004	.051**	.1
Age					.082***	.0
Upper class (1)					1.214*	.5
Middle class					.406***	.1
Education					.105***	.0
Gender					.127***	.1
Black (2)					-.849**	.3
White					-.457	.4
Colored					-.721*	.4
R	.210		.216		.299	
R2	.044		.047		.089	
Adj. R2	.044		.046		.086	

Table 7: Religiosity in South Africa[27]

Overall, in South Africa the same factors explain less variance than in the Swedish case. Morality still emerges as the main propelling factor explaining religiosity. Tolerance, as in Sweden, also shows some minimal influence. When socio-demographic variables are included, the percentage of explained variance doubles. Middle class and upper classes are more religious than lower ones. Indian people are the most religious group, followed by Whites, Coloreds and Blacks. Similar to Sweden, age and gender also show some small effect.

27. Beta is the standardized regression coefficient (unstandardized for dummy variables—class and race). S.E. the standard error. * Significant at the .05 level; ** significant at the, 005 level and *** significant at the, 000 level. (1) Reference: Lower class; (1): Reference: Indian. Dependent variable: Religiosity.

Overall, the percentage of explained variance in South Africa's level of religiosity is lower than in Sweden, meaning that factors that explain religiosity in South Africa are more diverse than in the Nordic case study.

CONCLUDING REMARKS

On a more general level, there are significant differences in the levels of religiosity between Sweden and South Africa.

Regarding the two items used to analyse "religious beliefs" there are huge differences between the two countries. With regards to the question of whether the respondent considers himself/herself as a religious person, 80 percent of the South African respondents replied in the affirmative, whereas this number is slightly over 34 percent for Swedish respondents. The number of atheists is also very high in Sweden (over 17 percent) compared to only 1.8 percent in South Africa. Another item related to beliefs, namely, whether the respondent believe in "a hell" yielded results of just over 30 percent more South Africans than Swedes believing in "a hell."

It is evident that there are substantial differences concerning religious values measured with items in what Inglehart and Norris called a "religiosity index." On items such as the "importance of God," the "confidence in churches," the "importance of religion in life," how "often they pray," and the "importance of religion in life" there are substantial differences between South African and Swedish population, confirming the high levels of religiosity in South Africa.

Furthermore, morality, in this case made up of three items, "support for abortion," "divorce," and "homosexuality" used in an index is the best predictor of high levels of religiosity. In a sense this is a division between "conservative" and "liberal" personal values. Again, we noticed important differences between the two nations, with Sweden liberal and South Africans, very conservative.

Finally, coming back to our initial points of departure regarding the thesis of secularization based on existential security on the one hand and, on the other hand, the cultural traditions axiom it is clear that there are vast differences between South Africa and Sweden on both these axioms. Existential security is an important "driver" of the higher levels of religiosity in South Africa, and as far as culture traditions are concerned a huge gap is noticeable between South Africans and the Swedish population.

BIBLIOGRAPHY

Inglehart, Ronald. *Cultural Shift in Advanced and Industrial Societies.* Princeton, NJ: Princeton University Press, 1990.

————. *The Silent Revolution: Changing Values and Political Styles among Western Publics.* Princeton, NJ: Princeton University Press, 1977.

Kotzé, Hennie J., and Karin Lombard. "Revising the Value Shift Hypothesis: A Descriptive Analysis of South Africa's Value Priorities between 1990 and 2001." *Comparative Sociology* 3–4 (2002) 413–37.

Lategan, Bernard. "Extending the Materialist/Post-Materialist Distinction." *Scriptura* 75 (2000) 409–420.

Myndigheten för stöd till trossamfund. "Faith Communities Eligible for State Funding." Online. https://www.myndighetensst.se/om-oss/in-english/faith-communities.html.

Norris, Pippa, and Ronald Inglehart. *Sacred and Secular: Religion and Politics Worldwide.* 2nd ed. Cambridge: Cambridge University Press, 2011.

Rokeach, Milton, ed. *Understanding Human Values.* New York: Free Press, 1979.

United Nations Development Programme (UNDP). "Table 1: Human Development Index and its Components." Human Development Reports. Online. http://hdr.undp.org/en/composite/HDI.

United States Department of State. "2010 Report on International Religious Freedom." Online. https://www.state.gov/j/drl/rls/irf/2010.

Van Deth, Jan W., and Elinor Scarbourough. *The Impact of Values.* Oxford: Oxford University Press, 1995.

The World Bank. "World Development Indicators." Data Catalog. July 10, 2019. Online. https://datacatalog.worldbank.org/dataset/world-development-indicators.

World Population Review. "South African Population 2018." Online. http://worldpopulationreview.com/countries/south-africa-population.

————. "Sweden Population 2018." Online. http://worldpopulationreview.com/countries/sweden-population.

World Values Survey. "Welcome to the World Values Survey Site." Online. http://www.worldvaluessurvey.org.

2

From "Prophetic Witness" to "Prophets of Doom"?

The Contested Role of Religion in the South African Public Sphere

DION FORSTER

The relationship between religious freedom and the safeguarding of human rights is complex in South Africa. Religion plays a very significant, and important, role in the public sphere. As recently as January 2017 the state has sought to regulate religious leaders and religious freedom under the "hate crimes" and "hate speech" bill. This, after a self-appointed prophet made headlines for using a deadly insecticide, Doom bug spray, to "heal" parishioners of various social, economic, and health ailments. The reasons given by the state for wanting to regulate religion and religious leaders was for the safeguarding of the human rights of South African citizens. Despite such religious abuses, South Africa remains a context where a great deal of trust is placed in religious leaders and religious organizations. Moreover, religious communities are extremely influential in society. Any move to curtail religious freedom must be very carefully considered, since as this chapter will show, the South African government (under apartheid) has previously used similar reasoning to try to silence the public witness of religious leaders and religious communities who were working against state sanctioned human rights abuses.

Considering the journey from "prophetic witness" to the "prophets of Doom," what role should religion play in the public sphere in South Africa today? This chapter aims to spend some time unpacking a complex set of intersectional realities in order to ask the question, "What is the role of South African religion in the public sphere, and what should it be?" Equally important, the chapter will seek to engage the question, "What religious freedoms should the state guarantee for its citizens?" In order to undertake this task we shall consider a previous instance in which the state sought to curtail religious freedoms with the expressed intention of protecting its citizens[1] and then relate what we can learn from that case for the current situation.

LEST WE FORGET: A REMINDER OF THE PUBLIC ROLE OF RELIGION IN OUR PAST

Christian churches, which make up the largest proportion of the religious community in South Africa, have a longstanding history of public witness for the common good of the nation's citizens. The *Message to the People of South Africa* (which was published in 1968, as the apartheid policy was moving towards its most violent implementation) had this to say about the public role, witness, and mission of the church in South African society:

> The task of the Church is to enable people to see the power of God at work, changing hostility into love of the brethren, and to express God's reconciliation here and now. For we are not required to wait for a distant 'heaven' where all problems will have been solved. What Christ had done, he has done already. We can accept his work or reject it; we can hide from it or seek to live by it. But we cannot postpone it, for it is already achieved; and we cannot destroy it, for it is the work of the eternal God.[2]

More recently, Russel Botman said in his inaugural address as Rector of Stellenbosch University, "Africa will yet rise to the challenge of the hope that God has for it and for its people. The church and theological education is crucial to this mission."[3] These admonitions seem as pertinent to the church and society today as they were in 1968 and in 2007 respectively.

1. I shall facilitate a conversation with a paper written by Robert Vosloo. In this article Vosloo presents a historical instance of conflict between the state and the South African churches over their public witness. He highlights the dangers of the state employing a *state of exception* to curtail religious freedoms. See Vosloo, "State of Exception."

2. Theological Commission quoted in Naudé, *My Land van Hoop*, 169.

3. Botman quoted in Smit, *Essays in Public Theology*, 58.

Indeed, the church does play a very significant role in South African society. In part this is because of its sheer number of adherents to this faith within the general population. Nieman comments that the "23 main religious groupings, with a membership of 37,157,820 in 2001 (84 percent of the population), represent a potentially powerful voice and resource."[4] However, the role and influence of religion in South Africa is also contested, as we shall see.

In 2015 the thirtieth anniversary of the South African Kairos document was celebrated.[5] This document challenged the church in South Africa to consider how its theological identity, and expression of faith in spirituality and worship, shaped its presence and witness in society at large.[6] The Kairos theologians challenged the church to move away from a theology that upholds and furthers the aims of oppressive power (with reference to the apartheid state—known as "state theology"), or that retreats from society and only focuses on the programmes and priorities of the church, or local congregation, (known as "church theology"), thus denying the challenges and opportunities that are faced outside of the confines of the gathered worshiping community. The Kairos theologians advocated for a "prophetic theology," and a "prophetic church," that would witness to God's will within the public of the church and the broader publics of society.[7] They said:

4. See Schoeman, "South African Religious Demography"; Nieman, "Churches and Social Development," 37.

5. See Kairos Theologians, Challenge to the Church.

6. The 1985 Kairos document identified three types of dominant theologies at that time in South Africa's history: a state theology that sought to uphold and support the ideology of the state through the church and theology. Next Kairos described a church theology that either sought a middle, "third way" of compromise or was completely disengaged from what was taking place in society and the political realm. See Forrester et al., Public Theology, 51). The document advocated for a prophetic theology that would stand on the side of the oppressed and speak truth to the power of the state, seeking to voice the disapproval and judgment of God on state oppression and the weakness of the church. See Kairos Theologians, Challenge to the Church, 15–17; Forrester et al., Public Theology, 51; Huber and Fourie, Christian Responsibility, 110–14; Boesak, Kairos, Crisis, and Global Apartheid, 15; Dion Forster, "State Church?"

7. For the use of the term "public" in this chapter, please refer to Smit, "What Does 'Public' Mean?"; "Does It Matter?"; Kim, Theology in the Public Sphere; De Gruchy, "Public Theology as Christian Witness." Then, please also see Smit, "Paradigm of Public Theology," for a helpful historical overview, and philosophical analysis, of the development of the term 'public theology' and development of the discipline of public theology in theological discourse. It is also worth noting that the discipline and terminology are contested in South African theological discourse. As two prominent examples of the diverse perspectives on the role and place of public theology in South Africa, see Maluleke, "Reflections and Resources"; Koopman, "Modes of Prophecy." Tshaka has a very insightful analysis of the debate, offering a balanced and nuanced view of the role

We as a group of theologians have been trying to understand the theological significance of this moment in our history. It is serious, very serious. For very many Christians in South Africa this is the KAIROS, the moment of grace and opportunity, the favorable time in which God issues a challenge to decisive action. It is a dangerous time because, if this opportunity is missed, and allowed to pass by, the loss for the Church, for the Gospel and for all people of South Africa will be immeasurable.[8]

The challenge from the Kairos document to the church remains as important today as it was thirty years ago. What the Kairos document achieved was to remind both the church and the state that each had a specific role to play within God's intended will for society. What makes the Kairos document important is that it not only pointed out the errors and shortcomings of the state, but passed judgment upon it.

The *Kairos Document* perceived that the church itself was a site of [the Apartheid] struggle. . . . Whereas Cottesloe and the *Message* did not challenge the legality of the State, the *Kairos Document* described the state as tyrannical and therefore one that had to be resisted through acts of civil disobedience.[9]

When the Church confronted the power of an errant state, it did not go unchallenged. John W. De Gruchy notes that the apartheid state sought to counter the contentions of the Kairos theologians by working "in tandem with right wing religious organizations."[10] In other words, parts of the South African church had become agents of the unjust state, expressing support for its views and acting as a social shield to deflect criticism against its policies, actions and theology. There is a fear that this unhealthy and uncritical support of state power (and state policy) is taking place once again.[11]

The Kairos theologians cautioned that those parts of the church that had either succumbed to "state theology," or were denying pressing social realities within a form of "church theology" were in theological error. They were denying their divine responsibility as the church. Dietrich Bonhoeffer noted concerning the state and the church—under Christ the responsibility of the pastoral office[12] of the church is both to care for its members, but also

---

of public theology in the South African context. See Tshaka, "Perspective," 4–5.

8. Kairos Theologians, *Challenge to the Church*, 1.

9. De Gruchy, *Church Struggle*, 198.

10. De Gruchy, *Church Struggle*, 197.

11. Forster, "State Church?," 61–88. See also Tandwa, "SACC."

12. Bonhoeffer understood that the "pastoral office is the power set in place by God to exercise spiritual rule with divine authority. It emerges not from the congregation

to make the "government aware of its failures and mistakes that necessarily threaten its governmental office."[13]

As will be shown, both the church and the state fail God and the common good of citizens when the relationship between the church and the government are polluted and compromised.[14] The church and the state each have a responsibility to safeguard the role and function of the other—in other words, the church has a role to play in the public sphere. The church has a specific responsibility within a democracy. Similarly, the state has a specific role and function in society—in particular, the safeguarding of its citizens, which includes the safeguarding of their religious freedoms. When one oversteps its bounds both are in error (one for committing the error, and the other for allowing it to take place).[15]

Many South African theologians are aware of this danger. It is important to remember that it is the same South African citizens who serve in the state (and other social institutions of power), who are members of the churches and adherents to the Christian faith. We all need to be reminded of our responsibility as members of the body of Christ, citizens of the nation, and for some, the responsibilities of elected service and governance for the common good.

THE STATE OF THE NATION AND ITS RELIGIOUS CITIZENS: DEMOGRAPHIC INFORMATION ON RELIGION IN SOUTH AFRICA.

As was mentioned, South Africa remains a deeply religious nation. In this section, we shall draw upon two important sources to gain some understanding of the demographic makeup of the religious population in South Africa, and consider how South Africans engage religion in their public lives.

The most recent survey of the South African population conducted by StatsSA was done in 2013. This survey shows that 84.2 percent of South Africa's citizens self-identified as Christian.[16]

---

but from God" (Green and DeJonge, *Bonhoeffer Reader*, 700).

13. Green and DeJonge, *Bonhoeffer Reader*, 714.

14. Also see Forster, "State Church?," 61–88.

15. See Green and DeJonge, *Bonhoeffer Reader*, 711.

16. Statistics South Africa, *General Household Survey*, 3. See Schoeman, "South African Religious Demography."

Religion (names as stipulated in the survey)	Numbers	Percentage
Christian	44,602,155	84.2
Muslim	1,042,043	2.0
Ancestral, tribal, animist, or other traditional African Religions	2,626,015	5.0
Hindu	529,471	1.0
Buddhist and Bahai	16,992	0.0
Jewish	101,544	0.2
Atheist and Agnostic	112,972	0.2
Something else	48,084	0.1
Nothing in particular	2,916,049	5.5
Refused or don't know	154,569	0.3
Unspecified	832,097	1.6
Total	52,981,990	100.0

Table 8: Religious Affiliation[17]

This is an increase of 4.4 percentage points from 79.8 percent in 2001.[18] Within the so-called Christian demographic of 84 percent, the largest percentage of Christians belong to a diverse conglomeration of churches and Christian groupings which are collectively categorized as "Africa independent" (40.8 percent) and "Other Christian" (11.96 percent). The Methodist Church of Southern Africa is the largest mainline Christian denomination (9.24 percent) followed by a collective grouping of Reformed Christian churches (Uniting Reformed Church, Dutch Reformed Church, Presbyterian Church, etc.) at 9.04 percent.

A 2010 Pew-report found that 74 percent of South Africans "indicated that religion plays an important role in their lives."[19] The World Values Survey (WVS), which you can read more about in Kotzé's chapter in this book, helps us to understand a qualitative aspect of this "important role." The WVS shows that religious organizations remain among the most trusted institutions in society, enjoying higher levels of public trust and confidence than either the state or the private sector.[20] The report notes that "while trust in political institutions recedes. In contrast, civil society organizations

17. Statistics South Africa, General Household Survey.

18. Hendriks and Erasmus, "Religion in South Africa," 3.

19. Lugo and Cooperman, "Tolerance and Tension," 3; Schoeman, "South African Religious Demography," 3–4.

20. Winter and Burchert, "Value Change," 1.

enjoy growing trust."[21] In this report the Church is classified within the 'civil society' grouping. Hennie Kotzé, the lead researcher on the WVS for South Africa, clarifies the situation further when he comments that, "Religion in general, and churches in particular, plays an important political socialization role [for South Africans]."[22]

From this short overview of the statistics in the recent *General Household Survey* (2013) and the World Values Survey on South Africa (2013), at least two things can be concluded:

- First, that South Africa remains a deeply religious nation with almost 85 percent of the population self-identifying as members of the Christian faith.[23]
- Second, that South Africans place a great deal of trust and confidence in their religious convictions, religious leaders, and faith communities. These remain among the most trusted personal and social institutions in South African at present.[24] This is particularly so for the Christian population, Christian leaders, Christian Churches, and Faith Based Organizations.

The Christian religion, and the Church, are clearly a significant social institution that garner a great deal of respect and trust among South African citizens.

FROM "PROPHETIC WITNESS" TO THE "PROPHETS OF DOOM": DEALING WITH THE PRESENT WHILE REMEMBERING THE PAST

With such large scale religious affiliation, and such deep trust in religious leaders and institutions, there is bound to be a complex and even contested relationship between the church and the state (as institutions of social influence and power). Dietrich Bonhoeffer suggests that a certain kind of relationship should exist between the church and the state for the good of its citizens:

21. Winter and Burchert, "Value Change," 1.

22. Kotzé, "Shared Values in South Africa?"; Kotzé and Garcia-Rivero, "Institutions, Crises," 33.

23. The *General Household Survey* has further interesting information on attendance at religious ceremonies, the age, race and gender breakdown of South Africa's religious population, and the decline and growth of different religions and Christian denominations. See Statistics South Africa, *General Household Survey*, 1–7.

24. Kotzé, "Shared Values in South Africa?," 439–40; Kotzé and Garcia-Rivero, "Institutions, Crises," 33.

Government and church are bound, and bound together, by the same Lord. Government and church are distinguished from each other in their task. Government and church have the same sphere of action, human beings . . . what matters is giving concrete room in every given form for the relationship actually established by God and entrusting the way it develops to the Lord over government and the church.[25]

A question that emerges from the quotation above is: what does it mean to give "concrete room in every form for the relationship established by God" between church and state in the interest of South Africa[26] and South Africans? What responsibility does the state have in relation to the church, for the safeguarding of its citizens rights? And, what responsibility does the church have in relation to the state and the citizens of a nation, some of whom may be members of the Christian faith, and other who are not?

On November 21, 2016, the South African media reported a story on the self-proclaimed neo-Pentecostal prophet, Lethebo Rabalago, who used a deadly insecticide (Doom) to "heal" members of his congregation from various physical, social and economic ailments.[27] This event marked a low point in the public perception of religion and the religious in contemporary South African society. In reaction to this event (and other similar crimes) the South African government intensified its efforts to pass the proposed Hate Crimes and Hate Speech bill. In particular, the Commission for the Promotion and Protection of the Rights of Cultural, Religious, and Linguistic Communities (CRL Rights Commission) called for stricter regulations to be applied to religious and cultural leaders, and practices by religious and cultural communities, in South Africa.[28] Their reasoning was supposedly to safeguard the rights and freedoms of South Africa's citizens.[29]

25. Green and DeJonge, *Bonhoeffer Reader,* 714–15.

26. I am somewhat hesitant to speak of God's will or desire for South Africa as a nation. This notion is problematic since it assumes that somehow God has a particular political preference for a nation state. Does God really care about the borders of the Republic of South Africa and the national ideals of this country? Or, is God's concern for persons, environs, creatures and creation that happen to fit into a political construct known as South Africa? For more on the complexity (and myth) of the notion of South African nationhood, please see Degenaar, *Nations and Nationalism;* "Beware of Nation-Building Discourse"; Smit, "Religion and Civil Society."

27. "South Africa's 'Prophet of Doom.'"

28. Masuabi, "Doom Pastor Causes Outrage."

29. The state's responsibility for the safeguarding of the rights of citizens is a complex, and contested, issue when it comes to religious freedoms. One of the most significant illustrative examples of this may be found in the *Charlie Hebdo* case in France on January 7, 2015. It was claimed that the attacks were orchestrated in response to a series

However, this does raise a dilemma—if such a large proportion of the citizenry are deeply religious, would the removal of religious freedoms not in some way deny or restrict the rights of the very citizens the state aims to protect?[30]

Of course, this is not the first time that the South African state has acted in relation to a complex intersectional dilemma between religion and law. Previously in South African history the state sought to curtail religious freedom for what it viewed as the protection of South African society. In the months of February–April 1988 a conflict emerged between religious leaders (predominantly from the mainline Christian Churches), and the governing South African National Party (NP), and in particular the party's president, Mr. P. W. Botha. The conflict surrounded the response of the religious leaders to the apartheid government's clampdown on its political opponents on February 24, 1988.[31]

In this instance, a number of anti-apartheid activists and political movements were shut down by the apartheid state as part of the "State of Emergency." The response of the religious leaders was to advocate for freedom of expression, freedom of association, and the right to protest against injustice. The state president, Mr. Botha, had numerous religious leaders arrested as they marched to parliament to hand over their statement. In a letter to Archbishop Desmond Tutu, Mr. Botha admonished the leaders:

> You are no doubt aware that the expressed intention of the planned revolution by the ANC/SACP alliance is to ultimately transform South Africa into an atheistic Marxist state, where freedom of faith and worship will surely be among the first casualties.[32]

---

of blasphemous portrayals of the Prophet Mohammed and Islam in the publication. Rolf Schieder discusses the complexity of the responsibility of the state to protect its citizens in Schieder, "Blasphemy." What Schieder illustrates is the collision of responsibilities (indeed a collision of values) between the state's responsibility to protect the religious freedoms of its citizens (which in this case finds expression in their freedom of speech and thought in relation to faith), and the responsibility to protect its citizens from physical and emotional harm.

30. Schieder suggests, in relation to the *Charlie Hebdo* case in France, that the freedom of religion "implies the freedom to blasphemy" (Schieder, "Blasphemy," 39). In other words, if the state is to ensure the rights of religious freedom, such freedom should include the right to religious difference—even religious opposition. However, in the case under consideration in this chapter the issue is qualitatively different. The expression of religious freedom has clear physical dangers and consequences because of Pastor Lethebo Rabalago's actions. Because of the contextual intersectionality complexity of each of these cases, further thought and reflection is necessary.

31. Vosloo, "State of Exception," 1.

32. Botha quoted in Vosloo, "State of Exception," 5.

Vosloo comments that the "notion of freedom of faith and worship is invoked to challenge the legitimacy of the churches' participation in the struggle for liberation."[33] The point is that the state, acting in the person of the president, seemed to be setting up a conflict between what it identified as two binaries, namely the "true" Christian faith, and Godless liberationary Marxism. The church leaders, however, sought to accentuate that their rights were bound up in both. They professed a form of Christian faith that could not be separated from justice, freedom, and equality. De Gruchy writes: "The struggle for liberation was related to the church struggle, and the extent to which it was a contest between two very different understandings of Christianity and the teaching of the Bible."[34] The struggle was thus not only a political struggle, but also a theological struggle.

Vosloo suggests that the state was appealing to a notion which the Italian philosopher, Giorgio Agamben has called a *state of exception*.[35] Agamben is critical of the manner in which contemporary democratic states seem to set up such "exceptions" against their citizens. A similar point is made, although for different reasons, by Rolf Schieder in relation to Germany's blasphemy laws.[36] When does the state have the right to deny common rights to a certain citizen (e.g., freedom of speech) for the protection of other citizens (e.g., a religious group who may take offence to a cartoon, or publication)? Furthermore, when does the state have the responsibility to deny common rights or for the protection of the rights of other citizens? Agamben cites the creation of the Boer war concentration camps, and the Nazi concentration camps, as examples of the worst teleological ends of a *state of exception*.[37]

> The camp is the space that is opened when the state of exception becomes the rule. In the camp, the state of exception, which was essentially a temporary suspension of the rule of law on the basis of a factual state of danger, is now given a permanent spatial arrangement.[38]

Agamben views such actions as having bio-political significance, since they seem to revolve around making political choices that have "a direct impact on the human body and its freedom."[39] Agamben points to Hitler as

33. Vosloo, "State of Exception," 5.

34. De Gruchy, *Church Struggle*, 205.

35. Vosloo, "State of Exception," 8–11.

36. See Schieder, "Blasphemy," 50.

37. Agamben, *Homo Sacer*, 168–69.

38. Agamben, *Homo Sacer*, 168–69.

39. Vosloo, "State of Exception," 9.

a historical illustration of the danger of such notions. Soon after his rise to power, Hitler's "Decree for the Protection of the People and the State" "suspended the Weimar Constitution's articles concerning personal freedoms."[40] George W. Bush's establishment of the Guantanamo Bay detention center in November 2001, that suspends person's individual rights and holds them without trial, is another example of such action.[41] Some would argue that the mistreatment of migrants and immigrants in Trump's America, or in parts of Europe, are further contemporary examples of such action. Across the world today, the *state of exception* seems to have been normalised. Citizens of democratic nations, Christians and members of Churches, seem to have accepted that their rights and freedoms can be summarily curtailed by the state without significant recourse or concern.

FREEDOM, RELIGIOUS FREEDOM, AND THE INTERSECTION OF CIVIL-RELIGIOUS RESPONSIBILITIES

While the causes, and consequences, of the state's interference with religious freedom is different in these two cases framed in this study (i.e., the apartheid state's suspension of religious freedom, the intention to curtail religious freedom in contemporary South Africa), they form helpful cases to discuss the relationship between the state and the church. Moreover, they bring into focus a critical aspect of the role of South African religion, and particularly Christian religion, in the public sphere within the context of religious freedom.

Religion has been a site of conflict in relation to human rights in South Africa. South Africa's Apartheid history is a complex mingling of racial, political, and economic realities in which religion played a significant role.[42] Indeed, while Apartheid was supported by, and even informed, by what Elphick and Davenport describe as heretical theology,[43] it was also challenged and deconstructed by faithful and courageous prophetic witness.[44] The relative freedoms that have been afforded to religious persons, religious communities, and faith based organizations in South Africa throughout recent history are thus not to be taken for granted. Faith has played, and continues to play, an important role in South African public life.

40. Agamben, *State of Exception*, 10.

41. Agamben, *State of Exception*, 3; Vosloo, "State of Exception," 10.

42. De Gruchy, *Church Struggle*, 51–101.

43. Elphick and Davenport, *Christianity in South Africa*, 370–82; Smit, *Essays in Public Theology*, 212–13.

44. Elphick and Davenport, *Christianity in South Africa*, 383–99; De Gruchy, *Church Struggle*; Plaatjies-Van Huffel and Vosloo, *Reformed Churches in South Africa*.

Since 2014 the relationship between South African faith leaders, Churches, and the State has also been called into question.

After 1994 the social actors of power in South African society changed from the National Party and the Dutch Reformed Church. The African National Congress (ANC) is now the governing party in South Africa, while the mainline, largely English speaking, Churches (such as the Anglican Church, and Methodist Church of Southern Africa etc.,) now occupy the positions of social prominence and dominance in the religious sphere. The nexus of power is once again challenging the witness and work of the Church, as well as the credibility of the government in South Africa. The church is once again facing the threat of becoming embedded in the actions and intentions of the national state.[45]

The concern at present is that both the church and the state seem to seek to misuse the relationship that exists between the state, political parties, and the church in order to engage one another for undesirable ends. From the side of the church it could be to build relationships that allow access to undeserved power and wealth in society. From the side of the state and political parties it could be to seek moral sanction for unethical behavior, or to co-opt the church as an electoral constituency, and in so doing negate the witness and work of the church. I shall cite one example to illustrate this point.

In the lead up to the 2014 national elections there was increasing rhetoric of a religious character in the speeches and pronouncements of ANC politicians. The most public display around this were the activities of the Revd Vukile Mehana (the Chaplain General to the African National Congress at the time), who defended President Jacob Zuma's statement that persons who voted for the ANC would go to heaven, while those who voted for other parties would not.[46] Just before the 2014 elections Revd Mehana, who is a senior minister in the Methodist Church of Southern Africa, MCSA (serving on the denomination's executive, holding the portfolio of human resources management) came in the spotlight for encouraging pastors in Cape Town to solicit votes for the ANC where he said, "You cannot have church leaders that speak as if they are in opposition to government.

---

45. Edwin Arrison notes that when the 2012 Kairos South Africa document was being discussed among church leaders in South Africa, Denise Ackermann warned the churches and their leaders to "engage, but not be embedded" in political parties and the aims of the state (Arrison quoted in Conradie and Pillay, *Ecclesial Reform*, 12). This in an important distinction in the current relationship between the church and state. For a more recent discussion of these issues, see Forster, "State Church?," 61–88.

46. Mehana, "Zuma's Remarks Explained."

. . . God will liberate the people through this (ANC) government."[47] Revd Mehana would have done well to heed Storey's warning that "the years since 1994 have surely persuaded us that democracy is not to be equated with the arrival of the reign of God."[48] As economic inequality has increased, suffering and poverty have remained, due to a lack of transfer of privilege, wealth and power from white South Africans to the majority of the population; coupled with government corruption and a lack of service delivery, political intolerance has increased. It has become a blight upon the church that it so openly supported a particular political party. In particular since it has only been two decades since the destructive and complicit relationship between the apartheid state and the Dutch Reformed Church was exposed.

As a result, some have come to ask: How did we move from the position, in our recent history, of being a nation in which religion and the religious contributed towards the deconstruction of apartheid and the establishment of a democratic nation, to a nation where religion is once again being used in dangerous ways to negate basic human rights?

This once again brings us to ask what responsibility, or right, the state has to impinge on the religious freedoms of its citizens to protect them from abuse by religions or religious persons?

This is not a simple question to answer. The answer is likely to be contextual, and possibly even to differ from situation to situation. However, there are some theological pointers that could aid the church in its role in public life. This in turn could help to inform the state in relation to its responsibilities.

THREE POSSIBLE WAYS IN WHICH THE CHURCH COULD WITNESS IN THE PUBLIC SPHERE

When we say that the Church plays an important role in the lives of South Africans, and holds a special place in South African society, what do we mean? This is a notion that requires some clarification.[49] A simplistic, or unqualified, discussion of the role and responsibilities of the Church and the churches in public life would be inadequate since each of the different forms of Church may have slightly different responsibilities and ways of enacting those responsibilities in relation to the nation and its citizens.

---

47. Phakathi, "Pastors Will Not Help ANC."

48. Storey, "Banning the Flag," 5.

49. This section is based, in part, on an edited version of previous research that I published on the public role and witness of the Church in Society. See Forster, "What Hope Is There."

When South Africans speak about the "Church" they are referencing a diverse range of understandings and concepts. What do we mean by the expression "church"? Dirkie Smit suggests that there are three general forms, or usages, of the notion of "the church" in academic and popular theological thinking.[50] I shall briefly present these below.

The Local Congregation

For many Christians this is most likely to be their primary perspective of the church, a localised community of Christians, organized around regular common worship. Philander points out that this is the place, and social group, that people often think of when they answer the question of where they go to church, or what church they are members of.[51] What role can this 'form' of church play in South African public life? As Smit rightly points out, this requires careful reflection. First, it is important to recognize that the largest grouping of South Africa's Christians belong to African Initiated churches. The last reliable census data showed that 40.82 percent of South Africa's Christian population fit into such church groupings,[52] with a further 31 percent belonging to other groupings that include the mainline denominations. Some scholars argue that these local communities provide a great deal of social cohesion, faith identity that fosters hope, and at times even concrete expressions of hope (such as feeding schemes, education, skills development, and social care).[53]

Quite apart from the immeasurable spiritual value and the work of moral formation added through local worshipping communities, there is another way in which such communities act as a witness in the public sphere.[54] This level of involvement in the local community is often described as first and second generation involvement, to use the development theory terminology of David Korten.[55] First generation engagement refers to relief and charity work (soup kitchens, child care, education, basic medical care etc.), whereas second generation engagement refers to the work of empowering a community, often through projects (such as skills development projects. Examples could include sewing classes, trades etc.).

---

50. Smit, "Oor Die Kerk"; *Essays in Public Theology*, 61–68.

51. Philander, "Die Rol van Die Kerk," 177.

52. For a thorough theological discussion, please see Hendriks and Erasmus, "Religion in South Africa." See also Schoeman, "South African Religious Demography," 1–7.

53. Nieman, "Churches and Social Development," 37–44.

54. Philander, "Die Rol van Die Kerk," 176–79.

55. Korten, *Getting to the Twenty-First Century*, 117–18.

However, we also cannot deny that while this form of church has potential for great good, it also has the potential for great harm,[56] as we saw with the "prophet of Doom" incident. Many of the leaders of these communities are self-appointed pastors who lack formal theological training and do not adhere to structures of governance or oversight that would be common in mainline denominations. The rampant spread of churches that preach a prosperity doctrine is alarming, as is the rise of fundamentalism and religious intolerance. Hence there are many ways in which this form of community could contribute negatively towards society. John de Gruchy notes that at times in South Africa's history, church worship, teaching and liturgy have been the cause of the preventing the gospel from taking hold in society.[57] Smit notes that this may not be the kind of contribution that theologians, or religious leaders, would like to see.[58]

The challenge is thus to engage this popular and ever-growing sector of Christian community with a theology that can aid them to work for the good of South Africans, while averting any possibly harmful social, religious and theological impact on society from such groupings.

The Institutional, Denominational, and Ecumenical Church

For many people the "church" refers primarily to the organizational or institutional structures. When some people hear the word "church" in this context they may think of the confessional community that they are a part of (e.g., Catholic, Orthodox, or Methodist). Philander notes that often this expression of church is what people would point to in answer to common questions, such as, "what does the church say about unemployment in South Africa?"[59] It could also refer to larger collective groupings such as Evangelical Christians, or even more formal groupings such as ecumenical bodies (like the World Council of Churches, or the World Communion of Reformed Churches). Smit notes that we must take care not to confuse the numerical prominence of a grouping with the social and theological contribution of that church.[60] Simply knowing how many Methodists or Charismatics there are in South Africa does not tell us much about their contribution to society. Some numerically smaller churches have had a very

---

56. "The Christian religion is also a dangerous power, and has been such and still is, in South Africa" (Smit, *Essays in Public Theology*, 63).

57. See Smit, *Essays in Public Theology*, 63; De Gruchy, *Cry Justice!*

58. Smit, *Essays in Public Theology*, 63.

59. Philander, "Die Rol van Die Kerk," 177.

60. Smit, *Essays in Public Theology*, 65.

significant impact on shaping South African society. The work and witness of Archbishop Desmond Tutu, and the Anglican Church, is one such example.

In previous decades this form of church would be understood to engage society with a third generation development strategy, namely to engage the policies of institutions in society (such as the policies and laws of government, and the decisions and policies of regulatory bodies in society etc.).[61]

A recent academic article on the changes in expectations of members, and the ministry models of South African churches, noted the demise of the ecumenical movement in South Africa.[62] The consequence is that the church has been left somewhat weakened and voiceless in the new dispensation. Perhaps it is for this reason that the state has sought to occupy the vacuum that has been created by the weakening of collective ecumenical identity and oversight.

Unlike the period leading up to 1994 there is thankfully no longer a "state church" that can speak on behalf of the people. Yet there is also no longer a "struggle church" linked to a strong functional ecumenical body, like the South African Council of Churches, that represents the collective will and intentions of the churches in South Africa. Smit notes that the ecumenical movement that was "strong during the apartheid years when many churches were committed to their common struggle against apartheid, has lost most of its appeal and influence."[63] Thus, there is a need to awaken and rebuild strong ecumenical bonds between the Churches and other faith bodies in order to both strengthen their collective work, and hold the state and the private sector to account, for justice and transformation.

The Church as Believers, Salt, and Light in the World

The third way in which people think of the church, is as individual believers who are 'salt and light' in the world, each involved in living out their faith on a daily basis in their own particular way.[64] This is a very important way in which the church can participate in the public sphere.

In an ideal situation this contribution of the church would be characterised as a fourth generation contribution, to use Korten's terminology

---

61. Korten, *Getting to the Twenty-First Century*, 119; Nieman, "Churches and Social Development," 8.

62. Forster, "What Hope Is There."

63. Smit, *Essays in Public Theology*, 66.

64. Smit, *Essays in Public Theology*, 68.

once again.[65] Fourth generation engagement is "akin to a social movement that makes extensive use of networks and people's independent mobilizing actions to work for justice and people's self-actualisation in society. It is guided by an alternative vision in society that mobilizes people to voluntary action."[66]

Gerald West challenged the church to recover the importance of people's theology in a paper he delivered at Stellenbosch University entitled, "People's Theology, Prophetic Theology, and Public Theology in Post-Liberation South Africa."[67] His challenge reminds us of Albert Nolan's description of the South African church, the majority church, which is frequently unrecognized in public life.

> The part of the Church that I am referring to is the oppressed part, the poor and the oppressed Christians of South Africa. . . . This cuts across all our Church denominations and includes leaders from various traditions. In fact, this part of the Church must now be, far and away, the majority of Christians in South Africa.[68]

Indeed, this is an important understanding of the church in South Africa. The church in South Africa remains largely poor, it is largely female, and it is largely between the ages of 15–65 (as the most recent statistics on the South African population[69] and Church membership[70] show). One could ask whether the leadership of church denominations, and academics in theological institutions, are engaging this church as we think about the future of South Africa, and the role of the church in that future? Moreover, in a country where 85 percent of the population self-identify as Christians, and many more as religious, it is Christians who are elected as political leaders, and Christians who lead major corporations and businesses. In a country where economic, social and political problems continue to contribute to suffering, there is a great deal that could and should be done by Christians in their daily life and work to witness and work for a better future for all.

---

65. Korten, *Getting to the Twenty-First Century*, 113–32.

66. Swart et al., *Religion and Social Development*, 8.

67. Professor West's paper appeared as a chapter in Claassens and Birch, *Restorative Readings*, 78–98.

68. Nolan, *God in South Africa*, 211.

69. Haldenwang, "20 Years of Democracy."

70. Nieman, "Churches and Social Development," 37.

A FINAL WORD (IN THE END)[71]

The discussion in this chapter has raised some questions about the relationship between the church and the state in South Africa in relation to religious freedom and responsibility. It has tried to probe the question of the role of the church in the public sphere, and offer some theological suggestions for how the three different 'forms' of church may contribute to the common good. The chapter has also cautioned against the state using its power as a *state of exception*, supposedly to protect the rights of its citizens. In relation to religious freedom, and the responsibility of persons who occupy identity within the Church and live within society at large, Stanley Hauerwas offers the following caution:

> The question is not whether we have freedom of religion and a corresponding limited state . . . but whether we have a church that has a people capable of saying no to the state. No state, particularly the democratic state, is kept limited by constitutions, but rather is limited by a people with the imagination and courage to challenge the inveterate temptation of the state to ask us to compromise our loyalty to God. Freedom of religion is a temptation, albeit a subtle one. It tempts us to believe that we have been rendered safe by legal mechanisms. It is subtle because we believe that our task as Christians is to support the ethos necessary to maintain the mechanism. As a result, we lose the critical skills formed by the gospel to know when we have voluntarily qualified our loyalty to God in the name of the state. We confuse freedom of religion with the freedom of the church, accepting the assumption that the latter is but a specification of the former. We thus become tolerant, allowing our convictions to be relegated to the realms of the private.[72]

What is clear is that we need deeper reflection and greater commitment to the responsibilities for justice and the common good from the state and the Church. In relation to the criminal abuse of citizens, such as when Lethebo Rabalago sprayed a pesticide on his members, the state should exercise its responsibility to protect its citizens from harm. This is possible within existing criminal law. It does not require the curtailing of religious freedom to protect one's citizens from such obvious physical abuse. It only requires the effective and consistent application of criminal law in instances where the

---

71. Deleted that may be included?—Telos and virtue (Aristotelian turn)—Faith and citizenship—Three forms of expression of conviction and belief—An ethics of care and an ethics of justice.

72. Hauerwas, *After Christendom?*, 7.

safety and well-being of the citizenry is under threat. On the other hand, the Church bears responsibility for greater reflection and cooperation in order to prepare its members for faithful service and a commitment to social and economic justice in society at large. This includes the formation and support of virtuous citizens who will act with justice and integrity in public life for the common good.[73] Moreover, local Churches and ecumenical bodies should care for their members, which includes holding themselves and the state to account for the principles of justice and freedom for all.

Perhaps what is necessary is the development of what Jürgen Moltmann has called a new "theo-political imagination."[74] Imagination is more fluid and open ended than legislation, and less binding than normative doctrine. Faithful and responsible imagination can inform how Christians in South Africa, who are members of the nation and the Church in their various forms, can safeguard the freedoms and rights of all.

BIBLIOGRAPHY

Agamben, Giorgio. *Homo Sacer: Sovereign Power and Bare Life.* Palo Alto, CA: Stanford University Press, 1998.

———. *State of Exception.* Chicago: University of Chicago Press, 2005.

Boesak, Allan Aubrey. *Kairos, Crisis, and Global Apartheid: The Challenge to Prophetic Resistance.* London: Palgrave Macmillan, 2015.

Claassens, Juliana, and Bruce Birch. *Restorative Readings: Old Testament, Ethics, Human Dignity.* Eugene, OR: Pickwick, 2015.

Conradie, Ernst M., and Miranda Pillay. *Ecclesial Reform and Deform Movements in the South African Context.* Stellenbosch: African Sun, 2015.

De Gruchy, John W. *The Church Struggle in South Africa.* Minneapolis: Fortress, 2005.

———. *Cry Justice! Prayers, Meditations, and Readings from South Africa.* Maryknoll, NY: Orbis, 1986.

———. "Public Theology as Christian Witness: Exploring the Genre." *International Journal of Public Theology* 1.1 (2007) 26–41.

Degenaar, Johan. "Beware of Nation-Building Discourse." In *Democratic Nation-Building in South Africa*, edited by Nic Rhoodie and Ian Liebenberg, 23–29. Pretoria: Human Sciences Research Council, 1994.

———. *Nations and Nationalism: The Myth of a South African Nation.* Johannesburg: Idasa, 1991.

Elphick, Richard, and T. R. H. Davenport. *Christianity in South Africa: A Political, Social, and Cultural History.* Oakland: University of California Press, 1997.

Forrester, Duncan B., et al. *Public Theology for the Twenty-First Century: Essays in Honor of Duncan B. Forrester.* London: A&C Black, 2004.

Forster, Dion. "A State Church? A Consideration of the Methodist Church of Southern Africa in the Light of Dietrich Bonhoeffer's 'Theological Position Paper on State and Church.'" *Stellenbosch Theological Journal* 2.1 (2016) 61–88.

73. See Koopman, "Towards a Human Rights Culture."

74. Moltmann, "Future of Theology," 9–11.

————. "What Hope Is There for South Africa? A Public Theological Reflection on the Role of the Church as a Bearer of Hope for the Future." *HTS Teologiese Studies* 71.1 (2015) 1–10.

Forster, Dion A., and Wessel Bentley. *Methodism in Southern Africa: A Celebration of Wesleyan Mission.* Kempton Park: AcadSA, 2008.

Green, Clifford J., and Michael DeJonge, eds. *The Bonhoeffer Reader.* Philadelphia: Fortress, 2013.

Haldenwang, Barbel. "20 Years of Democracy: Is Life Better or Worse for the 'Average' South African?" *Institute for Futures Research* 19.2 (2014) 1–6.

Hauerwas, Stanley. *After Christendom? How the Church Is to Behave If Freedom, Justice, and a Christian Nation Are Bad Ideas.* Nashville: Abingdon, 2011.

Hendriks, Jurgens, and Johannes Erasmus. "Religion in South Africa: 2001 Population Census Data." *Journal of Theology for Southern Africa* 121 (2005) 88–111.

Huber, Wolfgang, and Willem Fourie. *Christian Responsibility and Communicative Freedom: A Challenge for the Future of Pluralistic Societies.* Münster: LIT, 2012.

Kairos Theologians. *Challenge to the Church: A Theological Comment on the Political Crisis in South Africa [The Kairos Document].* Johannesburg: Kairos Theologians, 1985. Online. http://www.sahistory.org.za/archive/challenge-church-theological-comment-political-crisis-south-africa-kairos-document-1985.

Kim, Sebastian C. H. *Theology in the Public Sphere.* London: SCM, 2011.

Koopman, Nico. "Modes of Prophecy in a Democracy." In *Prophetic Witness. An Appropriate Mode of Public Discourse in Democratic Societies?,* edited by Heinrich Bedford-Strohm and Etienne De Villiers, 181–92. Münster: LIT Verlag, 2011.

————. "Towards a Human Rights Culture in South Africa. The Role of Moral Formation." *Scriptura* 48.1 (2007) 107–118.

Korten, David C. *Getting to the Twenty-First Century: Voluntary Action and the Global Agenda.* West Hartford, CT: Kumarian, 1990.

Kotzé, Hennie. "Shared Values in South Africa? A Selection of Value Orientations in the Field of Personal Ethics." *Scriptura* 75 (2016) 437–48.

Kotzé, Hennie, and Carlos Garcia-Rivero. "Institutions, Crises, and Political Confidence in Seven Contemporary Democracies. An Elite–Mass Analysis." *Journal of Public Affairs* 17.1–2 (2017) 1–17.

Lugo, Luis, and Alan Cooperman. *Tolerance and Tension: Islam and Christianity in Sub-Saharan Africa.* Washington, DC: Pew Research Center, 2010.

Maluleke, Tinyiko Sam. "Reflections and Resources the Elusive Public of Public Theology: A Response to William Storrar." *International Journal of Public Theology* 5.1 (2011) 79–89.

Masuabi, Queenin. "Doom Pastor Causes Outrage, Calls Increase for Religious Leaders to Be Regulated." *EWN News,* November 22, 2016. Online. http://ewn.co.za/2016/11/22/doom-pastor-causes-outrage-calls-increase-for-religious-leaders-to-be-regulated.

Mehana, Vukile. "Zuma's Remarks Explained—ANC Chaplain General." *PoliticsWeb,* February 7, 2011. Online. http://www.politicsweb.co.za/politicsweb/view/politicsweb/en/page71639?oid=220386&sn=Detail&pid=71639.

Moltmann, Jürgen. "The Future of Theology." *The Ecumenical Review* 68.1 (2016) 1–11.

Naudé, Beyers. *My Land van Hoop. Die Lewe van Beyers Naudé.* Cape Town: Human & Rousseau, 1995.

Nieman, Anna. "Churches and Social Development in South Africa." In *Religion and Social Development in Post-Apartheid South Africa*, edited by Ignatius (Naas) W. Swart, et al., 37–44. Stellenbosch: African Sun, 2010.

Nolan, Albert. *God in South Africa: The Challenge of the Gospel*. Grand Rapids, MI: Eerdmans, 1988.

Phakathi, Bekezela. "Pastors Will Not Help ANC Win Votes, Says DA." *Business Live*, February 6, 2014. Online. http://www.bdlive.co.za/national/politics/2014/02/06/pastors-will-not-help-anc-win-votes-says-da.

Philander, N. C. "Die Rol van Die Kerk as Een van Die Instellings in Die Samelewing Wat Mense Moreel Vorm." *Dutch Reformed Theological Journal* 52.1–2 (2011) 174–85.

Plaatjies-Van Huffel, Marry-Anne, and Robert Vosloo. *Reformed Churches in South Africa and the Struggle for Justice: Remembering 1960–1990*. Stellenbosch: African Sun, 2013.

Schieder, Rolf. "Blasphemy—A Civil-Religious Crime." In *Religion and Democracy: Studies in Public Theology*, edited by Torsten Meireis and Rolf Schieder, 37–54. Baden-Baden: Nomos, 2017.

Schoeman, Willem J. "South African Religious Demography: The 2013 General Household Survey." *HTS Teologiese Studies* 73.2 (2017) 1–7.

Smit, Dirk J. "Does It Matter? On Whether There Is Method in the Maddess." In *A Companion to Public Theology*, edited by Sebastian C. H. Kim and Katie Cannon, 67–94. Leiden: Brill, 2017.

———. *Essays in Public Theology: Collected Essays 1*. Stellenbosch: African Sun, 2007.

———. "Oor Die Kerk as 'n Unieke Samelewingsverband." *Tydskrif Vir Geesteswetenskappe* 2.36 (1996) 119–29.

———. "The Paradigm of Public Theology—Origins and Development." In *Contextuality and Intercontextuality in Public Theology*, edited by Heinrich Bedford-Strohm, et al., 11–23. Zürich: Lit, 2013.

———. "Religion and Civil Society in 'South Africa'? Searching for a Grammar for Life Together." In *The Role of Civil Society within a Participatory Democracy—On Religion and Civil Society in South Africa and Germany*, edited by Michael Welker, et al., 34–63. Stellenbosch: African Sun, 2015.

"South Africa's 'Prophet of Doom' Condemned." *BBC News*, November 21, 2016. Online. http://www.bbc.co.uk/news/world-africa-38051923.

Statistics South Africa. *General Household Survey 2013*. Pretoria: Statistics South Africa, 2014. Online. https://www.statssa.gov.za/publications/P0318/P03182013.pdf.

Storey, Peter. "Banning the Flag from Our Churches: Learning from the Church-State Struggle in South Africa." In *Between Capital and Cathedral: Essays on Church and State Relationships*, edited by Dion A. Forster and Wessel Bentley, 1–20. Pretoria: UNISA Research Institute for Theology and Religion, 2012.

Swart, Ignatius (Naas) W., et al. *Religion and Social Development in Post Apartheid South Africa: Perspectives for Critical Engagement*. Stellenbosch: African Sun, 2010.

Tandwa, Lizeka. "SACC Is Just a Government Mouthpiece—Student Leaders." *News24*, January 19, 2016. Online. http://www.news24.com/SouthAfrica/News/sacc-is-just-a-govt-mouthpiece-student-leaders-20160119.

Theological Commission of the South African Council of Churches. "A Message to the People of South Africa." *The Ecumenical Review* 21.1 (1969) 67–70.

Tshaka R. S. "A Perspective on Notions of Spirituality, Democracy, Social Cohesion and Public Theology." *Verbum Ecclesia Verbum et Ecclesia* 35.3 (2014) 1–6.

Vosloo, Robert. "The State of Exception and Religious Freedom: Revisiting the Church-State Confrontation Correspondence and Statements of 1988." *Studia Historiae Ecclesiasticae* 34.1 (2008) 1–17.

Winter, Susanne, and Lars Thomas Burchert. "Value Change in Post-Apartheid South Africa." *Konrad-Adenauer-Stiftung*, May 2015. Online. http://www.kas.de/wf/doc/kas_41566-1522-2-30.pdf?150609093459.

3

Exotic, Alien, Particular, Religious, and Dangerous?

The Complexity of Religion in European Public Spheres

Elisabeth Gerle

Freedom of Religion is one of the basic principles of Human Rights. It may even be seen as one of the earliest, and thus, foundational human rights principles, since expressions of religion, such as "teaching, practice, worship and observance," are closely related to freedom of expression and organization. Yet, this right is contested and debated in popular discourses. Is freedom of religion really necessary and, if so, for whom and why? According to the Universal Declaration of Human Rights this is a right to express your faith alone and in community:

> Everyone has the right to freedom of thought, conscience and religion; this right includes freedom to change his religion or belief, and freedom, either alone or in community with others and in public or private, to manifest his religion or belief in teaching, practice, worship and observance.[1]

I will leave to others to analyse this, or succeeding legal formulations, and the relationship between law and society. Rather, I will focus on present and

1. United Nations, "Universal Declaration of Human Rights" art. 18.

historical discourses, which can contribute to explaining the role of religion in the public sphere in Europe. This is also related to the notion "religion" as such. What is culture and what is religion? I will twist around and challenge some notions that may be interpreted and understood in different ways depending on historic, geographic, and political circumstances.

EUROPE—AN EXCEPTION?

Europe is sometimes described as an exception to other parts of the world. Due to the existence of broad national Churches many citizens in Europe today see themselves as belonging without believing, as well as believing without belonging, to refer to Grace Davie's famous formulation.[2] It may also be related to the influence of secularization theories that in parts of Europe have become a kind of world view in itself.

In the famous map of World Values Survey (WVS), religion and tradition is, for instance, set in opposition to the secular, and survival in opposition to self-expression.[3] Sweden, as a consequence, is situated in the utmost right corner scoring high on secular-rational values (less emphasis on religion, traditional family values and authority) and self-expression values (giving high priority to environmental protection, growing tolerance of foreigners, gay, and lesbian and gender equality etc.).

Many African countries are, on the other hand, placed rather low in the opposite corner scoring more in direction of traditional values (emphasis on the importance of religion, parent-child ties, deference to authority and traditional family values) and survival values (emphasis on economic and physical security). There are, however, also many East-European countries, often predominantly Orthodox, such as Belarus, Bulgaria, Ukraine, and Russia, which in the diagram are to be found a bit higher up than African countries in relation to the secular-rational, yet also emphasizing survival. Catholic Europe with countries such as Austria, Slovakia and Spain find themselves in the middle while France, Luxembourg and Andorra get a bit closer to the Protestant North. The survey can, however, also be seen as an example of how secularization and rationality are connected and treated as oppositional to more religious world views

A critical theory has been introduced by Tumoko Masuzawa who teaches European intellectual history and critical theory at the University of Michigan. She does not discuss the map of the WVS, but she claims that maps of world religions determine the outlook of "world religions."

---

2. Davie, *Europe*.

3. Inglehart and Welzel, *Modernization*.

Masuzawa makes quite broad claims, some of which may be debated.[4] She shows, though, how religion as a notion from the very beginning is woven into the emerging discourse of secularization. She thus argues that the discourse on religion is a discourse of othering.

In some areas, "being religious" is connected to practicing and often "related to personal and group identity in a way altogether different from the one usually assumed (i.e., assumed on the basis of the Western European denominational history of recent centuries)."[5] Hence, the question arises if it is very constructive with a sharp contrast between religious and secular any longer? Different contexts influence the connotation of both these terms. Many scholars have for decades, not only criticised their own secularization theories,[6] but also questioned the dichotomy between the religious/sacred and secular as a convincing contradiction.[7] Such a critique has most interestingly been exercised by theologians and philosophers.[8]

It may also be worth pondering the relationship between strong welfare states and decreasing dependency on traditional family. In a country such as Sweden this connection has developed in a state that for a long time has encouraged and facilitated emotional and economic individualism. This may, however, also be related to religio-cultural backgrounds. Different traditions of religion have had a great influence on various models of welfare in Europe. Charity that has shaped much of social work in Southern Europe has never been favored in Northern Europe where a Lutheran ethos has emphasized the need of other persons, not the cultivation of the moral development of the individual.[9] Hence, the needs of the other have been integrated into Nordic welfare politics inspired by this theological ethos.

4. Svenungsson, "Religionens återkomst," 12.

5. Masuzawa, *Invention of World Religions*, 5.

6. Casanova, *Public Religions*.

7. Van den Breemer et al., *Secular and Sacred?*, 312.

8. See Eagleton, *Reason, Faith*; Kristensson Uggla, "Gustaf Wingren"; Wyller, "Discovery"; Gerle, "Between Sun and Shadow."

9. Wejryd, "En svårförklarlig," 19–20.

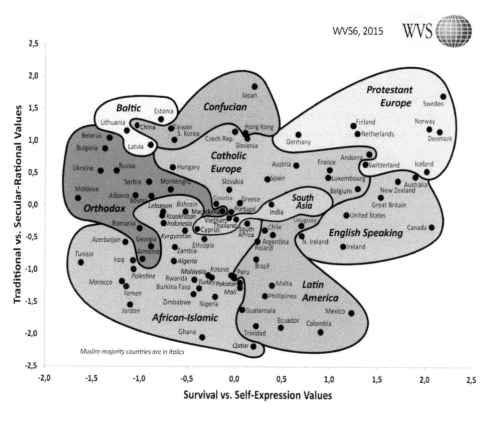

Figure 1: Cultural map—WVS wave 6, 2015

Europe may be exceptional, but it is not monolithic. Italy, France and parts of Germany with strong Roman Catholic backgrounds are very different from Northern Europe. In the Eastern parts of Europe, the tradition of orthodox churches has through centuries been closely connected to rulers and to nation states, thus playing an important role in contemporary identity formation emphasizing collective, often national, identities. There are also variations within countries and regions not only between them, even if certain trends may be discerned.

Protestant Europe negotiated with Modernity based on some deep Protestant beliefs focusing on the priesthood of all and the personal authority of the Christian to read and interpret the scriptures. These early theological convictions, similar to what later was developed in other terms by the Enlightenment, gave an opening to Modernity with its emphasis on individual reason. Maybe as an outcome of a rational(istic) understanding of Lutheran tradition, faith became seen as cognitive, affirming certain propositions and thus as related mostly to head and heart. This made it easy to regard religion as something for the individual, inner and private.

Hence, a more pluralist society with increasing visibility and presence of Muslim and Jewish practices becomes a challenge to a Universalist world view of the West. The non-Christian, or non-Secular, are thus described as the other, exotic, alien and sometimes as dangerous, always as particular. In the following I want to wrestle with some of these thoughts.

With Judith Butler I share the perspective that

> any generalizations we make about "religion" in "public life" are suspect from the start if we do not think about which religions are being presupposed in the conceptual apparatus itself, especially if that conceptual apparatus, including the notion of the public, is not understood in light of its own genealogy and secularization projects.[10]

She claims that it is very different "to refer to a secular Jew than to a secular Catholic"[11]; even when both "may be presumed to have departed from religious belief, there may be other forms of belonging that do not presume or require belief." She holds therefore that "secularization may well be one way that Jewish life continues as Jewish. And this, I think holds true for many more than Jewish traditions."[12]

With Butler I also share that we "make a mistake if religion becomes equated with Belief" and, as such,

> tied to certain kinds of speculative claims about God—a theological presumption that does not always work to describe religious practice. That effort to distinguish the cognitive status of religious and nonreligious belief misses the fact that very often religion functions as a matrix of subject formation, an embedded framework for valuations, and a mode of belonging and embodied social practice.[13]

Needless to say, I am putting myself in a liminal position, dealing mainly with cultural/religious/political trends, especially from my own region, which may be visible but not too easy to pin down and without providing references to legal texts or surveys. So, bear with me, as I am discussing new and old, re-emerging borders and binaries that I think are influencing the role of religion in Europe.

10. Butler, *Parting Ways*, 115.
11. Butler, *Parting Ways*, 115.
12. Butler, *Parting Ways*, 115.
13. Butler, *Parting Ways*, 115.

NAMING IS NOT INNOCENT—
ON THE IMPORTANCE OF NAMING YOURSELF

When others refer to you under a label this might be part of a naming that is unfamiliar to how you see yourself. Storytelling and selfhood are closely connected as is evident in the classic story told about the tragic love between Romeo and Juliet, belonging to competing families. Therefore, the tragedy of Romeo and Juliet is a tragedy of the name. Paul A. Kottman points out:

> For the tragedy of the name (and this is what is tragic about Romeo and Juliet) is that it is indifferent to the one who is named. This indifference is again the pain, even the death, that name-calling carries with it.[14]

He summarizes:

> The name carries death for the one who bears it, because the name has no regard for the life of its bearer: it is destined to survive that life, and thus announces its death.[15]

On the one hand the tragedy of Romeo and Juliet is theirs alone. Through the story we come to know *who* they were. On the other hand, "their tragedy is inseparable from the 'other' tragedy of the name, which is lethally indifferent to *who* they were."[16]

Naming is a way not to address who one is. As Judith Butler points out the crucial point is that naming produces a person's social existence. It is therefore "impacting what form that person's social existence will take." The one who is naming is often indifferent in relation to the one who is named. Hence, a person may be "confronted with a set of terms or names that do not seem to correspond at all with *who* he or she considers him/herself to be."[17]

This is crucial not only in relation to families, tribes or ethnic groups, who may be enemies or friends, but also for different religious groups.

In Europe of today, many Muslims do not recognize themselves in how they are being labelled and called. As a matter of fact, this holds true also for many Christians, who do not think that there is a problem to be "both secular and religious" as this is "more or less the content of faith" as there for all can only be "an embodied experience of the given world."[18]

---

14. Kottman, "Translator's Introduction," xxiii.

15. Kottman, "Translator's Introduction," xxiii.

16. Kottman, "Translator's Introduction," xxiii.

17. Kottman, "Translator's Introduction," xix.

18. Wyller, "Discovery," 264.

THE SO-CALLED CHRISTIAN OR SECULAR WEST— A DREAM OF HOMOGENEITY, PURITY, AND SUBORDINATION OF THE OTHER

In Western Europe, religion has increasingly been interpreted as something private and individual, such as holding certain attitudes or beliefs in private space. This might very well be an outcome of a Protestant negotiation with Modernity, adding weight to an interpretation of religion as private and invisible, in the head or heart. The theological struggles around dogmatic interpretations during the Reformation period may also have contributed to an understanding of faith as rational, related to brain and heart more than to the body. Faith is then understood as affirming certain propositional truths, more than participating in special practices. It can also be seen as related to theological trends to emphasize distinctly Christian features rather than to emphasize what Christians have in common with others. Such trends within Christianity, with several affinities with Enlightenment ideas on freedom of choice for individuals and groups, have been visible in Europe since the early twentieth century. Persuasive, often Pietistic, definitions of what it means to be a Christian have had a decisive role in defining a Christian as the other. While being a Christian during the nineteenth century simply meant to be a decent and trustworthy person, the meaning during the twentieth century has shifted to mean devoted, confessional, and often distinct from others.[19] He therefore claims that the definition of what it meant to be a Christian was in the hands of secularists and pietistic movements.[20]Particular interpretations to see oneself in contrast to others can, however, also be discerned in Judaism and Islam.

If privatization and individual choice can be traced back to Enlightenment, what is striking is that its effects have some resemblance with ancient Greece. As Hannah Arendt points out, the private was in Athens seen as pre-political. This was a sphere for the necessity of life, i.e., a sphere for women and slaves, for reproduction and survival. The public sphere on the other hand was related to politics. This political sphere was exclusively an arena for free men.[21] Modernity emphasized the binary between private and public; religion was thus pushed into the private and increasingly seen as

---

19. Religion historian David Thurfjell claims that what used to be described as Christian, relating to celebrating certain holidays, Christian names, dress codes, values (such as honesty, decency, etc.) more and more has come to be connected to special rites, teistic doctrines, and group organized activities. See Thurfjell, *Det gudlösa folket*, 38–39.

20. Thurfjell, *Det gudlösa folket*, 63.

21. Arendt, *Human Condition*, 30; cf. Gerle, *Passionate Embrace*, 72.

feminine, and as apolitical. Below I will argue that in a late, or post-modern, age a de-modernization process can be discerned, where some of these not so innocent borders between what is seen as private and public are being challenged in new ways.

Privatization and individualisation of religion may also be connected to a long history with monolithic societies where faith traditions, be they Roman Catholic, Protestant, or Greek, Serbian, Russian Orthodox, to mention some, basically have followed national borders. The Eastern part of Europe has been predominantly Orthodox with strong ties between the ruler and the Church hierarchy, something that is re-emerging in contemporary Russia.[22] Individualisation during Modernity thus became a way to escape oppressive structures from above.

CHRISTIAN MAJORITY CULTURE WITH INDIGENOUS PEOPLE, JEWS, AND MUSLIMS

Europe has, however, never been exclusively Christian. Indigenous people have continued to live here and have continued to nurture their spirituality. Jews have since the destruction of the second temple in Jerusalem been living in different parts of Europe. In 711 Muslim forces invaded and conquered the Iberian Peninsula. The multi-religious coexistence between Muslims, Christians and Jews in Granada until 1492 when Muslims and Jews were thrown out, killed or forced to convert, may have been somewhat idealised as a peaceful cohabitation. It is, however, obvious that these groups were able to benefit from each other. The following excerpt from the BBC suggests:

> Although Christians and Jews lived under restrictions, for much of the time the three groups managed to get along together, and to some extent, to benefit from the presence of each other. It brought a degree of civilisation to Europe that matched the heights of the Roman Empire and the Italian Renaissance.[23]

And the story continues:

> After the first victory, the Muslims conquered most of Spain and Portugal with little difficulty, and in fact with little opposition. By 720 Spain was largely under Muslim (or Moorish, as it was called) control. One reason for the rapid Muslim success was the generous surrender terms that they offered the people, which

22. Körtner, *Diakonie*, 35–57.
23. "Muslim Spain."

contrasted with the harsh conditions imposed by the previous Visigoth rulers.

The ruling Islamic forces were made up of different nationalities, and many of the forces were converts with uncertain motivation, so the establishment of a coherent Muslim state was not easy.[24]

The heartland of Muslim rule was Southern Spain or Andalusia. When Granada and Alhambra were conquered by Catholic Spain in 1492 the forced conversions are famous.

Enrique Dussel takes the close connection between church and state back to 1492. Ever since Jews and Muslims were deported from the Iberian Peninsula in 1492, or forced to convert to Catholicism, Europe has seen itself as a Christian continent. According to Dussel's analysis, the eviction of non-Christians should be read as the origin of European Imperialism expanding into the Latin Americas.[25] The conquest of the Islamic Kingdom of Granada in 1492 that ended the, possibly mythic, peaceful co-existence of the three Peoples of the Book on the Iberian Peninsula is a terrifying example of endless massacres and tortures, the demand that the conquered betray their religion and culture under threat of death or expulsion. Dussel argues that this was, in turn, the model for the colonisation of the New World.

When we eat paella it might be important to remember that the mixture of seafood and sausage is a dish aiming to expose who among those eating the dish were Jews. In *Kashrut*, the body of Jewish law dealing with what foods Jews can and cannot eat and how those foods must be prepared and eaten, seafood as well as pork is forbidden. *Marrano* is a term used about the Jews that were forced to convert to Catholicism or to leave Spain 1492, of whom many secretly continued to be practicing Jews.

During this time, it seems to have been a fairly open and moderate Islam practiced in what now is Andalusia, Southern Spain. These Muslims were, however, thrown out of Europe. Contemporary terror attacks from violent IS-crusaders may have nothing to do with ideas to reclaim Andalusia. What is obvious is, however, that their ideological motivation is far from any version of a tolerant or moderate Islam.

While the Church had been split in East and West since 1054, the Reformation created new splits in Central and Western Europe. After the Reformation 500 years ago, many countries followed the logic of Augsburg 1555 *cuius regio, eius religio,* claiming that the people ought to follow the

24. "Muslim Spain."
25. Dussel, *Invention*.

faith of the ruler. The Peace of Augsburg, also called the Augsburg Settlement, was a treaty between Charles V, the Holy Roman Emperor and the Protestant princes. It was signed on 25 September 1555. The principle from Augsburg in 1555 *cuius regio, eius religio* was intended to end religious warfare. The religion of the prince was the deciding factor as to which faith and what jurisprudence citizens in respective territory should follow and obey. It had very little to do with what we today mean with freedom of religion and individual freedom. Further, Calvinists and Anabaptists were not included in the treaty of Augsburg, but first at the Peace of Westphalia.

At the Peace of Westphalia in 1648 the principle *cuius regio, eius religio* was confirmed and combined with a concept of the state that focused on sovereignty. This created an international system that made nation-states possible in Europe, a system that through colonialism spread over the world. This had already started with the Spanish victory at Alhambra in 1492.

MONOLITHIC NATION STATES

The hyphen between, church and state, or nation and state, is not innocent because it created an impression that states could be, or ought to be, related to a nation, a people understood as *ethnos*. Hence, ethnicity became important. It also became connected with one religious faith, often seen as *the* world view.

In some North-European countries, e.g., in the Nordic region, Lutheran faith was used as a unifying, ideological force during nation building to such an extent that is was impossible to be an acknowledged citizen without being Lutheran. This meant that Jews, Reformed Christians or Roman Catholics, since the period of the Reformation, only gradually were allowed to live in these countries and for a long time with certain restrictions.[26] Indigenous people, like the Sami people in the North, were forced to speak Swedish and expected to leave their own religious traditions and inherited customs behind. Ethnicity, and religion, and later national language was thus used to create imagined communities of homogenous nation-states, something that today is being exploited by populist, nationalist forces in Europe. Hence, Fortress Europe, with increasingly higher walls between Europe and neighbouring countries and continents, has an ideological background that is intertwined with religious praxis and the close connections between national interests and organized religion. As Trond Skard Dokka points out:

26. See further Gerle, *Mångkulturalism*, 90.

The logic of "cuius regio eius religio" paved the way for a royal/ princely organization of churches with mandatory membership by all the king's subjects and with doctrinal homogeneity. The unity of the church resided in a king who in effect was summus episcopus, who often ruled over several principalities, and always over several quite different ethnic and linguistic groups.[27]

Needless to say, the allegiance to this "doctrinal homogeneity" where people were supposed to follow the faith of their king and with the king as the highest bishop was far from a pluralist society with tolerant co-habitation. It had little or nothing to do with what we today mean with freedom of religion or religious freedom for individuals and groups.

Gradually, religious authority as such has been met with suspicion. The emphasis on broader education, which was one of the great contributions of Protestant traditions, has gone hand in hand with an insistence on religious authority for all. Hence, there is a porous line to secularization as self-criticism and earthly responsibility that you find, e.g., in Bonhoeffer's writings as well as in Gogarten.[28]

In Roman Catholic contexts, with a stronger emphasis on Church callings and hierarchies, scandals related among other things to money and sexuality have led many Catholics to more of an indifferent or skeptical attitude. Yet, even those not practicing or attending Church often think of themselves as Catholics and have a strong affinity with, e.g., the Pope. In a butlerian perspective, they may be secular catholics. And many more than Catholics listen to the moral guidance from the Pope.

ENFORCED HOMOGENEITY MEETS A
NEW VISIBILITY OF RELIGION

However, against a background of enforced homogeneity in Europe many have interpreted freedom of religion as freedom *from* religion, i.e., the right to leave tradition behind and not to be bothered with expressions of faith, particularly not in public. The secular has become connected, not so much with Protestant faith as it actually could be,[29] as with freedom *from* traditional customs, from patriarchy and sexual control. This emphasis on freedom from is, however, often combined with a quite traditional longing for

27. Dokka, "Universal and Particular," 204.

28. See Persson, *Att tolka*, 22–28. Kristensson Uggla claims that there is an intimate relation between a Protestant, Lutheran emphasis on creation, the priesthood of all and on ordinary life and a healthy secularization. See Kristensson Uggla, "Gustaf Wingren," 103–7; *Katedralens hemlighet*. See also Gerle, "Var dags," 15–54.

29. See the argument in Kristensson Uggla, *Katedralens hemlighet*.

a monolithic society. Hence, a secular state, even a secular society, without visible expressions of faith has become the ideal for many. Sometimes the ideal of getting rid of religion altogether is expressing itself as an ideology, something I in earlier writings have labelled "secularism."[30]

At the same time as we are witnessing privatization and individualisation of religion we also experience a new visibility of religion as a collective force. Religion had, of course, never disappeared, but now it is back in the public sphere, often uniting people from different parts of the world. This challenge of globalization therefore becomes a threat to national ideas about homogeneity and clear borders.

Freedom of religion and religious expressions in public have increasingly been associated with different dress codes and with cultural customs, some more obviously religious than others. Wearing the headscarf, hijab, niqab, and praying five times a day are connected with Islam. With Orthodox Jews and conservative Christians many Muslims share the insistence on separate behavior in relation to men and women. Muslim migrants in Europe who claim the right not to shake hands with a woman, separate times for swimming, as well as separate curricula for girls and boys are, however, not understood as demanding pluralism but as a return to already overcome traditional European customs. In countries where gender equity for a long time has been interpreted as equality, indicating similarity and even sameness, such identity claims for pluralism and mutual respect are often seen as turning the clock backwards into patriarchal patterns of the past.[31] Emphasizing difference and complementarity between women and men in traditional societies has historically often been connected with patriarchal and homophobic attitudes. Further, as women are supposed to be inferior to men, homosexual men become an overt threat to this kind of masculinity formation, as some of these men are seen as behaving as women in same-sex relationships. In this kind of reading a man is supposed to rule, women to obey. Hence, sexual intercourse is an "act between unequals."[32] Religion and culture then becomes a site of struggle between conservative interpretations

30. Following Jürgen Habermas, I have drawn a distinction between secular and secularist in which a secularist perspective becomes totalitarian. A secular society is, for instance, not free from faith and religion, whereas this is an ideal for secularists. See, e.g., Gerle, *Farlig förenkling*; "New Kitchen"; "Between Sun and Shadow." Secularization can also entail a healthy measure of self-criticism and earthly responsibility, something that is found in Bonhoeffer. Both he and Gogarten made this distinction. See Persson, *Att tolka*, 22–28.

31. Okin, *Is Multiculturalism Bad for Women?*; Gerle, *Mångkulturalism*.

32. Greenberg, *Wrestling with God and Men*, 198.

of scriptures and traditions and those who claim the right to one's own body and the right to choose sexual orientation.[33]

These latter claims and rights are in Europe often understood as related to secularization theories, where everything that has to do with religious and cultural practices is supposed to disappear. It is further mostly connected to the others, to exotic, religious people, often of non-European origin. Neglecting that the world is highly asymmetrical, the reactions and demands of the majority societies in Europe are growing. "Adjust, assimilate, or leave." The French nationalist, populist leader Marine le Pen is quoted as saying that she thinks a French person first is French, then has a religion, then comes from a region.[34]

In such a discourse, religion is portrayed by the majority cultures as something conservative, and, even more, as a dress that you can put on or undress, like a hat or a jacket. When the Danish theologian, poet and historian N. F. S. Grundtvig in the twentieth century argued that he first of all was a human being, then a Christian, he was invoking a universal cord, challenging the dichotomy between Christianity and the World, or between the religious and the secular.[35]

Niels Henrik Gregersen, Bengt Kristensson Uggla, and Trygve Wyller claim that:

> For Grundtvig, faith, hope and love are basically the same phenomena within as well as outside Church and Christianity. Moreover, for Grundtvig, the major enemy of human life is death rather than sin.[36]

They further write about Grundtvig:

> With his principle, Human first, then Christian, Grundtvig argued that a broader understanding and appreciation of ordinary lived human experience is the underlying condition for a Christian way of life. Christian faith has to be lived in a humane way, in accordance with a shared sense of humanity.[37]

Quite contrary to this, religion among secularists in Europe increasingly is being seen as something outward, secondary, as an extra attribute. Religion is then understood as particular, not as universal and part of shared humanity, but as something for the other.

33. See Charlene van der Walt's chapter in this volume.

34. Küchler, "Le Pen."

35. See, e.g., Van den Breemer et al., *Secular and Sacred?*

36. Gregersen et al., "Reconfiguring Reformation," 27.

37. Gregersen et al., "Reconfiguring Reformation," 28; Allchin, *N. F. S. Grundtvig.*

The very existence of the term *marrano* is an example and a reminder that religious identity is deeper than a hat or a coat. However, these insights are not highlighted and affirmed. Rather, the majority culture demands homogeneity. Claims for purity re-emerge both among secularists and religious faith groups. While the purity of conservative religion is connected with expectations of female subordination, the purist claims of secularists argue in favor of women rights, as well as gay rights, against conservative interpretations within religions. Hence, these two positions reinforce and sometimes mirror each other.[38]

Pluralist advocates with an analysis of power relations, rightly claim that religious minorities have less power and therefore need extra protection. As Fatima Seedat and Charlene van der Walt hold in their chapters, an intersectional perspective provides a picture that is even more complex. Black women, or colored women, claim for instance that color is power, as well as gender and sex. Skin color, sex, gender, class, and religion add to each other. While women's movements claim that they can speak and act for themselves, the public debate moves around the need to protect women in highly patriarchal cultures, by the state, e.g., in suburbs through the law and the police.

Radical American feminist legal scholar Catherine McKinnon argues, however, that women who get support from the law often live in countries with more egalitarian values and thus with less need to be protected.[39] The question then returns; whose reality, or whose justice? MacKinnon points out that the liberal state is often permeated by the presumptions of the negative state, a view that government "best promotes freedom when it stays out of existing social arrangements," something that "reverberates throughout constitutional law."[40]

These values can be seen in rubrics such as the "requirement of equal protection law, in the law of freedom of speech, and in the law of privacy." Yet, as she further contends, women are already oppressed, prior to the law, "often in intimate contexts. The negative state cannot address their situation in any but an equal society—the one in which it is needed least."[41] In a pluralist Europe it is therefore important to remind police, lawyers and judges that equality in relation to the law includes women, independent of

38. Eagleton, *Reason, Faith*, 110, 114; Žižek, "In Defense of Lost Causes," 31; Gerle, "Between Sun and Shadow," 37.

39. MacKinnon, *Feminist*, 164.

40. MacKinnon, *Feminist*, 164.

41. MacKinnon, *Feminist*, 164. See also Nadar and Gerle, "Mediating the 'Sacredness.'"

origin or religious affiliation. The law of privacy may not be in the interest of women.

So called honour cultures have exercised power over especially young women in various cultural contexts, including in Europe. In traditional Christian families, young women's virginity has been seen as part of the family honour and thus important to protect. Such cultural patterns are now mostly connected with Islam. So, what does religion refer to in such a context?

All the examples above indicate that Islam is seen as the problem, but so is Jewishness and indigenous religious/cultural life. This is, of course, too simplistic. My argument, however, is that most religious practices and beliefs in Europe are being judged in relation to the majority culture. Christians see themselves as modern, often secular and enlightened, and thus to be trusted as citizens. The others are not. Often the others are described as dangerous. They represent threats to the homogeneity, purity and white, Christian hetero-patriarchal dominance, expressing itself anew in nationalist, populist movements.

Conservative interpretations of Christendom join forces with nationalists in many Eastern, or Central parts of Europe, such as Russia,[42] Poland, or Hungary. In the Western part we see secularists emerge as the new populist crusaders against, especially, Muslims but also against Jews and many other minorities in Europe, as can be seen in for instance The Netherlands. For them, secularists are the norm, and religious people the exception. Atheists, or at least agnostics, are seen as objective, universal and often as progressive, while religious people are described as subjective, particular and often as reactionary. But is atheism, or secularism, always more universal or more progressive?

Mazusawa understands this discourse as connected to the assumption of

> European hegemony, that is, on the basis of a monolithic, universalist notion of history as a singular civilizing process, of which modern Europe was the triumphant vanguard and all other civilizations and non-European societies merely markers of various interim phases already surpassed by the people of European decent.[43]

She also suggests that the European interest in "the future beyond religion" went hand in hand with a search for "the most primitive forms of religion,

---

42. Körtner, *Diakonie*, 35.
43. Masuzawa, *Invention of World Religions*, 12.

which were presumed to be equivalent, more or less, to the ones observable in the lives of contemporary savages, lives on the brink of disappearance."[44]

Once again, it is obvious that a line cannot be drawn between religious and secular people. Conservative or progressive interpretations and practices occur in both groups. And maybe the most interesting perspective comes from what Wyller calls the secular-religious other.[45] He holds that the "spirituality of every day" restores the significance of the secular-religious other as embodied, connected to the "experience of God's rootedness in all life."[46]

RELIGION AS NOTION—CONTESTED SPACE

So, what does religion, as a notion, mean? Talal Asad claims, in his *Genealogies of Religion*, that the very notion of 'religion' is a Western construction.[47]Asad's critical analysis has become widely influential and is something I am indebted to as well. However, I would claim that a similar analysis as the one on universalizing the notion of religion can also be applied to the notion secularism. But, let us first follow Asad's critique of the search for universal religion.

As a starting point for analyzing, and criticizing, the essence of religion as conceptually separate from the domain of power he chooses Clifford Geertz, *The Interpretation of Cultures* (1973). While Asad agrees with Geertz in making a connection between theory and practice, he is critical of seeing religion as

> essentially cognitive as a means by which a disembodied mind can identify religion from an Archimedian point. The connection between religious theory and practice is fundamentally a matter of intervention of constructing religion in the world (not in the mind) through definitional discourses, interpreting true meanings, excluding some utterances and practices and including others.[48]

Geertz's aim to create a universal, or anthropological, definition of religion[49] leads him to argue that in the West, the claim that religion must affirm

44. Masuzawa, *Invention of World Religions*, 12. See also the chapter written by Nokuzola Mndende on African Traditional Religion in this volume.

45. Wyller, "Discovery," 259.

46. Wyller, "Discovery," 255.

47. Asad, *Genealogies of Religion*, 24.

48. Asad, *Genealogies of Religion*, 44.

49. Asad, *Genealogies of Religion*, 29.

something specific about the nature of reality has shifted towards viewing religion as having a positive attitude toward the problem of disorder. This is, according to Asad, "a product of the only space allowed to Christianity by the post-Enlightenment society" namely the right to individual belief.[50] In the post-Enlightenment West this is one "indication of how marginal religion has become in modern industrial society as the site for producing disciplined knowledge and personal discipline."[51]

Asad describes this as a perspective, or as Marx viewed religion, as an ideology.[52] He reads Geertz as claiming that "religious belief stands independently of the worldly conditions that produce bafflement, pain and moral paradox, although that belief is primarily a way of coming to terms with them."[53] One example is that medieval valorisation of pain as a way of participating within Christ's suffering today is contrasted with a modern Christian perception of "pain as an evil to be fought against and overcome as Christ the Healer did."[54]

For Asad this understanding is "related to the Post-Enlightenment secularization of Western society and to the moral language, which that society now authorizes."[55] He describes this conception of religion as a "modern, privatized, Christian one because and to the extent that it emphasizes the priority of belief as a state of mind rather than as constituting activity in the world."

Asad claims that what Geertz calls the religious perspective is not everywhere the same.[56] On the contrary, Asad holds that religion contains "heterogeneous elements according to its historical character."[57] I would add that not only time but place, and location, influence what we mean with the notion religion and what we see as belonging to religious praxis, doctrines and rites. Religious interpretations are, just as political ideologies, sites of struggle. Hence, space, time, and history make religion somewhat contingent.

Patrik Fridlund holds that most scholars of religion see all religions as somewhat syncretic, as a "given religious tradition never comes from

50. Asad, *Genealogies of Religion*, 45.

51. Asad, *Genealogies of Religion*, 45.

52. Asad, *Genealogies of Religion*, 46.

53. Asad, *Genealogies of Religion*, 46.

54. Asad, *Genealogies of Religion*, 46.

55. Asad, *Genealogies of Religion*, 46–47.

56. Asad, *Genealogies of Religion*, 48.

57. Asad, *Genealogies of Religion*, 54.

nowhere."[58] Particular religions are always related to other religions as well as to ideologies, philosophies and historical circumstances.[59]

HISTORICITY AND SECULARISM

In my analysis something similar can be said about the secularist position. To emphasize "the priority of belief as a state of mind rather than as constituting activity in the world" is a late modern understanding. There is, at our stage of history, a growing insight that to be a convinced atheist is as much a matter of a faith, or belief, as religious faith, even if this understanding is still only held by a minority. As Jayne Svenungsson points out, the religion critic Richard Rorty concluded at the end of his life that neither those who affirm or deny the existence of God claim to have proofs for their views.[60] In academic thought the neo-atheist literature is not widely appreciated.[61]

The reception of what many academics call an outdated perception of rationality has, however, been given much more attention and appreciation in media and politics, where many have affirmed such perceptions and seen them as enlightened. Hence, for a secular majority in Western Europe, an agnostic or atheist position has come to be seen as more compatible with being a trusted citizen. If you needed to be a confessional Lutheran in the Nordic region during the seventeenth to nineteenth century, and practicing, or at least loyal to the Orthodox Church to count as reliable in Russia, you in secular Western Europe increasingly are expected to express scepticism against traditional religion. Hence, the logic of a monolithic society remains, but now with a secularist or a nationalist twist. Notions such as religious or secularist can be used to label the other in a way that is against that person's self-identification. Hence, labels, notions and naming are not innocent.

RELIGION FOR THE ALIEN AND EXOTIC

As I have pointed out above, when religion as a notion was introduced as a tool of analysis it also began to be seen as something that was disappearing in modern Europe. Jayne Svenungsson points out that religion then could be described as something with clear borders in relation to other spheres

58. Fridlund, "Rotten Syncretism," 153.

59. Fridlund, "Rotten Syncretism," 153.

60. Svenungsson, "Religionens återkomst," 10; cf. Rorty, "Antiklerikalism and Atheism."

61. Svenungsson, "Religionens återkomst," 10–11. Another example is Terry Eagleton and his critique of the outdated perception of rationalism held by Richard Dawkins and Christopher Hitchens. See Eagleton, *Reason, Faith*; Gerle, "Between Sun and Shadow"; *Farlig förenkling*.

of society.[62] While religion was seen as disappearing in Europe, or seen to be part of certain contained spaces, religion in other parts of the world remained as a socially present reality. It was seen as important in alien or "primitive" cultures that would be examined from outside through anthropological studies.[63] Religion is further described in pejorative terms as in the high modern critique of religion.[64] It is associated with words such as superstition, irrationality, and all the way from Kant, with women, and with Africa![65]

The notion "religious" in Europe is thus used to describe the other as exotic, superstitious and alien. To speak of "world religions" expresses a vague commitment to multiculturalism. Yet it is not merely a descriptive concept, the notion "world religions" is, according to Masuzawa, actually a particular ethos, a pluralist ideology.[66] She connects this to a hierarchical ordering of religions where "the idea of diversity of religions" may be seen as something that facilitates "a particular absolutism from one context to another—from the overtly exclusivist hegemonic version (Christian supremacist dogmatism) to the openly pluralistic one (world religions pluralism)."[67] She follows this line of thought in the logic and aspirations of early twentieth-century theologian Ernst Troeltsch, who embraced the pluralist logic of "world religions" and by so doing sought to reclaim the Universalist destiny of European modernity.

Weather she is absolutely right or not, it seems fair to conclude that religion is not a stable notion with the same meaning independent of time and context. Nor is secularism. Hence, it seems reasonable to be careful with labels.

RELIGION AS IDENTITY IN A MULTI-CULTURAL WORLD

Globalization has challenged the nation state and undermined homogeneity. While all this may be good in many aspects it creates a challenge to people's need to affirm their identity, where religious practices are important. Hence, we are now witnessing new challenges. Demands on rights are made and heard without any discussion about the relationship between rights and duties, or from a perspective where religion is seen as something that ought to

62. Svenungsson, "Religionens återkomst," 12.

63. Svenungsson, "Religionens återkomst," 12.

64. Svenungsson, "Religionens återkomst," 12.

65. Mulinari, "Ett postkolonialt, feministiskt," 208; Schott, *Feminist Interpretations of Immanuel Kant.*

66. Masuzawa, *Invention of World Religions.*

67. Masuzawa, *Invention of World Religions,* 326–27.

fade away and disappear from society. Identity politics wrapped in religious clothes may on the other hand be hijacked by extreme forces. If secularists with a neo-atheist agenda in some contexts pave the way for right wing conservative Christians who are claiming to be the only reliable Europeans, so are, for instance, evangelicals sometimes paving the way for populist leaders. Unification around white supremacy and resistance to abortion seems to be more important than universal human rights and international peaceful relations.

For strong, militant leaders it is an easy solution to point finger at people with another ethnicity or religion. Groups are then put against each other in ways that promote a kind of tribal justice. What Alain Touraine, in his book *Can We Live Together? Equality and Difference*, describes as de-modernization leads to a situation where individuals think of themselves as completely independent of everything and everybody except the market. While this may be introduced under the concept of freedom of choice, in reality it often leads to a situation where individuals increasingly are expected to solve problem that are socially constructed.[68]

If we once hoped that globalization would lead to wider circles of justice and companionship we now realise that we rather got almost feudal networks. With de-modernization followed not solidarity but the justice of enclaves, of sects and of xenophobia. Subcultures, be they mc gangs or gated privileged communities, are replacing a sense of wider collectivity.[69] Not only majority cultures are longing for homogeneity and purity. This can also be discerned in faith groups.

Further, the new visibility of religion has gone hand in hand with demands for collective rights, sometimes with arguments for the right not to have one's religious faith challenged. However, such claims do not take power relations, asymmetries and differences seriously. One always needs to ask for the rights of individuals, also to be dissidents, non-faithful, or the right to challenge traditional interpretations of religio/cultural practices. Feminist interpretations have, for instance, for decades been challenging patriarchal customs described as divine in all world religions.[70] Today they are joining forces with HBTQIA movements.[71]

---

68. This is something that Zygmunt Bauman pointed out at a public lecture attended by the author in Lund on March 31, 2015.

69. Toraine, *Can We Live Together?*, 43, 68; Rosenberg, *Plikten, profiten*, 233–34.

70. See, e.g., Fatima Seedat's chapter in this volume.

71. See, e.g., Charlene van der Welt's chapter in this volume.

CONCLUDING DISCUSSION

The Public sphere is a site of struggle, a site with many new voices who did not have the permission to speak in ancient Greece or who, during Modernity, where relegated to the private sphere. These voices and actors bring new questions. To quote Judith Butler:

> There is always a question: should I listen to this or not? Am I being heard or misconstrued? The public sphere is constituted time and again through certain kinds of exclusions: images that cannot be seen. Words that cannot be heard. And this means that the regulation of the visible and the audible field—along with the other senses—to be sure—is crucial to the constitution of what can become a debatable issue within the sphere of politics.[72]

Could old and new frameworks of human rights be strong enough to protect minorities who gradually have gained some protection from states and regional/ international treaties? If the logic of Westphalia is re-emerging, the risk is that majority cultures once again take the right to decide that freedom of religion must be defined by ethnic and hetero-patriarchal values, rather than to be a right for all living in a territory.

While Europe, both in East and West, seems to suffer from the heritage of imagined, homogenous communities and states, the normal way to function in many other parts of the world has been to live with respect and cohabitation both in multi-cultural, multi-religious and multi-linguistic terms.

One first step towards peaceful con-habitation may be to recognize that religion, according to Asad, have many "heterogeneous elements according to its historical character."[73] If the Westphalian logic only provided religious freedom for the princes, the logic of globalization tends to promote excessive rights for enclaves, but not for individuals. Hence, regional, global institutions are needed to guarantee religious freedom for real persons, not for collectives. To embrace the "secular-religious other," who defines herself as receiving life and living with respect for many sexual orientations and ethnic and religious backgrounds, could be one first step towards the future. An embedded understanding of human beings would need to argue in favor of religious interpretations with respect and care both for the human being as a bodily reality and for the future of the earth.

---

72. Butler, *Parting Ways*, 119. See also Rancière, *Politics*.
73. Asad, *Genealogies of Religion*, 54.

BIBLIOGRAPHY

Allchin, A. M. N. F. S. *Grundtvig: An Introduction to his Life and Work.* Aarhus: Aarhus University Press, 2015.

Arendt, Hannah. *The Human Condition.* Chicago: University of Chicago Press, 1998.

Asad, Talal. *Genealogies of Religion: Discipline and Reasons of Power in Christianity and Islam.* Baltimore, MD: John Hopkins University Press, 1993.

Bäckstöm, Anders, and Anders Wejryd. *Sedd men osedd. Om folkkyrkans paradoxala närvaro inför 2020-talet.* Stockholm: Verbum, 2016.

Butler, Judith. *Parting Ways: Jewishness and the Critique of Zionism.* New York: Columbia University Press, 2012.

Casanova, José. *Public Religions in the Modern World.* Chicago: University of Chicago Press, 1994.

Eagleton, Terry. *Reason, Faith, and Revolution: Reflections on the God Debate.* New Haven, CT: Yale University Press, 2009.

Davie, Grace. *Europe, the Exceptional Case: Parameters of Faith in the Modern World.* London: Darton, Longman, and Todd, 2002.

Dokka, Trond Skard. "Universal and Particular: Creation Theology and Ecclesiology in a Fragmented World." In *Reformation Theology for a Post-Secular Age: Løgstrup—Prenter—Wingren, and the Future of Scandinavian Creation Theology,* edited by Niels Henrik Gregersen, et al., 201–214. Göttingen: Vandenhoek & Rubrecht, 2017.

Dussel, Enrique. *The Invention of the Americas: Eclipse of "the Other" and the Myth of Modernity.* New York: Continuum, 1992.

Fridlund, Patrik. "The Rotten Syncretism that Opens the Spirit." *Swedish Missiological Themes* 102.2 (2014) 151–70.

Gerle, Elisabeth. "A New Kitchen for the World—Women, Politics, and Religion." *Feminist Theology* 22.1 (2013) 46–57.

———. "Between Sun and Shadow—Navigating between the Extremes and Beyond." *Feminist Theology* 24.1 (2015) 35–48.

———. *Farlig förenkling. Om religion och politik utifrån Sverigedemokraterna och Humanisterna.* Nora: Nya Doxa, 2010.

———. *Mångkulturalism för vem?* Nora: Nya Doxa, 1999.

———. *Passionate Embrace: Luther on Love, Body, and Sensual Presence.* Eugene, OR: Cascade, 2017.

———. "Var dags och varje människas upprättelse." In *Luther som utmaning, Om frihet och ansvar,* edited by Elisabeth Gerle, 15–54. Stockholm: Verbum, 2008.

Greenberg, Steven. *Wrestling with God and Men: Homosexuality in the Jewish Tradition.* Madison, WI: University of Wisconsin, 2004.

Rancière, Jacques. *The Politics of Aesthetics: The Distribution of the Sensible.* London: Continuum, 2006.

Inglehart, Ronald, and Christian Welzel. *Modernization, Cultural Change, and Democracy: The Human Development Sequence.* New York: Cambridge University Press. 2005.

Kottman, Paul A. "Translator's Introduction." In *Relating Narratives: Storytelling and Selfhood,* edited by Adriana Cavarero, xxiii. London: Routledge, 1997.

Kristensson Uggla, Bengt. "Gustaf Wingren and Scandinavian Creation Theology." In *Reformation Theology for a Post-Secular Age: Løgstrup—Prenter—Wingren, and the Future of Scandinavian Creation Theology,* edited by Niels Henrik Gregersen, et al., 253–65. Göttingen: Vandenhoek & Rubrecht, 2017.

———. *Katedralens hemlighet. Sekularisering och religiös övertygelse,* Skellefteå: Artos. 2015.

Körtner, Ulrich H. J. *Diakonie und Öffentliche Theologie.* Göttingen: Vandenhoeck & Ruprecht, 2017.

Küchler, Teresa. "Le Pen vill lämna dagens EU." *Svenska Dagbladet,* March 9, 2017.

MacKinnon, Cathriene A. *Towards a Feminist Theory of the State.* Cambridge: Harvard University Press, 1989.

Masuzawa, Tomoko. *The Invention of World Religions: Or, How European Universalism Was Preserved in the Language of Pluralism.* Chicago: Chicago University Press, 2005.

Mulinari, Diana. "Ett postkolonialt feministiskt samtal." In *Religionens offentlighet. Om religionens plats i samhället,* edited by Hanna Stenström, 205–216. Skellefteå: Artos & Norma, 2013.

"Muslim Spain (711–1492)." *BBC: Religions,* September 4, 2009. Online. http://www. bbc.co.uk/religion/religions/islam/history/spain_1.shtml.

Nadar, Sarojini, and Elisabeth Gerle, "Mediating the 'Sacredness' of Religion, Culture and Law in Contexts of Sexual Violence." *Agenda* 30.3 (2016) 104–114.

Okin, Susanne Möller, et al. *Is Multiculturalism Bad for Women?* Princeton: Princeton University Press, 1999.

Rorty, Richard. "Anticlericalism and Atheism." In *The Future of Religion,* edited by Santiago Zabala, 29–41. New York: Columbia University Press, 2005.

Rosenberg, Göran. *Plikten, profiten och konsten att vara människa.* Stockholm: Bonniers, 2003.

Schott, Robin May. *Feminist Interpretations of Immanuel Kant.* Pennsylvania: University of Pennsylvania State University Press, 1997.

Spinks, D. Christopher. *The Bible and the Crisis of Meaning: Debates on the Theological Interpretation of Scripture.* London: T. & T. Clark, 2007.

Svenungsson, Jayne. "Religionens återkomst—religionens slut?" *Signum* 8 (2016) 8–15.

Thurfjell, David. *Det gudlösa folket. De postkristna svenskarna och religionen.* Stockholm: Molin & Sorgenfri, 2016.

Toraine, Alain. *Can We Live Together? Equality and Difference.* Cambridge: Polity, 2000.

United Nations. "Universal Declaration of Human Rights." December 10, 1948. Online. https://www.un.org/en/universal-declaration-human-rights.

Van den Breemer, Rosemarie, et al. *Secular and Sacred? The Scandinavian Case of Religion in Human Rights, Law, and Public Space.* Göttingen: Vandenhoeck & Ruprecht, 2014.

Wejryd, Anders. "En svårförklarlig kyrka." In *Sedd men osedd. Om folkkyrkans paradoxala närvaro inför 2020-talet,* edited by Anders Bäckström and Anders Wejryd, 15–28. Stockholm: Verbum, 2016.

Wyller, Trygvde, "The Discovery of the Secular Religious Other in the Scandinavian Creation Theology." In *Reformation Theology for a Post-Secular Age: Løgstrup— Prenter—Wingren, and the Future of Scandinavian Creation Theology,* edited by Niels Henrik Gregersen, et al., 253–65. Göttingen: Vandenhoek & Rubrecht, 2017.

Žižek, Slavoj. *In Defense of Lost Causes.* London: Verso, 2008.

Part II

Freedom of Religion:
Perspectives from Kenya

4

Freedom of Religion

Individual and Collective as
Perceived by the Kenyan State

NEWTON KAHUMBI MAINA

The Constitution of Kenya guarantees freedom of religion and provides a legal framework that governs the operations and relations of different religions in the country. However, within an environment of religious pluralism, the functioning of these religions sometimes infringes upon the freedom of religion of others. Due the constitutional provisions, sometimes the government's attempt to control operations of religious groups and organizations through legislation has been interpreted as infringement upon freedom of religion. There are also accusations levelled against government's penchant for discriminating against some religions. It is noted that the threat of terrorism poses a challenge to the freedom of religion in the country, as individuals from some religions feel targeted by others for holding contrary religious opinions and beliefs,[1] while the government's war on terror has led to profiling of some religious communities. Based on the

---

1. Christians and Muslims face threats of harassment or terror attacks by virtue of professing a different faith from that of the attackers. There are examples shown in the article where alleged Muslim terrorists targeted Christians in a mall, public transport, and university by isolating them from Muslims. To avenge the attacks on Christians by suspected Muslim attackers, there are instances when Christians have also harassed or attacked Muslims in public vehicles.

constitutional provisions and other legal frameworks, this chapter attempts to interrogate forms of freedom of religion as expressed individually and collectively in the Kenyan state. The chapter explores the following issues: constitutional and legal provisions of freedom of religion in Kenya; religious demography and its implications for freedom of religion and expression; freedom of religion and government control; terrorism and its implication on freedom of religion, and the government response to the war on terror and its implication for freedom of religion.

CONSTITUTIONAL AND LEGAL PROVISIONS OF FREEDOM OF RELIGION IN KENYA

Freedom of religion in Kenya is founded upon, and governed by, two important articles in the Constitution. The first one is chapter 2, article 8, which defines the relations between religion and the state by spelling out that "there shall be no state religion."[2] According to this article, Kenya is a secular state. However, despite the absence of a state religion, many Kenyans recognize religious holidays which are gazetted by the government from time to time.[3]

The second and the most important article on freedom of religion is chapter 4 of the Bill of Rights, article 32, "Freedom of conscience, religion, belief and opinion."[4] This article is of great importance in relation to freedom of religion. It spells out clearly that:

1. Every person has the right to freedom of conscience, religion, thought, belief and opinion.

2. Every person has the right, either individually or in community with others, in public or in private, to manifest any religion or belief through worship, practice, teaching or observance, including observance of a day of worship.

3. A person may not be denied access to any institution, employment or facility, or the enjoyment of any right, because of the person's belief or religion.

2. Constitution of Kenya ch. 2, art. 8.

3. These holidays include Easter and Christmas for Christians, *Eid al-Fitr* and *Eid al-Adha* for Muslims and *Diwali* for Hindus. Indeed, the national anthem is a prayer (petition) to God, and prayers conducted by a Christian, Muslim, and adherent of African Religion, is an important component of the official opening of Parliament by the President, and during the celebration of national holidays such as *Madaraka* and *Jamhuri*, which mark the dates that Kenya attained Self-Government and Republic status, respectively.

4. Constitution of Kenya ch. 4, art. 32.

4. A person may not be compelled to act, or engage in any act, that is contrary to the person's belief or religion.

Another constitutional provision partly central to the freedom of religion is still found in chapter 4, article 27 on "Equality and Freedom from Discrimination."[5] This article stipulates that:

1. Every person is equal before the law and has the right to equal protection and equal benefit of the law.

2. Equality includes the full and equal enjoyment of all rights and fundamental freedoms.

3. Women and men have the right to equal treatment, including the right to equal opportunities in political, economic, cultural and social spheres.

The Constitution also provides for freedom of religion in a variety of ways. These include the *Kadhi* (Magistrate) courts,[6] recognition of Christian, Muslim, Hindu, and Cultural marriages through the Marriage Act.[7] The Education Act[8] provides for the teaching and promotion of religions by allowing religious groups to sponsor schools and promote the teaching of religious subjects which are taught and examined in primary schools and secondary schools up to the University. The subjects include: Christian Religious Education, Islamic Religious Education, Hindu Religious Education, and languages such as Arabic, Greek, Hebrew, and Gujarati. The component of African religion is integrated into the curriculum of religious studies in primary and secondary schools while at the university, African Religion is an area of specialisation at both undergraduate and postgraduate levels.[9]

Based on the above constitutional provisions and other legal frameworks, this chapter attempts to interrogate the freedom of religion as expressed individually and collectively in the Kenyan state. But first let us examine the Kenyan religious demography because it has implications for freedom of religion and its expression within this context.

5. Constitution of Kenya ch. 4, art. 27.

6. These are subordinate Islamic courts under the Judiciary, and which regulate Muslim personal law: marriage, divorce and inheritance enshrined in the Constitution of Kenya ch. 10, art. 170.

7. Republic of Kenya, "Marriage Act."

8. Republic of Kenya, "Education Act" ch. 211, sec. 26(2).

9. For example, at Kenyatta University, students taking Bachelor degree can choose units (courses) in African Religion, while at Masters and PhD levels, students can specialize in African Religion (see Kenyatta University, *Catalogue*).

RELIGIOUS DEMOGRAPHY IN KENYA
AND THE FREEDOM OF RELIGION

The latest data on the size of the Kenyan population (per 2018) by United Nations estimates is 51,263,793 people.[10] There is no reliable data on the different religious groupings in the country. The data largely depends on the sources, with some skewed in favor of some religious groups while others are skewed against these groups.[11] Generally, Kenya is a Christian majority country, with a significant Muslim minority. One of the latest sources gives the following estimates of Kenyan religious population: Christians, 81.0 percent; Muslims, 8.1 percent; adherents of African traditional religions 9.0 percent; Baha'is, 1.1 percent; Hindus, 0.5 percent; Buddhists, Sikhs, Jains, Zoroastrians and Jews 0.3 percent; Atheists and Agnostics about 0.1 percent.[12] Among Christians, the Protestants comprise 42.2 percent; Roman Catholics, 22.7 percent and Pentecostals/Charismatics 30.7 percent, Evangelicals 28.6 percent and African Initiated churches and denominations 13.0 percent.[13] While the Roman Catholic grouping is largely homogenous, the Protestants include the Anglican Church of Kenya, the Presbyterian Church of East Africa, African Inland Church, the Methodist Church, the Seventh Day Adventists (SDA), Baptist Church, Lutheran Church, among others. For Muslims, more than 70 percent are Sunni, while the Shi'a Muslims, together with the Ahmadiyya (a Muslim missionary group), constitute less than 20 percent of the Muslim population.

Regarding the geographical distribution of these religions, the majority Christians are distributed throughout the country while Muslims are predominant in the Coast and North Eastern provinces of the country. There are also some pockets of Muslims in the rural countryside and in the main urban areas where we also find Asian Muslim communities, Hindus, Buddhist among other marginal religious faithful. Followers of the African indigenous religions are dispersed among the rural communities especially among the Masai and the Samburu. However, most Christians in Kenya have integrated some aspects of African indigenous religions into Christianity, an aspect that is common in some parts of Africa as captured by Michael

10. Worldometers, "Kenya Population."

11. For example, Christian sources give a high population of Christians vis-à-vis Muslims and the converse is true. Oliana notes that Muslims constitute 6–10 percent, while Christians constitute 70 percent of the population. See Oliana, "Theological Challenges," 12. Muslim sources give Muslim figures ranging from 26 percent to 35 percent of the total population. See Brislen, "Christian Perceptions of Islam," 46–50; Oded, *Islam and Politics*, 11; Maina, "Christian-Muslim Dialogue," 184.

12. Murimi, "Christianity in Kenya," 605.

13. Murimi, "Christianity in Kenya," 605.

Brislen who argues that in Africa, Christianity has shaped African religio-cultural heritage and the converse also applies where African heritage is re-shaped by Christianity.[14] Integration of African religious beliefs could be said of some Muslim communities. For example, the Digo of the Kenyan coast are predominantly Muslim but they have integrated in their Muslim practices, African indigenous beliefs on magic, sorcery and witchcraft.[15] Indeed, in the words of John Mbiti, it is not possible to separate African religiosity from the life of an African, to the extent that it is not possible to isolate religion from their lives of Africans whether they are Christians, Muslims, or followers of other religions.[16]

The different religions in the country have formed umbrella organizations to promote their religious interests at the national level. For example, the Kenya Conference of Catholic Bishops represents the interests of the Roman Catholics while the National Council of Churches of Kenya is an organization for mainstream Protestant churches. The Evangelical Alliance of Kenya is the national umbrella organization of evangelical churches. The Supreme Council of Kenya Muslims and the National Muslim Leaders Forum represent the interests of Muslims at the national level while the Hindu Council of Kenya is the national organization that represents the Hindus. The Inter-religious Council of Kenya is an umbrella body that seeks to bring together all religions in Kenya and it is coordinated by all the main religious organizations.[17]

Within the environment of religious pluralism, generally there has been a spirit of tolerance, harmony and peaceful co-existence between the different religions in the country. In that regard, Kenya has not experienced the ignominy of religious war. However spatial competition between Christians and Muslims, the two leading faith communities in the country, sometimes creates an atmosphere of competition, acrimony and antagonism which infringes on the freedom of religion.[18]

Granted, the Constitution guarantees the freedom of "religion or belief through worship, practice, teaching or observance, including observance of a day of worship," furthermore, a "person may not be denied access to any institution, employment or facility, or the enjoyment of any right, because of the person's belief or religion."[19] However, the way the religious faith-

14. Brislen, "Christian Perceptions of Islam," 4.
15. Wanjiru, "Demonstration of Islamic Rituals," 15–23.
16. Mbiti, *African Religions and Philosophy*, 1.
17. Murimi, "Christianity in Kenya," 605.
18. Maina, "History of Christian-Muslim Relations," 17–20.
19. Constitution of Kenya, ch. 4, art. 32(2–3).

ful operationalise their religions through worship, practice and teaching sometimes borders on infringement of freedom of religion for those who do not subscribe to their belief(s) or opinion(s). We shall draw a few examples on religious tolerance, practice and worship to demonstrate how religious faithful infringe on freedom of religion for those profiled as "other." Largely, all the examples are drawn from Christian and Muslim faiths because of their predominance on the Kenyan religious landscape. As mentioned earlier, the contestation for space by the followers of the two religions has had ramifications on the freedom of religion in the country.

RELIGIOUS TOLERANCE AND FREEDOM OF RELIGION

The democratic space provided by the Constitution making Kenya a secular state has implications for religious tolerance and freedom of religion. Granted, all citizens regardless of their religious beliefs and world views are protected by the Constitution. Unfortunately, it is the constitutional provision that makes Kenya a secular state that Atheists in Kenya Society has used to agitate for the removal of religion in public sphere. The Society which was registered in April 2016 under the Society's Act has argued for the scrapping of religious studies in schools and colleges; banning of religious content in the media, and preaching in public sphere, terming it a nuisance and tantamount to "imposing beliefs on people."[20] The arguments by Atheists in Kenya Society could be interpreted not only as a strategy of drawing public attention for a newly registered organization, but also borders on religious intolerance which is an affront to freedom of religion for the majority of people who considers themselves to be religious.

There are also instances when some Muslims have seemingly exercised religious intolerance to the extent that followers of other religions, especially Christians, have perceived Islam as an intolerant religion. This perception has in the past bordered on cases of "Islamic fundamentalism" and most currently, terrorism which is discussed later in the chapter. For example, Muslim leaders in Kenya declared a death sentence on an identified author of a letter published in the mailbox of the *Standard newspaper* on July 22, 1994, which was critical of Islam. To many non-Muslims, the death sentence was an indication that Islam is an intolerant religion.[21] In the nineties, Muslim's intolerance in the eyes of other faithful was evident in the activities of the unregistered Islamic Party of Kenya which was extremely anti-government and behind the riots that engulfed the coastal

20. Sore, "Atheists Should Respect."
21. Maina, "Christian-Muslim Dialogue," 175.

town of Mombasa.[22] Religious intolerance is an affront to the freedom of speech in situations where followers of other religions feel insecure when they criticise religious extremities.

RELIGIOUS PRACTICE AND WORSHIP IN PUBLIC SCHOOLS

Religious practice and worship in educational institutions brings out some contestations that bring freedom of religion into focus, especially in public schools. Rosalind Hackett has captured the place of education in curtailing the freedom of religion as follows:

> Education has the potential for including or excluding minority religious groups and may be utilized as a powerful medium for the promotion, propagation, and spread of religion. It is also a location for segregation, victimization . . . harassment, and a point of conflict.[23]

DRESS CODE IN SCHOOLS AND FREEDOM OF RELIGION

In Kenyan educational institutions, religious practice on dress code has over the years put to test the freedom of religion in schools. This has been a contention mainly among Christian and Muslim adherents. In the early nineties, several heads of church sponsored public schools[24] were sued by Muslim parents for expelling their daughters from school because of wearing the *hijab* (veil) as part of the school uniform.[25] Muslim parents advocated for their daughters' religious rights on dress code to be respected in non-Muslim schools. There was also a general feeling that Muslim girls were being harassed because of their religion, in the schools which prohibited the *hijab*. It was not until a presidential directive that forbid forcing Muslim girls to dress in a manner that conflicted with their religion, that the matter came to rest.[26] From then on, many public schools continued to allow

22. Maina, "Christian-Muslim Dialogue," 175.

23. Hackett, "Regulating Religious Freedom."

24. In Kenya's education system, schools are categorized as either public or private. Public schools are funded by the government, while private schools are run by individuals or groups as private/business enterprise. According to the Republic of Kenya, "Education Act" sec. 8, a public school is supposed to have a "sponsor" mainly, a church, or an organization of churches or the local community. The sponsor is invariably the founder of the school.

25. Most of the schools affected by the *hijab* controversy were in Mombasa, e.g., Star of the Sea and Changamwe high schools—both sponsored by the Catholic Church.

26. Maina, "Christian-Muslim Relations," 6.

Muslim girls to wear the hijab but the issue resurfaced later in 2011, when a Muslim girl sought the court intervention to compel Kenya High School, in Nairobi, to allow her to wear the hijab in school.[27] The school administration however put up a tough defense with the Head teacher arguing that:

> Allowing the application would make Muslim girls look different, conspicuous, and special, favored and thus attract unprecedented and undesirable disruptive attention from the school community.[28]

The dress code in public schools affected Christians as well. In February 2012, there were two incidents pitting the followers of the Akorino Church against the schools' administration. The Akorino Church[29] requires women to wear headscarves. In the first incident, a girl from Jacaranda Primary School in Nakuru County was suspended and her parents advised to look for a school for Akorinos if they insisted on their daughter wearing a headscarf.[30] This act interfered with the freedom of religion since the girl was being denied access to the school on the basis of her belief contrary to the Constitution which stipulates that: "a person may not be denied access to any institution, employment or facility, or the enjoyment of any right, because of the person's belief or religion."[31]

The second incident involved a Form Two girl from Chogoria Girls Secondary School in Meru County who was also suspended because of wearing a headscarf. When similar conflicts of headscarf emerged in other schools in Mombasa, Naivasha and Machakos, the Permanent Secretary in the Ministry of Education issued a circular "stating that such attire might be accepted as long as they are in the colors of the school uniforms."[32] But this did not mark the end of the controversy surrounding the issue of dress code as the following other examples demonstrate.

In June 21, 2014, a parent went to court to challenge her daughter's suspension from Bura Girls High School, Taita Taveta County, over alleged boycott of Sunday mass and wearing *hijab*. The petitioner, explained that her daughter, together with 38 others, hid in a classroom to avoid being forced to attend a Christian service during the Holy month of *Ramadhan*. She added that the suspension was not just about the Sunday service mass,

27. Mutambo, "Religious War."

28. Mutambo, "Religious War."

29. Akorino Church is an African indigenous church that draws membership mainly from the Kikuyu community.

30. Mutambo, "Religious War."

31. Constitution of Kenya ch. 4, art. 32(3).

32. Mutambo, "Religious War."

but was a build-up of a disagreement over wearing *hijab* during prayer times and fasting period. The school asked the court to dismiss the case, arguing that the student chose the school out of free will and ought to adhere to its rules. In addition, the court was told that the Sunday mass was not about converting any person, but to make them good citizens.[33] While delivering the verdict, the judge ruled that schools' management should have a free hand in deciding the uniform that is good for the students in order to secure high and improved school standards. He noted that the school uniform should be the same for all learners regardless of culture, religion and socio-economic status, as different uniform encourages religious and status divisions.[34]

In a similar move, in 2015, an aggrieved parent of a Muslim girl sued the Methodist Church and St Paul Kiwanjani Secondary School in Isiolo—Muslim predominant county in Eastern Province of Kenya—over her daughter's suspension from school because of wearing *hijab* and trousers.[35] The Court of Appeal ruled in favor of the girl by noting that Muslim students should be allowed to wear *hijab* and trousers in addition to the school uniform. The Church appealed the ruling before the Supreme Court. The argument was having preferential treatment in schools would be tantamount to discriminating against others and would encourage defiance against school rules. The Teachers Service Commission—the umbrella government body that employs teachers in the country—was enjoined in this case as a respondent. It argued that the only way to resolve the dress code issue is through a policy by the Ministry of Education.[36]

The issue of religion and the dress code for girls in schools has however refused to abate as many schools still forbid the headscarves. There is no uniform legal position or opinion regarding dress code in schools, because sometimes the court supports the school management and other times the parents (students), as the discussion in this chapter has shown. The Ministry of Education has not developed a policy on dress code. Yet parents aggrieved by the schools' position of banning the *hijab* and other religious attire argue that the Constitution guarantee them the freedom of religion and worship which is superior to school regulations.[37] This argument stokes controversy and hair splitting as scholars and opinion leaders

33. Muthoni, "Uniform Is for All Students."
34. Muthoni, "Uniform Is for All Students."
35. Muthoni, "Uniform Is for All Students."
36. Muthoni, "Uniform Is for All Students."
37. Mutambo, "Religious War."

are drawn into the debate. A renowned educationist, Eddah Gachukia, once argued in support of banning headscarves by noting that:

> School uniforms enhance unity in school. . . . It would breed inequality and make it difficult for children to integrate. If every religious sect is allowed a dress code, the commonness created by school uniform shall cease and groups of students professing the same sect shall dress in a similar manner thereby disintegrating the uniform dress code.[38]

A contrary view in favor of headscarves in schools is seen in the remarks of a Muslim leader, the Secretary General of the Supreme Council of Kenya Muslims, Sheikh Adan Wachu who evokes the Constitution by saying that:

> The Constitution provides for religious rights of everyone and schools should not curtail them. I understand we must adhere to the rules of schools, but there should not be any religious compulsion for children to attend religious functions or practices they do not believe in. Children should be allowed to practice their religion and put on the attire according to their beliefs, as long as they are also putting on school uniforms. It would be religious animosity if any child, Muslim or Christian, is denied their religious rights.[39]

The views by Gachukia and Wachu above, rightly demonstrate how the dress code generates debates on freedom of religion in schools. It is anticipated that there will be more controversies in future stemming from the dress code and freedom of religion in schools.

PLACES OF WORSHIP IN SCHOOLS AND FREEDOM OF RELIGION

Another issue that engages freedom of religion in schools relates to the construction of places of worship in schools which is accentuated by the Education Act. The Act requires the school to provide places of worship for the students:

> Where the parent of a pupil at a public school wishes the pupil to attend religious worship or religious instruction of a kind which is not provided in the school, the school shall provide such facilities as may be practicable for the pupil to receive religious

38. Mutambo, "Religious War."
39. Mutambo, "Religious War."

instruction and attend religious worship of the kind desired by
the parent.[40]

The Act has implications for freedom of worship in schools regarding facilities. Many schools admit students from across the religious divide and
therefore it is hardly possible to provide adequate places of worship for
each religion. However, in most cases, schools which do not have a church,
mosque or temple, may improvise those facilities by converting classrooms
or school halls into places of worship during the day(s) of worship. Due
to this lacuna, there are cases when a religious group may feel obligated
to put a place of worship for their adherents in a school without consulting the school sponsor which amount to interference with the provisions
of freedom of religion and the Education Act.[41] A case in point was the
construction of a mosque, in a church sponsored school, in Isiolo in 1993.
The incident conflicted with the Education Act, because the religious traditions of the Catholic Church and other Christian groups who sponsored the
school, should have been respected. Although the Act[42] requires a school to
provide a place of worship and instruction for their children, this does not
mean an outsider should construct a place of worship without consulting
the sponsor. This was the situation at the school in Isiolo and Christians interpreted this act as tantamount to promoting Islam in a church sponsored
school and thus interfering with rights and essential freedoms provided by
the Constitution.[43]

RELIGIOUS PRACTICE/WORSHIP AND FREEDOM
OF RELIGION IN SCHOOLS

Conflicts arise where schools have to maintain a balance between students'
discipline and observing the freedom of religion. This happens when students are permitted to observe religious days or festivals outside the school
compound as it happened in a school in Meru County in 1993.[44] Muslim
girls who had gone for prayers in a mosque in town during *Ramadhan* were
suspended when they got late for the evening studies. This incident brought
the conflict between practice of religions and the constitutional provisions
for freedom of religion in schools. It also brought about conflict between

40. Republic of Kenya, "Education Act" ch. 211, sec. 26(2).

41. Republic of Kenya, "Education Act" ch. 211, sec. 8(1), shows that the religious
tradition of the sponsor of the school should be respected.

42. Republic of Kenya, "Education Act" ch. 211, sec. 26(2).

43. Constitution of Kenya ch. 4, art. 27(2).

44. Maina, "Christian-Muslim Relations," 6.

Christians and Muslims when local Muslim leaders stormed the school demanding unconditional re-admission of the girls and accusing Christians of "undermining the progress of Islam." They also demanded that fasting—which was banned in the school for both Christians and Muslims—be upheld. Since the school's administration could not budge, it forced the aggrieved parties to seek court redress. And the court ordered the unconditional re-admission of the Muslim girls, and equally gave them latitude to practice their faith without interference.[45]

Schools flout the constitutional provision of freedom of religion in article 32(3) due to perceived discrimination, when Christian sponsored schools deny Muslims admission into schools or refuse them to practice their religion, e.g., to conduct prayers and observe *Ramadhan*, and attend religious festivals such as *Iddul al-Fitr*.[46] The latter contravenes article 32(2). For example, in Meru County, the head of a church sponsored school was accused of refusing to admit Muslim girls. While in Nairobi and Nakuru counties, Muslim students, at two major boys' schools protested over lack of place and permission to pray. In Kiambu and Murang'a counties, Muslim students boycotted meals claiming that meat had not been ritually slaughtered according to Islamic principles, while in Limuru Girls School, there were complaints over a perception that pork was to be introduced into the school menu.[47] All these cases have a bearing on freedom of religion in schools, where there is a perception that the school management flouts the constitutional provisions. In the past this scenario has brought about conflicts between Christians and Muslims, especially when Muslim religious leaders intervene to demand that schools should observe the Constitution on freedom of religion.[48]

Besides Muslims, followers of the SDA Church have alleged discrimination of their faithful in non-SDA's schools. For example, in 2012, the SDA petitioned the High Court over alleged violation of the right to freedom of religion for the SDA students attending public schools across the country.[49] The students were allegedly denied the right to practice their religion in accordance with the fundamental tenets of their religion, under article 32 of the Constitution and section 26 of the Education Act that the Church claimed had been violated.[50] The petitioner alleged that SDA students

---

45. Maina, "Christian-Muslim Relations," 8.
46. Maina, "Historical Roots," 89.
47. Maina, "Historical Roots," 89.
48. Maina, "Historical Roots," 89.
49. Seventh Day Adventist Church v. Minister for Education.
50. Seventh Day Adventist Church v. Minister for Education.

had been suspended for failing to attend Saturday classes; that the schools conduct examinations on Saturdays; that they were not exempted from cleaning duties on Saturday and those who missed duties, classes or examinations on Saturday were suspended. The court's verdict neither found any violations of the rights nor discriminatory practices against SDA students in the schools.[51] But the case demonstrates how the practice of freedom of religion in schools is taken very seriously and especially where religious faithful feel their constitutional rights are violated.

EVANGELISATION AND COMPETITION FOR CONVERTS

The constitutional provision of freedom of religion ideally provides an atmosphere within which the various religions in the country can engage in activities of evangelisation and spreading of their belief through conversion. This therefore has set the stage for competition between the various religions especially Christianity and Islam. Spatial competition through evangelisation is a factor that engenders the environment of freedom of worship in the country as it is wrought with accusations and counter accusations especially between Christians and Muslims. The competition between the two religions provides fodder for propaganda purposes, with Muslims accusing Christians and Christian organizations of preaching against Islam, and counter attack of Christians accusing Muslims of undermining Christianity. There is no empirical evidence to prove that Christians and Muslims target each other in their evangelical work, but the claims and accusations demonstrate an atmosphere of competition which ultimately heightens tensions and engender freedom of religion in the country. This situation is accentuated by anti-Islamic rhetoric from the clergy of the mainstream churches. For example, the call by head of the Catholic Church in Kenya, Maurice Cardinal Otunga (1923-2003) in 1993 for "Christians to stand up and fight the spread of Islam in Africa" sparked off countrywide outrage and protests among Muslims with some perceiving the call as a prelude to religious wars in the country.[52] The following year, the Anglican Church of Kenya Bishop, Stephen Kewasis (1953) made a similar call for Christians to intensify evangelisation in North Eastern and Coast provinces of Kenya through building of churches as a method of challenging Islam. He claimed

51. Seventh Day Adventist Church v. Minister for Education.

52. Otunga's call was made during the opening ceremony of the Secretaries of the Episcopal Conference of Africa and Madagascar in Nairobi, January 12-16, 1993. He was equally critical of the Islamic teaching on Muhammad as the last prophet arguing that it is based on a lie because "it is clearly stated it is Jesus Christ." He further reportedly said that Muslims had joined all spheres of activity in order to fight Christianity. See Maina, "Christian-Muslim Dialogue," 174; "Christian-Muslim Relations," 11.

that Muslims were building mosques in all parts of the country. This call aroused the anger of Muslims who perceived it as a threat to freedom of religion in the country and an incitement of Christians against Muslims.[53] It could be argued that the reactions following such statements more often than not lead to denials but unfortunately the damage has already been done. This heightens mutual fears, suspicions and mistrusts between the religious groups.[54] And this does not portend well for the freedom of religion in an environment of religious pluralism largely dominated by Christianity and Islam.

One of the latest and common methods of evangelisation employed by followers of different religions, especially Christians and Muslims in Kenya, is what is commonly known in local lingo as *mihadhara*. Loosely translated *mihadhara* is Kiswahili for "street preaching" or "public religious rallies" or "open air preaching." *Mihadhara* is one of the latest *modus operandi* of Muslim outreach to Christians. It is a common feature in virtually all the major towns in Kenya. *Mihadhara* was perfected in East Africa by the South African preacher and author, Ahmed Deedat (1918–2005). Owing to the largely polemical nature of *mihadhara*, inter religious conflicts and physical confrontations occur resulting in injuries and destruction of life and property.[55]*Mihadhara* caused fights between Muslims and SDA Christians in Mumias town, Kakamega County, as result of remarks by Christian pastor.[56] In Bura, Tana River County, the arrest of a Muslim street preacher who aggressively preached against Christianity and Christians led to riots by Muslim youth who stoned a police station, torched and looted churches. The preacher, a former Christian pastor who converted to Islam preached offensive messages that incited Muslims against Christians.[57] This incident took place on June 13, 2003 and led to the razing of churches belonging to the Anglican Church of Kenya, Pentecostal Evangelism, Full Gospel Church of Kenya, East African Pentecostal Church, and Bethel Church.[58] Generally, *mihadhara* is an affront to the freedom of religion and expression in the country. Nevertheless, freedom of religious expression does not mean interfering with the fundamental rights of others through attacks and insults.

Freedom of religion implies that people should freely convert from one religion to another without any coercion whatsoever. But this has not always

53. Maina, "Historical Roots," 92.

54. Oded, *Islam and Politics*, 110.

55. Wandera, "Christian-Muslim Co-Existence," 95–104.

56. Maina, "Historical Roots," 92.

57. Maina, "Historical Roots," 92.

58. Maina, "Historical Roots," 92.

been the case. There are exceptional cases which are rarely documented or come to the public light—where people's lives have been threatened as a result of conversion especially from Islam to Christianity. This contravenes the freedom of thought, conscience and religion guaranteed by chapter 4, article 32 of the Kenyan Constitution and United Nations Conventions.[59] Fear and threats of attack due to conversion from one religion to another is a big indictment on the freedom of religion and sometimes causes inter religious conflicts especially between Christians and Muslims. For example, conflicts arose in Merti trading center north of Isiolo town in Eastern province, when some Waso Borana families converted to Christianity.[60] The next section of the chapter examines freedom of religion and the state/government control.

FREEDOM OF RELIGION AND
THE STATE/GOVERNMENT CONTROL

It has already been noted that Kenya is a secular state meaning that all religions should be granted the same status under the Constitution. But the presence of heavy Christian bureaucratic and political elite at the top of the leadership ladder makes the supposedly secular government to be brand-named "Christian government." The perception of the government as "Christian" has implications on the freedom of religion. This is the case especially when some religious groups point out apparent discrimination whenever the state/government fails to meet their political, social and economic expectations. In such instances, the government is accused of favoring some religious group(s) as opposed to others. In the past, before the introduction of devolution[61] Muslims expressed their displeasure in suc-

59. For example, the "Universal Declaration of Human Rights" states that: "Everyone has the right to freedom of thought, conscience and religion; this right includes freedom to change his religion or belief, and freedom, either alone or in community with others and in public or private, to manifest his religion or belief in teaching, practice, worship and observance" (UN, "Universal Declaration of Human Rights" art. 18). While the "International Covenant on Civil and Political Rights" states that: "Everyone shall have the right to freedom of thought, conscience and religion. This right shall include freedom to have or to adopt a religion or belief of his choice, and freedom, either individually or in community with others and in public or private, to manifest his religion or belief in worship, observance, practice and teaching" (UN, "International Covenant on Civil and Political Rights" art. 18. 1).

60. Maina, "Historical Roots," 93.

61. Devolution is a pillar of the Constitution which seeks political and economic empowerment of people at the grassroots. As a part of the implementation of the Constitution promulgated in 2010, Devolution led to the creation of 47 county governments after the General Elections on March 4, 2013.

cessive "Christian" governments which they accused of alleged discrimination and historical injustices[62] ranging from socio-economic and political marginalisation.[63] These sentiments do not augur well for harmonious coexistence between religious groups especially the predominant Christians and Muslims where the latter consider the Kenyan state as synonymous with Christians.[64]

Religious institutions such as churches, mosques, temples in Kenya are registered under the Societies Act, chapter 108. Indeed, it has been easy to register a "society,"[65] since all what is required is the name of the organization, details of the office bearers, and a copy of identity card, passport photos, and a copy of the Kenya Revenue Authority pin number. These minimal conditions have made it easy for an individual or group to register an institution and call it a religious entity.[66] Consequently, this has led to proliferation of religious groups, churches, mosques and temples in the country. This situation has brought about commercialisation of religion and exploitation of gullible Kenyans by rogue "pastors" and religious leaders who claim to solve a myriad of problems ranging from mundane ones such as financial to medical ones such treating incurable diseases such as AIDS. Besides, mosques have been used as focal points of radicalisation and religious extremism by radical Muslim clerics, through whom, radicalised Muslim youths had taken over the running of mosques in Mombasa and Nairobi. The teachings of radical clerics have been poisoning the minds of the young Muslims with the theological distortions that support violent ideology. This has made some of the youths to engage in acts of terrorism, an issue discussed later in the chapter.

An example of the commercialisation of religion was demonstrated in November 2014. A local television station, Kenya Television Network, aired a clip of a pastor of Salvation Ministries Church manipulating his congregation by performing tricks dubbed as healing miracles to lure the congregants to donate money.[67] The television footage was widely circulated

---

62. Oded, *Islam and Politics*, 101.

63. Mwakimako, "Muslim NGOs," 229.

64. Kellow, "Leave Religion Out," 17.

65. "Society" refers to any club, company, partnership, or other association of ten or more persons, whatever its nature or object, established in Kenya or having its headquarters or chief place of business in Kenya and any branch of a society. See Republic of Kenya, "Societies Act" ch. 108, sec. 2(8).

66. Noor, "Kenya's Bid to Regulate."

67. In the investigative television series dubbed *Jicho Pevu*, the flamboyant Pastor, Victor Kanyari, performed fake and dubious miracles cheating his gullible followers and listeners to give money and other gifts to the church with the promise of healing

through the print and social media thereby generating public outcry. The government reacted by imposing an indefinite suspension of registration of new religious institutions—associations, societies, churches, mosques, temples—and called for fresh registration of the existing ones.[68]The Attorney General issued a new raft of regulations called "Religious Societies Compliance Rules"[69]which were to be gazetted at the end of January 2016, and enforced a year later. The rules were to provide a framework for review of the Societies Act so that religious institutions were to become more accountable and transparent. Among others, the regulations would have required pastors, imams, rabbis, and other religious leaders to obtain a Certificate of Good Conduct from the police and clearance from the Ethics and Anti-corruption Commission. The government also required details of the religious institutions such as leaders, committee members and registered trustees and their location. The religious institutions were also to file annual returns and failure to comply with the Rules within 60 days, they were to have their licenses revoked.[70]Under the rules, were new Programming Code for Free to Air Broadcasting in which pastors were banned from making appeals for listeners to accept Jesus and for viewers to donate some money.[71] There was immediate reaction from the churches and other religious groups which saw the government's move as likely to curtail the freedom of religion in the country. Specifically, church leaders noted that the new regulations were "aimed at gagging and muzzling the Church in Kenya" and "a form of government persecution against churches."[72]

Owing to the stiff opposition, the new rules did not see the light of the day after religious leaders appealed to President Uhuru Kenyatta to intervene. After meeting the religious leaders, the president said: "the outcome will be development of firm and fair regulations that uphold the sacrosanct principles of religious freedom that underpin our democratic ideals as guaranteed by our constitution."[73] But even before the dust had settled, the latest move in March 2017 by the Registrar of Societies requiring churches to provide audited accounts before their licenses are renewed was interpreted by some Pentecostal Churches and Ministries as yet another attempt by the government to sneak the "Religious Societies Compliance Rules."

---

and financial prosperity. See Parsitau, "Taming Rogue Clergy and Churches," 7.

68. Noor, "Kenya's Bid to Regulate."

69. Noor, "Kenya's Bid to Regulate."

70. Noor, "Kenya's Bid to Regulate."

71. "Kenya's Government Curtails Freedom."

72. "Kenya's Government Curtails Freedom."

73. Osanjo, "Churches Divided," 13.

This move was unprecedented because prior to this, the churches were only required to file their annual returns with the Registrar of Societies. While the mainstream churches like the Anglican Church supported the idea, the Kenya National Congress of Pentecostal Churches termed this requirement "punishment" by the state to control the churches and their activities, a move that was likely to drive a wedge between Pentecostal churches and the government.[74] The Deputy Chairman of the Kenya National Congress of Pentecostal Churches and Ministries reportedly urged the Attorney General to reconsider the decision.[75] The demand for churches to submit audited accounts was yet another attempt by the government to control rogue churches and pastors especially those of the Pentecostal churches that revolve around individuals who commercialise religion at the expense of their congregants.

TERRORISM AND ITS IMPLICATIONS FOR FREEDOM OF RELIGION

The year 1998 marks the first act of terrorism attributed to religious radicalism and extremism on the Kenyan soil. On August 7, 1998, the USA embassy in Nairobi was bombed by alleged Al-Qaida terrorists killing 216 people and injuring scores. Since then, terror attacks intensified when the Kenya Defense Forces entered Somalia in 2011 to flash out Al-Shabaab.[76] Terror attacks have implications on the freedom of religion in the country. A characteristic feature of the attacks is the deliberate isolation of Muslims from Christians with the former spared while the latter are mercilessly massacred.[77] This has created fear among Christians who are largely targeted by people who profess the Islamic faith. Christians may not feel secure to practice their religion for fear of attacks. Indeed, in the past, some pastors

---

74. Njagi, "Registrar's Demand," 3; Osanjo, "Churches Divided," 13.

75. Osanjo, "Churches Divided," 13; Osanjo, "Githu on the Spot," 36; Njagi, "Registrar's Demand," 3.

76. Al-Shabaab has claimed responsibility for many of the terrorist attacks on Kenyan soil, e.g., killing 17 people in two churches in Garissa (July 1, 2012); the Westgate Mall attack in Nairobi that killed 70 people (September 21, 2013); killing 6 people in a Church in Likoni, Mombasa (March 23, 2014); killing 6 people in a food kiosk in Eastleigh, Nairobi (March 31, 2014); the Mpeketoni attack that killed more than 60 people (June 15–17, 2014); two attacks in Mandera—one in which 28 Nairobi bound passengers were killed (November 23, 2014) and the other 36 quarry workers (December 2, 2014); and the Garisssa University College attack, in which 147 students, mainly Christians, lost their lives (April 2015).

77. Ayman, "Why Al-Shabaab."

have appealed to the government to supply them with guns for self-defense against what they regarded as Muslim militants.[78]

Terrorism has led to irrational fear of Islam and Muslims or *Islamophobia* from the followers of other religions. *Islamophobia* is a socio-religious discourse that some Christian leaders of the Evangelical and Pentecostal churches employ through sermons to warn their followers about the Islam (Muslim) menace.[79] Apparently, *Islamophobia* is not congenial for freedom of religious expression and harmonious co-existence between various religions in the country.

The threat of terrorism has contributed to heightened levels of *Islamophobia* among Kenyans of different religions.[80] This is due to high levels of security and usual terror alerts that have become part and parcel of life. The threat of terrorism has prompted many public utilities and institutions such as schools, supermarkets, churches, temples, and mosques to invest heavily on security through hiring of security guards, security gadgets and closed circuit surveillance cameras. When worshippers troop to their worshipping places, they are thoroughly subjected to the security checks. This is a constant reminder about the threat and reality of terrorism, and that security cannot be taken for granted even in places of worship, hitherto considered places of refuge and safety for the faithful.

Terrorism has also led to a rising anti-Islamic rhetoric among Kenyans and "raised the tempo for the hostile climate towards Muslims."[81] Consequently, the fault lines between the religions especially between majority Christians and Muslims have widened.[82] Muslim opinion leaders have generally argued that the "terrorists are not Muslims"[83] or "terrorism is the work of the devil."[84] This kind of argument devoid of any substance has done little to absolve Muslims and Islam from blame as the attacks are committed by members who allegedly bear Muslim names and invoke the name of

78. Kellow, "Leave Religion Out," 17.

79. This was evident during the *Kadhi* courts debate that brought about a new constitution in 2010. See Maina, "Islamophobia," 53.

80. Maina, "Islamophobia," 53.

81. Ayman, "Why Al-Shabaab."

82. Kagwanja, "How Kenya Fiddled," 21.

83. This has become like a mantra in any forum where there is a discourse touching on radicalism and extremism, and where Muslims and Islam seem to be on the receiving end. For example, during the "Scientific Conference on 'Radicalism, Islam and World Peace'" held at the University of Nairobi, March 15, 2015, the statement was repeated by various presenters.

84. This was a response by the Supreme Council of Kenya Muslims condemning the Westgate Mall terror attack. See Kemei and Obuya, "Group Distances Islam," 11.

Allah. Hence the cliché "not every Muslim is a terrorist, but every terrorist is a Muslim" has gained currency as a blanket condemnation of Islam and Muslims. This has brought much tension between Muslims and members of other religions in the country partly because many non-Muslims may not distinguish the acts of an individual from those of a community and a religion. It is worth noting that while the Muslim community is blamed for terrorism, it has also suffered irreparably as members of the community have been victims of, and actually died from terror attacks.[85] Besides, Muslims residing in areas where they are a minority are looked upon with suspicion and sometimes subjected to discrimination and profiling by the non-Muslims, thus creating fear among them. For example, in the wake of Westgate Mall attack, ethnic Somali Muslims had to bear all sorts of harassment and discrimination such as insults, and being forcibly removed from public service vehicles.[86]

THE GOVERNMENT RESPONSE TO TERROR ATTACKS

Following the 1998 bombing of the USA Embassy, the government banned five Muslim Non-Governmental Organizations (NGOs) it alleged were aiding terrorists.[87] From the outset, Christians feared that some of the NGOs were going to interfere with the freedom of religion as they "had as their main goal making Kenya an Islamic country within the next two or three decades."[88] Many Kenyans and the government in particular were concerned about the growth of Islamic radicalism in the country. Consequently, in 2003, the government floated the Anti-terrorism Bill which was however withdrawn in the face of widespread criticism from Muslim leaders who argued that it was targeting Muslims. The Bill was later revived as the Terrorism Prevention Bill 2012 but it is still pending after criticism that some sections were infringing on basic human rights:

> Some sections of the law like the clause that gives powers to the
> police to detain people without consulting with the courts or

---

85. For example, there was a grenade attack targeting worshippers in a mosque in Nairobi Eastleigh, an area predominated by members of the Somali Muslim community. This attack led to death of two Muslims and inflicted serious injuries to the local Muslim Member of Parliament. Another attack in a bus in the coastal city of Mombasa killed four Muslims. See "Four Killed," 2.

86. Ayman, "Why Al-Shabaab."

87. These were: Mercy Relief International Agency; Al-Haramain Foundation; Help African People; the International Relief Organization; and Ibrahim Abd al-Aziz al-Ibrahim Foundation. See Oded, *Islam and Politics*, 84.

88. Oded, *Islam and Politics*, 84.

any other third party, making them both the judge and execu-
tioner, to be punitive and infringing on basic human rights.[89]

The government's war on terrorism has witnessed scores of Muslims being
arrested as terror suspects by the Anti-terror Police Unit. This provokes up-
roar from the Muslim community against the government. Muslim leaders
bitterly criticise the government of discrimination, polarisation and profiling the Muslim community and especially the Somali community, as terrorists.[90] It is our opinion that an atmosphere where a religious group feel
discriminated by a government that is supposed to protect them is not good
for freedom of religious co-existence.

CONCLUSION

Within an environment of religious pluralism, the Constitution provides the
central tenets of freedom of religion and worship in Kenya. The Constitution also provides a legal framework through various Acts of Parliament that
govern the operations of religions in the country. However, the operations
of these religions at either the individual level or collectively, sometimes
infringe on the freedom of religion for others. Undoubtedly, this freedom
is abused by the followers of the various religions especially Christians and
Muslims on one hand and the state/government on the other. The chapter
has concentrated more on Christians and Muslims because the followers of
two religions comprise the majority of the populace and their contestation
for the space bring issues of freedom of religion to the fore.

The chapter shows that the government has a constitutional mandate
to ensure that, firstly, religious groups and individuals enjoy the freedom
of religion. Secondly, the government has to provide a secure and peaceful
environment for religious practice and expression and mutual co-existence
among various religions. It is this context that the government's moves in
regulating religions and its response to terrorism should be understood.
However, the balancing act of the government in providing an enabling
environment for religions and regulating them at the same time is seen
to interfere with the freedom of religion. Therein lies the dilemma of the
government.

89. "Are Christian-Muslim Relations."
90. Abdullahi, "Kenyan Somalis," 20.

BIBLIOGRAPHY

Abdullahi, Ahmednasir. "Kenyan Somalis Treated like Second-Class Citizens." *Sunday Nation*, April 13, 2014. 20.

"Are Christian-Muslim Relations under Attack across East Africa?" *East African*, September 8, 2012. Online. https://www.theeastafrican.co.ke/news/Why-wave-of-Muslim-leaders-killings-in-EA-raises-alarm/2558-1500286-item-0-ugsfcd/index.html.

Brislen, Michael Dennis. "Christian Perceptions of Islam in Kenya: As Expressed in Written Sources from 1998 to 2010." PhD diss., University of Birmingham, 2001.

"Four Killed and Several Injured as Twin Explosions Rock Mombasa." *Sunday Nation*, May 3, 2014. 2.

Hackett, Rosalind I. J. "Regulating Religious Freedom in Africa." *Emory International Law Review* 25.2 (2011) 853–79. Online. https://heinonline.org/HOL/LandingPage?handle=hein.journals/emint25&div=22&id=&page=.

Kellow, Billow. "Leave Religion out of the Anti-Terror War." *Standard on Sunday*, April 6, 2014. 17.

Kemei, Timothy, and Peter Obuya. "Group Distances Islam from Raid." *Daily Nation*, September 21, 2013. 11.

"Kenya's Government Curtails Freedom for Religious Leaders in Worrying New Regulations." *Barnabas Fund*, January 21, 2016. Online. https://barnabasfund.org/en/news/Kenyas-government-curtails-freedom-for-religious-leaders-in-worrying-new-regulations.

Kenyatta University. *Catalogue 2014–2017*. Nairobi: Kenyatta University Press, 2014.

Maina, Newton Kahumbi. "Christian-Muslim Dialogue in Kenya." In *Quests for Integrity in Africa*, edited by Grace N. Wamue and Mathew Theuri, 171–84. Nairobi: Acton, 2003.

———. "Christian-Muslim Relations in Kenya: An Examination of Issues of Conflict." *CSIC Papers Africa* 17 (1995) 1–21.

———. "The Historical Roots of Conflicts between Christians and Muslims in Kenya." In *Interfaith Dialogue: Towards a Culture of Working Together*, edited by Frederic N. Mvumbi, 77–99. Nairobi: Catholic University of Eastern Africa, 2009.

———. "A History of Christian-Muslim Relations in Kenya, 1963–2015." In *Christian Responses to Terrorism: The Kenyan Experience*, edited by Gordon L. Heath and David K.Tarus, 12–32. Eugene, OR: Pickwick, 2017.

———. "Islamophobia among Christians and its Challenge in Entrenchment of Kadhi Courts in Kenya." In *Constitutional Review in Kenya and Kadhi Courts*, edited by Abdikadeer Tayob and Joseph Wandera, 49–55. University of Cape Town: Center for Contemporary Islam, 2011.

Mbiti, John S. *African Religions and Philosophy*. Nairobi: East African Educational, 1969.

Murimi, Susan. "Christianity in Kenya." In *Anthology of African Christianity*, edited by Isabel Apawa Phiri, et al., 604–613. Oxford: Regnum Books International, 2016.

Mutambo, Aggrey. "Religious War over School Dress Codes." *Daily Nation*, February 8, 2012. Online. https://www.nation.co.ke/news/Religious-war-over-school-dress-codes-/1056-1323080-4uryj6z/index.html.

Muthoni, Kamau. "Uniform Is for All Students Regardless of Religion, Nairobi Court Rules." *The Standard*, December 25, 2016. Online. https://www.standardmedia.

co.ke/article/2000227951/uniform-is-for-all-students-regardless-of-religion-nairobi-court-rules.

Mwakimako, Hassan. "Muslim NGOs and Community Development: The Kenya Experience." In *Islam in Kenya: Proceedings of the National Seminar on Contemporary Islam in Kenya*, edited by Muhammad Bakari and S. Yahya Saad, 233–34. Mombasa: MEWA, 1995.

Njagi, John. "Registrar's Demand for Audited Accounts Ruffles Churches." *Daily Nation*, February 7, 2017. 3.

Noor, M. Hawa. "Kenya's Bid to Regulate Religious Institutions." *Life & Peace Institute*, February 20, 2015. Online. http://life-peace.org/hab/kenyas-bid-to-regulate-religious-institutions-2.

Oded, Arye. *Islam and Politics in Kenya*. Boulder, CO: Lynne Rienner, 2000.

Oliana, Guido. "The Theological Challenges of Religious Pluralism: Towards a Christian Theology of Other Faiths." *Tangaza Journal of Theology and Mission* 1 (2010) 9–30.

Osanjo, Tom. "Churches Divided on Law on Financial Audit of Accounts." *Sunday Nation*, March 5, 2017. 13.

———. "Githu on the Spot over Proposed Churches Law." *Sunday Nation*, March 12, 2017. 36.

Parsitau, Damaris, S. "Taming Rogue Clergy and Churches: God, Scandals, Government, and Religious Regulation in Kenya." Unpublished paper. 2017.

Republic of Kenya. "Education Act." Kenya Law Reports. Online. http://kenyalaw.org/kl/fileadmin/pdfdownloads/Acts/EducationActCap211.pdf.

———. "The Marriage Act." *Kenya Gazette* s62.4 (2014). Online. http://kenyalaw.org/kl/fileadmin/pdfdownloads/Acts/TheMarriage_Act2014.pdf.

———. "Societies Act." Kenya Law. Online. http://kenyalaw.org:8181/exist/kenyalex/sublegview.xql?subleg=CAP.%20108.

Sore, Geoffrey M. "Atheists Should Respect Freedom of Religion in Kenya." *The Star*, October 12, 2015.

United Nations. "International Covenant on Civil and Political Rights (ICCPR)." March 23, 1976. Online. https://treaties.un.org/doc/publication/unts/volume%20999/volume-999-i-14668-english.pdf.

———. "Universal Declaration of Human Rights." December 10, 1948. Online. https://www.un.org/en/universal-declaration-human-rights.

Wandera, Joseph. "Christian-Muslim Co-Existence in the Light of Sacred Texts and Present Contexts, with Special Reference to Mihadhara in Nairobi." In *Christian-Muslim Co-existence in Eastern Africa*, edited by Fritz Stenger, et al., 95–104. Tangaza Occasional Papers 22. Nairobi: Pauline Africa, 2008.

Wanjiru, Musalia. "Demonstration of Islamic Rituals and Talismans by Digo to Assist the Traditional Healers as a Means to Restoring Health." *World Academic Journal of Demography and Population Studies* 2.1 (2014) 15–23. Online. http://docplayer.net/51057263-World-academic-research-journals.html.

Worldometers. "Kenya Population (2018)." Online. http://www.worldometers.info/world-population/kenya-population.

Court Cases

Seventh Day Adventist Church (East Africa) Ltd v. Minister for Education & Others (unreported). Civil Appeal No. 172 of 2014.

4

God in the Village

The Dynamics of Rural Pentecostalism and Development in Maasailand in Kenya

Damaris Parsitau

P entecostalism has undoubtedly become one of the major religious forces in the developing world, Africa in particular.[1] However, much discussion of African Pentecostalism has tended to focus on its impact on urban Africa, with little focus on its spread and impact on rural and deeply marginalized villages. Its impact on the social, cultural, political, and economic life of indigenous and marginalized groups is even less studied. More importantly and even less studied is how Pentecostalism transforms or is transformed by rural cultures, and whether indeed its interactions with rural communities and cultures constitutes "a radical break with the pasts" or "raptures with such cultures and traditions" or even how it domesticates and appropriates such cultures so as to thrive and spread. Other important questions are whether Pentecostalism shows any forms of continuities or discontinuities with local beliefs and values of such groups. This question is also related to the overall theme of this book wrestling with religious freedom for whom.

This paper examines the unprecedented spread of Pentecostalism in Maasailand in Kenya in the last one and a half decade or so. The Maasai

---

1. Jenkins, *Next Christendom*, 103–4, 123, 196, 260–61.

people are a deeply traditional, conservative and historically nomadic pastoralists who dwell in the southern parts of Kenya and Tanzania. As pastoralism was and still is the main economic activity of the Maasai people, livestock is very important to them. Cows in particular have huge social, cultural and political prestige. The Maasai People of Kenya and Tanzania are also easily recognizable by the red blankets and attire that they drape around their bodies. As such, Maasai People have long been considered by both locals and outsiders as the proud, tall, pristine and iconic tribe of Africa who have for years resisted the forces of modernization and globalization.[2] As a result, they have managed to maintain a strong sense of their traditional and cultural identity despite tremendous internal and external pressure to modernize and embrace development.[3] They have also endeavoured to retain and protect much of their traditions and cultural identity and have largely resisted attempt by outsiders and government to erode their traditions and culture.

According to Henri ole Saitabau,[4] the Maasai have tenaciously clung to their culture and resisted outside influence because they wanted to protect it from negative influence. In his view, "the Maasai have an independent way of thinking, are faithful to their kinship ties and maintain a very high regard for their own culture and way of life."[5] And while they are undergoing tremendous social changes brought about by colonization, modernity, education, globalization and development, they have still managed to keep much of their culture and traditions intact. For example, Maasai people have embraced and continue to embrace modern education for their children in the last two or so decades unlike in the past where they had resisted it. They are also redefining what it means to be Maasai in the twenty-first century.[6]

While, the complex processes of globalization and modernity have had far reaching impact on all people on the planet, including the Maasai people,[7] the Maasai are not passive recipients of such forces. In fact, they are resisting and contesting globalization on their own terms, adopting what they like and resisting what they don't. There are two areas in which Maasai people are embracing and contesting modernity in their own terms: education and new forms of religiosities and spiritualties. While Maasai people are now embracing modern education, their children still maintain

2. Kotowicz, *Maasai Identity*. See also Koissaba, "Effects of Globalization."

3. Kotowicz, *Maasai Identity*.

4. Saitabau, *Impact of Climate Change*.

5. Saitabau, *Impact of Climate Change*.

6. Kotowicz, *Maasai Identity*.

7. Salau, "Globalization."

much of their traditional cultures like mode of dress when they go back to their villages as well as participating in Maasai socio-cultural rituals. Maasai people are also embracing Pentecostalism without abandoning elements of their traditions that are not in contradiction with their new faith. In fact Pentecostalism in Maasailand is heavily appropriating certain elements of Maasai traditions to thrive and flourish in the rural areas.

Yet, while much attention has focused on the interactions between Pentecostalism and urban populations, even fewer studies have focused on the interactions between Pentecostalism and rural and indigenous cultures as well as the mutual influences born by such interactions. Studies on globalization have also ignored how globalization has created new opportunities for change and resistance as well as how indigenous people challenge their marginality by creating new spaces to reclaim their place and cultures. One such area in which Maasai people are contesting and navigating modernity is in how they have embraced Pentecostal Christianity.

This chapter explores the dynamics of rural Pentecostal Christianity in remote villages of Maasailand in Kenya and its impact on the social, cultural and political life and development among the Maasai people. In particular, I consider why rural Maasai communities are attracted to Pentecostalism and how it is transformed by Maasai culture and traditions and vice versa. I also consider how Pentecostal beliefs, teachings, and practices are impacting and transforming the cultures and traditions of conservative Maasai people that have resisted modernity for a very long time. In particular, I consider how rural Pentecostalism is transforming gender and family relations as well as the role of women in such church and communities. The research is guided by the need to understand how Maasai converts are negotiating and navigating modernity and Pentecostal spirituality in a deeply contested social and cultural space. Compared to other ethnic groups in Kenya, the Maasai have somehow managed to retain much of their cultural norms and values. These cultural norms and values I argue have been incorporated into Pentecostal Christianity to produce a sort of hybrid Maasai Pentecostal like type of worship and religiosity where both cultures transform and borrow from each other. As a result, I argue that Pentecostalism has spread and found a strong base throughout rural Maasailand because it has heavily appropriate elements of Maasai culture to spread, thrive and domesticate itself among this indigenous people. This mutual appropriation as we shall discuss shortly shows how Pentecostalism has been domesticate within Maasai socio-cultural and political millieu and vice versa.

This chapter examines, not just the fast and an unprecedented spread of Pentecostalism in rural villages in Maasailand but also how some of the dynamics that have allowed it to thrive in a heavily conservative social cultural milieu. I ask a number of questions such as its impact in Maasai culture and vice versa and as well as the dynamics that have allowed it to thrive alongside of Maasai Culture in less than two decades. More importantly, it considers how Pentecostalism is transformed by Maasai culture and how it is appropriating Maasai culture and traditions to thrive throughout Maasailand.

RESEARCH METHODOLOGY

This chapter is based on ethnographic research carried out in the rural Maasai County of Kajiado in Kenya in the last five years in the. It is further based on my own personal observations and analysis on the unprecedented spread of Pentecostalism in Maasailand in the last one and a half decades that went under the radar for many social, religious, and political observers of African and Kenyan Pentecostalism in particular. These observations aroused huge interests in me and I began to carry out ethnographic research in Maasailand. Since 2014, I have attended tens of social, cultural, religious and political events in Maasailand, which take place over most weekends but especially during school holiday months April, August and December. I have also attended more than ten church services and women conferences organized by Pentecostal churches in Maasailand.

In all the social, cultural and political meetings in Maasailand in the last ten or so years, a Pentecostal inspired kind of service preceded these meetings with people clad in their traditional Maasai attire praying in the spirit with hands raised up and many"slayed by the spirit" as Maasai praise and worship teams lead the masses in praise and worship. In such meetings, a new and popular kind of Pentecostal like Maasai gospel music is played through loud speakers, something that has increasingly become a defining feature of such meetings since the late 1990s to date.

This was something new for me personally having grown up in Maasailand in the 1970s where Mainline Churches such as the Anglican Churches of Kenya, the Catholic Church, the African Inland Churches as well as the Presbyterian Churches of East Africa were the only churches found in Maasailand. While Mainline churches are still operating in Maasailand, hundreds of newer Pentecostal church ministries, both huge and small today dot the rural villages of Maasailand and are inspiring social and cultural changes among this conservative ethnic group. In many cases, these churches are dwarfing the mainline churches that now have fewer and older members of the community. The newer Pentecostal churches are popular with the younger folks who are well schooled unlike many of their parents in mainline church traditions. The youth aspire to a modern Pentecostal type of worship and experience that is lacking in the traditional mainline churches mentioned above. This chapter also deals with how Maasai converts are negotiating and navigating modernity and Pentecostal spirituality in a deeply contested social and cultural space.[8]

This chapter is therefore based on ethnographic data collected through participant participation of church services, crusades and revival prayer meetings women fellowships, social and cultural events such as development projects commissioning, graduation parties, political rallies, marriage ceremonies, new home dedication ceremonies and many other such events. In rural villages, there are frequent social gatherings and political gatherings preceded by prayer and worship services mainly led by a Pentecostal clergy. I also carried out extensive interviews with church founders, senior and junior church leaders, youth pastors, women congregants, Maasai gospel artists and lay person. This was supplanted with media materials found in some church websites, church publications, social media chat forums as well as listening to Maasai vernacular radio stations and watching Maasai gospel music on you tube. Coupled with these ethnographic materials is literature on African Pentecostalism as well as my own personal analysis of new developments in Maasailand and beyond.

THE DYNAMICS OF KENYAN PENTECOSTALISM. MAPPING THE LANDSCAPE

Pentecostal Christianity originally started as an urban movement in America and as it spread to Africa and elsewhere it took root in urban centers, towns and cities.[9] In Kenya, the Pentecostal movement largely started in towns and cities like Nairobi, Nakuru, Kisumu, Eldoret, Kericho to name just but a few before it started to spread to the countryside and increasingly manifesting itself in the most rural communities in Kenya such as Maasailand.[10] Yet, the dynamics of Pentecostal Christianity in rural Kenya, as well as its impact on rural communities, has not received much academic attention. Urban Pentecostalism has been the focus of interest. This chapter seeks to fill this gap in Kenyan Pentecostalism.

Pentecostal and Charismatic groups are the fastest growing Christian movements in Kenya today, at least judging by the many numbers of buildings, structures and people who attend these churches. At present, Kenyan Pentecostalism represents the most visible evidence of religious renewal and

---

8. Kotowicz, *Maasai Identity*.

9. Freeman, *Pentecostalism in a Rural Context*; Anderson, *Introduction to Pentecostalism*; Gifford, *African Christianity*; Hollenweger, *Pentecostalism*; Martin, *Pentecostalism*.

10. Parsitau and Mwaura, "God in the City."

influence in the country. They also constitute the fastest growing group of churches within Kenyan Christianity.[11] The phenomenal rise in membership in these churches is validated by different statistics. A ten-nation survey by US based Pew Forum on Religion and Public Life reckons that Kenya was the most Pentecostal nation in Africa with 56 percent of its Christian population claiming to belong to Pentecostal and Charismatic movements. This accounts for more than half of Kenya's population beating even more populous nations such as South Africa and Nigeria at 34 and 26 percent respectively.[12]

The survey also found that approximately seven in ten Protestants in Kenya are either Pentecostal or Charismatic, and about a third of Kenyan Catholics surveyed can be classified as Charismatic. My research elsewhere suggests that what makes these numbers high is the fact that a significant number of mainline churches members describe themselves as Pentecostal or Charismatic due to the charismatisation and pentecostalisation of mainline Christianity in Kenya.[13] The modalities for arriving at such statistics might be debated. However, what is not debatable is the tremendous growth of these churches in Kenya. Similarly, Ogbu Kalu estimates that 14 percent of Kenyans are members of these non-mainstream churches.[14] Both the Pew Forum's figures and Kalu's estimates are further validated by other reports that appear to support this immense growth. Alex Ndegwa for example reported that the Registrar General's Office was overwhelmed by increasing demands for registration of these churches.[15] The former Attorney General, Amos Wako, while speaking at a workshop for church leaders revealed that the department was overwhelmed by an increasing demand for registration of churches and that the facility is facing difficulties in processing 6,740 pending applications by various religious organizations.[16]

The former Attorney General also revealed that there are about 8,520 registered churches and that about 100 applications are filed every month.[17] Some are eventually registered by the Registrar of Societies as the pastors' private properties, exclusively co-owned with their spouse and family, which explains the numerous protracted church ownership tussles that sometimes

11. Parsitau and Mwaura, "God in the City."

12. Pew Research Center, "Pentecostalism in Kenya."

13. Parsitau, "From the Periphery."

14. Kalu, *African Pentecostalism*, 5.

15. Ndegwa, "Over 6,000 Churches," 6.

16. Parsitau and Mwaura, "God in the City"; Gifford, *Christianity, Politics, and Public Life.*

17. Ndegwa, "Over 6,000 Churches."

end up in court. Although not all of these churches seeking registration are Pentecostal, the majority of them are of Pentecostal and Charismatic inclinations.

From these different sets of statistics, it can be argued that thousands of these newer Pentecostal and Charismatic churches have sprung up and sprouted in all major urban centers some within less than three to five kilometres of each other. While some are huge churches, others are small in size. Irrespective of whether they are mega churches or small churches, they cut across the various social classes of the country from urban to rural areas, richer to poorer, literate and illiterate.

Although Kenyan Pentecostalism is essentially an urban phenomenon, the movement has recently begun establishing itself in rural areas.[18] At present Kenyan Pentecostalism can be said to be a social force within the country. It has emerged as a popular form of religiosity for a significant majority of Kenyans. These movements have also changed, reshaped and reorganized the religious landscape of the country. They also point to how much power and influence the Pentecostal churches and the Christians can have in shaping their societies. Its impact also goes beyond demographic figures as its presence is powerfully felt in almost all areas of public life in Kenya.

GOD IN THE VILLAGE: THE DYNAMICS OF KENYAN PENTECOSTALISM IN RURAL VILLAGES IN MAASAILAND

As indicated above, Kenyan Pentecostalism in the last one and a half decade has begun to spread across the countryside into rural and sometimes very remote villages across the country. A case in point in these dynamics is the Ministry of Repentance and Holiness, one of the most prominent Neo-Pentecostal church movement in Kenya. This movement is under the leadership of the self-proclaimed prophet, David Owuor, established in 2004 when he claims to have given up his successful career as a scientist in the US and responded to God's call to return to Kenya to save the country from moral and spiritual decay.

The Ministry of Repentance and Holiness has since grown into a mass movement and Owuor has emerged as one of the most prominent figures in the Kenyan religious scene.[19] This Ministry that has morphed into a grassroot movement is now found in urban and rural areas in much of the countryside. Its "altars," as churches are referred to in this ministry, have spread to nearly every corner of the country from urban centers and large cities to

18. Parsitau and Mwaura, "God in the City."
19. Parsitau, "Prophets, Power." See also Parsitau, "Taming Rogue Clergy."

the deepest villages, but especially in the Rift Valley, Western Kenya, and Nyanza provinces. The Deliverances Churches of Kenya, one of the oldest Pentecostal churches in Kenya has also over the years spread into rural villages in many parts of the Kenya and East Africa more generally.

Yet it is the spread of Pentecostal Christianity in the deepest parts of Maasailand that I find most baffling given that the Maasai people have resisted any form of cultural intrusion for a long time. And while there are mainline churches such as the Roman Catholic Church, the Anglican Church of Kenya, African Inland Church, and the Presbyterian Church of East Africa that have long established themselves throughout Maasasiland, the entrance of the Neo-Pentecostal Churches in rural villages of Maasailand and its tremendous growth and spread within a relatively short time is baffling and requires special focus.[20]

Using the Dominion Chapel Ministries International (DCMI) founded and led by Maasai Pentecostal converts as an example, I examine this new phenomenon in a bid to understand its dynamics and impact on Maasai culture as well as how it has been transformed by its interaction with the cultures and traditions of the Maasai people. But first, a few words about the Maasai people as a background, so that we can appreciate the spread and impact of Pentecostal Christianity in this conservative culture.

THE MAASAI PEOPLE OF KENYA AND TANZANIA

The Maasai are Nilotic pastoralist communities found in the southern parts of Kenya and Northern Districts of Tanzania. In Kenya they occupy three counties: namely Narok, Kajiado and Samburu.[21] Maasai people speak Maa language. Pastoralism is the predominant livelihood of the Maasai of Kenya and Tanzania and contributes significantly to their economic and social livelihoods.[22] Livestock are at the heart of the Maasai socio-political economy and people and cattle, particularly cows, sheep and goats are more than just animals. Cattle, especially cows hold tremendous social, cultural, religious and political value to the Maasai people. Maasai men's love and relationship with their cattle is deep and nearly sacred. Cows, goats and sheep are markers and signifiers of social and cultural prestige, honor, wealth and spiritual value. The Maasai people believe that all cows belong to them and were given by God, or *Enkai*, in Maa language.[23]

20. Parsitau, "Engaging the Custodians."
21. Parsitau, "Engaging the Custodians."
22. Kipuri and Ridgewell, *Double Bind*.
23. Koissaba, "Effects of Globalization."

The Maasai are still generally known for the strong social-cultural practices and norms that govern all aspects of life. The Maasai political culture is complex and they practice an egalitarian system of social and political organization based on age-sets and have no system of centralized coercive authority. Popular public opinion based on custom places an obligation on people to carry out social duties, but no authority is exercised by particular individuals.

A dominant, but also culturally distinct, feature of the Maasai sociopolitical system is the age set system which mainly regulates the social and political organizations of the community. This complex system cuts through the clan system as well as the territorial organization and it defines the social division of labor.[24] The age set system stratifies adult males into age sets or age groups.

Within this age set system resides the linkages of alternating age sets. Certain individuals are worth to mention as tremendous, and special power and authority is vested upon them. Each local age set has its leader, called *oloiguanani*. He is publicly chosen and appointed at the *Eunoto* ceremony where young warriors graduate to become junior elders. Olaiguanani is responsible for discipline, order and ensuring conformity to customary law within the local age set. Uncircumcised boys provide the labor for the routine herding activities. The warriors are responsible for the military duties such as raids to restock their livestock, security for the community and their livestock and properties.[25]

Elders as well as traditional leaders wield tremendous political and spiritual power in Maasai land and they are deeply respected in Maa culture.[26] Social control among the Maasai rests ultimately on the general belief in the power of elders to bless and to curse, which is linked to their moral superiority in all spheres. The power of fire stick patrons over warriors, fathers over their children and all senior kin resides in their power to curse.

The Maasai people have a strong spiritual heritage with *Iloibonok*, or diviners, who can predict calamities and future events and provide remedy. There are several of these spiritual leaders but there is only one chief or Laibon. Laibons are consulted for advice during major community events such as major weather changes such as draught and health issues affecting both humans and animals. They carry out special prayers to Enkai for healing and mercy. Such spiritual and healing ceremonies are usually solemn

---

24. Kotowicz, *Maasai Identity*.

25. Koissaba, "Effects of Globalization."

26. Parsitau, "Engaging the Custodians."

events. These spiritual leaders use a collection of cultural paraphernalia such as gourds, special stones and herbs to carry out rituals for healing, cleansing and blessings. The religious or spiritual leader is a ritual expert whose function is to protect people and cattle from illness and misfortune, to cure diseases and perform rainmaking rituals. Nothing customary or religious can take place without his authority and the blessings of Oloiboni. The elders are expected to handle family affairs and manage family property, and they are the heads of livestock. As such, the Maasai Laibons wield tremendous social and spiritual control and command huge respect in their communities.[27]

In recent years, there has been significant worldwide progress towards gender equality across several key indicators in the social, economic, political and legal spheres. However, for Maasai women, not much has changed. The Maasai community is heavily patriarchal with minimum opportunities for women to challenge patriarchal ideologies and discrimination. The Maasai have strong socio-cultural practices and norms that govern all aspects of life in the community. These are so deeply ingrained in Maasai children's upbringing that it leaves little room from external and cultural influences and social change. Maasai cultural norms have negatively affected Maasai women who experience high levels of marginalization in their own culture.

First, Maasai women and girls are among the poorest and most marginalized groups in Kenya. Maasai women do not own livestock and land and other productive assets.[28] This makes them vulnerable and their vulnerabilities continue to become unstable in the face of emerging challenges. The Maasai women face great marginalisation socially, economically and politically. To start with, Maasai women lack property ownership rights. Besides, few options are available to control productive assets such as livestock and land and women are often unable to inherit property.[29] Economically, women remain important players in the pastoral and livestock economy, yet when it comes to ownership of livestock they are totally marginalized and excluded. Women are critical stakeholders in the pastoral/livestock economy, (the main source of pride for pastoralists). However, when it comes to the ownership and management of livestock, they are totally marginalised and excluded. And despite these multiple marginalisations, these women not only run their homes and families and raise children, they are also livestock managers and peace makers. On rare occasions they have managed to be elected into national office.

27. Kotowicz, *Maasai Identity*.
28. Parsitau, "Engaging the Custodians"; Kipuri and Ridgewell, *Double Bind*.
29. Kipuri and Ridgwell, *Double Bind*.

The status of a Maasai woman in the society is unseen, and their voices are unheard. At the same time, many lack access to social services and decision making power to make decisions concerning their lives for example, marriage, the number of children, education, access to healthcare services and voice to challenge husbands and spouses. Socially, Maasai women continue to be subjected to harmful social cultural and religious practices such as Female Genital Mutilation (FGM) and early marriage. They are often forcibly married off while still young in order to maximize on dowry and bride wealth systems. As such they continue to have less access to public services in areas that already lag behind. Women are also excluded implicitly or explicitly from community decision making which is firmly in the hands of male elders.[30]

Maasai girls are socialized early on to accept their roles as helpers to their mothers who are themselves subordinate to their husbands. In other words, they face multiple or even triple marginalities in the families and communities. They are marginalised as members of already marginalised and patriarchal structures. Women and girls are also marginalised by their gender. Being female in societies that equate women to girls is a huge obstacle to women empowerment. Marriage is an important part of pastoralist kinship relations, yet young women and men have little say in who they marry. Young girls are socialized to understand that marriage is the ideal for them and many aspire to grow and get married like their mothers. Early, arranged and forced marriages[31] are common among the Maasai people. Most marriages are arranged during adolescence or even earlier.

One reason for early marriages is the importance of bride wealth payments to the girl's family. With the rising level of poverty and diminishing land and livestock, women and girls are increasingly becoming commodified. Bride wealth, as well as discriminatory inheritance means that it is too difficult to seek divorce. At the same time, little has been done to improve women and girls access to education and health services. Statistics from Kenya show that women in remote pastoralist areas are seven times more likely to give birth without antenatal care.[32]

Politically, Maasai women are excluded explicitly or implicitly from community decision making, which is solely in the hands of male elders.[33] Women in the Maasai culture are traditionally viewed as novices where

---

30. Kipuri and Ridgwell, *Double Bind*. Parsitau, "Engaging the Custodians"; "How Young Men Can Change"; "How Girls Education."

31. Parasitu, "How Girls Education."

32. Kipuri and Ridgewell, *Double Bind*.

33. Parsitau, "How Girls Education."; Kipuri and Ridgewell, *Double Bind*.

leadership is concerned and are hardly given opportunity to show what they can do. Traditionally, Maasai women are not allowed to speak in public or in community meetings or even to participate in decision making, even those that have direct impact on their lives.

Besides, Maasai men own and control livestock, dominate politics and decision making. Men are heads of households, lineages, clans and community.[34] Women play secondary, supportive roles in livestock production and hold subordinate roles to their elders, fathers, husbands and sons. Decisions rest in the hands of elders and traditional leaders who are also custodians of authority and power.[35] This means that women have no power or voice and are under-represented at the village level, district level with community agenda often being determined by men.

Women also lack fora to challenge these oppressive practices and to speak out on issues that are important to them such as FGM, early and forced marriage, HIV and Aids, Reproductive health issues, healthcare, poverty and property ownership. This is worsened by the fact that many Maasai women at grassroots-level are illiterate.[36] This explains why there are fewer Maasai women in professional and public life, particularly in district organizations. The lack of educated women to fight for gender equality between Maasai men and women and to fight the patriarchal household structures has worsened women's situation, leaving them socially vulnerable and politically under-represented.

This complex social cultural dimension has negatively affected Maasai women who have experienced high levels of marginalization for many years. In short, the Maasai social and political system could be described as a government of men.[37] Women play secondary roles in the livestock economy and hold subordinate roles to their fathers, husbands, and brothers. Similarly, Maasai women have no voice and their health and status is adversely affected as well as their ability to fully participate in their communities. This is evident in their lack of property ownership including livestock, and in high mortality rates, low levels of education, forced marriages, heavy workloads and physical sufferings.

Maasai women are subjected to harmful customs and traditions such as FGM and early marriage.[38] Maasai women are also excluded from family and community decision making which is firmly in the hands of men, who

34. Kipuri and Ridgewell, *Double Bind*.
35. Parsitau, "How Girls Education."
36. Parsitau, "Engaging the Custodians."
37. Parsitau, "Engaging the Custodians"; Kipuri and Ridgewell, *Double Bind*.
38. Parsitau, "How Girls Education."

are also the custodians of tradition and customs. The Maasai community is heavily patriarchal with minimal opportunities for women to challenge these circumstances or to influence community decision making.

Polygamy is highly valued and men strive to marry many wives and have many children. The more wives and children a man has, the higher is his status in the community and his ability to cope with labour demands. For these reasons, Maasai women are arguably the poorest and most marginalized groups in the Kenyan society and their vulnerability is increasing in the face of climate change, globalization, modernity and unstable economies. They lack respect and appreciation and lack access to political power and frequently have development policies imposed on them. These tensions put Maasai women between a rock and a hard place. To appreciates, the impact of Pentecostalism on rural Maasai people, let us first understand how globalization is impacting on the Maasai communities.

MAASAI PEOPLE AND THE DILEMMA OF LIVELIHOODS POSED BY MODERNITY AND GLOBALIZATION IN THE TWENTY-FIRST CENTURY

The Maasai people as already stated above have managed to cling to their culture and traditions and maintained a strong sense of cultural identity in the face of incredible adversity where others have lost such identity.[39] The Maasai also face incredible pressure both externally and internally to adopt modernity and embrace modernity and development.[40] Although they are viewed by many outsiders and locals as a pristine iconic and traditional representation of Africa, the Maasai are actually undergoing many changes that are directly impacting on their livelihood and way of life. In an increasingly globalized world, the Maasai in the twenty-first century are faced with changes and challenges posed by globalization and modernity. Due to increased external pressure from colonialism, globalization and modernity as well as pressure from government, the Maasai people, who had for a long time resisted outside influence, are beginning to crack.

Viewed by many outsiders and locals as the pristine iconic and traditional representation of Africa, the Maasai are being redefined and presented in many ways. This presentation affects not only the external perception and ideas about the Maasai but what it means to be one. Firstly, the Maasai who are predominantly pastoralists are finding pastoralism increasingly difficult to maintain. It is important to understand the significance of identity

39. Kotowicz, *Maasai Identity.*
40. Kotowicz, *Maasai Identity.*

in social change especially in the face of globalization and modernity. With such challenges, the Maasai are changing and evolving in many ways. There are several areas where change is already evident.

First, the Maasai pastoralist and nomadic lifestyle is changing. Maintaining a pastoralist lifestyle and economy is becoming increasingly difficult in the face of climate change, environmental degradation, diminishing land and human wildlife conflicts. Secondly, the Maasai people are experiencing rapid social and political changes like never witnessed before. Their traditional ways of life and cultural practices are undergoing transformation in so many ways. In fact, the Maasai identity is fast evolving and is being transformed and redefined.

The changes are multi-dimensional occurring both nationally and globally. Yet, the Maasai are not just passive about such changes. In fact, they are also active participants in social change and the resultant social transformation. For example, more and more girls are going to school than before and women's economic status is changing. Yet, the single most important change that is sweeping Maasailand and which is the focus of this study is the spread of Pentecostalism in deep rural and remote villages of Kajiado and Narok County.

GOD IN THE VILLAGE: THE CASE OF THE DOMINION CHAPEL MINISTRIES IN INTERNATIONAL (DCMI) IN KENYA

One aspect of the changes that many societies in Africa are undergoing is the emergence of Pentecostalism as one of the dynamic movements as well as a formidable force for change. In Kenya's urban centers as well as in rural villages, Pentecostalism is not only changing the social, cultural, economic and political dynamics of communities and cultures that were hitherto unchanged. It is also constructing how individuals understand themselves in relation to it.

In Kenya, Pentecostalism is not only constructing how individuals understand themselves but it is also changing the social dynamics of the group and culture. Using the case of the Dominion Chapel Ministries International (DCMI) in the deepest and remotest villages of rural Maasailand, I show the ways in which this Neo-Pentecostal church movement has spread into deep villages of Maasailand. I argue that in such communities, Pentecostalism has become a vector of change and modernity among the Maasai people and beyond. I further examine the impact of globalization on rural cultures and how it is transforming local experiences. Further, I examine the dynamics of rural Pentecostalism and its expansion and influence in different societies and cultures and how it transforms those cultures in significant ways. Below, I discuss the fast spread of the Dominion Ministries in Maasailand in Kenya and its impact on culture and traditions of the Maasai people.

SPREADING THE FIRE! THE SPREAD AND GROWTH OF THE DOMINION CHAPEL MINISTRIES INTERNATIONAL (DCMI)

In less than two decades, the Dominion Chapel Ministries International (DCMI) has spread throughout Maasailand to cover the two major counties of Kajiado and Narok, both predominantly Maasai counties. The DCMI was founded in 2002 by Bishop Peter Ole Mankura, a Maasai man born in 1971 in Oloirien location in Kajiado County and his wife Sophie Mankura, who co-pastors with her husband.[41] Ole Mankura went to primary school at Olooseos Primary School and Oloitokitok high school for his secondary education. While in form one, he joined the Christian Union, also popularly known as CU, and soon rose to become its chairperson. He also served as a school head boy where he honed his leadership skills.

After his secondary school education in 1992, he started the first Interdenominational Youth Alliance Ministry called Soul Winners Evangelistic Ministry (SWEM) which sought to spread the gospel and evangelize the whole of Maasailand in Kenya and Tanzania. In particular, SWEM focused on evangelistic outreaches to secondary schools, colleges and universities where there are large constituencies of youth. SWEM also organized youth crusades, conferences, rallies, outreaches, all night prayer rallies and weekend challenge rallies. Bishop Ole Mankura led SWEM for nearly ten years before he moved and founded the DCMI ministries. SWEM brought great spiritual revival to the entire Maasai regions also in Tanzania where there are Maasai people. And while there are other Pentecostal churches in Maasailand, the Dominion Ministry is the most popular and has had the greatest impact.

Since founding the DCMI in 2002, Bishop Ole Mankura has founded Dominion ministries also called "Assemblies" throughout Maasailand. In just less than one and a half decade, he had planted well over 300 Assemblies under the Dominion umbrella. These Assemblies are divided into around seven local regions all headed by Maasai youthful Pastors appointed and anointed by Bishop Mankura and commissioned to carry out evangelist works in those regions. In fact, these Pentecostal pioneers in Maasailand are

---

41. Dominion Chapel Ministries, "Bishop Dr. Peter Ole Mankura."

predominantly young Maasai men and women in their teens and early 20s and 30s. Many of these youth were school leave outs or colleges graduates who got born again and exposed to Pentecostal Christianity and modernity in institutions of higher learning where most went to school. The regions where most of the Dominion churches are found include Kiserian, Suswa, Kitengela, Kajiado, Narok South, Narok North, and Trans Mara regions. Each region is headed by a regional overseer who is in charge of several districts. All these regions are headed by Maasai clergy who serve under Bishop Mankura. Many of them are former students or classmates who worked with him in SWEM and whom he also mentored in the work of the Ministry.

Bishop Mankura also runs an International Missions Ministry as well as a School of Ministry that aims to build capacity for pastors and followers. He has preached in the USA, Europe, South Africa, and Tanzania. Further he preaches on the Kenyan media scene especially on Maasai radio stations such as Nosim FM and others. His Dominion ministry has helped spread the gospel throughout Maasailand. Based on my ethnographic material, I found that the Dominion Ministry has at least five main ministries or wings that I think are transforming Maasai people as well as having an impact on their social and cultural lives, namely: Youth Alive, Turning Point, Men of Purpose, Kings Daughters, and Children Ministry.

THE IMPACT OF DCMI IN MAASAILAND

The DCMI ministry is inspiring social change and social transformation throughout Maasailand through those five different ministries. Notable change is already visible in a number of areas particularly in certain con-stituencies such as youth, men and women that are impacting gender as well as cultural changes which I discuss below.

TRANSFORMING YOUTH THROUGH THE GOSPEL

The DCMI is a youthful ministry. Most of these young people are secondary school and a few college graduates who became born gain in high school or universities and went back to their communities to evangelize and spread the fire throughout their villages. In DCMI, the youth go through elaborate spiritual training to prepare them well for evangelism and ministry. Most of the trainings take place at the DCMI headquarters at Kiserian. Here, the youth ministry is formulated to cater for the needs of the communities. For example, the ministry organizes events such as annual Christian camps; youth outreach activities and conferences throughout the year. In such meetings, the youth are taught how to navigate their Christian life in a way that leads not just to personal but social transformation as well. They are for example taught how to become people of integrity. Virtues of honesty, accountability, self-control, discipline, faithfulness, righteousness, and holiness are heavily stressed here. These virtues are expected of every youth who is a member of this ministry. Here, they develop leadership skills and values of integrity, honesty and accountability. But they are also trained and taught to shun certain aspects of their culture that is not compatible with their new faith. For example, they are taught about relationships and given tools to navigate relationship spaces using spiritual resources. They are encouraged to abstain from sex outside marriage and observe fidelity in marriage. Monogamy is presented as the ideal form of marriage which is contrary to Maasai culture which is highly polygamous. Many of the young men I interviewed, the majority of whom come from polygamous families, do not find it compatible with their new Christian faith. Pentecostalism appeals to upward looking young men who desire to turn away from cultural practices that are at odds with their new-found faith. So such teachings have inspired a new generation of Maasai men and women who espouse monogamous ideals, something inconceivable only a few decades go. This is also having an impact on women and family dynamics which I will discuss below.

MEN OF PURPOSE

The DCMI also runs annual and quarterly programmes solely designed for men, popularly known as the Men of Purpose programmes. This programme focuses on transforming Christian or "born again" men into men of purpose and honour. Here the men, who are members of this ministry, are taught how to raise strong Christian families. They are taught how to be better fathers and spouses to their wives and good leaders for the society. Similarly, men of purpose fellowship takes place in every region where there are DCMI churches in a bid to build capacity for men in those regions using spiritual resources to transform men into men of honour and integrity. In these meetings, men are trained on how to become good fathers to their children and better and supportive spouses to their wives. In a wedding ceremony I attended at Oloshoibor village in which the bride and groom and bridal troup all dressed in a modern but Maasai inspired attires, Bishop Mankura who presided over the wedding taught about monogamy as the ideal Christian marriage where the husband treats his wife as a companion and loves her as Christ loved the church. In church and wedding ceremonies monogamy and fidelity within marriage is highly stressed and promoted. This is portrayed as the ideal Christian trait for Maasai men to embrace.

This is important for Maasai men who have been raised in a heavily patriarchal culture like that in Maasailand where men: elders, fathers, young warriors are the main decision makers and where polygamy is a highly valued cultural practice. A significant contribution of DCMI as well as Pentecostal churches in general is how they strive to bring about social and cultural change as well as its ability to reshape gender roles and gendered identities in new ways.[42] DCMI is helping young men embrace and promote ideals of monogamy, love and fidelity within marriages which is significant in Maasailand where the older generation is heavily polygamous. Most Maasai children including pastors at DCMI come from polygamous families.

A visible change throughout Maasailand now is the emergence of a generation of younger married men who espouse the virtues of monogamy in a heavily polygamous culture. While conversion to Pentecostalism is not the only reason for this kind of social change taking place throughout Maasailand, there are indications that DCMI is promoting monogamy through its youth outreaches activities as well as ordained pastors serving in this ministry, of whom most testify to being married to one wife in a bid to stem out polygamy among younger generations. The question whether this is helping to transform masculinities of Maasai men by turning them into men who espouse virtues of fidelity to one spouse in a culture that frowns upon weak men is debatable. What DCMI has succeeded in doing is to aim at directing Maasai men to become more committed to nuclear family ideals and embrace an alternative vision and ideal of a "transformed born again Maasai man." In a society where cultural masculine standards and traits of bravery, physical strength and polygamy defined what it means to be Maasai, the transformation taking place in respect of marriage and family life in Maasailand is significant. Based on my interactions with youthful Maasai converts, it seemed to me that Pentecostal churches like DCMI appeal to a new generation of young educated and "born again" converts who desire modernity and a different life away from the Maasai culture they are accustomed to.

WOMEN'S EMPOWERMENT

DCMI, like many Pentecostal churches, is in every sense of the word a church for women. The majority of its members are women who fill its pews every Sunday and weekly services. The churches also run a number of programmes for women, programmes that aim to empower them spiritually, socially as well as in their private and public lives. The role of women in Pentecostal churches has been heavily researched as opposed to that of its

42. Lindhardt, "Men of God."

impact on men. One such programme is the 'Kings Daughters Ministry' which is the women wing of the DCMI church. This programme was created by the Rev Sophia Mankura, the wife of Bishop Peter Ole Mankura.

The purpose of this annual conference is to bring together all women from the Dominion Ministries throughout Maasailand for a weeklong intensive training. This conference which takes place every April of each New Year attracts women from all walks of life across Maasailand to be trained in ministry and empowerment. Women clergy from other Pentecostal churches are invited to speak to these women and mentor them in their spiritual journey. Women such as Rita Lai, Ida Adoyo, Josephine Kitonga, and Esther Obasike Kitonga, all wives of leading Pentecostal clergy, minister to women in this conference as well as other church meetings that focus on women.

The ministry aims to transform Maasai women in their ministry and outreach, homes and society. Common themes I found during participant observations in these conferences revolve around epithets of empowerment, growth, development, impact, leadership and Ministry. Here women are taught how to run their homes, how to bring up strong families, few children, the benefits of education for their children both boys and girls, how to support their husbands, entrepreneurship and business, leadership and social transformation. I have, however, not come across teachings on gender equality. But a general trend that runs in many Pentecostal churches as well as the DCIM ministry is that women are in charge of the domestic sphere and that it is their role to ensure that the home sphere runs smoothly. I also came across teachings that appear to help the woman become a better wife and mother. In this case, the kind of empowerment preached here is of a kind that does not promote gender equality. Instead, it aims to produce domesticated wives, mothers and sisters. Yet, and for Maasai women who have suffered hugely under a heavily patriarchal culture, Pentecostalism has offered them huge relief from gender-based violence, in particular Female Genital Mutilation and forced marriage. Pentecostal clergy in Maasailand are speaking against such vices and challenging converts to resist cultural oppression of women which I think is important for Maasai women. In my work with girls' education, I have worked and trained with Pentecostal clergy to support girl's education and speak up against gender based violence.

In this sense, it is correct to say that Pentecostal churches like the DCMI are helping Maasai "born again" Christians to contest and embrace development. In one meeting attended by this researcher, Bishop Mankuru, who had been invited to pray over a new house that had just been finished, preached a sermon about development. He praised the house owner for putting up a beautiful home for his family and decried the Maasai culture where women are the ones responsible for house building. He argued that the culture that expects a woman to put up a house was oppressive to women and urged all Maasai men to build decent homes for their families. He further urged men to embrace girls' education and women empowerment and to denounce wife beating, a common practice in Maasailand.[43] Bishop Mankuru and his fellow DCMI clergy have also chosen to focus on the youth constituencies, who are trained to become agents of change in their societies.

A significant body of research in Africa, Southern Europe and Latin America has shown how participation in Pentecostal and Charismatic churches benefits women in a number of ways.[44] There are many ways in which I think the DCMI has changed the lives of a significant number of Maasai women. One fact to start with is that the DCMI ministry through the creation of a number of regional and district churches has seen a large creation of DCMI pastors who minister in these branches with their wives.

It is now a common feature to see Maasai "born again" female clergy who serve in ministry with their husbands, as well as media pictures showing men with their wives on church magazines and in social media, something that was virtually non-existing less than two decades ago. This has enlarged both the private and public roles of such women who serve alongside their husbands in ministry. For these reasons, Pentecostal churches offer rural women like Maasai women with minimal education (literacy levels in Maasailand are very low), and whose main domain of operation has mainly been the private/home sphere, new platforms for public and semi-public participation.[45]

These women now serve as preachers, faith healers, worship leaders, prophetesses, Sunday school teachers, translators, event organizers and many other such public roles.[46] This is a very significant change for Maasai women who come from an extremely patriarchal culture where women's place and role remains largely in the private home sphere, tending children, cattle, the old and the sick as well as taking care of the homestead.

Secondly, as Martin Lindthardt has pointed out, the situation for women improves when their husbands convert, as the converted man tends to become more oriented to the domestic sphere and leave behind old patterns of consumption (drinking and womanizing among others).[47] In the

43. Sermon preached by Bishop Mankuru at Oloshoibor village during a house dedication service, December 2016.

44. Brusco, *Reformation of Machismo*; Cucchiari, "Between Shame and Sanctification"; Lindhardt, "Narrating Religious Realities"; Soothill, *Gender, Social Change*.

45. Lindhardt, "Men of God."

46. Lindhardt, "Narrating Religious Realities."

47. Lindhardt, "Men of God."

case of Maasai men converts, their wives benefit when their husbands shun a culture of violence against women such as FGM, early marriage, other forms of gender based violence, especially wife beating, as well as abandoning polygamy, and other masculine traits promoted by culture such as bravery, strength, aggressive behavior, virility and disregard for women's voice. Now women can preach at the pulpit and speak against oppressive cultures and traditions of the Maasai People. Besides, Maasai women whose husbands are not "born again" learn from their churches strategies that enable them to navigate life with "non-born again" husbands as they acquire a new set of interpretative frameworks for understanding aggressive and irresponsible male behavior.[48] Women fellowships further offers space to minister to each other and form circles of spiritual support for one another.

At the same time, Maasai Pentecostal clergy are promoting social change in the area of family life. Pentecostal clergy like to show off their wives and testify that they are married to one wife as a good Christian man is expected to. This is significant for Maasai girls and women who come from a long line of polygamous families. It presents a new and desirable trait for younger girls and women who aspire to be in monogamous unions. Culturally, a Maasai man who also is the head of family can marry as many wives as he wishes and has powers and authorities to choose spouses for his children to marry. In short, the scholarly literature[49] coupled with my own observations of the new changes sweeping across Maasailand seem to suggest that participation in Pentecostal churches offers women certain empowerment both in private and in public spheres.[50]

INSPIRING BROADER SOCIAL CHANGE

The DCMI and its leadership are inspiring broader social change. Bishop Mankura and his fellow clergy from DCMI preach vehemently against Female Genital Mutilation, early marriage, gender-based violence, polygamy, the exclusion of women in society and decision making and promote girls and women education and gender empowerment. This is significant in Maasailand where literacy levels are low and where FGM still stands at 79 percent.[51]

However, even as Pentecostalism (or DCNI) seeks to create broader social change within Maasailand, it is also interesting to note that there are

48. Mariz and Machado, "Pentecostalism and Women."

49. "Impact of Globalization." See also Kipuri and Ridgewell, *Double Bind*; Kotowicz, *Maasai Identity*.

50. Kotowicz, *Maasai Identity*.

51. Parsitau, "Engaging."

several areas in which the Dominion Ministry appropriate Maasai culture. Notable areas of cultural appropriation include Maasai dress and beads work as well as leveraging social capital of the Maasai community. Thus, it is interesting to see how Pentecostalism embraces and contest Maasai traditions and how this transform both Pentecostalism and Maasai culture. This I argue has been one of the many reasons why Pentecostal ministry has been largely successful in Maasailand.

PERFORMING PENTECOSTALISM: GOSPEL MUSIC, IDENTITY, AND THE INTERPLAY BETWEEN MAASAI CULTURE AND PENTECOSTALIST SPIRITUALITY

A relatively new phenomenon sweeping across Maasailand is the evolution of gospel music that incorporates indigenous cultural influences in the performances, commercial recording, and production of this type of music to produce a hybrid gospel music inspired by Maasai culture as well as Pentecostal spirituality. Maasai gospel music, which has grown in popularity throughout Maasailand in the last one and a half decade now incorporates the use of Maasai beads and singing and dancing styles. This type of music is now played in most Maasai homes as well as in social functions such as weddings, funerals, graduation ceremonies and political events. It is also played in urban centers throughout Maasai counties in many homes and in urban centers where Maasai people reside. It is also played in public transport vehicles. People download their favorite tunes into their phones as their ringtone or ring back tones. Maasai gospel music is also popular among the Maasai in Diaspora, particularly in North America and England.

The dynamics of this type of popular music, suggests a dynamic re-contextualized genre of music that involves the appropriation of Maasai indigenous culture in Pentecostal worship and spirituality. Many believers and non-believers alike see this type of hybrid gospel music as a medium through which they articulate their faith as intimately connected to their traditional, religious and cultural identity and spirituality.[52] Further it provides believers with a means of expressing a modern Pentecostal aesthetic that incorporates the best of their culture and traditions fused with modernity. Many believers see Maasai gospel music as a medium through which they articulate their faith as intimately connected to their religious cultural identity. Maasai Gospel music also provides believers with a means of expressing a modern Pentecostal aesthetic. The significant point here is that worldliness, modernity and culture are compatible and that Maasai

52. Butler, "Performing."

culture is beautiful as well, worthy of being appropriated by Christians. It also suggests to the Maasai people that culture and modernity, when combined together, is a beautiful thing. Music is an important cultural practice that easily finds acceptance not just among believers but also non-believers alike. Growing up in Maasailand, I understood that music and dance are an integral part of Maasai culture. Maasai people love to sing and dance. All social, cultural and political events are preceded by cultural dances and singing. Pentecostal Christianity successfully incorporated this cultural practice in its dance and worship in a way that has enhanced both Maasai cultural dance and Pentecostal forms of worship.

For Maasai people, this suggests that modernity and culture are compatible and that Maasai culture and traditions are worthy of being appropriated by Pentecostals. It also suggests that culture and modernity when combined together allows Maasai Pentecostal Christians to live out their faith with the best of their traditions while the use and appropriation of Maasai cultural attire suggests on-going negotiation of identity and spirituality. Women, who are doing particularly well in this area, like to dress in Maasai cultural attire suggesting an on-going negotiation of identity as well appropriation of culture.

A fascinating feature of this music is that women constitute the majority of musicians although there are also male gospel artists. Popular Maasai female gospel musicians include Maryanne Tutumua, Charity Tajeu, Dorcus Karei, and Semeyian Kaori among many others. Charity Tajeu, a popular gospel artist is the winner of the 2015 Rift Valley region for the song of the year.[53] The lyrics cover spiritual issues as well as social issues. For example, Maryanne Naipasoi Tutumua hit song, *enkisoma*, is a popular song about education and its benefits. The song encourages the Maasai community to embrace education and educate their children, especially girls, because education changes lives. Organizations working with girls' education are using such music to promote girl's education and rally communities to embrace education and development.[54]

Gospel music has also led to the increased visibility of Maasai women in the public sphere as artists in their own rights, and as women inspiring social change through their music. For Maasai women who have been invisible in public life as well as public spaces, gospel music has granted them space and voices to articulate not just their spirituality but also issues of concern to them, such as girls education, gender and sexual violence. For such

53. Butler, "Performing."

54. My own non-profit organization, "Let Maasai Girls Learn," uses this song to encourage parents to embrace girl's education.

women, gospel music has enabled them space to contest spirituality, social, political and economic spaces. Maasai female gospel artists are considered celebrities and are invited to perform in social events such as weddings, funerals, thanksgiving services, educational events and political events. For these reasons, it is safe to say that gospel music performances are some of the spaces for women to contest not just empowerment but also space, voice and public life that are a direct impact of Pentecostal spirituality.[55]

SOCIAL CAPITAL AND CULTURAL APPROPRIATION OF MAASAI CULTURE BY PENTECOSTALS

Aside from gospel music, there are also other ways in which Pentecostal churches are appropriating Maasai culture in order to penetrate Maasailand. Some of these areas include the Maasai social, cultural, political and community events and activities including thanksgiving celebrations, graduation ceremonies, wedding ceremonies, funeral rites, political events, other community/cultural rites such as boy's circumcision ceremonies and warriors' cultural graduation events and many others. In all such events, Pentecostal clergy especially from the DCMI are often called upon to preside over such meetings through leading prayers for thanksgiving. A new and emerging trend in Maasailand is the praying and anointing of new homes and cars, as well as other assets, or when a child does well in national examinations or graduates with a degree.

In all such events, Bishop Mankuru or his other pastors are invited to pray and bless the functions. The blessing of community functions is a common traditional practice that has a long history throughout Maasai land. Such functions were often carried out by traditional Maasai leaders popularly known as *iloibonok*. And because the roles of traditional leaders are gradually diminishing in Maasailand, especially with the advent of modernity, Christian clergy are now performing such tasks. In fact, the role of spiritual Maasai leaders are now being replaced by Pentecostal clergy, who preside over all sorts of social functions. Such clergy see no tension in this new-found role, which simply is a continuation of the old Maasai traditional and spiritual role carried out by elders. For these reasons, Pentecostalism has taken root in Maasailand because it is successfully challenging and appropriating the cultures and traditions of the Maasai people to produce a new hybrid of Maasai Christians, who want to embrace both modernity and certain aspects of their culture that are compatible with their spirituality.

---

55. Parsitau, *Then Sings My Soul*.

CONCLUSION

This chapter has explored the dynamics of rural Pentecostalism in Maasailand in Kenya. It has shown how the initial appeal of Kenyan Pentecostalism was felt in cities and urban centers before it gradually moved into the remotest parts of Maasailand. Through the case of the DCMI and guided by rich ethnographic data as well as questions that guided this study from the beginning of the paper, I showed how this particularly Neo-Pentecostal Ministry is inspiring new models of change and bringing out new and alternative visions of social transformation to various constituencies, namely, youth, men and women. More important is how rural communities embrace Pentecostalism in their own terms and as well as how they are both transformed by such encounters. As well I examine how Maasai people are navigating, appropriating and contesting modernity and Pentecostalism and how Pentecostalism is appropriating Maasai culture to thrive and spread in Maasailand and in the process inspiring social and spiritual change in a contested social cultural and political terrain.

In conclusion, I suggest that rural Pentecostalism is not only growing popular in Maasailand but it is also creating shifts in values as well as legitimizing new aspirations among constituencies such as youth and women converts to create broader social and gendered transformation. It is also having impact on development issues such as education, women and gender empowerment and leadership. The chapter also shows how this particular Neo-Pentecostal Ministry is thriving by appropriating certain elements of Maasai culture in a bid to thrive and gain acceptance in Maasailand as well as contesting cultural elements that are at odds with modernity and Pentecostal spirituality such as FGM, child marriage, wife beating, polygamy, women (dis)empowerment, decision making and other development issues. Consequently, the chapter shows how both Pentecostalism and culture transform each other.

BIBLIOGRAPHY

Brusco, Elizabeth E. *The Reformation of Machismo: Evangelical Gender and Conversion in Colombia*. Austin, TX: University of Texas Press, 1995.

Butler, Melvin L. "Performing Pentecostalism: Music, Identity, and the Interplay of Jamaican and African American Styles." In *Rhythms of the Afro-Atlantic World: Rituals and Remembrances*, edited by Mamadou Diouf and Ifeoma Kiddoe Nwankwo, 41–54. Ann Arbor: University of Michigan Press, 2010.

Cucchiari, Salvatore. "Between Shame and Sanctification: Patriarchy and Its Transformation in Sicilian Pentecostalism." *American Ethnologist* 17.4 (1990) 687–707.

Dominion Chapel Ministries International. "Bishop Dr. Peter Ole Mankura." November 18, 2014. Online. http://dominionchapelministry.org/2014-11-18-13-59-54/meet-the-bishop.

Freeman, Dena. "Pentecostalism in a Rural Context: Dynamics of Religion and Development in South East Ethiopia." *PentecoStudies* 12.2 (2013) 231–49.

Gifford, Paul. *African Christianity: Its Public Role in Uganda and Other African Countries*. Kampala: Fountain, 1999.

———. *Christianity, Politics, and Public Life in Kenya*. London: Hurst & Co., 2009.

"The Impact of Globalization on the Maasai." *Group 2 Anthropology* (blog), July 25, 2014. Online. http://group2anthropology.blogspot.com/2014/07/the-effect-globalization-has-on-maasai.html.

Jenkins, Philip. *The Next Christendom: The Coming of Global Christianity*. Oxford: Oxford University Press, 2011.

Kalu, Ogbu. *African Pentecostalism: An Introduction*. New York: Oxford University Press, 2008.

Kipuri, Naomi, and Andrew Ridgewell. *A Double Bind: The Exclusion of Pastoralist Women in the East and Horn of Africa*. London: Minority Rights Group International, 2008.

Koissaba, B. R. Ole. "Effects of Globalization in the Maasai Family." Unpublished paper, 2013. Online. https://www.researchgate.net/publication/249994886_Effects_of_globalization_in_the_Maasai_Family.

Kotowicz, Allison Marie. *Maasai Identity in the Twenty-First Century*. MSC diss., University of Wisconsin-Milwaukee, 2013.

Lindhardt, Martin. "Men of God: Neo-Pentecostalism and Masculinities in Urban Tanzania." *Religion* 45. 2 (2015) 252–72.

———. "Narrating Religious Realities, Conversion, and Testimonies in Chilean Pentecostalism." *Suomen Anthropologi: Journal of the Finish Anthropological Society* 34.3 (2009) 25–43.

Mariz, Cecília Loreto, and María das Dores Campos Machado. "Pentecostalism and Women in Brazil." In *Power, Politics, and Pentecostals in Latin America*, edited by Edward L. Cleary and Hannah W. Stewart-Gambino, 41–45. Boulder, CO: Westview, 1997

Martin, David. *Pentecostalism: The World Their Parish*. Oxford: Blackwell, 2002.

Ndegwa, Alex. "Over 6,000 Churches Awaiting Registration." *Standard*, September 4, 2007. 6.

Parsitau, Damaris Seleina. "Engaging the Custodians of Tradition and Culture: Leveraging the Role Multiple Actors in Maasai Girls' Education." *Brookings*, November 7, 2017. Online. https://www.brookings.edu/research/engaging-the-custodians-of-tradition-and-culture-leveraging-the-role-of-multiple-actors-in-maasai-girls-education.

———. "From the Periphery to the Center: The Pentecostalization of Mainline Christianity in Kenya." *Missionalia: Southern Africa Journal of Missiology* 35.3 (2007) 83–111.

———. "How Girls Education Intersects with Maasai Culture in Kenya." *Brookings*, July 25, 2017. Online. https://www.brookings.edu/blog/education-plus-development/2017/07/25/how-girls-education-intersects-with-maasai-culture-in-kenya.

————. "How Young Men Can Change Gender and Social Norms of the Maasai People to Support Girls Education." *Brookings*, November 7, 2017. Online. https://www.brookings.edu/blog/education-plus-development/2017/11/07/how-young-men-can-change-gender-and-social-norms-of-the-maasai-people-to-support-girls-education.

————. "Prophets, Power, Authority, and the Kenyan State: Prophet Owuor of the National Repentance and Holiness and Ministry." In *Religious Freedom and Religious Pluralism in Africa: Prospects and Limitations*, edited by Pieter Coertzen, et al., 233–56. Stellenbosch: African Sun, 2016.

————. "Taming Rogue Clergy and Churches: God, Scandals, Government, and Religious Regulations in Kenya." In *Religious Pluralism, Heritage, and Social Development in Africa*, edited by M. Christian Green, et al., 241–57. Stellenbosch: African Sun, 2017.

————. "Then Sings My Soul: Gospel Music as Popular Culture in the Spiritual lives of Kenyan Pentecostal/Charismatic Christians." *Journal of Religion and Popular Culture* 14.1 (2006) 3–33.

Parsitau, Damaris Seleina, and Philomena Njeri Mwaura. "God in the City. Pentecostalism as an Urban Phenomenon in Kenya." *Studia Historiae Ecclesiaticae (SHE) Journal of the Church History Society of Southern Africa* 36.2 (2010) 95–112.

Pew Research Center. "Pentecostalism in Kenya." *Religion and Public Life*, August 5, 2010. Online. https://www.pewforum.org/2010/08/05/historical-overview-of-pentecostalism-in-kenya.

Saitabau, Henri Ole. *The Impact of Climate Change on the Livelihoods of Loita Maaasai Pastoral and Community Related Indigenous Knowledge Adaptation and Mitigation.* Nairobi: National Museums of Kenya, 2014.

Salau, Daniel. "Globalization Entrenches Itself on the Maasai." *Global Policy Forum*, September 2002. Online. https://www.globalpolicy.org/component/content/article/162/27587.html.

Soothill, Jane E. *Gender, Social Change, and Spiritual Power: Charismatic Christianity in Ghana.* Leiden: Brill, 2007.

Part III

Freedom of Religion:
Perspectives from South Africa

6

Freedom of Religion: Individual? Collective?
As Perceived by the South African State

Keith Matthee, SC

In terms of section 2 of the Constitution of the Republic of South Africa, 1996 (hereafter "the Constitution"), the Constitution is the supreme law of South Africa and any "law or conduct inconsistent with it is invalid, and the obligations imposed by it must be fulfilled."

Accordingly, the question to be answered is, does the Constitution perceive the Freedom of Religion as an individual, or as a collective right?

The argument in this chapter will be that in effect in the Constitution the foundation for the collective right is the individual right to freedom of religion. However, that such protection is at risk of being trumped by what the 11 women and men of the Constitutional Court decide is reasonable, under the guise of merely extrapolating and then applying the "objective normative value system"[1] from the Bill of Rights.

GERMANE CONSTITUTIONAL PROVISIONS

Central to answering this question is section 167(3)(a) of the Constitution, which reads: "The Constitutional Court . . . is the highest court in all constitutional matters." Thus, where the Constitutional Court has pronounced

---

1. Carmichele v. Minister of Safety and Security.

on an issue, such a pronouncement is binding on all organs of state and all people residing in South Africa.

Turning to the issue of whether the Freedom of Religion is perceived as an individual or a collective right by the South African State, the Constitutional Court has made a number of pronouncements which are germane. Where the Constitutional Court has not pronounced on an issue, one must attempt to extrapolate answers from the text of the Constitution itself. (chapter 2 of the Constitution, where the various rights referred to below are contained, hereafter is termed the "Bill of Rights.")

Section 15(1) of the Bill of Rights reads as follows:

Freedom of Religion, Belief and Opinion

Everyone has the right to freedom of conscience, religion, thought, belief and opinion.

Section 30 of the Bill of Rights reads:

Language and Culture

Everyone has the right to use the language and to participate in the cultural life of their choice, but no one exercising these rights may do so in a manner inconsistent with any provision of the Bill of Rights.

Section 31 of the Bill of Rights reads:

Cultural, Religious, and Linguistic Communities

Persons belonging to a cultural, religious or linguistic community may not be denied the right, with other members of that community-

> a. to enjoy their culture, practice their religion and use their language; and
>
> b. to form, join and maintain cultural, religious and linguistic associations and other organs of civil society.

The rights in subsection (1) may not be exercised in a manner inconsistent with any provision of the Bill of Rights.

Applicable sections of the Constitution for interpretation and application include the Preamble and sections 7, 36, and 39 of the Bill of Rights.

In the Preamble we see that a central purpose of the Constitution is to "Heal the divisions of the past and establish a society based on democratic values, social justice and fundamental human rights."

In section 7(1) we read: "This Bill of Rights is a cornerstone of democracy in South Africa. It enshrines the rights of all people in our country and affirms the democratic values of human dignity, equality and freedom." Section 7(3) reads: "The rights in the Bill of Rights are subject to the limitations contained or referred to in section 36, or elsewhere in the Bill."

Section 36 states:

Limitation of Rights

The rights in the Bill of Rights may be limited only in terms of law of general application to the extent that the limitation is reasonable and justifiable in an open and democratic society based on human dignity, equality and freedom, taking into account all relevant factors, including—

a. the nature of the right;

b. the importance of the purpose of the limitation;

c. the nature and extent of the limitation;

d. the relation between the limitation and its purpose; and

e. less restrictive means to achieve the purpose.

Except as provided in subsection (1) or in any other provision of the Constitution, no law may limit any right entrenched in the Bill of Rights.

Section 39(1)(a) reads:

(1) When interpreting the Bill of Rights, a court, tribunal or forum—must promote the values that underlie an open and democratic society based on human dignity, equality and freedom.

For our purpose the obvious question is whether Freedom of Religion is protected in the collective rights of sections 30 and 31, or in the individual rights contained in section 15(1).

EX FACIE READING OF THE CONSTITUTIONAL PROVISIONS

Before we look at some of the decisions of the Constitutional Court, it would be instructive to reflect on the wording and phrasing of the Constitution itself.

Section 15(1)

The holder of these rights is "Everyone." Thus they are clearly individual rights. Furthermore, the "freedom of conscience, religion, thought, belief and opinion," which the section grants to "Everyone," by necessary implication has no other requirement than that an individual believes what she claims to believe.

The State arguably could limit these individual rights if reference was made only to religion, by stating that to qualify as a religion it must be shown that a collective holds certain beliefs which qualify it as a religion. Thus, in effect the collective rights could be used to restrict an individual's Freedom of Religion. However, by including conscience, thought, belief and opinion in the section, it is clear that the section is addressing the convictions of an individual.

Sections 30 and 31

From the wording of these sections, it is clear that central to the exercise of these collective rights, once again, is the choice of an individual. The difference to section 15 is that to enjoy the benefits of the choices protected by sections 30 and 31, an individual will have to show that a religious, or cultural, or linguistic collective she wants to be a part of, actually exists.

Whilst cultural or linguistic collective rights would seem to be qualified by this requirement, section 15(1) has no such qualification for the Freedom of Religion. Thus, arguably neither section 30 nor section 31 adds anything to section 15(1), when it comes to the right to Freedom of Religion. This is important as *ex facie* the Bill of Rights, the further qualification in sections 30 and 31—that the rights in these sections may not be inconsistent with any provision of the Bill of Rights—does not apply to section 15.

Accordingly, the only qualifications to the Freedom of Religion in section 15(1) are sections 36 and 39 of the Bill of Rights. However, on closer scrutiny of these sections, we see that central to interpreting and applying the Bill of Rights is the promotion of the values that underlie an open and democratic society, based on human dignity, equality, and freedom, and the concept of reasonableness. This dilutes the distinction between section 15 on the one hand, and sections 30 and 31 on the other.

The only meaningful distinction accordingly is that section 15 is grounded on what the individual believes, irrespective of whether or not anyone else shares her belief.

CONSTITUTIONAL COURT INTERPRETATIONS

With these introductory observations, I now turn to the interpretation of these rights by the Constitutional Court.

Three seminal decisions of the Constitutional Court which have a direct bearing on the question posed are:

- *Christian Education SA v. Minister of Education*, 2000 (4) SA 757 (CC) (hereafter, *Christian Education*).

- *Prince v. President, Cape Law Society*, 2002 (2) SA 794 (CC) (hereafter, *Prince*).

- *MEC for Education: KwaZulu Natal v. Pillay*, 2008 (1) SA 474 (CC) (hereafter, *Pillay*).

The central question in the *Christian Education* matter was the constitutionality of a prohibition on corporal punishment in schools given the right to the freedom of religion. Although it recognized that the use of corporal punishment was part of a certain set of religious belief, the court held that the limitation of this religious belief was reasonable and justifiable and ordered that parents of children in independent schools could not authorise teachers, acting in their name and on school premises, to use corporal punishment to fulfil what they regarded as their biblically-ordained responsibilities.

In the *Prince* case the question before the court was whether the limitation of the religious freedom of Mr Prince, to use dagga for religious purposes, was justifiable or not. The majority of the court held that the limitation was reasonable and justifiable.

The *Pillay* decision concerned the right of a teenage girl to wear a nose stud to school, as it was part of her culture and religion. The basis for her claim was her right to equality, unfair discrimination, and her right to freedom of religion and culture. The Constitutional Court held in her favor.

Commenting on the *Christian Education* and *Prince* matters, Woolman, et al., write:

> In Christian Education, South Africa, the court unanimously assumed that a statute prohibiting corporal punishment of juveniles in schools infringed the claimant's right to freedom of religion. It found, however, that any such infringement would be justified under the limitation clause. In Prince, the court found that there was a violation of section 15 as well as section 31 vis-a-vis adherents of the Rastafarian religion as a result of the prohibition on the use or possession of cannabis in two statutes. The

majority of the court hearing the case found, however, that the infringement is justified under section 36 of the Constitution.[2]

Dealing with the interrelatedness of sections 15 and 31, in *Prince*, Justice Ngcobo writes:

> Sections 15(1) and 31(1)(a) complement one another. Section 31(1)(a) emphasizes and protects the associational nature of cultural, religious and language rights. In the context of religion, it emphasizes the protection to be given to members of communities united by religion to practice their religion.

At [38] he writes:

> This court has on two occasions [in Solberg and Christian Education South Africa] considered the contents of the right to freedom of religion. On each occasion, it has accepted that the right to freedom of religion at least comprehends: (a) the right to entertain the religious beliefs that one chooses to entertain; (b) the right to announce one's religious beliefs publicly and without fear of reprisal; and(c) the right to manifest such beliefs by worship and practice, teaching and dissemination. Implicit in the right to freedom of religion is the 'absence of coercion or restraint.' Thus 'freedom of religion may be impaired by measures that force people to act or refrain from acting in a manner contrary to their religious beliefs.'

(Although Justice Ngcobo wrote a minority judgment on behalf of four of the nine justices, there was no disagreement about the content of the above two paragraphs.)

In the same matter, The Majority held:

> The right of an individual to practice his or her religion is part of the section 15(1) right. The associational right, to practice religion in association with others, is protected by section 31. The appellant relies on his individual right to use cannabis in the privacy of his home and elsewhere, and on his associational right to use cannabis with other Rastafari on appropriate occasions.

The relationship between section 15 and section 31 is most clearly set out in the partially dissenting judgment of Justice O'Regan in the *Pillay* matter. I deal at length with her treatment of culture and religion, as I am of the view that it is instructive for the purposes of this chapter.

---

2. Woolman et al., *Constitutional Law*, 41 (legal point 22, 23).

In this case, the applicant argues that the conduct of the school constituted unfair discrimination on the grounds of culture and religion. . . . I am in complete agreement with the Chief Justice's consideration of these arguments and have nothing to add. Before turning to the question of unfair discrimination, I consider it necessary to consider briefly the constitutional approach to culture and religion.

Culture and Religion

Both "culture" and "religion" are terms that resist definition. And it is not desirable in this case to seek to identify a determinative definition of either. However our Constitution does treat them differently. And that different treatment gives us some understanding of where the difference between the two concepts lies. Section 9 of the Constitution prohibits discrimination on the grounds of both culture and religion,[3] but section 15 entrenches the right to freedom of "conscience, religion, thought, belief and opinion" and does not mention culture or cultural identity. Here the different constitutional treatment of the two concepts arises.

Section 30 entrenches the rights to language and culture, without mention of religion, in the following terms—

"Everyone has the right to use the language and to participate in the cultural life of their choice, but no one exercising these rights may do so in a manner inconsistent with any provision of the Bill of Rights."

Section 31 provides for certain rights to members of cultural and religious communities in the following manner—

"(1) Persons belonging to a cultural, religious or linguistic community may not be denied the right, with other members of that community—

a. to enjoy their culture, practice their religion and use their language; and

b. to form, join and maintain cultural, religious and linguistic associations and other organs of civil society.

3. "The state may not unfairly discriminate directly or indirectly against anyone on one or more grounds, including race, gender, sex, pregnancy, marital status, ethnic or social origin, color, sexual orientation, age, disability, religion, conscience, belief, culture, language and birth. . . . No person may unfairly discriminate directly or indirectly against anyone on one or more grounds in terms of subsection (3). . . . Discrimination on one or more of the grounds listed in subsection (3) is unfair unless it is established that the discrimination is fair" (Constitution of the Republic of South Africa sec. 9[3–5])

(2) The rights in subsection (1) may not be exercised in a manner inconsistent with any provision of the Bill of Rights."

Although it is not easy to define a sharp dividing line between the two, it does seem to me that our Constitution recognizes that culture is not the same as religion, and should not always be treated as if it is. Religion is dealt with without mention of culture in section 15, which entrenches the right to freedom of belief and conscience. *By associating religion with belief and conscience*, which involve an individual's state of mind, religion is understood in an individualist sense: *a set of beliefs that an individual may hold regardless of the beliefs of others.* The exclusion of culture from section 15 suggests that culture is different.

The inclusion of culture in section 30 and section 31 makes it clear that by and large culture as conceived in our Constitution, involves associative practices and not individual beliefs. So, section 31 speaks of the right of persons who are members of religious, linguistic or cultural communities "with other members of that community" to enjoy their culture. This formulation is drawn almost directly from article 27 of the United Nations International Covenant on Civil and Political Rights, which provides that people who belong to a particular "minority" shall not be denied "in community with other members of the group" the right to enjoy their own culture. In this sense, it is understood that individuals draw meaning and a sense of cultural identity from a group with whom they share cultural identity and with whom they associate. As Currie and De Waal reason:

> The right of a member of a cultural or linguistic community cannot meaningfully be exercised alone. Enjoyment of culture and use of language presupposes the existence of a community of individuals with similar rights. . . . Therefore an individual right of enjoyment of culture assumes the existence of a community that sustains a particular culture.[4]

By including religion in section 31, the Constitution makes plain that when a group of people share a religious belief, that group may also share associative practices that have meaning for the individuals within that religious group. Where one is dealing with associative practices, therefore, it seems that religion and culture should be treated similarly. In the case of an associative practice, an individual is drawing meaning and identity from the shared or common practices of a group. The basis for these practices may be a shared religion, a shared language or a shared history. Associative practices, which might well be related to shared religious beliefs, are treated

---

4. Currie and de Waal, *Bill of Rights Handbook*, 623–24.

differently by the Constitution because of their associative, not personal character.

Religion however need not be associative at all. A religious belief can be entirely personal. The importance of a personal religious belief is more often than not based on a particular relationship with a deity or deities that may have little bearing on community or associative practices. Where one is dealing with personal and individualised belief, religion is to be considered differently to culture, as the Constitution makes clear. In such circumstances, it is appropriate for a court to ask whether the belief is sincerely held in order to decide whether a litigant has established that it falls within the scope of section 15. If a sincere religious belief is established, it seems correct that a court will not investigate the belief further as the cases cited by the Chief Justice in his judgment makes plain. A religious belief is personal, and need not be rational, nor need it be shared by others. A court must simply be persuaded that it is a profound and sincerely held belief.

A cultural practice on the other hand is not about a personal belief but about a practice pursued by individuals as part of a community. The question will not be whether the practice forms part of the sincerely held personal beliefs of an individual, but whether the practice is a practice pursued by a particular cultural community. This distinction needs to inform how we deal with discrimination on the grounds of religion and culture. Where one is dealing with an associative religious practice such as protected by section 31, religion and culture will be treated very similarly. In this regard it is worth noting that some religions are far more associative in character than others. Many African religions and traditions are profoundly associative in character. Our Constitution recognizes this and does not privilege one form of religion over another, although associative practices are treated differently to what can be loosely described as personal beliefs. Where one is dealing with religious belief that is personal, as contemplated by section 15, it will be treated differently to culture. At times, this line may be difficult to draw but that is not the case here and nothing further need be said at this stage.

> I set out the difference between the constitutional protection of religion, on the one hand, and associative religious and cultural practices, on the other, because I am uneasy with the approach taken by Langa CJ on two issues. The first is whether religious and cultural practices are to be dealt with on the basis of the sincerely held beliefs of a particular complainant.

Dealing with culture the Justice picks up later in her judgment:

Understanding the right to cultural life against the background of human dignity emphasizes that the rights in sections 30 and 31 *are associative rights exercised by individual human beings and are not rights that attach to groups.*[5] They foster association and bolster the existence of cultural, religious and linguistic groups *so long as individuals remain committed* to living their lives in that form of association.[6] . . .

However, there is a constitutional limit on the protection of associative practices. The rights may not be exercised in a manner inconsistent with other provisions of the Bill of Rights. . . .

How then should we approach culture? The Chief Justice's answer to this question is that courts should urge respect for the sincerely held beliefs of those who assert cultural rights. My difficulty with that approach is threefold. First, it does not acknowledge sufficiently that cultural practices are associative and that the right to cultural life is a right to be practiced as a member of a community and not primarily a question of a sincere, but personal belief. If the right to cultural life 'cannot be meaningfully exercised alone' then an individualised and subjective approach to what constitutes culture is faulty. In probing whether a particular practice is a cultural practice, some understanding of what the cultural community considers to be a cultural practice, is important. . . . Cultures are not generally unified and coherent but are dynamic and often contested. Nevertheless, the need to investigate whether a particular asserted practice is shared within the broader community, or portion of it, and therefore properly understood as a cultural practice rather than a personal habit of preference, is central to determining whether a cultural claim has been established.

APPARENT INDIVIDUAL RIGHTS TRUMPED BY THE JUSTICES OF THE CONSTITUTIONAL COURT?

The importance of Justice O'Regan's distinction is that the Freedom of Religion, as opposed to the freedom of culture, in the Bill of Rights is only dependent on whether or not an individual sincerely holds a belief. It is thus clearly an individual right. In effect, it can be argued that the associative rights in sections 30 and 31 are redundant when it comes to religion. The rights in sections 30 and 31 are protected by section 15 as individual rights.

5. My emphasis.
6. My emphasis.

However, on closer scrutiny it can be argued that these individual rights are trumped by another collective, that of the 11 women and men of the Constitutional Court.[7]

The gateway to this trumping of the freedom of religion as an individual right by a collective, are sections 36 and 39(1)(a) of the Constitution, which in effect make "reasonable and justifiable" central to the hermeneutic of the Constitutional Court. Linked to this is the view of the Constitutional Court that the Bill of Rights contains "an objective normative value system."[8]

In *Christian Education* Justice Sachs at one point states:

> More precisely, the proportionality exercise [in other words, primarily the application of sections 36 and 39] has to relate to whether the failure to accommodate the appellant's religious belief and practice by means of the exemption for which the appellant asked, can be accepted as reasonable and justifiable in an open and democratic society based on human dignity, freedom and equality.
>
> Before setting out to apply the above approach to the facts of this case, I feel it necessary to comment generally on difficulties of proportionality analysis in the area of religious rights. The most complex problem is that the competing interests to be balanced belong to completely different conceptual and existential orders. *Religious conviction and practice are generally based on faith. Countervailing public or private concerns are usually not and are evaluated mainly according to their reasonableness.*[9]

This breath-taking assertion by Justice Sachs, that unlike in Theism, non-Theist conceptual and existential orders are based on their reasonableness, is an open invitation to use sections 36 and 39 to impose a non-Theist world view where the Theist world view is deemed unreasonable, notwithstanding the purported religious freedom granted to individuals, as individuals, in section 15. Central to this trumping is the collective view/opinion of the 11 men and women on the Constitutional Court of what is reasonable and justifiable.

In *De Lange v. Presiding Bishop of the Methodist Church of Southern Africa for the Time Being and Another,*[10] Justice van der Westhuizen in a minority concurring judgment wrote:

7. Sec. 167(1) of the Constitution reads: "The Constitutional Court consists of the Chief Justice of South Africa, the Deputy Chief Justice, and nine other judges."

8. Carmichele v. Minister of Safety.

9. My emphasis.

10. De Lange v. Presiding Bishop.

In this Court Sachs J said in *Christian Education*:

"The underlying problem in any open and democratic society based on human dignity, equality and freedom in which conscientious and religious freedom has to be regarded with appropriate seriousness, is how far such democracy can and must go in allowing members of religious communities to define for themselves which laws they will obey and which not. Such a society can cohere only if all its participants accept that certain basic norms and standards are binding. Accordingly, believers cannot claim an automatic right to be exempted by their beliefs from the laws of the land. At the same time, the State should, wherever reasonably possible, seek to avoid putting believers to extremely painful and intensely burdensome choices of either being true to their faith or else respectful of the law." . . .

The Constitution is the supreme law of the land. It allocates powers to the State and enshrines the fundamental rights of its citizens. But it is more. It also states the values on which we have agreed. The Constitution is the credo that binds our nation together. It was born from our sad history of the violation of virtually all human rights and embodies our national vision of the future. It is the yardstick by which we have to measure our achievements and failures. A constitution has been referred to as the "autobiography of a nation," the "window to a nation's soul" or the "mirror in which a society views itself."

So, can one say that the Constitution does not reach our private religious and social spheres? I am not persuaded that we can. Is it not rather the case that the Constitution—as a set of values and protected fundamental rights—indeed reaches even into the most intimate spaces; *but* carries with it *all* the rights and values it recognizes? This would include not only equality and non-discrimination which is of high importance in our constitutional constellation, but also privacy, freedom of association and the autonomy of choice that necessarily goes with the recognition of human dignity. All of these were violated during our undemocratic past. . . .

In *Christian Education* the following was stated: "Special care has been taken in the text expressly to acknowledge the supremacy of the Constitution and the Bill of Rights. Section 31(2) ensures that the concept of rights of members of communities that associate on the basis of language, culture and religion, cannot be used to shield practices which offend the Bill of Rights. These explicit qualifications may be seen as serving a double purpose. The first is to prevent protected associational rights of members of communities from being used to 'privatise'

constitutionally offensive group practices and thereby immun-
ise them from external legislative regulation or judicial control.
This would be particularly important in relation to practices
previously associated with the abuse of the notion of pluralism
to achieve exclusivity, privilege and domination. The second
relates to oppressive features of internal relationships primarily within the communities concerned, where section 8, which
regulates the horizontal application of the Bill of Rights, might
be specially relevant." . . .

The closer courts get to personal and intimate spheres, the
more they enter into the inner sanctum and thus interfere with
our privacy and autonomy. In a slightly different context Ackermann J said in *Bernstein*[11]: "Each right is always already limited
by every other right accruing to another citizen. In the context
of privacy this would mean that it is only the inner sanctum
of a person, such as his/her family life, sexual preference and
home environment, which is shielded from erosion by conflicting rights of the community. This implies that community
rights and the rights of fellow members place a corresponding
obligation on a citizen, thereby shaping the abstract notion of
individualism towards identifying a concrete member of civil
society. Privacy is acknowledged in the truly personal realm, but
as a person moves into communal relations and activities such
as business and social interaction, the scope of personal space
shrinks accordingly."

In *Magajane*[12] it was explained how *Bernstein* had "described
what can be seen as a series of concentric circles ranging from
the core most protected realms of privacy to the outer rings that
would yield more readily to the rights of other citizens and the
public interest." By analogy, it could be argued that the closer
the tension between, for example, equality on the one side and
privacy and free choice of association on the other gets to the
core of our private inner sanctum, the less suitable courts are to
pronounce on the balancing of these rights. . . .

Is it contradictory to say that the Constitution does have
a role to play in every sphere, but that we do not want a court
to intrude into private spaces with the bluntness of its orders?
After all, the Constitution is law; we mostly want law to be enforceable; enforcement is important for the rule of law, because
unenforceable law can hardly "rule." The Constitution is more
than law, however. It is the legal and moral framework within

11. Bernstein and Others v. Bester and Others.
12. Magajane v. Chairperson.

which we have agreed to live. It also not only leaves, but guarantees space to exercise our diverse cultures and religions and express freely our likes, dislikes and choices, as equals with human dignity. In this sense one could perhaps talk about a "constitutionally permitted free space." This is quite different from contending that certain areas in a constitutional democracy are beyond the reach of the Constitution, or "constitution-free."

This case does not require answers to the above vexed questions. It shows a glimpse of the complexity of the issues that cases of this kind may raise. This Court would need the benefit of more reflection and legal argument before giving definite answers. If and when necessary, to be debated and decided properly, procedural compliance, the correct forum and maximum participation by all interested parties—to name a few things—are necessary. . . .

That in short—is why I concur with the reasoning and conclusion in the judgment by Moseneke DCJ.

Justice van der Westhuizen cites Justice Sachs's qualification of the individual right to the freedom of religion in *Christian Education*—"Such a society can cohere only if all its participants accept that certain basic norms and standards are binding."

In his own argument that the Constitution itself may permit a "free area" when it comes to individual freedom of religion, once again, and I might add, unavoidably so, he in effect also qualifies this "free area" by making the assertion that the Constitution "states the values on which we have agreed." He continues:

> Is it not rather the case that the Constitution—as a set of values and protected fundamental rights—indeed reaches even into the most intimate spaces; but carries with it all the rights and values it recognizes? . . .
>
> The Constitution is more than law, however. It is the legal and moral framework within which we have agreed to live. It also not only leaves, but guarantees space to exercise our diverse cultures and religions and express freely our likes, dislikes and choices, as equals with human dignity. In this sense one could perhaps talk about a 'constitutionally permitted free space.'

But once again, central to what we define as the values "on which we have agreed" are the words "reasonable and justifiable" in section 36. It is thus a circuitous argument dependent on agreement about the practical content of the values "on which we have agreed." It begs the question.

In the same vein, in *Carmichele* above at 961 F, Justice Ackerman and Justice Goldstone stated:

> Our constitution is not merely a formal document regulating public power. It also embodies, like the German Constitution, an objective normative value system. As was stated by the German Federal Constitutional Court: 'The jurisprudence of the Federal Constitutional Court is consistently to the effect that the basic right norms contain not only defensive subjective rights for the individual but embody at the same time an objective value system which, as a fundamental constitutional value for all areas of the law, acts as a guiding principle and stimulus for the Legislature, Executive and Judiciary.' The same is true of our Constitution. . . . It is within the matrix of this objective normative value system that the common law must be developed.

In *Minister of Home Affairs and Another v. Marie Adriaana Fourie and Another*[13] (hereafter, *Fourie*), Justice Sachs wrote:

> In the open and democratic society contemplated by the Constitution there must be mutually respectful co-existence between the secular and the sacred. The function of the Court is to recognize the sphere which each inhabits, not to force the one into the sphere of the other. Provided there is no prejudice to the fundamental rights of any person or group, the law will legitimately acknowledge a diversity of strongly-held opinions on matters of great public controversy. I stress the qualification that there must be no prejudice to basic rights. . . .
>
> The hallmark of an open and democratic society is its capacity to accommodate and manage difference of intensely-held world views and lifestyles in a reasonable and fair manner. The objective of the Constitution is to allow different concepts about the nature of human existence to inhabit the same public realm, and to do so in a manner that is not mutually destructive and that at the same time enables government to function in a way that shows concern and respect for all.

While the Constitution entrenches the right to life, dignity, and equality as fundamental to this new moral order, it of itself provides no guidance to Justice Sachs and the other Justices of the Constitutional Court as to the practical moral content of these rights and the impact they should have on institutions in South Africa and the daily lives of people living in South Africa. Thus, for example, whilst grounding its jurisprudence in dignity, the

---

13. Minister of Home Affairs and Another v. Marie Adriaana Fourie and Another.

Constitution does not tell us what our dignity is. Furthermore, the Constitution provides no value-based hermeneutical key in this regard, other than human reason and autonomy, which as stated above, begs the question. As Berkman and Mattison III write, when referring to the 1948 Nuremberg Declaration as an example: "(It) took one particular universal ethics path to articulating universal agreement on certain moral standards without articulating the moral basis for them."[14]

CAUSE FOR CAUTION

At the moment the moral landscape of South Africa is being transformed by the Justices of the Constitutional Court under the guise that the Bill of Rights contains an "objective normative value system" which must be implemented in South Africa. The traditional Christian faith–based communities in South Africa have been marginalised in this regard. Central to this process is, in my present opinion, the flawed view that "a strict neutrality is (being) maintained between . . . (the secular and the religious)."[15] As Justice Sachs states in *Fourie* above:

> The hallmark of an open and democratic society is its capacity to accommodate and manage difference of intensely-held world views and lifestyles in a reasonable and fair manner. The objective of the Constitution is to allow different concepts about the nature of human existence to inhabit the same public realm, and to do so in a manner that is not mutually destructive and that at the same time enables government to function in a way that shows concern and respect for all.

However, in the previous paragraph of the same judgment Justice Sachs adds the following qualification:

> In the open and democratic society contemplated by the Constitution there must be mutually respectful co-existence between the secular and the sacred. The function of the Court is to recognize the sphere which each inhabits, not to force the one into the sphere of the other. Provided there is no prejudice to the fundamental rights of any person or group, the law will legitimately acknowledge a diversity of strongly-held opinions on matters of great public controversy. *I stress the qualification that there must be no prejudice to basic rights.*[16]

14. Berkman and Mattison III, *Searching for a Universal Ethic*, 6.

15. Ackerman, *Human Dignity*, 42.

16. My emphasis.

This qualification by Justice Sachs once again begs the question. How do the Constitutional Court Justices determine what these basic rights are and what content to give them? Which reference point do they use and how do they arrive at this reference point? An analysis of the reasoning of the Constitutional Court will reveal that the reference point is the purported "objective normative value system" which the collective on the Constitutional Court has determined is contained in the Bill of Rights. Once again, the question presents itself, which reference point does the collective on the Constitutional Court use to unlock this objective normative value system? It is thus a circuitous argument. Touching on this problem in principle Davis, et al., write: "This controversy and complexity about indeterminacy."[17]

CONCLUSION

The result is that by commission or omission the Constitutional Court may be imposing one specific theological or philosophical world view on South Africans. This would be destructive of the Constitutional Court's stated objective of allowing "different concepts about the nature of human existence to inhabit the same public realm, and to do so in a manner that is not mutually destructive and that at the same time enables government to function in a way that shows concern and respect for all." (*Fourie* above)

More importantly, for our purposes, the individual right to the Freedom of Religion contained in section 15(1) is in danger of being fundamentally compromised by the collective opinion of the Constitutional Court as to what, according to section 36 of the Constitution, is "reasonable and justifiable in an open and democratic society based on human dignity, equality and freedom."

BIBLIOGRAPHY

Ackerman, Laurie. *Human Dignity: Lodestar for Equality in South Africa.* Cape Town: Juta, 2012.
Berkman, John, and William C. Mattison III, eds. *Searching for a Universal Ethic.* Cambridge: Eerdmans, 2014.
Currie, Iain, and Johan de Waal. *The Bill of Rights Handbook.* 5th ed. Lansdowne: Juta & Co., 2005.
Davis, Dennis, et al. *An Inquiry into the Existence of Global Values Through the Lens of Comparative Constitutional Law.* Oxford: Hart, 2015.
Woolman, Stuart, et al. *Constitutional Law of South Africa.* Cape Town: Juta, 2008.

17. Davis et al., *Inquiry*, 454.

Court Cases

Bernstein and Others v. Bester and Others NNO 1996 (2) SA 751.

Carmichele v. Minister of Safety and Security 2001 (4) SA 938 CC at 961F.

Christian Education SA v. Minister of Education 2000 (4) SA 757 (CC).

De Lange v. Presiding Bishop of the Methodist Church of Southern Africa for the Time Being and Another (CCT223/14) [2015] ZACC 35; 2016 (1) BCLR 1 (CC); 2016 (2) SA 1 (CC).

Magajane v. Chairperson, North West Gambling Board 2006(5) SA 250 (CC).

MEC for Education: KwaZulu Natal v. Pillay 2008 (1) SA 474 (CC).

Minister of Home Affairs and Another v. Marie Adriaana Fourie and Another 2006(1) SA 524 (CC).

Prince vs. President, Cape Law Society 2002 (2) SA 794 (CC).

7

Freeedom of Religion in South Africa

MARY-ANNE PLAATJIES-VAN HUFFEL

In this chapter, attention will be given to the notion of religious freedom and religious pluralism in South Africa as well as the constitutional provisions thereof. The chapter is divided into three parts. Part one attends to constitutional provisions related to their freedom of religion in apartheid South Africa as well as in post-apartheid South Africa. Part two examines freedom of religion with regard to religious observance at public schools in a religiously pluralistic South Africa. Part three attends to the "South African Charter of Religious Rights and Freedoms." These sections will give the reader a broad picture of the relationship between the government and religions, as well as freedom of religious expressions in public institutions in South Africa. The terms religious diversity and religious pluralism are used interchangeably in this chapter.

RELIGION IN SOUTH AFRICA

Historically, religion was used in South Africa to theologically justify apartheid. The role of religion in politics was thus relatively common-place, and largely undisputed, up to 1994. In apartheid South Africa, the Dutch Reformed Church (DRC) played a pivotal role in presenting the Apartheid State as a Christian State.[1] For example, in point 49.6 of *Human Relations and the South African Scene in Light of Scripture* the DRC gave

---

1. See *Human Relations; Story of the Dutch Reformed.*

theological justification "for a constitutional system based on differentiated development for different population groups."[2] Jan Hendrik Petrus Van Rooyen states categorically that apartheid "extended over every aspect of a people's life—national, social and religious."[3] The Afrikaans Reformed churches went to great lengths to scripturally justify the policy of apartheid that was followed by government of that time. In apartheid South Africa the state gave official recognition to the majority religion, namely Christianity. This ultimately led to what Anna Triandafyllidou would refer to as the "privileged position of one religion by the state over against minority religions for example exemption from taxation, state subsidies, and official recognition of some religious celebrations."[4] Members of other religions and even those who were not adherents to any religion were marginalized during apartheid in South Africa and were subjected to mistreatment. During this period the preferential treatment of adherents of the Christian religion led to the marginalization of other religions. Paul Prinsloo rightly deduced that in the pre-1994 dispensation "a specific version of Protestant Christianity informed apartheid policies and legislation."[5]

According to Simon Shetreet, the relationship between the church and the state can be reflected in different forms. He suggests that five models can be discerned, namely "the theocratic model, the absolute-secular model, the separation of state and religion model, the established church model, and the recognized religions model."[6] The theocratic model suggests that religion will dominate the state.[7] In a theocratic model there is only one officially recognized religion and the rest are marginalized or forbidden. The state-religion relationship in apartheid South Africa has some coherence to the theocratic model. The apartheid state identified with one particular religion (namely Christianity).[8] Moreover, Christianity was recognized in law by the apartheid government and this recognition was contained in the preamble of the Constitution:

> We declare that we are conscious of our responsibility towards God and man; Are convinced of the necessity of standing united and of pursuing the following national goals: To uphold Christian values and civilized norms, with recognition and protection

2. *Story of the Dutch Reformed*, 14–15.

3. Van Rooyen, *Die NG Kerk*, 54.

4. Triandafyllidou, *Addressing Cultural*, 29–30.

5. Prinsloo, "South African Policy," 32.

6. Shetreet, "Model of State and Church Relations," 88.

7. Shetreet, "Model of State and Church Relations," 88.

8. *National Policy on Religion*, 3.

of freedom of faith and worship. To safeguard the integrity and
freedom of our country.[9]

In article 2 of the Constitution, the sovereignty and guidance of "Almighty
God" is further acknowledged.

According to Shetreet, the separationist model refers to the separation
of state and religion.[10] The contemporary South African state's legislation
is secular (in this sense) since no single religion, or religious tradition, is
preferred over any other. In principle the contemporary state embraces a
position of neutrality towards all religions and other worldviews. In France,
India, post-Communist Russia, and the United States, the separationist
model endeavours to divorce the religious and secular spheres of a society
entirely.[11]

In the established church model, or recognized religions model, the
state officially recognizes one religion as a state religion. For example, the
recognition of the Anglican church in United Kingdom, or the Lutheran
church in some Northern European countries.[12] In this model the state and
the church assist each other. In the recognized community model as portrayed in Austria, Hungary, Belgium, Luxembourg, Germany, and in some
Swiss cantons, there is, according to Archimandrite Nikodemos Anagnostopoulos, no official state religion or recognized church.[13] Rather all communities of faith are recognized equally before the law. According to James
Richardson the repressionist model adopts a hostile stance towards religion
and is based on premise that the state must repress religion.[14] Both the theocratic model and the repressionist model are rejected in the "National Policy
on Religion and Education."

According to Sinača Zrinščak the co-operative model is characterized
by a constitutional separation between church and state coupled with mutual agreements between the state and various recognized religions.[15]

South Africa, at present, upholds a form of the co-operative model.
According to the "National Policy on Religion" two separate spheres for religion and the state were established by the Constitution. However, provision
is made for interaction between the two.[16] The best way to describe South

9. Constitution of South Africa art. 2.

10. Shetreet, "Model of State and Church Relations," 88.

11. "National Policy on Religion," 5.

12. Eberle, *Church and State*, viii, 2.

13. Anagnostopoulos, *Orthodoxy and Islam*, 9.

14. Richardson, *Regulating Religion*, 301.

15. Zrinščak, "Church, State in Society," 159.

16. "National Policy on Religion" sec. 3.

Africa is to describe it as a constitutional democracy. Michele Graziadei asserts that freedom of religion is an essential part of the constellation of freedoms in modern democracies.[17] Simon Shetreet asserts that it is the responsibility of a democratic state to ensure, and preserve, the rights of religion for its citizens.[18]

The 2001 South African census was the last census that explicitly asked about religion and specific religious affiliation among the population of South Africa. The 2011 census did not ask about religion. Therefore, the *South Africa Statistics* 2001 are used in this chapter in references made to the breakdown of adherents of the different religions in South Africa. The statistics indicate that of the total national population of 44.8 million, 30 million or 79.8 percent are Christians.[19] The statistics also indicate that South Africa is a deeply pluralistic society. Protestantism is the largest denominational or theological identity among the Christian grouping.

The great majority of South Africans are Christians, but the Christian majority can be further subdivided. For example, the Zion Christian Church (3,867,798), the Dutch Reformed Church (3,527,075), the Roman Catholic Church (3,426,525), the Methodist Church of Southern Africa (2,808,649), the Pentecostal/Charismatic Churches (2,204,171), the Anglican Church of Southern Africa (1,600,001), the Apostolic Faith Mission (1,124,066), the Lutheran Church (1,051,193), the Presbyterian Church in Southern Africa (726,936) et cetera. Other major religious groups are Muslims (553,585), Hindus (537,428), and Jews (68,058). A large percentage of South Africa's population regard themselves as traditionalists (holding to African Traditional Belief (17,085) or with no religious affiliation (4,638,897) and others refused to state their religious affiliation (3,746,706).[20] Thus, we can see that South Africa is a country with a high level of religiosity. In this chapter religious minorities refer to any sub-group within a culture which is singled out for differential and unequal treatment. This is a longstanding reality in South Africa. As early as 1971 Van der Merwe stated that minority status carried with it the exclusion from full participation in the life of society.[21]

---

17. Graziadei, "State Norms, Religious Norms," 30.

18. Shetreet, "Model of State and Church Relations," 89.

19. *South Africa Statistics*, 25.

20. *South Africa Statistics*, 25.

21. Van der Merwe, "What is a Minority Group?," 11.

CONSTITUTIONAL PROVISION IN SOUTH AFRICA
FOR FREEDOM OF RELIGION

Freedom of religion in South Africa is protected by both national legal instruments as well as the international legal instruments to which South Africa subscribes. Article 18 of the "Universal Declaration of Human Rights" (1948) states the following:

> Everyone has the right to freedom of thought, conscience and religion; this right includes freedom to change his religion or belief and freedom, either alone or in community with others and in public or private life, his religion or belief in teaching, practice application.

This article influenced the drafting of the provisions in the Constitution of South Africa that relate to religion.

In South Africa religious freedom does not mean freedom *from* religion, but rather entails freedom *of* religion. Freedom of religion is protected in the Constitution of the Republic of South Africa no. 108 (1996).[22] The preamble is an important indicator of the fundamental values embedded in the Constitution. The preamble ends with the words: "May God protect our people. God bless South Africa" (*Nkosi Sikilel' iAfrica*). Kristin Henrard rightly notes that it can be deduced that the Constitution of South Africa makes a position choice *for* religion and not *from* religion.[23] According to Prinsloo, the term "secular state" was deliberately not included in the 1996 Constitution of South Africa.[24] The Constitution is therefore not a religiously neutral document.[25] Choices were intentionally made *for* religion, yet not for Christianity as major religion, in the Constitution. These are important, yet subtle, distinctions to keep in mind when reflection on the Constitution.

For example, section 9(1) of the Constitution states that everyone is equal before the law and has the right to equal protection and benefit of the law. This equality includes the full and equal enjoyment of all rights and freedoms, including the freedom of religion, thought, and conscience (section 9[2]). Section 9(3) further emphasizes that it is unconstitutional

---

22. See, for example, the sections on Equality (section 9); Human Dignity (section 10); Freedom of Religion, Belief, and Opinion (section 15); Freedom of Expression (section 16); Freedom of Association (section 18); and Cultural, Religious, and Linguistic communities (section 31).

23. Henrard, "Accommodation of Religious."

24. Prinsloo, "South African Policy," 31.

25. Henrard, "Accommodation of Religious," 55.

to unfairly discriminate directly or indirectly against anyone on one or more grounds, including race, gender, sex, pregnancy, marital status, ethnic or social origin, color, sexual orientation, age, disability, religion, conscience, belief, culture, language and birth.

Section 15(2) of the Constitution provides that "religious observances may be conducted in state or state-aided institutions, such as hospitals, schools and prisons on condition that that it is conducted on an equitable basis and attendance at them is free and voluntary." Section 15(3) of the Constitution, recognizes religious traditions and legal systems alongside the South African legal system. Section 15 of the Constitution states that everyone has the right to freedom of conscience, religion, thought, belief, and opinion. The right to religious freedom is guaranteed in section 15.

With regard to freedom of expression section 16(1) of the Constitution makes provision that everyone,

has the right to freedom of expression, which includes freedom of the press and other media; freedom to receive or impart information or ideas; freedom of artistic creativity; and academic freedom and freedom of scientific research.

However, this right does not include "propaganda for war; incitement of imminent violence; or (c) advocacy of hatred that is based on race, ethnicity, gender or religion, and that constitutes incitement to cause harm" (section 16[b]).

Section 18 of the Constitution guarantees the right to freedom of association. Furthermore section 31(1) makes provision

that persons belonging to a cultural, religious or linguistic community may not be denied the right, with other members of that community to enjoy their culture, practice their religion and use their language; and to form, join and maintain cultural, religious and linguistic associations and other organs of civil society.

The "South African Charter of Religious Rights and Freedoms" states that Section 31 of the Constitution makes provision for the protection of "the right of persons belonging to a religious community to practice their religion together with other members of that community and form, join and maintain voluntary religious associations."[26] Yet, in spite of this, it is important to note that the right to religious freedom is not absolute. Section

---

26. "South African Charter," 4.

31(2) makes it clear that the above rights may "not be exercised in a manner inconsistent with any provision of the Bill of Rights."

The Bill of Rights is a foundation stone of democracy in South Africa (chapter 2 of the Constitution). Section 7 places the responsibility on the state to "respect, protect, promote, and fulfil the rights in the Bill of Rights," including therefore the right to religious freedom (section 15) and the rights of religious communities (section 31).[27] The right to freedom of religion is guaranteed in the Bill of Rights.[28] General limitations of the Constitution are protected in section 36 of the Constitution:

> The rights in the Bill of Rights may be limited only in terms
> of law of general application to the extent that the limitation
> is reasonable and justifiable in an open and democratic society
> based on human dignity, equality and freedom.

Section 185 and section 186 of the Constitution makes provision for the constituting of a "Commission for the Promotion and Protection of the Rights of Cultural, Religious, and Linguistic Communities" of South Africa.[29] The primary objects of the Commission are:

a. to promote respect for the rights of cultural, religious and linguistic communities;

b. to promote and develop peace, friendship, humanity, tolerance and national unity among cultural, religious and linguistic communities, on the basis of equality, non-discrimination and free association; and

c. to recommend the establishment or recognition, in accordance with national legislation, of a cultural or other council.

The Constitution of the Republic of South Africa no. 108 (1996) protects the rights of every citizen, unlike the Constitution of South Africa 1983 which safeguarded the rights of a select group (in that instance, the majority religion, Christianity). The Constitution of 1996 expects the State to safeguard the right to religious freedom of all citizens. Section 1 states "that human dignity; the achievement of equality and the advancement of human rights and freedoms are the founding values of the Republic." The right to human dignity, freedom of expression, and freedom of association, relate according to Rassie Malherbe indirectly to the protection of religious freedom.[30] Section 10 of the Constitution states clearly that everyone has

27. *Response to the CRL*, 12.
28. Malherbe, "Background and Contents," 1–2.
29. Malherbe, "Background and Contents," 1–2.
30. Malherbe, "Background and Contents," 1–2.

inherent dignity and the right to have their dignity respected and protected. The Constitution furthermore accommodates religious diversity. These stipulations are important, since Constitution is the supreme law of the Republic of South Africa, and will regulate social life and protect the rights of individuals and minority groupings.[31]

Huge strides have been made since 1994 to accommodate the diversity of identities, beliefs, and convictions of the population of South Africa. The Constitution of the Republic of South Africa no. 108 (1996) also warrants freedom from coercion. All faith communities, and even those who profess no religion at all, are equal before the law. The Constitution enshrines freedom of religion as a fundamental right. Therefore, there is a legal obligation to accommodate religious minorities, religious beliefs and practices, in South Africa. Freedom of religion includes the freedom to practice one's religion. It also implies an obligation to accommodate the variety of religions, religious practices and beliefs. This is important since South Africa is a deeply pluralistic society. The country consists of different social groups and systems of personal law and cultural or religious beliefs. Constitutionally, protection is granted against any form of unfair discrimination. According to Grant S. Shockley the essence of religious pluralism is not regalia but relationships.[32] One could argue that the emphasis on relationship led to the emergence of a measure interreligious tolerance and co-operation in South Africa.

Taking all of the constitutional provisions discussed above into account, it is clear that post-apartheid South Africa does not embrace the theocratic model, separationist model, established church model, recognized religions model, or the repressionist model. Rather South Africa seems to adhere to the general characteristics of the co-operative model. In South Africa there is not a strict separation between religion and the state. A secular state is viewed to be a state with no state religion. Secularism is a political and legal system which has to do with the separation between the church and the state as well as the neutrality of the state. According to Joselyn Maclure and Charles Taylor secularism means that the state should be separated from religion and religious beliefs.[33] In other words, a secular state must be neutral in matters of religion. Secularism also has to do with the distinction between the public sphere and the private sphere. There should be an appropriate relation between religion, the public sphere, and public institutions. Two aims of this view of secularism today are the respect of the

---

31. Malherbe, "Background and Contents," 1–2.

32. Shockley, "Religious Pluralism," 140.

33. Maclure and Taylor, *Secularism and Freedom*, 3.

moral equality of individuals and the protection of freedom of conscience and of religion.[34] For a long time in South Africa religious tolerance meant either an exclusion, or marginalization, of certain religions or worldviews. Secularism in South Africa's context should therefore be understood within the broad framework of diversity of beliefs and values that the citizens of South Africa embrace. According to Maclure and Taylor secularism is a political and legal system whose function is to established certain distance between the state and religion.[35] It has to do with the separation between the church and the state as well as the neutrality of the state.

FREEDOM OF CONSCIENCE AND RELIGION AT PUBLIC SCHOOLS

Maintaining religious freedom can be a complex affair. Problems of complying with the constitutional provisions regarding freedom of conscience and freedom of religion came to the fore in post-apartheid South Africa in relation to the emergence of public schools. The school boards did not take sufficient cognizance of the provisions for the freedom to practice one's religion in public institutions. In particular many private schools missed the important point that freedom of belief and practice necessarily implies an obligation to accommodate other religions. The Constitution prescribes a legal obligation to accommodate minorities, religious beliefs and practices. Many private schools in South Africa came to embrace a Christian ethos. This highlighted the tension between the rights to religious freedom as set out in the Constitution, and the ways in which certain choices for religious identity can lead to a denial of the equal status of other religions. According to Kristin Henrard from around 1652 until the start of the post-apartheid era, unequal legal status was accorded to the different belief systems in South Africa.[36]

In 1967 the "National Education Policy Act of 1967" was adopted by the government of South Africa. Christian National Education became the national education policy for state schools in South Africa.[37] Henceforth education in all state-supported schools had a Christian ethos and nationalistic character.[38] The educational content was Christocentric in nature and religious education held a central place in the formal education system.[39]

34. Maclure and Taylor, *Secularism and Freedom*, 4.
35. Maclure and Taylor, *Secularism and Freedom*, 3.
36. Henrard, "Accommodation of Religious," 52.
37. Van Niekerk, *Die Ontstaan*, 10.
38. Van Niekerk, *Die Ontstaan*, 33.
39. Van Niekerk, *Die Ontstaan*, 36.

Paul Prinsloo states categorically that Christian National Education "endorsed and promoted a version of Protestant Christianity and excluded other Christian denominations, other religions and African traditional religion from curricula, access to learners and representation in curricula."[40] Henrard concurs that Christian National Education was characterized by Protestant hegemony. State-subsided schools were obliged to be opened and closed with Scripture reading and prayer during that period.[41] The "National Education Policy Act" indicated that religious education should preferably be taught within the first half of the school day. According to Henrard these courses in religious studies or biblical studies, had a conservative theological perspective and hardly anything was said about other world religions.[42] Parents with conscientious objections could request a written exemption from religious education for their children.[43] In general the majority religious calendar, namely that of Christianity, was accommodated within the school programme.

The "National Policy for General Education Affairs Act" of 1984 attempted to accommodate the different education approaches of the different culture groups in South Africa, namely that equal education opportunities should be pursued regardless of race, color, religion, or gender. The Act dealt with education content in section 2(i), (ii), and (iv), and provides: (i) that equal education opportunities, including equal education standards, for each resident, regardless of race, religion, or gender, should be pursued (ii) recognition of both the commonality and the diversity of religious and cultural living and the languages of the inhabitants. Article 14(a) and (b) of the Constitution of 1993 determined that "every person has the right to freedom of conscience, religion, thought, conviction and opinion and that religious practice in state or state-supported institutions had to take place on an equitable basis, although attendance should be voluntary." The Christian National Education system imposed the Christian religion on all public institutions.

The "White Paper on Education and Training" of 1995 confirmed that education and training is a basic human right which obliges the state to care for every citizen regardless of race, class, gender, religion, or age. Henrard concludes that there was a total absence of a balanced, multi-faith programme of religious studies in state-funded schools during apartheid.[44]

---

40. Prinsloo, "South African Policy," 32.

41. Henrard, "Accommodation of Religious," 52.

42. Henrard, "Accommodation of Religious," 52.

43. Van Niekerk, *Die Ontstaan*, 90.

44. Henrard, "Accommodation of Religious," 52.

She further states that emphasis was placed on the teaching of Christian values in state schools.

With the establishment of the Government of National Unity on April 27, 1994 a new period in the education history of South Africa and the safeguarding of religious freedom and religious equity was introduced. During 1996 the "South African Schools Act" based on the constitutional provisions regarding religious freedom and equity was promulgated. The "South African Schools Act" recognizes two categories of schools: public (also known as state-controlled schools) and independent schools (also known as privately governed schools):

> Subject to the Constitution and any applicable provincial law, religious observances may be conducted at a public school under rules issued by the governing body if such observances are conducted on an equitable basis and attendance at them by learners and members of staff is free and voluntary.[45]

The "South African Schools Act" of 1996:

> upholds freedom of conscience, religion, thought, belief and opinion, and freedom from unfair discrimination on any grounds whatsoever, including religion, in all public education institutions.[46]

The "National Education Policy Act" of 1996 indicates in article 4(a)(vi–vii) that every person has the right to the freedoms of conscience, religion, thought, belief, opinion, expression and association within educational institutions. The "National Education Policy Act" of 1996 and the "South African Schools Act" of 1996 as well as the 1997 Curriculum 2005 (Grades 1–9) did not address diverse ideas and approaches of religious communities adequately. After lengthy consultations with religious groups the department of education drafted a national policy on religion and education.[47]

In 2003 Kader Asmal, Minister of Education, declared the "National Policy on Religion and Education" as policy in terms section 3(4)(1) of the "National Education Policy Act" of 1996. It was promulgated on August 4, 2003. The "National Policy on Religion and Education" meritoriously barred confessional, sectarian religion from public schools, but permitted the teaching of Religion Studies as an academic subject and allowed for religious observances, under the proviso that these were offered in a fair and

---

45. "South African Schools Act," sec. 7.
46. "National Policy on Religion and Education."
47. Van der Walt, "Religion in Education," 1.

equitable manner.[48] The "National Policy on Religion and Education" gives full expression to the constitutional provision regarding freedom of religion and conscience that is set out in the Constitution of South Africa. The "National Policy on Religion and Education" introduced a curriculum in which learners were introduced to a variety of world religions (including African traditional religion).[49] The state attempted to assume a position of fairness with religions and worldviews. However, in the recent past numerous case studies surfaced in post-apartheid South Africa that highlighted the complexity, and conflicts, surrounding religious freedom in private schools. Some public schools have prohibited religious minorities from exercising their religious freedoms. For example, children from a family of practicing Muslims were barred from wearing the *hijab* (a headscarf worn by some Muslim women which covers the head, hair and neck) or the *jilbab* (a dark cloak covering everything but the head, hands and feet), a *burka* that covers even the eyes,[50] or the fez.[51] Incidents that prevented learners from attending public schools because of clothing associated with the Islamic faith surfaced on a regular basis in post-apartheid South Africa. Notwithstanding provisions in the "National Guidelines on School Uniforms"[52] and the "National Policy on Religion and Education" children were regularly told to remove the headscarf or fez as it wasn't seen as part of the school dress code.

Article 29 of the "National Guidelines on School Uniforms" states that:

> The school uniform policy or dress code should take into account religious and cultural diversity within the community served by the school. Measures should be included to accommodate learners whose religious beliefs are compromised by a uniform requirement. (2) If wearing particular attire, such as yarmulkes and headscarves, is part of the religious practice of learners or an obligation, schools should not, in terms of the Constitution, prohibit the wearing of such items. Male learners requesting to keep a beard as part of a religious practice may be required by the school to produce a letter from their religious teacher or organization substantiating the validity of the request. The same substantiation is applicable to those who wish to wear particular attire.

---

48. Van der Walt, "Religion in Education," 1.

49. Prinsloo, "South African Policy," 5.

50. Bennoune, "Secularism and Human Rights," 381, 410.

51. See Antonie v. Governing Body Settlers High School; Pillay v. MEC for Education, KwaZulu-Natal; MEC for Education, KwaZulu-Natal v. Pillay.

52. See "South African Schools Act"; "National Guidelines on School Uniforms."

To prohibit learners from wearing yarmulkes and headscarves at school amounts to non-compliance with the South African Constitution of 1996 and the "National Guidelines on School Uniforms." Schools cannot prohibit the wearing of certain items which are part of a pupils' religious practice. The parents of these learners considered the wearing of the *hijab* or the *jilbab* as a religious duty. The school boards at some public schools in South Africa did not see the ban on headscarves (and the like), as a violation of the freedom of religion of their learners. These schoolboards usually made reference to the code of conduct of the school which entails amongst other things, rules with regard to the ethos and the dress code of the school. The parents of the affected learners argued that the schoolboard's prohibiting the wearing of the *hijab* (a headscarf) or the *jilbab* (a dark cloak) instead of the school uniform violated their right to freedom of religion as stated in article 9 of the Constitution. They in turn saw such prohibitions as a violation of their human rights. Among others they invoked their right to manifest their religion under article 9 of the Constitution.

Kader Asmal states that as "a democratic society with a diverse population of different cultures, languages and religions South Africa is duty bound to ensure that through the diversity a unity of purpose and spirit is being developed that recognizes and celebrates the diversity of the people of South Africa."[53] The intention was thus to ensure that in public schools a particular religious ethos must not exercise excessive control or authority over others. Kader Asmal's understanding was that the equal rights of all students at schools should be ensured and protected whilst also upholding their right to have their religious views recognized and respected. The "National Policy on Religion and Education" therefore tries to ensure and protect the rights of all pupils to have their religious views recognized and respected at schools. Furthermore, the "National Policy on Religion and Education" encompasses a co-operative model and aims to protect young people from religious discrimination or coercion. The co-operative model combines constitutional separation and mutual recognition. According to article 1 of the "National Policy on Religion and Education," public schools have an educational responsibility for to teach their pupils about the various religions. South Africa embraces a co-operative model regarding religious education. The co-operative model provides a framework for religion and for education in the democratic South Africa. Furthermore, this model encourages an ongoing dialogue between religious groups and the state in areas of common interest and concern.[54] According to Paul Prinsloo the

---

53. "National Policy on Religion," foreword.
54. "National Policy on Religion," 68.

promotion of the role of religion in education, teaching about religion, as well as the teaching about secular worldviews, are encapsulated in the "National Policy on Religion and Education" (2003).[55] South Africa's context should thus be understood under a broad framework of a diversity of beliefs and values that the citizens of South Africa embrace.

According to Maclure and Taylor, public institutions such as schools and universities, are institutions belonging to the nation, under the protection of the state, and as such they ought not to be identified with a particular religion otherwise this will hamper bridging diversity.[56] They should rather serve the common good of all citizens of the nation. The premise of Maclure and Taylor is that citizens have the right to display their religious affiliations both in the private sphere and in the public sphere.[57] Freedom of religion refers on the one side the freedom to practice one's religion but implies on the other side an obligation to accommodate other religions.[58] Hence, South Africans have a legal obligation to accommodate and protect the religious beliefs, practices, and rights of minorities. Mutual respect among cultural, religious, and linguistic communities should be fostered. Education is seen as one of the areas which can be utilized to engender such values in a diverse society.

Provision is made in the "National Policy" to regulate religion education, religious instruction and religious observances at all public schools. Section 57 of the "Schools Act" makes provision for "Public Schools on Private Property with a recognized religious character, which also have the right to specify a religious ethos and character, subject to an agreement with the provincial authorities." The provisions regarding religious instruction and religious observances as prescribed by the "National Policy on Religion and Education" (2003) are not applicable in the case of public schools on private property. These include both independent schools and religious schools. Parents who send their children to a denominational school, rather than a public school, should take cognisance of the ethos and identity at these schools which may include the religious observances and commitments of a particular faith. Most public schools in South Africa do not adhere to the "National Policy on Religion and Education" (2003). Research shows that most of them have simply continued to operate as they had before the introduction of the "National Policy." School boards should be reminded of the importance of upholding and enacting the "National Policy" in keeping

---

55. Prinsloo, "South African Policy," 31.

56. Maclure and Taylor, *Secularism and Freedom*, 38.

57. Maclure and Taylor, *Secularism and Freedom*, 40.

58. "Commission for the Promotion and Protection."

with the Constitution. Since religious observance is not a compulsory part of the school day at public schools, schoolboards should make appropriate provision for pupils who do not participate in religious observances, ensuring that they are not made to feel excluded.

According to section 17–20 of the "National Policy" the "programmes for religion education should purposefully pursue the moral and ethical development of pupils, whilst they learn in a factual way about the various religions and beliefs which exist." The "Policy" emphatically states that public schools should avoid adopting a particular religion, or a limited set of religions, that advances sectarian or particular interests. For example, they should avoid only singing Christian hymns or songs during assemblies. Schools should build respect for diversity. The group, *Organisasie vir Godsdienste-Onderrig en Demokrasie* (OGOD), has recently been in the South African media. This group advocates against a single-faith approach to religion in public schools. Although provision is made in the "National Policy" for religious education, freedom of conscience, conviction and religion should be recognized in the curricula.

The "National Policy" states categorically:

> that religious instruction is primarily the responsibility of the home, the family, and the religious community. Under religious instruction is being understood the instruction in a particular faith or belief, with a view to the inculcation of adherence to that faith or belief. It refers to a programme of instruction which is aimed at providing information regarding a particular set of religious beliefs with a view to promoting adherence thereto.[59]

Facilities at public schools utilized for religious instruction should be used:

> in a manner that does not interrupt or detract from the core educational purposes of the school provided that opportunities be afforded in an equitable manner to all religious bodies represented in a school, that no denigration or caricaturing of any other religion take place, and that attendance at such instruction be voluntary.[60]

The "National Policy" therefore makes provision for voluntary gatherings and meetings of religious associations during break times. This "Policy," in line with the Constitution and "South African Schools Act" of 1996, "encourages the provision of religious instruction by religious bodies and other accredited groups outside the formal school curriculum on school

---

59. "National Policy on Religion," 54.
60. "National Policy on Religion," 54.

premises." In most cases governing bodies in South Africa choose to safe-guard the major religious grouping they are serving. Provisions for minority religions are not made on an equitable basis. Article 8 of the "South African Schools Act" makes provision for a governing body of a public school to adopt a code of conduct for the learners after consultation with the learners, parents, and educators, of the school. Research shows that most schools use this provision to develop a code of conduct based on the religious prefer-ence of the majority religion in their constituency, and in doing so they exclude the minority religions from their constitutional right to equity.

The 1996 Constitution of South Africa contains a provision allowing for religious observances to be conducted at state or state-aided institutions, provided they follow public authority rules, they are conducted on an equi-table basis, attendance is free and voluntary, and they also provide for the recognition of religious legal systems and marriages that are not inconsis-tent with the Constitution.[61] "The constitutional right to practice one's reli-gion . . . is of fundamental importance in an open and democratic society. It is one of the hallmarks of a free society."[62] The prospect of the Constitution is to allow religious observances in public institutions, ensuring fairness in the way they are conducted, also ensuring that no-one is forced in any way to participate or not to participate. The aim of these provisions is to foster a spirit of respect and tolerance in a multi-religious society.

The "National Policy" also makes provision for religious observances. The latter refers to "activities and behaviors which recognize and express the views, beliefs and commitments of a particular religion and may include gatherings of adherents, prayer times, dress and diets."[63] Religious obser-vance includes acts of formal worship within a particular faith tradition as well as any activity that is specific to a particular religion and would not be practiced by members of other faith communities for example faith-specific worship (singing Christmas and Easter hymns), dietary rules (eating ko-sher food or halal food, fasting during Ramadan), and dress code (wearing turbans). The multi-religious nature of public schools has been ignored by schoolboards with regard to the organization of religious observance as an official part of the school day. In 2009 *Organisasie vir Godsdienste-Onderrig en Demokrasie* (OGOD) instituted proceedings in the Johannesburg High Court, against six public schools with a "Christian ethos" who espoused co-called Christian values. OGOD states that they endeavour to promote

61. Henrard, "Accommodation of Religious," 55; Constitution of South Africa sec. 15.

62. Prince v. President.

63. "National Policy on Religion," sec. 59.

in-depth, fact-based education about the religions of the world; eradicating religious indoctrination in public schools; identifying and exposing religious counter-knowledge and magical thinking; shielding children from the psychological dangers of religious damnation; promoting a democratic, secular and human rights based South African society, and eradicating religious elitism.[64] The high court issued the following order:

> (a) It is declared that it offends s.7 of the Schools Act, 84 of 1996 for a public school

> (i) to promote or allow its staff to promote that it, as a public school, adheres to only one or predominantly only one religion to the exclusion of others; and

> (ii) to hold out that it promotes the interests of any one religion in favor of others.[65]

The verdict clearly supports the notion that religious observance could take place in public schools, as longs as such observances are undertaken on a fair basis and attendance is voluntary. Religious observance should not be practiced in public institutions in order to promote confessional or sectarian approaches to religion. However, as has already been stated, the reality in South Africa is that numerous school governing bodies are not adhering to the "National Policy," and so they continue to exclude minorities through their religious observances. Provisions should be made by school boards of public schools to ensure equitable recognition and observance of all religious groupings.[66]

SOUTH AFRICAN CHARTER OF RELIGIOUS RIGHTS AND FREEDOMS

In 1990, Judge Albie Sachs, Justice of the Constitutional Court of South Africa (1994–2009), wrote:

> Ideally in South Africa, all religious organizations and persons concerned with the study of religion would get together and draft a charter of religious rights and responsibilities. . . . It

64. Pietersen, "Press Release."

65. Organisasie vir Godsdienste-Onderrig en Demokrasie v. Laerskool Randhart and Others.

66. "National Policy on Religion," 64.

would be up to the participants themselves to define what they consider to be their fundamental rights.[67]

The Constitution of the Republic of South Africa of 1996 makes provision that Charters of Rights consistent with the provisions of the Constitution can be adopted. On April 6, 2010 a charter of religious rights and freedoms, called the "South African Charter of Religious Rights and Freedoms" was drawn up by South African religious and civil organizations.[68] The "South African Charter" is the first public charter to be developed under section 234 of the Constitution of South Africa.

The intention of the "Charter" is to define the freedoms, rights, responsibilities and relationship between the "State" of South Africa and her citizens concerning religious belief.[69] The "South African Charter of Religious Rights and Freedoms" (SACRRF) has been endorsed by signatories from the different religions as well as organizations, commissions and broads.[70] Since 2010 the number of persons who endorsed the "Charter" has grown to over 20 million making the "Charter" a force to be taken account of when dealing with the relationship between the state and the church regarding freedom of religion.[71] The endorsement of the "Charter" by millions of South Africans from diverse religious backgrounds explicitly affirmed their constitutional rights regarding freedom of religion and opinion. After the public endorsement of the Charter, the *South African Council for the Protection and Promotion of Religious Rights and Freedoms* was established. One of the tasks of the *Council* is to seek ways and means to protect and promote religious rights and freedoms in South Africa.

The SACRRF outlines what the legal and civil manifestations of the right to freedom of religion are for individuals, groups and official

67. Sachs, *Protecting Human Rights*, 46–47.

68. South African Council, *Minutes*, 1.

69. "Explanatory Notes on the Charter," 4.

70. The National House of Traditional Leaders; the Buddhist Religion; the Rastafarians; the Anglican Church; the Roman Catholic Church; the Bahá'í Faith; the Dutch Reformed Church; the Hatfield Christian Network (representing some 100 churches across the country); the Black Evangelical Leadership; the Jami'atul 'Ulamâ (Council of Muslim Theologians); the Religious Editorial Board of the SABC; the Executive of the National Religious Leaders' Forum; the General Secretary of the South African Council of Churches; the Chairperson and Members of the Commission for the Promotion and Protection of the Rights of Cultural, Religious, and Linguistic Communities; Members of the Reformed Churches in South Africa; Members the Nederduitsch Hervormde Kerk in Afrika; the Muslim Judicial Council; the Chief Rabbi of the Jewish Religion in South Africa; the Apostolic Faith Mission; tomen's organizations; Youth movements; and the Church of Jesus Christ of the Latter Day Saints. See *South African Charter*, art. 5.

71. South African Council, *Response by the Council*, 1.

organizations, within a South African context.[72] The "Charter" defines the freedoms, rights, responsibilities, and relationship between the state and the citizens of South Africa with regards to religious belief in eleven articles. The "Charter" takes account of the provisions in the Constitution sec. 185(1)(c) "to recommend the establishment or recognition, in accordance with national legislation, of a cultural or other council or councils for a community or communities in South Africa"

Article 7 of the "Charter" affirms with regarding to education that

> Parents may withdraw their children from school activities or programs inconsistent with their religious or philosophical convictions; Every educational institution may adopt a particular religious or other ethos, as long as it is observed in an equitable, free, voluntary and non-discriminatory way, and with due regard to the rights of minorities; Every private educational institution established on the basis of a particular religion, philosophy or faith may impart its religious or other convictions to all children enrolled in that institution, and may refuse to promote, teach or practice any religious or other conviction other than its own. Children enrolled in that institution (or their parents) who do not subscribe to the religious or other convictions practiced in that institution waive their right to insist not to participate in the religious activities of the institution.[73]

The *South African Council for the Protection and Promotion of Religious Rights and Freedoms* was admitted as one of the friends of the court in the high court case of *Organisasie vir Godsdienste-Onderrig en Demokrasie v. Laerskool Randhart and Others*. The *Council* should take cognisance of the judgment of the court that it is unconstitutional for public schools to hold a particular religious ethos and values, to promote a particular religion or to primarily associate itself with a particular religion. Article 7 of the "Charter" is therefore redundant and should be revisited by the *Council*. The declaratory order of the High Court makes it clear that public schools cannot promote a system that adheres predominantly to only one religion to the exclusion of others, or a propose system of education that promotes the interests of one religion over others.

72. "South African Charter" art. 5.
73. "South African Charter" art. 7.

CONCLUSION

In post-apartheid South Africa Christianity does not have any legal preference over other religions. Rather freedom of religion is a fundamental right in South African society. This right is enshrined in the Constitution of South Africa 1996. A shift has taken place from a country which embraced a theocratic model of the relationship between the state and religion (official recognition was given to the majority religion, namely Christianity, and members of other religions and even those who were not adherents to any religion, were marginalized), to a country which embraces constitutional democracy, freedom of religion or belief. Freedom of religion in South Africa therefore includes the freedom to practice one's religion without prejudice. South Africa is not a Christian state or a secular state. Rather, it embraces a co-operative model. This implies an obligation to accommodate a diversity of religions in public institutions. The non-compliance to constitutional and legal provisions regarding freedom of religion and conscience in public institutions (such as public schools), which occurs on a regular basis in post-apartheid South Africa, is being redressed by the provisions in the "National Policy on Religion and Education" (2003). In the watershed case for religious freedom in South Africa brought by OGOD the high court found that it was against the Education Act to "promote one faith or one religion primarily at the expense of others or allow school staff to do it."[74] The judgment upholds section 15(2) of the Constitution, which grants provision for religious observances at State or State-aided institutions. This chapter has highlighted some of the complexities of protecting religious freedom in South Africa, while allowing for freedom of expression and practice in public schools.

BIBLIOGRAPHY

Anagnostopoulos, Nikodemos. *Orthodoxy and Islam: Theology and Muslim-Christian Relations in Modern Greece and Turkey*. Culture and Civilization in the Middle East. New York: Routlegde, 2017.

Bennoune, Karima. "Secularism and Human Rights. A Contextual Analysis of Headscarves, Religious Expression, and Women's Equality Under International Law." *Columbia Journal of Transnational Law* 45.2 (2007) 367–426.

Commission for the Promotion and Protection of the Rights of Cultural, Religious, and Linguistic Communities Act, 2002. Act No. 19 of 2002. Online. http://www.saflii. org/za/legis/num_act/cftpapotrocralca20021086.pdf.

Comments on the CRL Rights Commission's Report on the "Commercialisation" of Religion. February 28, 2017.

---

74. Organisasie vir Godsdienste-Onderrig en Demokrasie v. Laerskool Randhart and Others.

Du Plessis, Lourens. "Religious Freedom and Equality as Celebration of Difference: A Significant Development in Recent South African Constitutional Case-Law." *PER* 12.4 (2009) 10–34.

Eberle, Edward J. *Church and State in Western Society: Established Church, Cooperation and Separation.* London: Routlegde, 2011.

Graziadei, Michele. "State Norms, Religious Norms, and Claims of Plural and Normativity under Democratic Constitutions." In *Religious Rules, State Law, and Normative Pluralism: A Comparative Overview*, edited by Rossella Bottoni, et al., 29–43. Berlin: Springer, 2016.

Henrard, Kristin. "The Accommodation of Religious Diversity in South Africa." *Journal of African Law* 45.1 (2001) 51–72.

Maclure, Jocelyn, and Charles Taylor. *Secularism and Freedom of Conscience.* Cambridge: Harvard University Press, 2011.

Malherbe, Rassie. "The Background and Contents of the Proposed South African Charter of Religious Rights and Freedoms." *BYU Law Review* 3 (2011) 613–35.

National Education Policy Act. No. 39 of 1967.

National Education Policy Act. No. 27 of 1996.

National Guidelines on School Uniforms 2006. Online. http://us-cdn.creamermedia. co.za/assets/articles/attachments/02561_notice173.pdf.

National Policy for General Education Affairs Act. No. 76 of 1984.

"National Policy on Religion and Education." September 12, 2003. Online. https://www. gov.za/sites/default/files/religion_0.pdf.

Nederduitse Gereformeerde Kerk in Suid-Afrika. *Human Relations and the South African Scene in the Light of Scripture.* Kaapstad: NG Kerk-Uitgewers, 1974.

———. *The Story of the Dutch Reformed Church's Journey with Apartheid 1960–1994: A Testimony and a Confession.* Pretoria: General Synodal Commission of the Dutch Reformed Church, 1996.

Pietersen, Hans. "Press Release: Organisasie vir Godsdienste-Onderrig en Demokrasie." August 20, 2014. Online. https://www.ogod.org.za/wp-content/uploads/ogod-litigation-press-release-aug2014.pdf.

Prinsloo, Paul. "The South African Policy on Religion and Education (2003). A Contradiction in a Secular State and Age?" *Alternation Special Edition* 3 (2009) 31–54.

Republic of South Africa. *Constitution of the Republic of South Africa. Act 110 of 1983.*

———. *Constitution of the Republic of South Africa. Act 200 of 1993.*

———. *Constitution of the Republic of South Africa. Act 108 of 1996.*

Richardson, James T. *Regulating Religion: Case Studies from Around the Globe.* New York: Plenum, 2004.

Sachs, Albie. *Protecting Human Rights in a New South Africa: Contemporary South African Debates.* Cape Town: Oxford University Press, 1990.

Shetreet, Simon. "The Model of State and Church Relations and Its Impact on the Protection of Freedom of Conscience and Religion: A Comparative Analysis and a Case Study of Israel." In *Religion in the Public Sphere: A Comparative Analysis of German, Israeli, American, and International Law*, edited by Winfried Brugger and Michael Karayanni, 87–161. Berlin: Springer, 2007.

Shockley, Grant S. "Religious Pluralism and Religious Education: A Black Protestant Perspective." In *Religious Pluralism and Religious Education*, edited by Norma H. Thompson, 138–70. Birmingham: Religious Education, 1988.

South African Charter of Religious Rights and Freedoms. Pretoria, 2010.

South African Council for the Protection and Promotion of Religious Rights and Freedoms. *Minutes of the South African Charter of Religious Rights and Freedoms*. Pretoria: South African Council for the Protection and Promotion of Religious Rights and Freedoms, 2010.

———. *Response by the Council for the Protection and Promotion of Religious Rights and Freedoms to CRL Rights Commission Report on the Commercialisation of Religion and Abuse of People's Belief Systems*. Pretoria: South African Council for the Protection and Promotion of Religious Rights and Freedoms, 2017.

South African Schools Act. No. 84 of 1996. Online. https://www.gdeadmissions.gov.za/Content/Files/SchoolsAct.pdf.

Statistics South Africa. *Census 2001: Primary Tables South Africa Census '96 and 2001 Compared*. Pretoria: Statistics South Africa, 2004. Online. http://www.statssa.gov.za/census/census_2001/primary_tables/RSAPrimary.pdf

Triandafyllidou, Anna. *Addressing Cultural, Ethnic, and Religious Diversity Challenges in Europe: A Comparative Overview of 15 European Countries*. Rev. ed. Accept Pluralism Project. Florence: European University Institute, 2012. Online. http://cadmus.eui.eu/handle/1814/19254.

United Nations. "Universal Declaration of Human Rights." December 10, 1948. Online. https://www.un.org/en/universal-declaration-human-rights.

Van der Merwe, H. W. "What Is a Minority Group?" In *South Africa's Minorities*, edited by Peter Randall, 11–12. Fordsburg: Golden Era, 1971.

Van der Walt, Johannes L. "Religion in Education in South Africa: Was Social Justice Served?" *South African Journal of Education* 31 (2011) 381–93.

Van Niekerk, Elsabe Francina. *Die Ontstaan, Verloop en Toekoms van Christelik-Nasionale Onderwys in Suid-Afrika*. Pretoria: UNISA, 1997.

Van Rooyen, Jan Hendrik Petrus. "Die NG Kerk, apartheid en die Christelike Instituut van Suidelike Afrika." PhD diss., Universiteit van die Witwatersrand, 1990.

White Paper on Education and Training. Notice 196 of 1995. Cape Town: Parliament of the Republic of South Africa, 1995. Online. https://www.education.gov.za/Portals/0/Documents/Legislation/White%20paper/White%20paper%20on%20Education%20and%20Training%201995.pdf?ver=2008-03-05-111656-000.

Zrinščak, Sinača. "Church, State in Society in Post-Communist Europe." In *Religion and the State: A Comparative Sociology*, edited by Jack Barbalet, et al., 157–82. London: Anthem, 2011

Court Cases

Antonie v. Governing Body Settlers High School 2002 (4) SA 738 (C).

MEC for Education, KwaZulu-Natal v. Pillay 2008 (1) SA 474 (CC).

Organisasie vir Godsdienste-Onderrig en Demokrasie v. Laerskool Randhart and Others (29847/2014) [2017] ZAGPJHC 160; [2017] 3 All SA 943 (GJ); 2017 (6) SA 129 (GJ) (27 June 2017).

Pillay v. MEC for Education, KwaZulu-Natal 2006 (6) SA 363 (N).

Prince v. President, Cape Law Society 2001 (2) BCLR 133 (CC) at par 25 per Ngcobo J.

8

African Traditional Religion and Freedom of Religion in South Africa

Nokuzola Mndende

South Africa, like many other African states have undergone some socio-political changes from pre-colonial through colonial and apartheid regimes to the present democratic dispensation. All these changes had some effects in influencing the history and the nature of the country. New concepts that did not apply to the general population, except for the privileged minorities in the country, were now made to be available to all. The Bill of Rights of the country's Constitution emphasized that freedom and equality for all should be among the basic tenets of the country's liberation strategies. This led to new policies being formulated so as to accelerate some important changes to try and accommodate everybody who lives in the country irrespective of race, class, religion, gender and geographical area.

It will therefore be crucial that before engaging in African Traditional Religion and freedom of religion in South Africa, that one should consider what were the causal factors that promoted inequalities and what were the effects of such changes in the country. Before colonialism, the African indigenous communities were living a communal way of life without compartmentalizing their way of life into different fields of beliefs and practices.[1] Spirituality is an internal relationship between an individual and the Spiritual World where the Creator and ancestors are believed to reside. Such

1. Makgoba, "Patterns of African Thought," 27–28.

spiritual activities are acted out using cultural tools that are available so as to unite families and communities. It is the introduction of the Abrahamic faiths, for good or for bad, that tried to separate spirituality from the actions and morals of the people. It tried to confine it to the documented history of the Jews which is found in their Bible.

Because of the different approaches to religion and its doctrines, the new imposed religion brought by missionaries displaced the indigenous forms of spirituality and relegated them to exclusive and supposedly outdated cultural practices of the Black population of South Africa. Religion, Christianity, and Western culture were incorrectly implied to be synonymous with one another. Hence, those attending Western schools were referred to as *Abantu basesikolweni* (school people), or *Amagqobhoka* (people with holes referring to converts), or *Amakhumsha* (those who speak English). This change of identity was preceded by the giving of a new name, called a 'Christian name.' These names stemmed from Jewish, Roman, Dutch, or English names. The African indigenous names were referred to as heathen or pagan names. These so-called Christian names were given to each child during baptism since Christian baptism was an entry to Western schooling and job seeking in government and broader society. This practice of the imposed Christian names is explicated by Sybil Maureen Dickens when she cites the instruction that were given by the Catholic Church that:

> Pastors shall see to it that the person baptized is not given a name that is alien to the Christian sense. Pastors should see to it that a Christian name is given to the person baptized. The church has always upheld the pious custom of bestowing a Christian name on the baptized.[2]

Ritual practices, and any relationship with ancestors, were never classified as religious practices within this cultural and religious framework. Any knowledge of a Creator (God) that was not related to the Triune God (Father, Son, and Holy Spirit) of the Christian Bible was also never regarded as truly religious. The early Southern African missionary, Johannes van der Kemp, in his letter to the London Missionary Society which sent him to convert amaXhosa of South Africa said the following:

> If by religion we understand reverence of God, or the external action by which that reverence is expressed: I never could perceive that they had any religion, nor any idea of the existence of a God.[3]

2. Dickens, "Western Influence," 670.

3. Johannes van der Kemp quoted in Chidester, *Savage Systems*, 75.

This attitude was not isolated to the amaXhosa. Rather, it was a common practice throughout the region at that time. Eventually the whole government in South Africa came to be associated with one religion, namely. The country was later declared a Christian country hence for entry into all government departments one had to declare his or her Christian affiliation. This situation led to a situation in which all schooling operated within the Christian tradition. Hence, even the educational, moral, social and religious aims of the Education system were based on the Christian Bible. Whether the subject was Biblical Studies or Religious Education or Religious Instruction, it was all based on the Bible and Christian teachings irrespective of which religion one was affiliates with.

All government departments were automatically Christianised, be it the Health services, Police service, Prison service, Defense force, Statistical services, it was the same. With the Department of Defense for instance, all Black soldiers had to affiliate with Christianity. Hence, they were forced to be buried by Christian military chaplains since there were no military Chaplains representing African Traditional Religion. Thus, even though military personnel needed to have access to counselling services from trained professionals from their religious backgrounds, African Traditional Religion military workers were disadvantaged, and suffered, because they were counselled by people who did not recognize their cultures, religions, and spirituality. This was, and still is, a violation of human rights by people who claim to be God's ambassadors.

African Traditional Religion could only be freely practiced in the rural communities and then, not as a religion, but rather as an aspect of African culture. On Sundays these persons had to make sure that they go to church in order to declare their public adherence to the Christian faith. This resulted in split social and religious identity, where one had to pretend to be something she or he is not during the day, (because of socio-political and religious circumstances), yet at night or in secret she or he lived a normal life and communicated with her or his ancestors. This conflation of missionary work, Western schooling, and colonialism was also experienced by AbaMbo of the Eastern Cape where on May 14, 1835, they were made to take an oath under a milkwood tree (*umqwashu*) led by Reverend John Ayliff. The pledge written on their behalf by Reverend Ayliff was recited by AbaMbo. They had to make the following promises:

- to be faithful to God;
- to be loyal to the British king;
- to do all in their power to support their missionaries; and
- to educate their children.[4]

4. Ayliff, *History of AbaMbo*, 34.

One has to bear in mind that to promise to be faithful to God implies an understanding of God in Westernised, Missionary, Christian terms. Hence, even today for most Black Christians in South Africa, to be non-Christian implies that one does not believe in any God. This misconception skewed understandings of the concept of freedom of religion. Many think that by allowing African Traditional Religion to be part of the multi-religious demographic nature of the country, they are including atheists—which is how many view African Traditionalists.

There are many other factors from colonialism and apartheid which made African Traditional Religions to be understood as a lesser form of religion by Black South African Christians. The exclusion of African Traditional Religion in the list of religions in South Africa during the colonial period was deliberate. The government agents of the time were very racist. This is evidenced in the way in which the national census of the time was carried out. All races which came to South Africa were asked about their religious affiliations. However, when it came to Black Africans, they were only asked which denomination they belonged to, with the assumption that they were all Christians. That oversight resulted in the absence of an African Traditional Religion category in the census. This, in turn, led to the assumption that the religion does not exist, and the associated assumption that all Black people are Christians.

Mission schools also played a significant role in the destruction of African culture and religion, and promotion of Western culture religion. E. M. Uka, commenting the effects of these imported schools and their religion, states that mission schools and churches

> spared no efforts in condemning everything African as worthless, pagan, primitive and poor. Consequently young educated Africans, through Western indoctrination not only lost interest in African beliefs but despised them as if they themselves were white men. In this way the vitality of the African Traditional Religion suffered a severe setback as the Africans themselves began to lose confidence in anything African.[5]

Okot p'Bitek further defines them as follows:

> Their works were 'apologies' for the colonial system, their task was to demonstrate the superiority of Western culture over those of the colonized peoples.[6]

5. Uka, *Reading in African Traditional Religion*, 332.
6. p'Bitek, *African Religions*, 104.

The state of the indigenous people, as explained above, resulted in their religion being removed from the center and being shoved to the periphery. Alternatively, it was forced into underground exile. As Christianity in South Africa had become a state religion, Africans were denied any other form of religion on the basis that such religions were different from the dominating religion of the visitors (missionaries).

In 1994 political and religious domination of this nature began to change in South Africa. This was the year that the country obtained its independence from colonialism and apartheid. With the above in mind it can be seen that in the last few centuries the country travelled a journey from a mono-religious country that was based on racism, to a multi-faith state as declared by the Constitution. Section 15(1) and (2) of the Constitution states that everyone has a right to freedom of religion and freedom of conscience. Other sections of the Constitution which aim at bringing the varied religions, and facets of religious life, into equal status were instituted by the government so that all inequalities could be dealt with. Chapter 9 institutions (Section 185), are particularly important in this regard. One such institution, is the *Commission for the Promotion and Protection of the Rights of Cultural, Religious, and Linguistic Communities.* The vision for the establishment of this Commission was good but instead of promoting the under-representation of African Traditional Religions, it once again fell into the trap of 'Christendom' by focusing almost exclusively on African Initiated (Christian) churches.

Several international organizations have lobbied countries to commit themselves to the implementation religious rights and freedoms, since they believe that such freedoms are inherent natural rights for all individuals. However, it will be important for one to consider how these principles are enacted so that everyone in society has their religious views respected and has the opportunity for their voice to be heard.

The second question relates to the implementation of such principles and policies so as to avoid a repetition of the kinds of abuses that were perpetuated during colonialism and apartheid. How can the elements of suspicion be removed from those who were victims of conversion, when initiators and implementers of the processes of freedom of religion are the very same people who see these victims as their potential cultural and religious converts? How genuine is this process when those who were excluded happen to be the poor and are now invited by the rich, who belong to the missionary religions, this creating a significant imbalance of power in such interactions? This leads to another question, whether there will ever be equality of religions in South Africa as the poor still depend on the rich, and the rich open these dialogues with some terms and conditions, or with strings attached that favor their sponsorship? It is difficult for the voiceless to engage the rich on how they (the voiceless) would like to participate in the religious debates on freedom of religion and equality. This gets to the heart of the matter and is a clear example of the social, political, and economic complexities that thwart open an equal engagements on freedom of religion in South Africa.

During the term of the Truth and Reconciliation Commission (TRC) in South Africa, where the oppressors pleaded for forgiveness to those they oppressed, it was never seen as necessary that Christianity had to plead African Traditional Religion for forgiveness for the atrocities it performed against that religion. Instead the very oppressor religion was made to be the champion of this process, to take the lead in forcing their oppressed counterparts to plead for forgiveness. This implies that atrocities carried out by "the men of God" are Godly. They therefore do not need forgiveness because "that's what the Bible says." To this date there has not yet been a formal recognition of the evil that was perpetrated by these so-called people of God. Some would go so far as to argue that oppression is now more severe for African Traditional Religions than during colonialism. It is more severe because it hurts to be side-lined by your own people, who themselves accepted that religion is one of the tools that separated the indigenous people. Hence, one is either a convert, a pagan, or a heathen as classified by the religions that came to the Southern tip of Africa with the Christian missionaries. To add more salt to the wound, the very same clergy that were oppressive during the apartheid era have now become the new leaders in "democracy." They only shifted with governments (from apartheid to democracy). The same content and weapons used by the missionaries were brought forward to continue suppression. Yet it now comes clothed in religious regalia and not primarily along racial lines. There is now a shift from racial oppression to religious oppression. Oppression is oppression, it must not be condoned.

The voice that you are hearing today, one must bear in mind, is a voice from the indigenous spirituality of South Africa, a voice whose spirituality is still being suffocated by customary laws and spiritualities of other countries that came to South Africa.

It is liberating when the indigenous spirituality hears about freedom of belief, conscience, and equality for all. It raises some hopes that one day the dream for total liberation will be a reality, the dream of equality for all will no longer be just an unfulfilled promise, it will become a reality. A dream that one day all humans will be treated equally irrespective of race and spiritual origin. Yet, what is happening at present is that indigenous spiritualities find themselves as members of a spiritual diaspora. African Traditional

Religion adherents are in most cases analysed as being disingenuous when they insist on their independence.

Freedom of Religion and belief is a fundamental right for every individual irrespective of religion, race, class or geographical divide. Talking about freedom and equality within religion and amongst other religions is for now only an ideal. Instead, religion has become central in championing inequalities, discrimination, and the suppression of the other. The same champions of religious freedom and equality in many cases use their religious convictions as a central ingredient and a causal factor of religious suppression and alienation of the under-privileged. For the indigenous peoples to experience freedom, there are terms and conditions prescribed by the privileged religions in order for them to be given public space. Even in the media what one experiences is fake African Traditional Religions. What is presented comes from a point of departure where Judeo/Christian religions sponsors dictate what they want and not what actually happens in these communities. Because African Traditional Religion does not have economic means to express its own practices in an unfettered and authentic manner, they have to endure watching the mockery of their religion by other people. We hope that one day the world will be interested to hear how the practitioners would like to be promoted and be part of the interfaith debates. Unfortunately, politicians are interested in numbers so no one can rely on them, they are like chameleons.

The above introduction indicates that though religion is a fundamental right for each individual who feels entitled to it, the practicality of attaining freedom of religion by every citizen has proven to be near impossible to achieve. This is caused by different countries being governed by the Constitutions that have to conform to the dictates of the international laws and politics. These seem to perpetuate the social and religious domination of majority cultural and religious groupings over historically subjugated religions. Each country is obliged to develop policies that are to be in line with the Constitution of that particular country but many of them have failed to consider the prospect of Freedom of Religion and equality for all, in spite of religious freedom being enshrined in their respective Constitutions, in theory at least. It is in the formulation of the Constitutions and policies where the oversight of religious freedom and equality becomes conspicuous. Also, in the drafting of policies there are serious gaps and flaws that are not considered as the causes of further denial of religious freedom and equality.

This chapter will try and analyse these inequalities by judging from the experience of the underprivileged and the marginalised religious affiliations and also from the perspective of indigenous spirituality. Few policies in support of these views will be used in this chapter. Today it is unfortunate that politics, economic class, and mental racism are playing a major role in propelling religious suppression and inequalities within and from outside.

The fact of the matter is that the religion of the wealthy, who are able to attract the needs of the underprivileged, always dictates on how freedom of religion should be defined and upon which guidelines it should be based. As religious equality can never be reached within one country because of inherent inequalities, it is doubtful that there could be equality of religions in any state where there are inequalities amongst religious groupings.

As the laws that govern countries are not necessarily based on the indigenous religious practices and doctrines of those respective countries; there are certain limitations in practicing certain religions freely. In countries where there are people practicing different religions, equality is only an ideal as there is a tendency to quantify and politicise religious participation without unpacking the causal factors of some groupings being numerically stronger than others. The chapter will also try to evaluate the possibilities within which religious practitioners of different religions could stay together in freedom without jeopardizing those who are different from themselves. Empirical evidence could be cited on how freedom of religion and equality disadvantage the spiritual reality of the poor, and how religion has resulted into mental and spiritual racism.

When South Africa was liberated, the oppressed had many expectations that they 'dreamt' would give rise to holistic liberation. The religious and culturally suppressed expected that they:

- would be allowed to be honest and not to pretend to belong to 'recognized' cultures and religions;
- would not be forced to explain the authenticity of their religious practices to the Black leadership of the country;
- would come out of the spiritual cocoon, into which they were forcefully driven by colonialism and apartheid, without fear of marginalization;
- would be free to define themselves and not to be defined by people of other faiths;
- would be free to represent themselves and not to be represented by people of other faiths;
- would be free from indoctrination, spiritual denial and harassment;
- would be included in all interfaith debates without any strings attached.

What actually happened is the opposite, the voiceless are more silenced if they do not know the line that is if they fight for their independence and not to allow Black Christians to be the spokespersons of African Traditional Religion. Simon S. Maimela puts it right when he says:

> For what happened during the process of independence was merely a replacement of one form of oppression by another, that is, a substitution of a European oppressor for an African oppressor. Consequently, if Africans are to experience authentic liberation, they must go beyond replacing one oppressor by another—oppressive powers must themselves be destroyed.[7]

AFRICAN TRADITIONAL RELIGION AND FREEDOM OF RELIGION

The question that needs to be asked is how far are the rights of the indigenous cultural, religious and linguistic communities promoted and protected in this present dispensation? The answer is simple; though the Constitution may appear liberating, the truth is that the indigenous religion is still trampled upon by the religions that were privileged in the past. This situation still exposes the indigenous religion to still suffer from the very same pain, namely, that of being defined from an outside perspective by the very same Black people in this democracy.

The South African government does not take into consideration the fact that the religions that are practically recognized, even in formal government documents, are those that came to Southern Africa in the last 400 years. Krüger, Lubbe, and Steyn summarize the dates at which the religions in discussion came as follows:

- Christianity in 1652
- Buddhism in 1860
- Hinduism in 1860 (16)
- Judaism in 1804
- Islam in 1658
- Bahai Faith in 1911.[8]

The approaches to religious freedom by the government are very selective. Their approach implies the inclusion of the other Ibrahamic faiths (Islam and Judaism) in the status quo of Christianity, and also the religions of the East and Far East. There are no genuine discussions with African Traditional Religion because Black Christians themselves claim that no Black

---

7. Maimela, *Culture, Religion, and Liberation*, 4.
8. Krüger et al., *Human Search for Meaning*, 14–16.

person could claim that she or he is not a Christian since they have attended Western schooling. This mentality is the same as explained earlier by Philip Mayer namely, that Christianity and Western schooling are regarded as synonymous.[9] That is why one would wonder why the Department of Police, for example, has a Hindu Chaplain yet there are very few Hindus in the country, far less than adherents of African Traditional Religions. Yet, there is no African Traditional Religion Chaplain. Wande Abimbola has also noticed the exclusion of African Traditional Religion in interfaith discussions. Abimbola also noticed the imbalances found in the discussions between these self-imposed 'people of God' in Africa and the indigenous peoples of the land and he argues as follows:

> The dialogues that the Christian missions have staged so far have been half-heated and insincere. To start with, the dialogues have been held only with Islam and Judaism for the most part. Sometimes, these dialogues have included the Buddhists and the Hindu religions and some other religions of the Far East. When they included African indigenous religion at all, Christian evangelists often represent them by masquerading as scholars or practitioners of so-called African Traditional Religion (ATR).[10]

Abimbola further makes an analogy to emphasize the seriousness of these assumed dialogues in an African land by foreigners by stating the following:

> These past dialogues can be likened to an attempt by a person who wants to hold consultations with members of his households, but who deliberately neglects some members of that household, either because he does not like them or perhaps because he wishes they were dead or lost.[11]

Even today when one looks at the government calendars, only the holidays of these visitor religions appear in all government calendars. An example could be cited from the 2017 *Diary* published by the "Republic of South Africa" only the following religions appear under the heading "Environmental Calendar & Religious Holy Days":

- Bahai Faith's Holy days
- Christian Holy Days
- Hindu Festivals
- Islamic Holy Days

9. Mayer, *Townsmen or Tribesmen*, 29.

10. Abimbola, "African Traditional Religions," 17.

11. Abimbola, "African Traditional Religions," 17.

- Jewish Holy Days.[12]

DEPARTMENT OF DEFENSE

Icamagu Heritage Institute has been flooded with requests from some military members to intervene because of the deliberate and continuous exclusion of African Traditional Religion's code in the Departmental forms reflecting religious affiliation. These codes help the department to know how many soldiers belong to a particular denomination or a particular religion. This declaration to a particular religious affiliation helps the individual in many instances like counselling, or being buried in military custom, by a Chaplain who belongs to one's religion. When it comes to African Traditional Religion, there is a shift from moving African Traditional Religion from the periphery to the underarm of Christianity. Though there are definitely less Hindus, Muslims and Jews than African Traditional Religion adherents in South Africa, there are Chaplains for these minority religions but no African Traditional Religion Chaplains. Several requests to the departments fall on deaf ears. This is clearly an indication that we are sold by our own people, our own comrades.

DEPARTMENT OF EDUCATION

The government, during the time of the late Professor Kader Asmal, as the national minister of Education, formulated a "Policy on Religion in Education." This policy was formulated to cater for all students in South African schools. Section 63 and 64 of the "Policy on Religion in Education" states the following:

> A school assembly has the potential for affirming and celebrating unity in diversity, and should be used for this purpose. Public schools may not violate the religious freedom of pupils and teachers by imposing religious uniformity on a religiously diverse school population in school assemblies. Where a religious observance is included in a school assembly, pupils may be excused on grounds of conscience from attending a religious observance component, and equitable arrangements must be made for these pupils.
>
> Since the state is not a religious organization, theological body, or inter-faith forum, the state cannot allow unfair access to the use of its resources to propagate any particular religion or religions. The state must maintain parity of esteem with respect

12. South African Government. "Public Holidays in South Africa."

to religion, religious or secular beliefs in all of its public institutions, including its public schools.[13]

The reality in Black schools are operating contrary to the above two sections. They still adhere to the apartheid religious education in schools
something different from former Model C schools which were basically for
White children. There are options that are suggested by the policy but in
Black schools the old assemblies are still used. One teacher even told me
that pupils are punished by teachers if they do not close their eyes when
singing the Christian Lord's prayer.

The subject, Life Orientation, is deeply insulting to African Traditional
Religions. This undermines any confidence in African Traditional Religion
among school going children. African Traditional Religion is either omit-
ted by some authors[14] or devalued by being ranked far below all other
religions that came into the country.[15] The content on African Traditional
Religion presented by W. Buys for instance is confusing. In fact, it looks like
the author only included the religion to satisfy government requirements.
The author seems not to be interested in knowing the proper name of the
religion as there are different, and even confusing names (see the italicized
letters), some are in lower case letters while others are written in upper case
letters; "*T*raditional *A*frican *R*eligion," or "*T*raditional African religions," or
"*t*raditional *A*frican *r*eligion," or "*A*frican *t*raditional *r*eligion." When writing about African Traditional Religion symbols he writes as follows:

> Spiritual symbols are simple and easily missed. A green twig
> hanging above the door of a hut is often a sign that the forefa-
> thers are present. The best-known symbol of traditional African
> religion is probably the clay pot (associated with inyangas) and
> the ritual sacred spear.[16]

The above information is all incorrect and is demeaning. Some readers
would even doubt the mental state of the practitioners of the religion as
explained by Buys. One must understand that the information above is at
Grade 7 leaner level. How does one expect such a pupil to understand and
be proud of such content? Buys seems to show a disregard for a respectful
display of multi-faith issues in a normal class of learners from a diverse
society, learners who are expected to respect each other.

---

13. "Policy on Religion in Education," 23.

14. Matthee and Swanepoel, *Life Orientation for Today*.

15. Buys, *Exciting Life Orientation*.

16. Buys, *Exciting Life Orientation*, 70.

As long as the Education Department runs parallel with promoting the country's morality and is suppressing the country's indigenous values there could never be peace in the country. The law of the land based on ancestral teachings of its people at least had a way of prescribing the norms and values so that there is tolerance and acceptance among people living in one community. The curriculum needs to be written in a manner that promotes the law of the land and in so doing does not import foreign laws that are sometimes contradictory of the indigenous way of life.

PROMOTION OF SYNCRETISM

Instead of promoting independence of African Traditional Religion the Black leadership of South Africa has no shame to publicly parade with the promotion of syncretism as a defining factor of Black affiliation in religion. As Blacks were forced to live in two worlds which are an African world during the week and then a Judeo-Christian world on Saturday and Sunday, they now force everybody to be part of that confusion. There is no promotion of indigenous religion unless it agrees to be an exclusive culture or sangoma (diviner) or one of the African Initiated Churches. African Traditional Religion is thrown in the stream to swim or sink unless it agrees to exist at the 'mercy' or sympathies of its Black clergy. In other words, African Traditional Religion is in underground spiritual exile and the Black leadership has now become the spokespersons of the White church.

When talking about African Traditional Religion, Black Christians always speak in the third person plural. The very same people who claim to recognize African Traditional Religion as their religion, even though they are Christians, always speak of African Traditional Religion in the past tense. Yet the true practitioners always use the present tense because it is the religion that they practice in this present dispensation. These 'stand on the fence' practitioners like to refer to the religion as this worldly and as an exclusive culture.

As said earlier the stand of these African opportunists is causing more harm to the African identity. These two tongued practitioners are in their homes syncretistic (both African Traditional Religion and Christian) and on Sunday they claim to be Christian. In order to justify their confusion they use the Judeo-Christian Bible where they tell African Traditional Religion practitioners that *uThixo uthi kuqala okwenyama kugqibele okomoya,* (God says that it's flesh first then the spiritual). They cite from Paul's first letter to the Corinthians (1 Cor 15:46) where he said "But it is not the spiritual that is first, but the physical, and then the spiritual." As Africans who live in Africa, how can they use Paul's letter to the people of Corinth in Europe and the Middle East to justify their confusion in the furthest part of Africa (South Africa)? According to their limited analysis of what we call African Traditional Religion they equate the religion as something that is relevant in this life, that is, with the flesh; and what was brought to them by missionaries, that is Christianity; which they interpret as of the spirit and is heavenly, that is why to them God is Christian. This is an insult to their forebears who died before Christianity came into this country and those who died without conversion to this new religion as to them it means that they died without the spiritual aspect.

Those who are vocal and are claiming to be representatives of African Traditional Religion are the nominal Christians, the syncretic group.

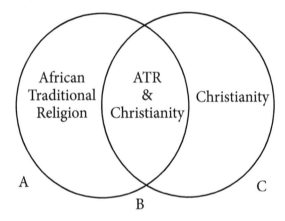

Figure 2: Religious Affiliations of Black People in South Africa.

The above diagram is an example of the religious affiliation of Black people in South Africa. Its aim is to give a mental picture and dispute the claim that the majority of Black people in South Africa are Christians. A represents the African Traditional Religion faith specific group, B representing the two-tongued group who are comfortable with practicing rituals for their ancestors while also going to church on Sunday for their 'spirituality,' and C represents Christianity as a faith specific group.[17] If the subset (B group) belongs to both A and B how can one classify them as Christians?

If that is the case where does one put the religious affiliation of group B if religion is defined from a phenomenological approach. A phenomenological approach defines religion as a phenomenon with the following aspects:

1. Myth

2. Personal

17. Mndende, *Tears of Distress*, 9.

3. Social

4. Doctrinal

5. Ritual

6. Ethical

7. Life after death

If group B believes in the dualistic nature of each of the above, that is in practicing both African Traditional Religion and Christian aspects at the same time, where would they be classified since they have one foot in A and the other in B? It would therefore be better that they represent African Christianity.

The other deliberate inaccuracy and misleading tendency which is due to ignorance by some practitioners is the misinterpretation of Matthew 5:17. Where Jesus is cited as saying, "Do not think that I have come to abolish the law or the prophets; I have come not to abolish but to fulfil," it is very much distorted to justify syncretism. This verse is frequently used to justify the centrality of ancestors in the practice of Rituals, as in the Rites of passage, and to be a Christian at the same time. In indigenous languages the verse is misinterpreted as if Jesus was saying, *andizanga kuchitha amasiko ndizokuwazalisekisa* (I have not come to abolish rituals, I have come to fulfil them).

Rituals are performed by clan members and the community as a collective for individuals and also addressing ancestors. During each ritual performance there is a central belief that ancestors, as intermediaries between the living and the Creator, must indicate that they have accepted the ritual. The indication of acceptance in the Xhosa community is the bleating of a goat or bellowing of an ox before it is slaughtered. That belief cuts across Christians and African Traditional Religion adherents and both groups are concerned if it shows some signs of rejection and the animal is not slaughtered until the reason is known. In the church congregants participate in the Eucharist and with African Traditional Religion the Holy Communion is called *umoshwamo* which is the first taste of the members of that particular clan. The B group believes in ancestors and Jesus; they also claim to be healed by the blood of a sacrificial animal and also by the blood of Jesus.

When the African Traditional Religion faith specific group claims its own space independent of the nominal Christians, they are denied that space and are labelled unrealistic. This claim of being unrealistic is based on the fact that the syncretic group, which is unfortunately in the political leadership, always claim that they do not see any contradictions in practicing two religions which in effect heal them. On the other hand, the African

Traditional Religion faith specific does not have any problem with the syncretic group's beliefs but require to be given its own space as a group of indigenous practitioners who do not practice Christianity. The request for independence is not that it is impossible because it is the same space that is easily given to other faiths like Hinduism, Islam, Judaism, Bahai, and even Rastafarianism. If racism can be directly related to Christian religious bigotry, surely it would give sense that persons who hold to indigenous faiths would want to be liberated from Christianity.

One other aspect of demeaning the spirituality of African Traditional Religion, more especially in interfaith debates, is the insistence of the inclusion of witchcraft as one of the aspects of African Traditional Religion, as if witchcraft is not a universal phenomenon. Last but not least, the colonial perception among Black Christians that portrays God as a Christian will take decades to make them realise that they are still captured by colonial thinking and categories of thought. To the dualists by explaining that God is above all religions is blasphemous as they equate God with the Christian religion. Under such circumstances, how can one even start to think that colonialism has gone and there is freedom of religion?

It is a positive and constructive approach that the world focuses on international human rights. What is lacking is the correct form of implementation so that these initiatives should heal wounds and not to scratch them to bleed again. How does one justify for instance the shift from exclusion of African Traditional Religion to further distortions by the very same people who oppressed it? As explained earlier for example the exclusion of African Traditional Religion category in the census forms during the colonial period, what happens in this democracy is once again opening wounds of African Traditional Religion adherents. Statistics South Africa's 2015 *General Household Survey* has a confusing categorization of religious affiliation named "Ancestral, tribal, animist or other traditional African religions."[18] How can one still write about animist or ancestral religion in the twenty-first century if colonialism had been defeated? This shows that amongst religions there are some that are seen as holier than other religions, according to the authors of these reports, and if so there is no freedom, and then there is no equality. The positive thing is that the government has now recognized that African Traditional Religion exists in South Africa, unlike in the colonial period, but what is still demeaning is to use the terms that are foreign and insulting to the groups that are being referred to.

The governments should give the voiceless and the downtrodden the space to speak for themselves and open up dialogues that will be on

18. *General Household Survey*, 4.

a horizontal level and not a top down approach because the downtrodden have not got access to resources.

As long as the government is claiming to be religious neutral, or impartial, but is in a campaign to promote Christianity only, we cannot speak of freedom of religion in South Africa. No religion should be made to be an appendage of another religion as that denies the rights and freedoms of the subordinated religion. Denial will also lead to silencing of the suppressed in a democratic society. Until African Traditional Religion is liberated from its own place of birth, no one can talk about freedom, equality and democracy in South Africa. No one can talk about a loving and a liberating God while marginalizing and suppressing others.

Lastly, as long as African Traditional Religion is still in chains its rights and freedom are still violated. Racism and religious discrimination are two sides of the same coin. Africans fought against racial oppression but they took all the tools used by Whites to oppress Black people and have imposed them over their own indigenous beliefs and practices. Black South Africans are now, sadly, agents of religious discrimination.[19]

BIBLIOGRAPHY

Abimbola, Wande. "African Traditional Religions and Interfaith Dialogue." In *Changing the Present, Dreaming the Future: A Critical Moment in Interreligious Dialogue*, edited by Hans Ucko, et al., 16–21. Geneva: World Council of Churches, 2006.

Ayliff, John. *History of AbaMbo*. Butterworth: Gazette, 1912.

Buys, W. *Exciting Life Orientation, Grade 7*. Cape Town: Nasou Via Afrika, 2005.

Bitek, Otek. *African Religions in Western Scholarship*. Kampala: East African Literature Bureau, 1970.

Chidester David. *Savage Systems: Colonialism and Comparative Religion in Southern Africa*. Cape Town: University of Cape Town Press. 1996.

Department of Education, Republic of South Africa. "National Policy on Religion and Education." *Government Gazette* 459.25459 (2003). Online. https://synapses.co.za/uploads/2009/09/National-religion-policy.pdf.

Dickens, Sybil Maureen. "Western Influence on the Zulu System of Personal Names." MA thesis, Rhodes University, 1985.

Krüger, J. S., et al. *The Human Search for Meaning: A Multireligious Introduction to the Religions of Humankind*. Pretoria: Van Schaik, 2009.

Maimela, Simon S. *Culture, Religion, and Liberation*. Pretoria: EATWOT, 1994.

Makgoba, M. W. "Patterns of African Thought: A Critical Analysis." In *Faith, Science, and African Culture: African Cosmology and Africa's Contribution to Science*, edited by C. W. Du Toit, 27–32. Pretoria: Unisa, 1998.

Matthee, S., and P. Swanepoel. *Life Orientation for Today*. Johannesburg: Vivilia, 2004.

Mayer, Philip. *Townsmen or Tribesmen: Conservatism and the Process of Urbanization in a South African City*. Cape Town: Oxford University Press, 1961.

19. Mndende, *Flying with Clipped Wings*, 105.

Mndende, Nokuzola. *Flying with Clipped Wings: Under the Sword of Proselytization in a Secular State*. Dutywa: Icamagu Institute, 2016.

———. *Tears of Distress: Voices of a Denied Spirituality in a Democratic South Africa*. Dutywa: Icamagu Institute, 2009.

South African Government. "Public Holidays in South Africa." Online. https://www.gov.za/about-sa/public-holidays.

Statistics South Africa. *General Household Survey 2015*. Statistical Release P0318. Pretoria: Statistics South Africa, 2016. Online. http://www.statssa.gov.za/publications/P0318/P03182015.pdf.

Uka, E. M. *Reading in African Traditional Religion*. Bern: Peter Lang, 1991.

9

Building Bridges or Walls?

Human Rights and Religious Freedom:
A South African History

SELINA PALM

The relationships between human rights and religion in South Africa are fraught with historical ambiguity. Selected Christian doctrines have been, and are still, used here by some to undergird a narrow understanding of religious freedom that denied emerging claims of universal human rights as of the Devil. However, an alternative trajectory exists where Christian leaders and theologians (often alongside those of other faiths) employed their religious freedom, not to deny universal human rights but to actively struggle for their realisation as a central part of public Christian witness. This latter tradition reflects what have been termed "minority prophetic voices" for human rights, existing within multiple religious traditions and in need of reclaiming today.[1] This chapter traces this place-based engagement between human rights and Christian faith in the South African context to suggest that whether religious identity is defined narrowly against human rights or in synergy and interdependence with its claims will shape the public witness of faith communities here today.

---

1. Witte, "Introduction."

SOUTH AFRICAN CHURCHES—
FOR OR AGAINST HUMAN RIGHTS?

Social attitudes statistics show that over 80 percent of South Africans identify as active Christians with high unquestioned beliefs in God, 77 percent seeing Jesus as "the solution to all the world's problems" and a strong preference towards literalist interpretations of sacred texts.[2] Christian churches still form one of the most trusted institutions in the country, higher than the police, law courts or government, making them an important social factor for enabling change.[3] Christianity has also historically held a privileged position in relation to the state with a Christian Constitution in place until the 1990s. Despite the formal separation between church and state today, religion and public life often remain intertwined with South Africa seen as a religiously neutral rather than a secular state.[4]

Christianity has played an ambiguous public role in South African society historically, entwined with the discourses of civilisation, colonialism and commerce, and often giving a doctrinal overlay of moral purpose to ideologies of empire, white supremacy and apartheid. Scholars note that theologised missions of conquest have often misshaped churches here into legitimating ideological tools for the status quo who surrender their prophetic task and spurn talk of universal human rights as "the work of the Devil."[5] However, at the same time, other South African Christian faith leaders such as Beyers Naudé, Allen Boesak, Frank Chicane, and Desmond Tutu, took up protest roles against this theological abuse to struggle for human rights as public acts of Christian witness, grounded in local theologies for human rights.[6] Beyond these two paradoxical extremes were thousands of racially segregated churches in which most ordinary South Africans sat weekly. Some saw human rights involvement as an inappropriate socio-politicisation of the church and argued it should focus on a spiritual mission leaving socio-political reconstruction to other stakeholders. Others called churches to maintain a post-apartheid public presence on implementing human rights as part of a wider commitment to justice.[7]

Twenty years into South Africa's new constitutional era, while the gap between human rights rhetoric and practice remains, concerning the public

2. Rule and Mncwango, "Christianity in South Africa."

3. Schoeman, "South Africa Religious Demography," 5.

4. Green and Van Der Vyver, "Foundations and Future of Law," 337.

5. Villa-Vicencio, *Theology of Reconstruction*, 19.

6. De Gruchy, *Church Struggle*. See also Nolan, *God in South Africa*.

7. Smit, "Revisioning through Reconstruction." 51. See also Villa-Vicencio, *Theology of Reconstruction*.

prophetic voices of churches seem less prominent on human rights than in the struggle years. Reversals are even being seen with some churches using claims of religious freedom not to progress human rights struggles but to claim exceptional status from them on issues of gender equality, gay rights, corporal punishment,[8] child education and cultural practices.[9] Concerns have also been raised regarding the rise of so-called New Religious Movements and their abuse of power over congregants.[10] Many church leaders are seen to be "missing the opportunity to challenge entrenched perceptions and practices contrary to a human rights culture based on the dignity of all human beings."[11] South African public theologian Dirk Smit notes that in the new dispensation, Christians and churches may speak up for their own rights, but are far less likely to speak up publicly for the rights of others.[12] At the same time, South African Anglican Archbishop Thabo Makgoba suggests that the shared struggle to protect a human rights culture is "perhaps the most challenging one confronting us today" requiring a courageous taking of responsibility by the next generation to make the realisation of rights a reality for all[13] and has embodied this from his pulpit. It is historically unquestionable that churches can perpetuate dominating dynamics and underlying theological justifications for abusive social patterns, creating a dangerous atmosphere of unquestioned authority. However, history also suggests that they can also engage difficult ethical topics in concrete ways locally in solidarity with those who are right-less. Feminist theologians in South Africa have long insisted that the contradictory relationship between human rights and religion here cannot be ignored and point to human dignity as at the heart of both the Constitution and a Christian understanding of being human, offering common ground on which to build.[14]

An empirical study of the link between human rights and religious attitudes in post-apartheid South Africa concludes that religious ideas and institutions still have a significant impact on a post-apartheid young generation's attitudes to human rights.[15] Assessments of Christian attitudes to God, evil, salvation, Jesus and other religions showed that the theology

8. Palm, "Church Outrage."

9. Concerning practices in unregulated churches led to a formal investigation by the Commission for Religious Freedom in 2015. This points to ongoing tensions between religious freedom and constitutional values here.

10. Pretorius, "Religious Cults, Religious Leaders."

11. Pillay, "Solidarity in Suffering," 142.

12. Smit, "On the Impact of the Church," 69.

13. Makgoba, "New Struggle to Protect."

14. Ackermann, "Freedom of Religion."

15. van der Ven et al., *Is There a God of Human Rights?*

embraced had correlations to high school students' human rights attitudes. It concludes that the task of embedding theologies for human rights into churches has not taken place consistently. Ecclesial attitudes arguably shape individual views on human rights in both positive and negative ways showing that churches still hold a critical role in developing the attitudes which "sit at the heart of building a human rights culture."[16] However, it notes that the post-apartheid theological relationship between Christianity and human rights remains marked by a "haze of ambivalence"[17] which mitigates against positive institutional action by most churches for concrete human rights realisation.

A recent backlash by a number of vocal conservative religious leaders and institutions employs the constitutional language of "religious freedom" narrowly to claim exceptional status from wider human rights claims, rather than to advocate for their realisation. This is demonstrated by the organization "Freedom of Religion South Africa."[18] Recently it has mounted legal challenges against constitutional decisions around human rights including same sex relationships, corporal punishment of children, gender equality and religious education. In so doing, it explicitly perpetuates a literalist approach to Scripture underpinned by multiple God-ordained hierarchies of domination and submission. Its theological arguments using some rights (e.g., parental) over others bear similarities to those used to defend slavery, colonialism and apartheid, whilst claiming to stand in the prophetic tradition of challenging unjust laws. A 2016 press statement by one of its church members in negative response to recent constitutional shifts on the corporal punishment of children states,

> Holy Scripture has clear instructions on the discipline of children . . . including spanking. . . . It is outrageous to propose spanking as administered by loving Christian parents committed to the best interest and welfare of their children. . . . State legislation forbidding this would be a direct rejection of biblical authority. . . . We must obey God rather than men.[19]

This approach taken against human rights for all in the name of a religious freedom giving rights only to some is at clear odds with other Christian theologians and faith leaders in South Africa, who instead employ their religious freedom to call churches and people of faith forwards into progressive social

16. van der Ven et al., *Is There a God of Human Rights?*, 81.

17. van der Ven et al., *Is There a God of Human Rights?*, 583.

18. For more on this particular organization and its various press releases on human rights, see FORSA, "Welcome!"

19. Baptist Union of Southern Africa, "Press Release."

action on human rights, in the light of endemically high levels of family violence, abuse of women and children and violence against LGBTIQ+ persons in contemporary South Africa.[20] A call for careful contextual engagement with sacred texts in the light of their implications for concrete human bodies, stands in contrast to a return to hierarchical theologies often inherited from a chequered religious past. I suggest that this reflects an internal crisis of religious freedom itself and that a narrow approach to religious freedom as utilised against other human rights needs to be set within the wider historically troubled relationship between religion and human rights in South Africa. Its history has also nurtured a broader understanding of religious freedom that is deeply committed to a holistic, liberational understanding of human rights that goes beyond the law to form a people-centerd, moral-spiritual imperative from below. Which type of religious freedom is embraced by churches today has significant implications for Christian public witness on human rights. I suggest that these present dilemmas are shaped by a complex past to which detailed attention must be paid.

RELIGION AND HUMAN RIGHTS—
A GLOBALLY TROUBLED RELATIONSHIP

This contested reality in contemporary South Africa reflects what some theologians have termed a globally "troubled relationship" between Christianity and human rights today, where "many Christians define their theologies in a way that leads them to both misinterpret and reject rights talk,"[21] a theme receiving renewed attention worldwide. Whilst a global theological shift was made in the 1970s in the formal relationship of many churches to the human rights movement, local relationships between these two ideas remain contested today.[22] Recently some human rights scholars have called for more practical engagement with religious ideas, as a gap in the human rights movement[23] whilst social ethicists ask religion to "keep faith" with human rights in ways that take note of feminist and post-colonial critiques to help rearticulate its contours for a new era.[24] Despite the need to bridge this potentially widening gap between religion and human rights,[25] some dissenting religious voices still claim that these remain competing ideologies that preclude each other in an irreconcilable conflict, viewing human

20. West et al., "When Faith Does Violence."
21. Wolterstorff, *Hearing the Call*, 148.
22. Shepherd, *Christianity and Human Rights*, xxvi.
23. Cox, "Human Rights," 1.
24. Hogan, *Keeping Faith with Human Rights*, 5.
25. Williams, *Faith in the Public Square*, 160–75.

rights as "godless secular values" that are destroying society and creating a culture of entitlement.[26] This positions human rights as a contradiction of the theological principle of human dependence on God, a view remaining influential within the wider African continent today.[27] Influential Western theologians such as Stanley Hauerwas can reinforce this rights-scepticism by polarizing rights and virtues and suggesting that Christians are to remain uninvolved in the politics of society.[28] In contrast, others seek to ground human rights essentially in Western Christianity, highlighting the significant role of Christians in their historical development[29] and even suggesting that the idea may be incoherent if removed from its Christian roots.[30] While these voices add important plurality to the prevalent idea of human rights as a secular ideology, they can unwittingly mitigate against building an overlapping consensus that acknowledges multiple foundations. In South Africa, this may cause understandable suspicion regarding the imposition of human rights on other traditions, especially if it is positioned as a white, western, civilizing import.[31]

Exploring South Africa's historical relationship between human rights and religion may benefit from a more pragmatic, empirical lens than either of the above. Scholars such as Abdullahi An-Na'im from Sudan and John Witte from North America point to emerging liberating hermeneutics for human rights within all faith traditions, that begin with confession, proceed with suspicion, pay attention to history and engage with interdisciplinarity.[32] This approach builds congruencies between religious traditions and human rights discourse without grounding human rights essentially in only one faith tradition.[33] It sees religions as respected dialogue partners but not as the sole ground of human rights, and recovers prophetic voices of dissent within faith traditions to help build a human rights culture from below. This can play a role in nurturing internal religious legitimacy for human rights

---

26. Phillips, "Human Rights," 115–7.

27. Atiemo, *Religion and the Inculturation of Human Rights*.

28. Hauerwas, *Community of Character*, 74. However, in recent response to critics, he has articulated his skeptical position further on human rights. See Hauerwas, "How to Think Theologically about Rights." However, he reflects a concerning tendency to place responsibility over rights similar to those employed problematically in early South African apartheid discourses of "responsible trusteeship."

29. Nurser, *For All Peoples and All Nations*.

30. Perry, *Towards a Theory of Human Rights*, 12.

31. Mutua, *Human Rights*, 20. See also Huber, "Human Rights and Globalization."

32. Witte, "Introduction," 13.

33. An-Na'im, "Synergy and Interdependence," 20.

in South Africa's still emerging democracy.[34] Theologies for human rights emerged here historically in minority protest voices held against the larger religious establishment. Reclaiming this complex faith history may nurture contemporary action to realise human rights in the hearts, minds and lives of people here today.

Over the last few decades, a number of scholars have traced multiple genealogies of the idea of human rights, seen not just as abstract givens but as emerging historically in different contexts.[35] Southern histories are however often "missing"[36] with a human rights narrative still dominated by the West, despite South Africa being viewed by many as one of the most successful historical human rights struggles of the twentieth century.[37] Its complex history on human rights and the ambivalent role of religion may offer an important contribution. According to historian Saul Dubow, in South Africa, rights discourse itself strongly resists a single history with both liberating and abusive uses.[38] Its story of many stories can help re-dress West-centric over-simplified ways in which the intellectual history of human rights is often written,[39] helping human rights to take more sustainable root within African societies. Nigerian historian Bonny Ibhawoh emphasizes that the association of human rights with Western world views in the public imagination to cease if they are to become "the heritage of all humankind." developed, struggled for and won by people in all societies.[40] It is aspects of this South African history that offer a validity from below, not merely imposed from above.

SOUTH AFRICA: A FAITH-SHAPED HUMAN RIGHTS GENEALOGY

Dubow notes that a rights-resisting Protestant Christianity came with the 1862 settler ships as a by-product of European commerce, one reacting against liberalizing trends elsewhere and also entwining race and religion. Emerging rights discourse often became a bargaining chip between colonial powers, one tied to religious ideology. The Dutch concept of *rechten van der mensch* in the early 1800s, was crushed by a British administration in favor of a discourse of colonial citizenship that took root over that of common

34. Palm, "Liberating Human Rights?," 104.

35. See Hunt, *Inventing Human Rights.*

36. Stammers, "Hidden Actors."

37. Mutua, *Human Rights,* 126.

38. Dubow, *South African Struggle,* 11.

39. Dubow, *South African Struggle,* 16.

40. Ibhawoh, *Imperialism and Human Rights,* 27.

humanity.[41] With the 1799 British occupation, came the rise of missionary humanitarianism. John Phillips was one missionary recorded as taking a strong stand on equal relations between black and white people, championing the rights of black Africans against those who saw South Africa as "white man's country."[42] Phillips was instrumental in forming Ordinance 50 in 1828, named by Dubow as the "earliest human rights document on African soil" and pioneering calls for African rights to land, labour and the law. It introduced the idea of common personhood across race and culture, grounded in both Christian faith and natural law but Dubow notes that this lost out historically to a drive for the rights of whites."[43]

A lesson can be learned here about the early ambivalent use of rights talk to both bolster legal exploitation and to protest it in the name of common personhood, entangled from the start in theological narratives about who was fully human. Phillips is one early minority protest voice within Christian tradition, theologically challenging the use of religion to undergird rights abuse and sent home as a result. Arguments on the gospel's social implications continued as colonial powers trekked inwards where the church remained theologically divided over rights and placed limits through heresy trials on the religious freedom of its congregants and clergy.[44]

As South Africa entered the twentieth century, two discourses developed on human rights.[45] White supremacy and minority rights were formally reinforced through the 1910 Union as the legal, social and moral norm, removing even small rights-gains made by African populations.[46] Land Acts drove dispossession and a segregationist approach led to the 1948 election of the National Party with a narrative of South Africa as a chosen land for whites, underpinned by a theology.[47] Church and state formed a conservative formal alliance in the name of a Christianity that embraced a white trusteeship model of duties and rejected the language of rights for all.[48]

---

41. Dubow, *South African Struggle*, 21–23.

42. De Gruchy, *Church Struggle*; Dubow, *South African Struggle*, 25–32.

43. Dubow, *South African Struggle*, 30.

44. See De Gruchy, *Church Struggle*, for more detail on this historical contestation in the churches.

45. Dubow, *South African Struggle*, 50. Human rights were tied to race, entrenching hierarchical dignity.

46. For more on the battles around removal of voting rights and other "prior rights," see Cameron, *Justice*, 19–20.

47. Dubow, *South African Struggle*, 45. See also De Gruchy, *Church Struggle*, 27–36.

48. Dubow, *South African Struggle*, 60.

It is well known that Reformed theologians provided politicians with theological backing for the apartheid ideology for many years. Many believed that it was the preordained will of God that whites, who represented the "only true" religion and civilization, had to colonize Southern Africa three hundred years ago to evangelize its people.[49]

At the same time, the emerging African National Congress (ANC) utilised a universal human rights discourse from early on. Its 1912 formation was grounded in protest against the racist Union to articulate a vision of universal suffrage and human dignity for all[50] standing in the common personhood tradition of Ordinance 50. ANC founder Pixley ka Seme spoke of cooperation "not just with kith and kin . . . but with all peoples and with all life" emphasizing the right to be the same and the right to be different as "children of one household who must learn to live together."[51] The ANC used human rights as a practical, decolonizing language of protest, calling in 1923 for a Bill of Rights on land, law and political rights as a "substantial statement of human rights grounded in the claims of African humanity, over and against the reigning and exclusivist ideology of the times."[52] It offered a theological counter-claim to the Afrikaner Christian narrative, by pointing out that "sons of this earth have God-given right to ownership of land, to be contributors and to secure a right to equality."[53] The ANC formally accepted a progressive Bill of Rights in 1943, predominantly drafted by black African struggle leaders. This lesson counters critiques of human rights as merely an abstract list hegemonically decided by an elite group of Western allies in 1948 and imposed down on the rest. Human rights were asserted earlier in South Africa within a post-colonial vision and in concrete protest of systemic unjust treatment made from the bottom-up.

By 1948, South Africa's position on human rights was divided. Formally, universal human rights were being systematically disregarded in favor of minority group rights with South Africa one of only 8 countries to abstain from endorsing the Universal Declaration on Human Rights (UDHR). Informally however, a grassroots protest language on human rights was developing in concrete, holistic and vibrant ways. Religion and politics had combined in a formal alliance against universal human rights,

---

49. Du Toit, "Religious Freedoms."

50. See Asmal et al., *Legacy of Freedom,* which reproduces primary historical sources of the day.

51. Cited in Asmal et al., *Legacy of Freedom,* 34.

52. Asmal et al., *Legacy of Freedom,* 7.

53. Cited in Asmal et al., *Legacy of Freedom,* 43.

developing an exclusivist ideology of apartheid which led to a systematic removal of rights from black populations and the crushing of all dissent.[54] This alliance consistently decried universal human rights as "humanistic nonsense" using the language of minority group rights for an Afrikaner elect aligned with a distorted Calvinism that gave full, God-given authority to the sovereignty of the state in a form of Christian nationalism.[55] Resistance to universal human rights was then made in the name of conservative Protestant Christianity. At the same time, ANC leaders, many themselves educated in mission schools and people of faith, were campaigning against unjust laws. They used human rights clams as a communal protest language of moral struggle to develop the 1955 Freedom Charter as a human rights document ahead of its time, holding together rights holistically in advance of the United Nations Covenants as a "contribution towards world human rights literature of which South Africans can be proud."[56]

In 1961, South Africa became a Republic. However, its new Constitution reinforced the supremacy of the legislature and ongoing structural racism, while also "framed in humble submission to Almighty God and pledges to uphold Christian values and civilised norms"[57] John Dugard notes that both lawyers and politicians of the day argued that Christian values and God's sovereignty trumped humanistic values such as human rights where "the Christian premise of the sovereignty of God stands in radical opposition to the humanistic point of departure which makes man the sovereign consideration."[58] For President Kruger "the testing right was from the Devil."[59] However, at the same time, other Christian leaders began to mobilise a more coordinated resistance to apartheid theologies around human rights. Afrikaner pastor Beyers Naudé formed the Christian Institute in defiance of his denomination in 1961, law professor Johann van der Vyver was sacked from the University of Potchefstroom in 1978 due to his theological-ethical criticisms of apartheid and ran an important human rights conference in Cape Town in 1978. Some theological colleges were opening up to theologies of liberation to mobilise a new generation of activists while Biko's black consciousness movement shaped the rise of

---

54. For more on rights-abusive legislation, see Liebenberg, *Human Development*.

55. Dugard, *Human Rights*.

56. Sachs, *Advancing Human Rights*, 50.

57. Villa-Vicencio, "God, the Devil," 232.

58. Dugard, *Human Rights and South African*, 41.

59. Villa-Vicencio, *Theology of Reconstruction*, 62.

black theology.[60] Dubow notes that churches were an important, overlooked source of human rights thinking in South Africa.[61]

By the 1980s, human rights language was again being popularised both in the grassroots struggle and by ANC leaders who signed up to international human rights documents.[62] More faith leaders found a shared voice on human rights, in line with the positive momentum generated globally between religion and human rights in the 1970s where South African faith leaders such as Boesak and Tutu had been influential. By the 1980s, a significant shift was seen in religious engagement on human rights and prominent church leaders took direct action in the struggle using human rights language. In 1985, Beyers Naudé explicitly described apartheid as a violation of human rights and dignity with theological roots of evil, pointing to the urgent need to "go beyond pious words to action."[63] Conferences like Cottesloe (1960), and public declarations such as the Message to the People of South Africa (1968) and the Belhar Confession (1982) were watershed moments for many churches. Multi-racial theological voices became vanguards in the struggle for human rights, finding unity in the rejuvenated South African Council of Churches (SACC) and pioneering theological reflection on human rights that emphasized apartheid as a heresy to motivate active protest by faith communities both at home and abroad.[64]

Key events mobilized by local faith leaders included the Kairos Document of 1985, the Standing for the Truth Campaign of 1988, the Call to Prayer to End Unjust Rule, and the Peace March in 1989 of 30,000 people headed by interfaith leaders in Cape Town. This testifies to the convening power of religion for good if mobilized around human rights as an effective call to action even if this prophetic voice was not characteristic of most churches. Kairos theology emerged as a uniquely South African contribution from the people, challenging the churches theologically to reject domination and quietist theologies and to take sides for human rights.[65]

---

60. Black theology proponents in the later years of the struggle used human rights and dignity to reflect on the black experience and challenge narratives of inferiority to offer a liberating, intersectional ethic.

61. Dubow, *South African Struggle*, 83.

62. Dubow, *South African Struggle*, 87–88. Dubow points to a "genuine sense of epiphany" in the 1980s in the ANC where belief in the efficacy of armed struggle lost out to those emphasizing rights in the negotiations (Dubow, *South African Struggle*, 114).

63. Boesak, "Time for Pious Words," 225.

64. De Gruchy and Villa-Vicencio, *Apartheid is a Heresy*.

65. Kairos Theologians, *Challenge to the Church*; Nolan, *God in South Africa*.

Theologians have called in recent years for a "renewed Kairos" in South Africa that needs to be passed on to new generations.[66]

The historical lesson of the dangers of a systematic polarizing of rights and Christianity needs to be acknowledged as it has an ongoing legacy today. However, it can be held in tension with the reality of active, influential prophetic minority faith voices that in time, helped reshape the narrative from within. In the transition years of the 1990s, the ANC's Charterist tradition of universal human rights shaped both the Bill of Rights and strong calls to build a human rights culture. South Africa was seen globally as a triumph of human rights struggle[67] with its new Constitution noted as a "milestone in the history of human rights in South Africa by moving beyond paying merely lip service to the interconnectedness of human rights and giving them concrete effect by making them judicially enforceable."[68] While some saw this achievement as the end of the human rights struggle, others suggested it was only the beginning of a new struggle for their concrete realisation in practice, where, "if the Constitution is not about actual rights for real human beings, and if those rights are not upheld without fear or favor, then it is nothing."[69] Deep interconnections between poverty and human rights abuses were identified here and churches were asked to help place the most excluded at the heart of their realisation.[70] Some faith leaders, such as Frank Chicane, crossed over into formal political life on human rights while the contested Truth and Reconciliation (TRC) process in the late 1990s was a way in which other faith leaders remained publicly prominent in ways focused on the creation of a political culture respectful of human rights. However, scholars have suggested in looking back at the TRC, that its task of embedding legal norms of human rights into ordinary social norms was, in many ways, ineffective, and that many of its practical recommendations were ignored.[71]

New sites of human rights struggle emerged here around issues such as HIV/AIDS where human rights discourse was employed again in paradoxical ways to both to reinforce and to challenge neoliberal claims[72] and where

---

66. Le Bruyns, "Rebirth of Kairos," 465; Boesak, "Time for Pious Words," 225; Saayman, "Sky is Red," 27.

67. Mutua, *Human Rights*, 126.

68. Liebenberg, *Human Development*, 8. She notes that no distinction is made between justiciable "first generation" rights and "second generation rights" in this Constitution in line with the spirit of the UDHR (Liebenberg, *Human Development*, 10).

69. Sachs, *Advancing Human Rights*, 214.

70. Liebenberg, *Human Development*, 28–30, 992.

71. Gibson, "Truth, Reconciliation," 5.

72. Cameron, *Justice*, 76–91.

churches again became both a challenge and a challenger. Some scholars saw the new state as over-reliant on rights discourse as the engine of change. They pointed to the double-edged malleability of rights talk that could reinforce oppression[73] and the need to develop a cross-culturally legitimate creed of human dignity. They insisted that mainstreaming human rights into institutional machinery was not enough and that maintaining their counter-hegemonic historical power as a transforming ethics of responsibility was also needed.[74] In the new dispensation, many churches struggled to admit their historical complicity in human right abuses or to find a post-struggle identity. Ecumenical conferences called churches to stand up against any government that violates human rights and to "take sides with all who remain oppressed in one form or another to defend the human rights of all."[75] The move from the unity of one church struggle to fragmented, plural struggles required a holistic commitment to human rights.[76] A dignity-enriched human rights discourse was called for to engage new threats posed by economic globalization.[77] Christians were asked to engage with rights and grapple with their plurality rather than seeking a return to Christian hegemony but many failed to respond to this call.[78]

Lessons from South African history highlight the paradoxical nature of rights talk but also its grassroots power to adapt and mobilise change from below. From Ordinance 50, to ANC protests, a Charterist tradition, an anti-apartheid struggle, rights-based Constitution, the TRC and HIV/AIDS, human rights have consistently been re-claimed here by those on the margins with prophetic faith leaders playing an ongoing important role. The struggle for human rights has played out more from below than above in concrete African circumstances. South African history challenges those who may see human rights merely as an abstract, white, liberal and individualistic preoccupation of the 1 percent elite. However, rights have also been misused by colonial and patriarchal powers. This history is also a reminder of the selective use of rights, the paradoxical role that faith can play both for and against them, and the need for their ongoing theological

---

73. Mutua, *Human Rights*, 121, 128, 151. He suggests that rights can be used to protect the powerful and the status quo just as easily as they can be wielded to advance the interests of the excluded. See Mutua, *Human Rights*, 137.

74. Koskenniemi, "Human Rights," 47, 55.

75. De Gruchy, "Becoming the Ecumenical Church," 19.

76. De Gruchy, *Church Struggle*, 229–55.

77. Botman, "Human Dignity and Economic Globalization."

78. Botman, "Human Dignity and Economic Globalization," 256–60.

decolonisation if a localised transformational ecclesiology for human rights is to be nurtured here in South Africa.[79]

HUMAN RIGHTS IN CONTEMPORARY SOUTH AFRICA

Human rights remain enshrined at the heart of national discourse today. However, they face multiple obstacles to their concrete realisation.[80] Human rights reports[81] note serious issues related to abuse, violence, xenophobia, crime, sexual violence, child poverty and hunger, unemployment and ineffective access to justice and an increasing tendency to harass rights defenders and protesters. A troubling resurgence of African Nationalism under previous President Jacob Zuma called for "cultural exceptionalism" on human rights, seeking to decenter the Constitution from forming the foundation of how citizens think about their interactions with one another.[82] Statements by Zuma[83] regarding the need to change things in the Constitution shows that attempts to frame human rights as a form of neo-colonial white supremacy that prevents transformation continue today. Reclaiming a historical grassroots human rights tradition can counter claims that human rights are a colonial import of the West and help reclaim their transformative radicality. This requires engaging all social actors in building a bottom-up culture of human rights if the gap between constitutional rhetoric and the realities of many lives is to be bridged.

> One may have a society where, from a legal point of view, human rights are guaranteed but unless a culture exists, created for people by people, where the citizens recognize their own rights and deeply respect those of others, without such a culture, the legal frame is merely superficial.[84]

In South Africa, constitution-making from above is important but it is not enough. The task of developing a human rights culture from below requires going beyond the law to change hearts and minds.[85] Without placing the needs of the vulnerable at the heart of rights, they can remain ambivalent, selectively employed by the powerful and proving ineffective over private entities. This is an opportunity in which faith could play an ongoing role.

79. Palm, "Always Reforming," 336.
80. Ahmed, "IJRC Interview."
81. Amnesty International, "South Africa."
82. Cameron, *Justice*, x.
83. Huber, "Human Rights and Globalization."
84. Botman and Sporre, *Human Rights Culture*, 10.
85. Dubow, *South African Struggle*, 125. See also Viljoen, *Beyond the Law*.

Formal human rights education often remains highly law-oriented and framed only in secular terms. This may be a mistake if human rights are to be better "enculturated" into the lives of people for whom religious values remain a significant moral force.[86] Religion can be an important partner for human rights and therefore the absence of churches overall in South African human rights forums is noteworthy. They are more likely to be seen today as a liability on issues of gender and sexuality, corporal punishment, and traditional cultural practices. Reclaiming voices of religious freedom for human rights offers an alternative to a religious freedom that positions religion against them. A 2008 Durban conference questioned how to install respect for the law in South Africa when it prohibits deeply-rooted beliefs and practices. Conference reports concluded that "changing the hearts and minds of people cannot be imposed from the top down but must be cultivated from the bottom up"[87] where religion remains an important moral force.

> For millions in all walks of life, religion provides support and nurture and a framework for individual and social stability and growth, Religious belief has the capacity to awaken concepts of self-worth and human dignity which form the cornerstone of human rights. It affects the believer's view of society and founds the distinction between right and wrong.[88]

The South African human rights story offers a locally rooted, people-centerd, African genealogy, as one contingent story of human rights and its ambivalent relation to religion. Here faith leaders have been both powerful allies and dangerous enemies. Minority prophetic voices offered compelling public witness to the power of faith for human rights, reshaping hearts, minds and actions of both oppressed and oppressors in ways that went beyond the law into the relational nature of human beings. From John Phillips in 1828 to Bishop Colenso in 1860, Beyers Naudé in 1960 and Desmond Tutu, Allan Boesak and Frank Chicane in the 1970s and 80s and beyond, prophetic faith leaders have pointed to common personhood and human dignity as a subversive claim of Christian witness for human rights, equipping them to move beyond pious words to action and the mobilisation of others. I have argued elsewhere that churches remain a missing link today that could assist human rights claims to become sustainably rooted in line

86. Ter Haar, "Religion and Human Rights," 296.

87. Green and Van der Vyver, "Foundations and Future of Law," 337–56. Witchcraft accusations, circumcision, virginity testing, and lobola all have socio-religious overtones challenged by rights legislation.

88. Christian Education v. Ministry of Education.

with a long prophetic movement for human rights.[89] This call for churches to take up their human rights task was made at the time, a call to which I now turn.

TOWARDS POST-APARTHEID HUMAN RIGHTS ENGAGEMENT FOR SOUTH AFRICAN CHURCHES

Charles Villa-Vicencio has charted the influential role of religious voices in the South African human rights struggle.[90] Yet, he noted that many churches remained trapped in apartheid and it was minority prophetic voices that enacted their faith in relation to human rights practice. At the start of the new dispensation, he called for the ongoing public engagement of churches in relation to the realisation of human rights.[91] His call to build a liberating culture of human rights as an essential part of nation-building was framed as part of the church's liberating obligation to society, a prophetic responsibility in the light of historicised oppression, where its primary task is "to facilitate Christians to promote and appropriate the values of a human rights culture."[92] This goes beyond proclamation to implementation and the nurturing of communal commitment requiring further Africanisation of human rights theologies.[93]

Villa-Vicencio suggests that this revolutionary theological task could equip South Africans to see human rights as at the center of human co-existence and help to prevent them becoming mere decoration or even misused tools concealing the harsh realities of abuse and exploitation.[94] However the historical co-optation of theology to serve power, requires locating the church in solidarity with those who suffer to counteract a social bias that favors the powerful. Instead "exploited people should form the norm and not the exception to a human rights agenda."[95] Theology can help Christians connect to their traditions to motivate action for all human rights as a faith imperative that situates religious freedom in the service of nurturing other freedoms. The diagnosis remains, however, that tragically "few churches have seen the need to make human rights issues an integral part of

---

89. Palm, *Reimagining the Human*; "Always Reforming."

90. Villa-Vicencio, *Theology of Reconstruction*. See also Masuku, "Prophetic Mission."

91. Masuku, "Prophetic Mission," 15.

92. Masuku, "Prophetic Mission," 126.

93. Villa-Vicencio, "God, the Devil," 241.

94. Villa-Vicencio, *Theology of Reconstruction*, 45.

95. Villa-Vicencio, *Theology of Reconstruction*, 16.

their liturgy, preaching and practice."[96] To the question, "Do human rights need God?" he notes "it depends on your God. The God of Verwoerd and the God of Tutu are not the same"[97] South Africa's history, current empirical realities and this primarily unanswered post-apartheid call all suggest that the content of theology matters. Portuguese scholar De Sousa Santos has recently claimed that in a place-based engagement with human rights, contextual liberating hermeneutic re-engagement with religions can show their post-secular potential as a "source of radical energy towards counter-hegemonic human rights struggles,"[98] by generating the moral indignation and normative politics required for change. For an example of this "revolutionary genealogy" in South Africa that depicts God as a human rights activist, I turn to the theology of Desmond Tutu.

EMBODYING A THEOLOGY FOR HUMAN RIGHTS— DESMOND TUTU.

Archbishop Emeritus Desmond Tutu is recognized as a global human rights icon with multiple awards for his contributions to human rights.[99] His role in the anti-apartheid struggle is well documented and he has also spoken out consistently on rights-related issues such as reconciliation, LGBTIQ+ rights, Palestine, corruption, women in the church, HIV/AIDS and euthanasia. Tutu notes that Christians "must hang our heads in shame when we survey the gory and shameful history of the Church of Christ on human rights."[100] His willingness to grapple publicly with the power-laden history of his faith tradition and yet still hold to its potential for human rights realisation offers an alternative form of religious freedom to a narrow view that still sees holistic human rights claims as a threat to Christian faith.

At the heart of Tutu's theology for human rights is a conviction "that to be human is to be free"[101] underpinned by his relational understanding of the person. He stresses freedom to choose as a significant endowment of the Bible. In line with the holistic vision of the 1948 Universal Declaration

96. Villa-Vicencio, *Theology of Reconstruction*, 6, 24–25.

97. Villa-Vicencio, "God, the Devil," 236.

98. De Sousa Santos, *If God Were*, 2, 64.

99. Desmond Tutu was ordained as an Anglican priest in South Africa in 1961, was a teacher at the radical black theology seminary FEDSEM from 1967, recipient of the 1984 Nobel Peace Prize for human rights, President of the SACC from 1978 and the All African Council of Churches since 1987. In 1986 he became the first black Archbishop in South Africa and led, alongside other religious leaders, the 30,000 strong non-violent protest Freedom March in Cape Town. See "Archbishop Desmond Tutu."

100. Tutu, "First Word," 6.

101. Tutu, "First Word," 1.

of Human Rights (UDHR), he includes freedom from fear, insecurity, want and penury but also freedom-for expression, movement, association, togetherness, meaningful work, creativity and community. For Tutu, this relational freedom is what religious traditions can help to contribute to wider society. It reminds people that everything is a gift and belongs to God by using a principle of grace, not to negate rights by seeing people as undeserving,[102] but instead to ground a radical egalitarianism.[103]

Tutu sees humans as created for community and draws on African spirituality by using the theme of *ubuntu* to reinforce an ethic of interconnection where our humanity is caught up in that of all others.[104] Jonny Hill suggests that Tutu's pioneering, practical use of the *imago dei* motif to demand the rights of an oppressed group revealed that apartheid was at heart, a theological problem.[105] Instead of a divine monarch who dominates within God-ordained hierarchical structures, he models an egalitarian model of mutuality where people are free for each other in healthy relationships. Tutu's ability to link God-images with concrete social behaviors enabled him not only to theologically legitimate the anti-apartheid struggle as a Christian imperative but has continued in relation to emerging human rights issues in churches such as the status of LGBTIQ+ people.[106] He rethinks reconciliation as an ongoing participatory social task with God to help God's children become more fully human. This Trinitarian sense of inviolable human dignity contests the suffering in the world to fire protest struggles for social change, reaching backwards to a subversive creational claim of value and forwards to anticipate a more just future together. This conviction took him, alongside others, beyond words into costly action and the defiance of unjust laws and church doctrines.

> This incredible sense of the infinite worth of each person created in the image of God, being God's viceroy, God's representative, God's stand-in, a God-carrier, a sanctuary, a temple of the holy spirit, inviolate, possessing a dignity that was intrinsic with an

102. See Du Toit, "Religious Freedom," 683, who notes that apartheid theologies claimed that sinful humans have no rights before God, as everything comes as undeserved gifts. Tutu offers an opposing interpretation to this approach, interpreting grace as supporting rather than undermining human rights.

103. Tutu, "First Word," 4.

104. Tutu, *No Future*, 145.

105. Hill, *Theology of Desmond Tutu*, 43.

106. LGBTIQ+ rights have been a consistent concern for Tutu post-apartheid, who states: "The church has joined the world in committing the ultimate blasphemy—making the children of God doubt that they are children of God, lesbians and gays have been made to reject God. . . . If the church, after the victory over apartheid, is looking for a worthy moral crusade, then this is it; the fight against homophobia and hetero sexism" (Tutu, "Foreword," x).

autonomy and freedom to choose that were constitutive of human personality, it is this that fired our apartheid struggle.[107]

Tutu's liberatory hermeneutic for re-interpreting sacred texts enables him to claim that the Bible makes "staggering assertions about human beings that came to be the foundations of the culture of basic human rights that have become so commonplace in our day and age."[108] This offers a unifying force that binds all liberations as interconnected corporeal violations of human dignity, enabling him to move from the apartheid struggle seamlessly into new human rights tasks. This approach sees God from the perspective of the poor, outcast, disenfranchised and humiliated and acts accordingly, mobilizing churches under the banner of a God who liberates both the oppressed and the oppressor.[109] Tutu is convinced that the human rights struggle formed a theological message of what God was doing in the world and was not merely a secular strategy for social transformation.[110] His human rights hermeneutic mounted a theological protest by seeing all humans as God-carriers where, "to oppress another human, to trample them underfoot is not just evil or painful but it is blasphemous—tantamount to spitting in the face of God."[111] His eschatological vision inaugurates a diverse rainbow community that restores relationships, breaking the hierarchical bonds of racial, ethnic, religious, economic and other differences.[112]

At the start of the new dispensation, Tutu continued to embody a public role for the church on human rights as a visible part of the TRC. While this role has been contested, it remains an important example of positive faith leader engagement in nation-building and offers an alternative to the prevalent ecclesiological influence of rights-skeptical theologians such as Hauerwas noted earlier.[113] For Tutu, a theological imperative drives Christian involvement in the struggle for human rights where not to stand up against injustice and oppression is to disobey God. It becomes an internal religious duty to condemn and redress any violation of "the rights of God's stand-in," galvanizing Christians as active protectors of the rights of all persons.[114] Churches can become change agents in the world, nurturing theolo-

---

107. Tutu, "First Word," 5.

108. Tutu, "First Word," 1.

109. Hill, *Theology of Desmond Tutu*, 96, 123.

110. Hill, *Theology of Desmond Tutu*, 11. Secular can be defined in this way as excluding religious contributions.

111. Tutu, "First Word," 3.

112. Hill, *Theology of Desmond Tutu*, 110.

113. Hill suggests that a Hauerwasian ecclesiology can lead to a lack of concern for changing social structures in contrast to the more prophetic tradition of Desmond Tutu. See Hill, *Theology of Desmond Tutu*, 190–92.

114. Tutu, "First Word," 3.

gies that reshape the liturgical, sacramental, pietistic and biblical practices of faith as concrete ways to challenge the roots that fuel human rights violations.[115] Tutu employed his religious freedom as a Christian to nurture theologies for human rights that positioned God as a human right activist. His public stand in defiance of all unjust theologies motivated others to do the same. He arguably stands in a Protestant tradition of protest going back to figures such as John Phillips in 1828 and further to Luther's claiming of religious freedom against both church and societal injustices. This protest sits at the heart of the right to religious freedom, a summons to all people of faith to exercise their conscience around theology's impact on those who suffer, with whom, Tutu insists, God always stands.

CONCLUSION

South Africa has a complex and multi-faceted Christian history of theological engagement with human rights. Churches and faith leaders here played multiple roles as moral endorsers of violations, silent bystanders and active, influential protesters in human rights struggles. Today however, their voices are rarely perceived as assets in the contemporary task of building a human rights culture. A militantly secular and exclusively legal framing of rights can also leave little room for genuine theological engagement. However, a historic minority strand of prophetic resistance nurtured forms of theological resistance tied into human rights and dignity and offers resources for new generations of South African Christians. Passing on this complex history can help them navigate new manifestations of this struggle with regard to religious freedom and its relationship to other human rights. New manifestations of domination and quietist theologies that have been historically rights-violating are re-emerging. Nurturing new prophetic voices of theological dissent in churches remains critical.

If Christians understand and employ their religious freedom to play a transformative role that motivates holistic action-for-human rights as a core part of their faith, they can help to better embed human rights locally. Human rights organizations can also re-find the often missing link with religions and build authentic alliances with faith-based movements. Churches could be spaces where the inviolable dignity of every person is reinforced and where grassroots discussions on human rights can help ordinary South Africans become part of the shared task of building a liberating human rights culture from below.

Unlike some contemporary theologians who speak dismissively of human rights, South African faith leaders such as Tutu engaged publicly to embody a theological praxis for human rights in specific relation to building

---

115. Hill, *Theology of Desmond Tutu*, 91, 125, 202.

a liberating human rights culture. They offer a revolutionary place-based politics for a human rights discourse from below that is grounded in concrete voices of pain. In this task, history shows that theology matters and has concrete implications for human rights. An embrace of the broken body of God as a divine protest of all those pushed to the social margins calls congregations to practice relational embodiment in solidarity with the bodies of the abused, requiring liberating hermeneutical reappraisal of its traditions. This approach builds bridges from religious freedom towards other human rights, not walls to keep them out. Faith communities can then become authentic allies in building a liberating human rights culture as acts of public Christian witness, inspired by prophetic church history to see this as a missional task central to their identity.

BIBLIOGRAPHY

Ackermann, Denise. "Freedom of Religion and the Equality and Dignity of Women: A Christian Feminist Perspective." In *Building a Human Rights Culture: South African and Swedish Perspectives Today*, edited by Russel Botman and Karin Sporre, 180–93. Falun: Högskolan Dalarna, 2003.

Ahmed, Kayum. "IJRC Interview with Kayum Ahmed, CEO, South Africa Human Rights Commission." *Int'l Justice Resource Center* video, 20:49. October 12, 2012. Online. http://vimeo.com/51933658.

Amnesty International. "South Africa: Key Human Rights Concerns in South Africa: Amnesty International's Submission to the UN Universal Periodic Review, May–June 2012." *Amnesty International*, February 7, 2012. Online. https://www.amnesty.org/download/Documents/16000/afr5300320012en.pdf.

An-Na'im, Abdullahi. "Synergy and Interdependence of Religion, Human Rights and Secularism." In *Human Rights and Responsibilities in the World Religions*, edited by Joseph Runzo, et al., 20–40. London: One World, 2014.

"Archbishop Desmond Tutu Laureate of the 2012 UNESCO/Bilbao Prize for the Promotion of a Culture of Human Rights." *UNESCO*, November 28, 2012. Online. http://en.unesco.org/news/archbishop-desmond-tutu-laureate-2012-unescobilbao-prize-promotion-culture-human-rights.

Asmal, Kadar, et al., eds. *Legacy of Freedom: The ANC's Human Rights Tradition*. Cape Town: Jonathan Ball, 2005.

Atiemo, Abamfo O. *Religion and the Inculturation of Human Rights in Ghana*. London: Bloomsbury, 2013.

Baptist Union of Southern Africa. "Press Release: Response to the South African Human Rights Commission's Proposal to Outlaw Spanking." February 1, 2016. Online. https://www.baptistunion.org.za/index.php/fi/downloads/downloads/file/153-press-release-response-to-the-south-african-human-rights-commission-s-proposal-to-outlaw-spanking.

Boesak, Allen. "The Time for Pious Words Is Over: Beyers Naudé, Decision, Conscience, and Courage in the Struggle for Justice." In *Reformed Churches in South Africa and the Struggle for Justice: Remembering 1960–1990*, edited by Mary-Anne Plaatjies-Van Huffel and Robert Vosloo, 213–25. Stellenbosch: African Sun, 2013.

Botman, H. R. "Human Dignity and Economic Globalization." *NGTT* 45.1 (2004). Online. http://ojs.reformedjournals.co.za/index.php/ngtt/article/view/318/610.

Cameron, Edwin. *Justice: A Personal Account*. Cape Town: Tafelberg, 2014.

Cox, Larry. "Human Rights Must Get Religion." *OpenDemocracy*, April 14, 2014. Online. https://www.opendemocracy.net/openglobalrights/larry-cox/human-rights-must-get-religion.

De Gruchy, John. "Becoming the Ecumenical Church." In *Being the Church in South Africa Today*, edited by N. Barney Pityana and Charles Villa-Vicencio, 12–26. Johannesburg: SACC, 1995.

———. *The Church Struggle in South Africa*. Cape Town: David Phillips, 1979.

De Gruchy, John, and Charles Villa-Vicencio, eds. *Apartheid Is a Heresy*. Grand Rapids: Eerdmans, 1983.

De Sousa Santos, Boaventura. *If God Were a Human Rights Activist*. Stanford: Stanford University Press, 2015.

Du Toit, Cornel W. "Religious Freedoms and Human Rights in South Africa: After 1996, Responses and Challenges." *BYU Law Review* 3 (2006) 677–98.

Dubow, Saul. *The South African Struggle for Human Rights*. Cape Town: Jacana, 2012.

Dugard, John. *Human Rights and the South African Legal Order*. 1978. Reprint, New York: Princeton University Press, 2015.

Freedom of Religion South Africa. "Welcome!" Online. http://forsa.org.za.

Gibson, James. "Truth, Reconciliation, and the Creation of a Human Rights Culture in South Africa." *Law and Society Review* 38.1 (2004) 5–40.

Green, Christian M., and Johann Van der Vyver. "The Foundations and Future of Law, Religion and Human Rights." *African Human Rights Law Journal* 8.2 (2008) 337–56.

Hauerwas, Stanley. *A Community of Character: Toward a Constructive Christian Social Ethic*. Notre Dame: University of Notre Dame Press, 1981.

———. "How to Think Theologically about Rights." *Journal of Law and Religion* 30.3 (2015) 402–413.

Hill, Jonny B. *The Theology of Martin Luther King and Desmond Tutu*. New York: Palgrave MacMillan, 2007.

Hogan, Linda. *Keeping Faith with Human Rights*. Washington, DC: Georgetown University Press, 2015.

Huber, Wolfgang. "Human Rights and Globalization: Are Human Rights a Western Concept?" *NGTT* 55.1 (2014) 117–37.

Human Rights Watch. "World Report 2014: South Africa." January 2014. Online. https://www.hrw.org/world-report/2014/country-chapters/south-africa.

Hunt, Lynn. *Inventing Human Rights: A History*. New York: W. W. Norton, 2007.

Ibhawoh, Bonny. *Imperialism and Human Rights: Colonial Discourses of Rights and Liberties in African History*. New York: State University of New York Press, 2007.

Kairos Theologians. *Challenge to the Church: A Theological Comment on the Political Crisis in South Africa [The Kairos Document]*. Johannesburg: Kairos Theologians, 1985. Online. https://kairossouthernafrica.wordpress.com/2011/05/08/the-south-africa-kairos-document-1985.

Koskenniemi, Marti. "Human Rights: Mainstreaming as a Strategy for Institutional Power." *Humanitarianism and Development* 1.1 (2010) 47–58.

Le Bruyns, C. "The Rebirth of Kairos Theology and Its Implications for Public Theology and Citizenship in South Africa." *Missionalia* 43.3 (2015) 460–77.

Liebenberg, Sandra. *Human Development and Human Rights: South African Country Study Paper for Human Development Report 2000*. UNDP. Oxford: Oxford University Press, 2000.

Makgoba, Thabo. "New Struggle to Protect Our Human Rights Culture." *Sunday Independent*, March 22, 2015. Online. http://www.iol.co.za/sundayindependent/new-struggle-to-protect-our-human-rights-culture-1.1835413#.Vl3pCnYrLIU.

Masuku, T. M. "Prophetic Mission of Faith Communities during Apartheid South Africa, 1948–1994: An Agenda for a Prophetic Mission Praxis in the Democratic SA." *Missionalia* 42.3 (2014) 151–67.

Mutua, Makau. *Human Rights: A Political and Cultural Critique*. Philadelphia: University of Pennsylvania Press, 2002.

Nolan, Albert. *God in South Africa: The Challenge of the Gospel*. Cape Town: David Phillips, 1979.

Nurser, John. *For All Peoples and All Nations: The Christian Churches and Human Rights*. Geneva: WCC, 2005.

Palm, Selina. "Always Reforming? Nurturing a Church for Human Rights in South Africa." *Stellenbosch Theological Journal* 4.1 (2018) 321–46.

———. "Church Outrage against Spanking Ban Aids Violence against South Africa's Children." *Conversation*, January 14, 2018. Online. https://theconversation.com/church-outrage-over-spanking-ban-aids-violence-against-south-africas-children-88098.

———. "Liberating Human Rights? Insights from Abdullahi An-Na'im for Present Day South Africa." *Acta Academia* 46.4 (2014) 93–116.

———. "Reimagining the Human? The Role of the Churches in Building a Liberatory Human Rights Culture in South Africa Today." PhD diss., University of Kwa-Zulu Natal, 2016. Online. http://researchspace.ukzn.ac.za/handle/10413/13037.

Perry, Michael. *Towards a Theory of Human Rights: Religion, Law, Courts*. Cambridge: Cambridge University Press, 2006.

Phillips, Melanie. "Human Rights and its Destruction of Right and Wrong." In *Does God Believe in Human Rights? Essays on Human Rights and Religion*, edited by Nazila Ghanea, et al., 115–20. Leiden: Martinus Nijhoff, 2007.

Pillay, Miranda. "Solidarity in Suffering in the Context of HIV/AIDS." In *Building a Human Rights Culture: South Africaan and Swedish Perspectives Today*, edited by Russel Botman and Karin Sporre, 142–63. Falun: Högskolan Dalarna, 2003.

Pretorius, Stephen. "Religious Cults, Religious Leaders, and the Abuse of Power." *International Journal for Religious Freedom* 6.1/2 (2013) 203–216.

Rule, Stephen, and Bongiwe Mncwango. "Christianity in South Africa: Theory and Practice." In *South African Social Attitudes: 2nd Report. Reflections on the Age of Hope*, edited by Benjamin Roberts, et al., 185–98. Cape Town: Human Sciences Research Council, 2010.

Saayman, Willem. "'The Sky Is Red so We Are Going to Have Fine Weather': The Kairos Document and the Signs of the Times, Then and Now." *Missionalia* 36.1 (2008) 16–28.

Sachs, Albie. *Advancing Human Rights in South Africa*. Oxford: Oxford University Press, 1992.

Schoeman, W. J. "South African Religious Demography: The 2013 General Household Survey." *HTS Teologiese Studies* 73.2 (2017). Online. https://doi.org/10.4102/hts.v73i2.3837

Shepherd, Frederick, ed. *Christianity and Human Rights: Christians and the Struggle for Global Justice*. New York: Lexington, 2009.

Smit, Dirk. "On the Impact of the Church in South Africa after the Collapse of the Apartheid Regime." In *Essays in Public Theology: Collected Essays 1*, edited by Ernst Conradie, 57–74. Stellenbosch: African Sun, 2007.

————. "Revisioning during Reconstruction: Contemporary Challenges for the Churches in South Africa." In *Essays in Public Theology: Collected Essays 1*, edited by Ernst Conradie, 41–56. Stellenbosch: Sun, 2007.

Stammers, Neil. "The Hidden Actors and Missing Histories of Human Rights." *OpenDemocracy*, September 25, 2013. Online. https://www.opendemocracy. net/openglobalrights/neil-stammers/hidden-authors-and-missing-histories-of-human-rights.

Ter Haar, Gerrie. "Religion and Human Rights: Searching for Common Ground." In *Religion and Development*, edited by Gerrie Ter Haar and James Wolfensohn, 295–314. New York: Columbia University Press, 2011.

Tutu, Desmond. "The First Word: To Be Human Is to Be Free." In *Christianity and Human Rights: An Introduction*, edited by John Witte Jr. and Frank Alexander, 1–17. Cambridge: Cambridge University Press, 2010.

————. "Foreword." In *Aliens in the Household of God: Homosexuality and Christian Faith*, edited by Steve De Gruchy and Paul Germond, ix–x. Cape Town: David Phillip, 1997.

————. *No Future without Forgiveness*. New York: Doubleday, 1999.

van der Ven, Johannes A., et al. *Is There a God of Human Rights? The Complex Relationship Between Human Rights and Religion: A South African Case*. International Studies in Religion and Society. Leiden: Brill, 2004.

Viljoen, Frans, ed. *Beyond the Law: Multidisciplinary Perspectives on Human Rights*. Center for Human Rights in South Africa. Pretoria: Pretoria University Law Press, 2012.

Villa-Vicencio, Charles. "God, the Devil, and Human Rights: The South African Perspective." In *Does Human Rights Need God?*, edited by Elizabeth Bucar and Barbra Barnett, 225–42. Grand Rapids: Eerdmans, 2005.

————. *A Theology of Reconstruction: Nation Building and Human Rights*. Cape Town: Cambridge University Press, 1992.

West, Gerald, et al. "When Faith Does Violence: Reimagining Engagement Between Churches and LGBTI Groups on Homophobia in Africa." *HTS Teologiese Studies* 72.1 (2016). Online. http://dx.doi.org/10.4102/hts.v72i1.3511.

Williams, Rowan. *Faith in the Public Square*. London: Bloomsberg Continuum, 2012.

Witte, John. "Introduction." In *Christianity and Human Rights: An Introduction*, edited by John Witte and Frank S. Alexander, 8–43. Cambridge: Cambridge University Press, 2010.

Wolterstorff, Nicholas. *Hearing the Call: Liturgy, Justice, Church, and World*. Grand Rapids: Eerdmans, 2011.

Court Cases

Christian Education SA v. Ministry of Education. 2000 (4) SA 757: 2000 (10) BCLR 1051 (CC) para. 36.

10

Intersections and Assemblages

*South Africans Negotiating Privilege and
Marginality through Freedom of Religion and
Sexual Difference*

FATIMA SEEDAT

Beyond an analysis of the freedoms available to religious communities as a collective, this chapter explores the operations of state and religion in the realisation of the constitutionally guaranteed right to freedom of religion as it pertains to unrepresented and marginalised segments of religious communities, namely women and people with queer sexualities. The primary ways in which the South African state engages religious communities is through simultaneous recognition of religious authorities and non-involvement with religious doctrine. Together these two modes of engagement result in the state maintaining both a measure of political recognition and a measure of legal distance in relation to religious authorities. My concern is for how this combined political recognition and legal distance from the effects of that religious authority functions within the religious community.

My argument is that state recognition of the mainstream of authority in a religious community produces closeness between the state and the religious authorities which foregrounds the concerns of the mainstream of the religious community. Privileging these religious authorities however means that other voices within the religious community are marginalised and may subsequently also loose the protection of the state. In more egregious situations, religious institutions may co-opt state authority while they practice doctrines that violate the constitutional rights of minority groups within religious communities. This situation is a result of the state's commitment to both the constitutional guarantee for freedom of religion and the legal doctrine of judicial non-entanglement which limits the state's legal or legislative involvement in the religious community and so too its ability to ensure that constitutional protections including freedom of religion extend to unrepresented and marginalised minority interests within a religious community. Consequently, I argue, that the 'theological-political' intersection produced in recognizing and working with religious authorities emboldens and privileges mainstream religious authority and opinions within religious communities while simultaneously neglecting or marginalizing minority interests within religious communities; by simultaneously courting religious authorities and remaining uninvolved in the doctrinal matters of faith which discriminate against minority interests in religious communities the state consequently produces a 'theological-political' convergence which simultaneously protects the rights of religious communities and also abdicates a responsibility to protect the rights of minorities within these communities.[1]

Theoretically, I propose to view these dynamics of state and religion through the "intertwined relations of intersectionality and assemblages,"[2] to glean insights into the multiple mechanisms of control and discipline between state authority and religious authority. Through an analysis of Jewish, Muslim and Methodist struggles in South Africa, it becomes evident that guarantees of freedom of religion do not extend similarly to non-normative or queer and female religious adherents as they do to the mainstream religious authority and adherents of a faith tradition. Unless the state also finds mechanisms to engage these minority interests within religious communities, such individuals are circumscribed within the doctrinal limits prescribed by the mainstream of religious authority. State failure to address the intersectional and assembled powers at work in the lives of religious communities has the potential to produce ranks of privilege and marginalisation within religious communities living in constitutional contexts. The

---

1. I draw here on the concept of the "theological political" suggested in Leatt, "Faithfully Secular."

2. Jasbir Paur's reflections on "the operations of religion and homonationalism as the entwined connections of intersectionality and assemblage," are useful for understanding how religious authority and state authority articulate in the South African context.

examples used here pertain to Jewish divorce, Muslim prayer spaces, the legal recognition and regulation of Muslim marriage, and same sex marriage in a Methodist community.

OVERVIEW

Annie Leatt explains that after 1994, South Africa's democratic elections marked a shift from the "theological-political" dynamic of apartheid times toward a commitment to secularism as "an overt political and legal stance."[3] Democratic secularism in South Africa has been guided by constitutional guarantees for freedom of religion; in practical terms this means the South African state facilitates the democratic presence of religious communities in the public sphere but does not promote a single religious doctrine. Accompanying this position is a commitment to avoid judicial entanglement, a formal legal stance that avoids the state becoming excessively involved with the internal matters of religious communities.[4]

The three locations for religious freedom in the South African Constitution are sections 9, 15, and 31. Respectively, the equality clause, section 9, prohibits unfair discrimination on various grounds including religion and section 15, which states that everyone has the right to freedom of conscience, religion, thought, belief and opinion, provides for the recognition of religious systems of personal law. Section 31 protects the right of persons belonging to a religious community to practice their religion together with other members of that community, and to form, join and maintain voluntary religious associations. The analysis below suggests that constitutional guarantees of freedom of religion as well as other rights do not extend similarly to female and queer worshipers as they do to those in the mainstream of religious doctrine and authority. The theological-political dynamic that emerges through state relations with religious communities demonstrates the marginalisation of minority interests within religious communities and brings into question the ways in which the constitutional guarantees for freedom of religion are limited. Once the intersections of religion, authority and sexuality are brought to the fore, it would appear that these freedoms do not extend to minority interests within religious communities.

Accordingly, I argue here that recognizing and working with religious communities through their religious authorities emboldens and supports these religious authorities and their religious opinions; remaining simultaneously uninvolved in the doctrinal matters of faith which discriminate against minority interests within these religious communities consequently

3. Leatt, "Faithfully Secular," 36.
4. Kenneth, "Entanglement Test."

leaves minority groups within religious communities unprotected by the state and proscribed by those religious authorities in their access to other constitutionally guaranteed rights. These dynamics of gender, state and religion in the exercise of the constitutional guarantees for freedom of religion operate through intersections and assemblages, two theoretical frameworks which help reveal the multiple ways in which doctrinal contestations within religious communities are proscribed through the political-theological convergence of state and religious authority[5] speaking to the complexity of social relations in law-making, legal adjudication and constitutionality in the interactions of South African religious communities with the South African state.[6]

DOCTRINAL ENTANGLEMENT

Inherent to the political-theological dynamic of religion and state is the legal concern for doctrinal entanglement, i.e., state reluctance for judicial and legislative involvement in contested matters of religious doctrine, which is motivated by the twin concerns for excessive state involvement in religious communities and excessive state support for any one religion. Aimed at managing the legal and administrative relationship between state authority and religious authority, the judicial intent informing the doctrine aims to avoid "excessive government entanglement with religion," and Judge Farlam, in the matter of *Ryland v. Edros* (1996) confirmed this reluctance in South African jurisdictions.[7] While intended to avoid excessive entanglement in the doctrine of a religious tradition it is also true that practically, this has meant that religious communities are free to enact contested religious practices and doctrines which are potentially unconstitutional but which the state also remains reluctant to engage. An example of this reluctance was evident in 1994, when the South African Law Commission produced a *Report on Jewish Divorces*, prompted by concerns of women in the Jewish community who were divorced through the civil courts but not through Jewish law and therefore could not remarry according to Jewish law unless their husbands also agreed to a Jewish divorce (*gett*).[8] Moved by their concerns, the Commission suggested legislative amendments that would subsequently ensure that women are not 'chained' to husbands who refused to pronounce a religious divorce. However, to legislate directly on the matter of Jewish divorce

5. Paur, "I Would Rather Be," 49–66. Paur suggests reflecting on the dynamics of state and religion through the intertwined relations of intersectionality and assemblages.

6. Paur, "I Would Rather Be," 49–66.

7. Ryland v. Edros; Ashraf, "Divorce Amendment Act," 495–6.

8. South African Law Commission, *Report on Jewish Divorces*.

law risked the state's doctrinal entanglement in religious law, as a result of which the subsequent Divorce Amendment Act 95 of 1996 was religiously non-specific. The full name of the act explains its intent:

> To amend the Divorce Act, 1979, so as to empower a court to refuse to grant a decree of divorce if it appears to the court that the spouses are bound by their religion to effect a divorce in accordance with their religion before a decree of divorce will have full effect; and to provide for matters connected therewith.

In this interaction of religious doctrine and state law, the amendment did not affect couples who were married only by religious law (and not by civil law). It only conditioned the practice of divorce where couples were married by both civil law and religious law. The reason, it explained, was because "the constitutional guarantee of freedom of religion" required "the shaping of legislative regimes to protect persons in religiously distinctive positions from losing state benefits or being subject to particular hardships in the operation of the law."[9] In legal terms this meant that Jewish husbands could no longer divorce their Jewish wives in court without also divorcing them in terms of religious laws.

In practice, however, Jewish husbands do continue to access state divorce without also pronouncing a religious divorce, arguably because the state has legislated on the civil divorce and not the religious divorce. To illustrate, in the case of *Amar v. Amar* (1999), a husband withheld the *gett* because he was unhappy with the financial provisions of the civil settlement agreement signed by the parties. As a result, the judge granted the civil divorce while ordering the husband to pay spousal maintenance until he granted the religious *gett*.[10] Evidently, while the court remained ostensibly outside the religious law, it did attempt to influence its practice; using the provisions of section 5A of the Act, the judge intended to prompt the reluctant husband to pronounce a *gett* and thus release his wife from the marriage.[11] However, there is little guarantee that the burden to pay spousal maintenance may always act as a prompt to end the marriage and grant the *gett*; a wealthy husband could continue his payments for years to avoid granting the *gett* and to prevent his (ex-)wife from remarrying. Contrary to its intent, I argue, in maintaining its distance from the religious law, the state has in fact perpetuated its inequalities.

9. South African Law Commission, *Report on Jewish Divorces*, 81.
10. See Amar v. Amar; Bonthuys, "Obtaining a Get."
11. Bonthuys, "Obtaining a Get."

The Report motivating the 1995 amendment argued for legislation as a means of protecting religious persons from "losing state benefits" or creating "hardships" in the operation of the law, which for spouses in civil marriage would include legal claims to a spouses pension, spousal maintenance, benefits of shared proprietary and taxation regimes, the possibility of financial partnerships and other legal protections and privileges that accrue to married couples.[12] Over the twenty-four years since democratic rule in South Africa, the courts have received a number of applications addressing the hardships created in the operation of Muslim marriages which are as yet not formally recognized or legislated upon in South African law.[13] For Muslim wives, hardships include the failure to inherit, the inability to initiate and pursue spousal maintenance claims and failure to receive pension benefits of deceased spouses.

Since 1994 Muslim wives have approached the courts for relief, as a result of which the case of *Rylands v. Edros* (1997), overturned *Ismail v. Ismail* (1983), confirming that Muslim marriage is not offensive to social mores, and is constituted as a contract from which flows the responsibility for maintenance, which responsibility may also be brought to court.[14] The *Amod v. Mutilateral Motor Vehicle Accident Fund* (1999) case followed, to allow a Muslim widow to sue for loss of support upon the death of her husband in a car accident and the court ruled she was entitled to death benefits.[15] In *Daniels v. Campbell NO and Others* (2004), a Muslim wife in a monogamous marriage was recognized as a spouse for purposes of inheritance in terms of intestate succession.[16] Continuing this stream of approaches to the court for remedies for Muslim wives, through *Hassam v. Jacobs NO and Others* (2008), for purposes of contract the courts recognized a polygynous wife in a Muslim marriage as a spouse who cannot be discriminated against and for whom the Constitutional Court confirmed her rights to equality, religion and culture.[17] Following upon *Khan v. Khan* (2005), parties in a polygynous Muslim marriage are entitled to interim maintenance after divorce as the claim falls within the ambit of the Maintenance Act (Rule 43), and most recently, in *Moosa NO and Others v. Harnakar* (2017), the court

---

12. South African Law Commission, *Report on Jewish Divorces*, 81.

13. In August 2018, the Cape High Court passed judgment on an application to prompt the state toward making legislation. See *Women's Legal Center v. The President* 9.

14. Rylands v. Edros; Ismail v. Ismail.

15. Amod v. Multilateral Motor Vehicle.

16. Daniels v. Campbell NO.

17. Hassam v. Jacobs NO.

allowed for two wives in a polygynous union to inherit the estate of their deceased husband.[18]

Evidently, Muslim wives have used various judicial processes to approach the state for relief from the effects of a theological-political dynamic where the state refuses to recognize Muslim marriages, but the democratic dispensation allows the practice of Muslim marriage without restriction. Over the years of Muslim presence in South Africa, Muslim marriage has been variously regulated and limited until it was finally rendered *contre bono mores*. The case of *Ismail v. Ismail* (1983) above, preceded by *Kader v. Kader* (1972), *Seedat's Executors* (Natal 1917), *Ebrahim v. Mahomed Essop* (1905) and *Bronn v. Fritz Bronn Executors* (1860), rendered all Muslim marriages outside the norms of the public policy by virtue of being potentially polygamous.[19] Consequent to this denouncement of Muslim marriage, alongside apartheid state politics allowed communities to ignore or boycott the state, and Muslim marriages were regulated through an alternative system of Islamic law derived from the originating cultures of Muslim slaves, indentured labourers, and merchants who made up the various South African Indonesian, Indian and Zanzibari Muslim communities. But this system of Islamic law preceded *Ismail v. Ismail* by almost a generation wherein formal Muslim judicial bodies had earlier arrogated to themselves the capacity to regulate Muslim marriage, divorce and other aspects of daily Muslim life.

While initially not as institutionalised as they are presently, over the period of almost two generations, the Muslim Judicial Council, the *Jamiatul Ulama* and Sunni *Jamiatul Ulama*, amongst others, gradually came to acquire positions of leadership in the western and north-eastern parts of the country respectively, until 1994 at which point they have also come to be identified as *de facto* representatives of the Muslims of South Africa nationally.[20] The new South African state has engaged the Muslim community variously since 1994, firstly by recognizing these Muslim judicial bodies, frequently to the exclusion of other Muslims groupings, and secondly by maintaining a distance from the effects of their authority within the community of Muslims.[21] The resultant theological-political dynamic points to the complexities of law-making and constitutionality in the interactions of South Africa's religious communities with the South African state.

18. Khan v. Khan; Moosa NO and Others v. Harnakar; "Maintenance Act of 1998."

19. Kader v. Kader; Seedat's Executors (Natal); Ebrahim v. Mahomed Essop; Bronn v. Fritz Bronn Executors.

20. For a history on Islam in the Cape and KwaZulu-Natal respectively, see Da Costa and Davids, *Pages from Cape Muslim History*; Vahed "Indian Muslims in South Africa."

21. For Muslim responses post-1994, see Vahed, "Changing Islamic Traditions."

In addition to the matter of marriage, which I return to below, congregational prayer spaces further reflect the impact of state recognition of religious authorities

CONGREGATIONAL PRAYER

This pertains to the incident of the Unity *Eid Gah*, an outdoor congregational prayer, first held at the Moses Mabhida stadium in Durban in 2011. The stadium, a state-owned facility, was built for the FIFA World Cup 2010 using tax payer monies and made available to the Muslim community upon their request for what organizers called a Unity *Eid Gah*, which was to bring together the numerous smaller congregations that ordinarily take place in and around Durban on the morning of *Eid ul Adha*. The dynamics of *Eid* congregations are characteristically reflective of local sectarian and class politics and so securing a stadium that could accommodate most of the community was a significant feat for the organizers. The municipal authorities appear to have also been glad to facilitate this attempt to promote unity allowing the group to rent the prestigious venue at a nominal fee.[22]

One particular congregation, however was excluded from the call for unity, which was also the only congregation which included women.[23] While less contentious elsewhere, the presence of women in congregational prayer is a matter of religious contestation in South African Indian communities in KwaZulu-Natal and Gauteng, the majority refusing to allow women into mosque spaces, a few permitting only marginal forms of inclusion and a small handful advocating inclusive gender practices in the prayer space.[24] Against significant local pressure, the Family *Eid Gah* had begun in 2004 with a small congregation of a few hundred people. By the time of the Unity *Eid Gah*, it was the primary project of a group called TIP (Taking Islam to the People), which had been operating for more than 6 years and drew a sizeable congregation of Muslims from across the South African demographic.[25] Focused on inclusivity and a progressive reading of Islam,

22. Telephone inquiry with Moses Mabhida administrative staff, August 2011, verified in private conversation with Chairperson of the TIP Family Eid Gah, R. Mahomed, Durban August 2018.

23. "Women and the Eid Prayer." Also, the author is themselves an organizer of this congregational event.

24. For more on gender struggles in Muslim prayer spaces in South Africa see Ismail, "Eid Prayer in South Africa." For a more recent analysis of women's attempts to access Muslim prayer spaces, see Ismail, "Female Musallees"; "Struggling to Find God"; Surtee, "They Don't Have Prayer."

25. For further background to the beginnings of the TIP Family Eid Gah see Asmal, "South African Women."

what has become the TIP Family *Eid Gah* is intentionally inclusive of Muslims of various racial, class, and national backgrounds, Muslims of various sexual orientations, accessible to the elderly, people with disabilities, and welcoming of children and youth. The organization pursues a developmental philosophy, mentoring youth into leadership positions and its events are marked by racial, generational and gender representation guided by commitments to an inclusive reading of Islam.[26] The leadership of the group is primarily female and adopts a position of gender inclusivity.

While invitations to join the Unity *Eid Gah* were extended to other congregations, none were extended to the TIP Family *Eid Gah*. The intention to exclude them from the Unity *Eid Gah* was confirmed publicly through the accompanying advertising materials; the posters and pamphlets read "Strictly for Men Only."[27] In spite of their objections to being excluded from this event through representations to the municipality not to make the venue available until women were included, the event went ahead at the municipal venue. Finally, the municipality showed support for the event when the mayor of Durban himself, Mayor James Nxumalo, addressed the all-male congregation of the morning.[28]

Politically, it appears the municipality approved and supported the event. Theologically, however, the state, through the municipality, offered not only tacit support for the event by making available the prestigious venue, but, through presence of the mayor of Durban at the inaugural event, also supported the doctrinal position of the organizers of the Unity *Eid Gah* and the commitment that congregational prayer is "Strictly for Men Only."[29] Consequently, not only has the state legitimised the exclusion of Muslim women from congregational prayer, it has also legitimised the use of a state resource, the venue, to facilitate the doctrine that excludes women from congregational prayer. Emboldened by state resources and state authority, the organizers of the Unity *Eid Gah* are under no pressure to transform their stance excluding women from the main prayer space. The Unity *Eid Gah* continues as a twice-yearly event into 2018, seven years later and is now likely the largest *Eid Gah* congregation in the city. Officially, it also remains exclusive of women.[30]

26. See *Taking Islam to the People*; Rai, "'Apartheid' of Spaces."

27. Islam Today, "One Ummah." Rai's dissertation includes a picture of the poster. See Rai, "'Apartheid' of Spaces" fig. 1.

28. Omar, "Nxumalo Hailed."

29. This article, produced by the Jamiatul Ulama, illustrates some of the arguments against women's presence in public prayer spaces. See "Women Attending the Eid Gah."

30. A small group of women have over the past year begun to pray in the same venue but at a distance from the congregation. In response, the organizers have taken

NIKĀḤ

A second example is in a legislative process that began 24 years ago with the intention to recognize Muslim family law and give legal recognition and regulation to Muslim marriage. The stream of legal cases cited above reflects the impact of non-recognition of Muslim marriage and the processes of court adjudication that Muslim wives must continue to pursue to first establish their legal status as wives and then to argue for the legal protections and benefits that ordinarily accrue to wives in a South African civil marriage.

Prompted by the lack of legal recognition of Muslim marriage, in 1987 the South African Law Commission initiated an investigation into recognition and regulation of Muslim marriage and divorce, and soon after the elections of 1994 the ANC government established the Muslim Personal Law Board.[31] By 1996, the South African Law Reform Commission (SALRC) recommended a Project Committee (No. 59) which would eventually also produce draft legislation to recognize and regulate South African Muslim marriage in accordance with the new Constitution.[32] Established in March 1999, the next year, Project Committee No. 59 produced an issue paper *Islamic Marriages and Related Matters* (2000) which was followed by a discussion paper *Islamic Marriages and Related Matters* in the latter parts of 2001.[33] Following the review of public submissions made early in 2002, by July 2003 the Committee submitted the *Islamic Marriages and Related Matters Report*, including submissions made by various community stakeholders. In addition, the report presented newly drafted legislation (the SALRC draft Bill), to the Minister of Justice and Constitutional Development.[34] Over a period of seven years thereafter, the Ministry regularly promised to move forward on the legislation, making progress until, eventually, in 2010, Cabinet approved the newly formulated "Muslim Marriages Bill" (2010), published for public comment in the *Government Gazette*.[35] Submissions closed at the end of May 2011, and for another seven years, until 2018, there has been no further movement on the "Muslim Marriages Bill."

In the interim, by 2013, a court application, resulted in the court directing the Minister of Justice to report on the progress of the legislation

---

to concealing their presence through a make-shift screen placed in front of the group.

31. Amien, "Overcoming the Conflict."

32. Amien, "Overcoming the Conflict."

33. South African Law Commission, *Islamic Marriages and Related Matters* 15; *Islamic Marriages and Related Matters* 101.

34. The original draft was issued in 2001. *Islamic Marriages and Related Matters. Report*; Republic of South Africa, "Muslim Marriages Bill."

35. Republic of South Africa, "Muslim Marriages Bill."

making process.[36] Rather than renewing interest in the Bill, the state re-sponse shifted the matter of Muslim marriages from the Ministry of Justice to the Ministry of Home Affairs; instead of returning to the stalled Bill, the state began a campaign to register Muslim *Imams* as Muslim Marriages Of-ficers. Most recently and at the time of going to print a new judgment in the matter of *Women's Legal Center v. The President of the Republic of South Africa* (2018), directed the President once again to ensure the recognition and regulation of Muslim marriages, this time within a period of two years. The judgment has been appealed, and the state is presently proposing a new 'omnibus Bill' which, it argues, will address the needs of all religious communities.[37]

The community dynamics of the 24-year long process of creating legis-lation, namely a process of consultation marked by contestations of Islamic legal doctrine which resulted in a tacit sense of community consensus on the outcomes of the process, and the further processes of making represen-tations to government, has meant that the authority and institutionalisation of religious bodies has increased over time. Concomitantly, state recogni-tion of these religious bodies also increased. Over the course of the past 24 years as a constitutional democracy, the nature and form of the community of Muslims in South Africa has also changed; increasingly, it is becoming more reflective of the diversity of South Africans. The implications of those developments are threefold.

First, in South Africa, the systems of Muslim family law which func-tion in parallel to the system of civil marriage, partnership and divorce have been developed through religious scholars schooled in foreign, namely middle-eastern and sub-continental madrassas, using historical systems of Islamic law and financed by local Muslim business.[38] Primarily male in their constitution and patriarchal in their ideologies these scholars are established in religious bodies which officiate marriage and divorce. The South African Muslim community is composed of a mixture of conservative and progressive views, and the former holds sway amongst the recognized Muslim judicial authorities. Once the SALRC draft was made public in 2003 it became obvious that mainstream conservative views of Islamic mar-riage would dominate the new legislation. These include unilateral divorce or *ṭalāq*, polygyny without spousal consent and a marriage of dominion established through the payment of dower. Progressive Muslim representa-tions to the SALRC indicated the inequalities and potential constitutional

36. Faro v. Bingham NO and Others.
37. Women's Legal Center v. The President.
38. Amien, "Overcoming the Conflict."

conflict should these recommendations become law.[39] Further, between 2003 and now, the geo-politics of Muslim communities have shifted significantly; globally, Muslim communities are characterised as intolerant of gender equality and South African Muslims have not escaped similar problematisation. Compounding this, the community of local Muslims has also felt the effects of the international impulse toward securitisation of Islam and Muslim practices, which are the result of conflict oriented and racist civilisational discourses.[40] Finally, the international prevalence of radical over progressive Muslim approaches reflect in the increasing conservativism amongst segments of South Africa's Muslim community.[41] At its initial stages the law reform process had the support of a majority of the most influential judicial bodies, since then a number of these have withdrawn and even opposed the process and at present only a few of the original groupings remain committed to new legislation which would recognize and regulate Muslim marriage and divorce. Across the board however, these Muslim judicial authorities preside over a system of marriage and divorce law that favors husbands over wives through unilateral divorce rights and unregulated polygyny for husbands, strictly limited divorce options for wives which may only be accessed through these Muslim judicial institutions, and the prohibition of communal property rights for wives or spousal maintenance for divorced women, as was illustrated in the string of legal cases presented earlier in this chapter.

Second, in promoting the registration of *Imams* as Muslim Marriage Officers, the state has also strengthened their authority within the community. Politically, the move may indicate a shift in policy from an imperative to recognize and regulate Muslim marriage and divorce to a new imperative to regularise the population register, which reflects an international trend to improve national population registers as a means of managing migration and internal movements of people subsequent to the new security paradigms that followed after 9/11.[42] Consequently, there are now a few hundred Muslim *Imams*, who are now also authorised to conduct marriage under the South African Civil Marriages Act.[43] In retrospect, the campaign promoted

39. See the submissions of Muslim Youth Movement and Shura Yabafazi in the SALC Report. *Islamic Marriages and Related Matters. Report.*

40. See Ewi and Els, "Is a Terrorist Attack Imminent?"

41. See an early article on Muslim conservatism in South Africa, Moosa, "Muslim Conservatism in South Africa."

42. See Ministry of Home Affairs, "Deputy President Kgalema Motlanthe"; "Minister Gigaba."

43. Ministry of Home Affairs, "Minister Gigaba." In the absence of state recognition of Muslim marriages, it is common practice that the majority of Muslims marry

a number of political goals, namely improving the registration records of married Muslims, (with benefits for tax and population registration), and allowing the ruling party to garner support in the elections that followed soon after.

The individuals chosen for the state training programme were identified through mainstream Muslim judicial bodies.[44] None of these include women or identifiably queer individuals and as a result the state naturally excluded these individuals from the training programmes. As a consequence of selecting the trainees from mainstream Muslim religious bodies, the state privileged their demographic make-up and also their doctrinal perspectives. In terms of their demography, the numbers of ethnically African *Imams* in these groups are marginal, and there are no female *Imams* amongst them. Doctrinally, these groups do not recognize marriage outside the legal paradigm of *Nikāḥ*, which has been described by classical and contemporary Muslim legal scholars as a marriage of dominion, nor do they recognize the possibility of same-sex marriage.[45] Given that contemporary Islamic thought regulates sexuality and reproduction through marriage, the realisation of sexual and reproductive health rights is located in the recognition of Muslim marriage and divorce.[46] As a result, only the locations of religious authority and forms of Islamic marriage that these religious authorities consider legitimate have been given the possibility of simultaneous state recognition through the registration of a civil marriage. The alternate interpretations of Islamic marriage, contrary to the traditional concept of marriage as dominion, and a queer interpretation of Islamic marriage as a partnership between same-sex individuals, are thus excluded from the state's recognition of Muslim marriage. In recognizing the authority of Muslim Marriage Officers, without regulating the form of Muslim marriage, the state is now complicit if not directly entangled in the application of the doctrines of Islamic marriage selected by judicial bodies or individual *Imams*.

Finally, the current strategy to register a civil marriage for Muslims who marry under Islamic law functions in the place of legislation, which would recognize and regulate Muslim marriage, and has led to the consequent lack of legislative protection for Muslim wives. In the absence of

---

without the state. For the state's purposes, Muslim men and women who are not married under civil law are considered single. Their children were not considered legally theirs/legitimate until 1994. See Amien, "Overcoming the Conflict."

44. Private communications with the Ministers office indicate that recruitment was conducted through the major theological bodies.

45. See Ali, *Marriage and Slavery*, for a detailed discussion of marriage as dominion in Islamic law.

46. Ali, *Marriage and Slavery*.

legislation Muslim wives are not automatically recognized as beneficiaries of a joint marital property regime, nor as spouses for the purpose of inheritance, pension benefits, spousal support and other legal privileges that ordinarily accrue to women as wives married under the Civil Marriages Act and the Customary Marriages Act or as partners under the Civil Unions Act. Summarily, in avoiding legislation, the state enables the perpetuation of these bodies and the continued practice of a system of religious marriage and divorce laws that discriminate against South African Muslim wives. In creating a new cadre of Muslim marriage Officers, the state also supports *Imams* who implement a system of marriage and divorce law which discriminates against women as wives.

SAME-SEX MARRIAGE

The situation is not very different in majority faith traditions in South Africa; a further instance of state recognition of religious authority accompanied by distance from the effects of that authority in the religious community comes from the Methodist Church of Southern Africa (MCSA). In the case of *Ecclesia de Lange v. Presiding Bishop of the Methodist Church*, a ministers same sex marriage lead to her dismissal from her position as minister in the MCSA.[47] Raising "her constitutional right to equality and dignity and her right to keep her religious beliefs intact," she approached the courts to rule on the labour practices that allowed her dismissal.[48] MCSA objected to De Lange's same-sex civil union on doctrinal grounds that allowed for heterosexual marriage only. Whereas the MCSA argued for her dismissal on grounds of labour law, De Lange argued that her dismissal was on doctrinal grounds. Siding with the MCSA, Judge Dikgang Moseneke, who is also a lay preacher in the Methodist church, relied on the provisions of South African labour law to argue that the minister had not followed the appropriate internal guidelines to take up a dispute with the Church, thereby upholding the Church's decision to terminate De Lange's employment.[49]

In the recognition of the authority of the MCSA as an employer, labour laws gave sanction to the doctrinal positions of the mainstream Methodist church. The unexpected result is to consequently also marginalise the doctrinal positions advanced by de Lange in her own capacity as religious leader and minister. The distinction lies between the recognized religious authority of the mainstream MCSA and the authority of de Lange and her

47. De Lange v. Presiding Bishop.

48. Easthorpe, "Bruised but Not Broken," 115–23.

49. De Freitas, "Doctrinal Sanctions." My appreciation to Prof D. Forster for their insights on this decision.

colleagues who advance an alternate doctrine of MCSA views on Christian marriage. Upholding the authority of the church here as employer results in also sanctioning the doctrinal positions that exclude married lesbian women from church leadership.

RELIGION'S AGENCY IN THE STATE

Abdulkader Tayob (2015) argues for the ways in which "religions may reflect the nation, but are also very likely to invert, subvert and ignore it."[50] Further to this, the examples above illustrate some of the ways in which the agency of religion is exercised by also co-opting the state. Through the Unity *Eid Gah*, the community of mainstream Muslims co-opt the power of the state through the subsidised venue and the mayor's participation in an event that explicitly excludes women, and which might have been easily challenged at the Equality Court.[51]

Through their refusal to marry through civil marriage law, the Muslim community subverts the state's power to marry its citizens, and in doing so they also create a parallel system of Islamic law which discriminates against Muslim wives. In the convergence of Islamic divorce law and the states refusal to recognize and regulate Muslim marriages, the state subjects Muslim wives to a series of religiously sanctioned inequalities which increasingly prompts their claims in civil courts. Through their participation in the training of Muslim Marriage Officers, Muslim cis-het male clerics again co-opt the state, even as they earn recognition from the state, and practice their marriage officer duties based on a heteronormative model of marriage as dominion. In the Methodist church, labour law allows for the church to use its power as an employer who is regulated by labour law to restrict the sexual and marital options available to its employees, ensuring that lesbian church ministers do not marry without losing their jobs.

While intending to avoid doctrinal entanglements, the instances above illustrate how the state can and effectively does become entangled in doctrinal matters when it recognizes religious authorities without also engaging minority religious views or without challenging religious authorities and practices that also produce inequality. This also illustrates the privileged position that the state allots itself in negotiating religious freedoms, arguably in deference to Section 15 of the Constitution. The legal cases brought by

50. Tayob, "One and the Many," 122.

51. Given that section 15 of the Constitution allows "religious observances in state and state-aided institutions, provided they follow public authority rules, they are conducted on an equitable basis and attendance is free and voluntary," this event might easily have been challenged on grounds of discrimination and inequality.

Muslim wives and Methodist lesbian women reveal the various legal implications of the reluctance of the state to legislate on matters of equality within religious communities. Consequently, systems of religious law offer religious communities a space to operationalise doctrines that may otherwise not be legally or constitutionally acceptable. This space protects the potentially discriminatory doctrinal positions which discriminate against minority interests within religious communities. I suggest that in real terms, this form of engagement may also be viewed as a form of doctrinal preference on the part of the state. Co-opting the state in this way, religious authorities enjoy the benefits of the state's recognition to manipulate state resources and interests to maintain their own privilege.

The theological-political intersection produced in state-recognition of religious communities draws the state to mainstream religious authorities; at the same time not engaging with minority interests and non-interference of the state in the doctrinal hegemonies within religious communities produces a theological-political dynamic where the state also abdicates its responsibility and cannot meaningfully protect the interests of minority segments within religious communities.

INTERSECTIONAL ASSEMBLAGES: WOMEN AND QUEER ADHERENTS NEGOTIATING RELIGIOUS RIGHTS

An intersectional analysis moves away from a single-axis analysis of oppression and challenges the temptation to treat oppression through mutually exclusive categories of identity. We've had detailed analysis of the 'dangers of a single-story' in oppressions that result from gender, race, and class differences, but less theoretical effort has been applied to the place of religion in an intersectional analysis of power.[52] While gender, race and class are common-place markers in the matrix of oppressions that operate in constitutional and secular societies, the intersectional effects of religion and state are less frequently theorised. This distorts an analysis of the religious experience and has the potential for theoretical erasure of subjects that function at the intersection of multiple vectors of oppression within religious communities. This erasure extends to a lack in conceptualizing, identifying and remedying the challenges of religious freedom faced by vulnerable and unrepresented segments within religious communities. As a theory of oppression rather than identity, an intersectional analysis locates South Africans at various confluences in the matrices of oppression that operate within a constitutional democracy. Mediated by the dynamic interplay of

52. Crenshaw, "Demarginalizing the Intersection"; Singh, "Religious Agency and the Limits."

class, race, gender, religion and other aspects of political and social location, an intersectional analysis reflects the multiple subjectivities that operate in the production of religious freedom for vulnerable members and minority interests within religious communities.

An analysis of assemblages surfaces further elements of "discipline and control" that operate in the interplay of the twin constitutional guarantees of equality and religious freedom and the secular imperative to avoid doctrinal entanglement. While the state grants recognition to Jewish, Muslim and Methodist leadership at state events and through recognition of religious bodies, it simultaneously stands back and thus also enables the oppression of vulnerable members and minority interests amongst the collective of Jewish, Muslim and Methodist adherents. South Africa was one of the first nation states to guarantee constitutional protection for minority sexual orientations and accordingly same-sex unions are now legally recognized. Yet this does not entitle a MCSA minister to a public same-sex marriage, and while married same-sex couples enjoy the privileges of a state recognized union, lesbian Methodist ministers and Muslim same-sex or heterosex couples married under religious laws may not. While Muslim women may marry within or outside of state recognition, when they choose to marry by religious rites only (and not through a civil marriage) they are excluded from state recognition and the benefits and protections that ordinarily accrue to couples married under state laws in South Africa do not apply to them. Polygynous marriages performed in the context of African customary law may also enjoy the recognition and protection of the state and couples married therewith can enjoy the benefits that accrue to married couples, but not so for polygynous unions performed under Islamic or other religious laws. Muslim and Jewish wives can also not claim the full protection of the state when held ransom by unscrupulous husbands who refuse to release them from a religious marriage through either a *ṭalāq* or a *gett*.

Reflecting on the dynamics of state and religion through the 'intertwined relations of intersectionality and assemblages,' it is evident that within the sphere of their religious communities, religious authorities hold powers, akin to the capacities for discipline and control exercised by the state, through religiously authorised systems of legal and social sanction, protection and benefit. When these same authorities also co-opt the authority of the state to augment their authority, the resultant assemblage of religious and state mechanisms of discipline and control produce a powerful central authority, increasingly alien from vulnerable segments of the religious community; similarly, the authority of the state within the religious community is consolidated through religious leadership. In these configurations of power, women and queer individuals have neither the options of being goddesses nor cyborgs, as an analysis of intersectionality and assemblages may suggest. They are neither elevated through romanticised notions of non-liberal forms of agency, nor are they privileged individuals who cross boundaries that innovate new assemblages of power. Instead, they are rendered aberrant adherents whose humanity is differentially negotiated through the proclamations of piety and policy issued through the political-theological dynamics operating amongst ministers of religion and ministers of state. The contest between the two suggests overlapping loyalties, and a metaphorical contest for territorial legitimacy; is Muslim marriage the location of state authority or religious authority? What are the theological-political options for queer Muslims and Methodists, or for Jewish, Muslim and lesbian Methodist wives whose marriages and piety are not similarly protected by the constitutional democracy?

As a political entity, the state has the responsibility to fashion a public space that promotes government efficiency and a "unified politics."[53] It is in the interests of a democratic state to produce and maintain a secular public space through the exclusion of religion from the state and or through the possibility for a number of religions to function simultaneously within the public space. Secularism also allows for different religious communities to coexist requiring not only that each religion tolerate others, but that the state too tolerates the public exercise of religious authority. In return, for the well-being of the religious community, its religious authorities must also give recognition to the authority of the secular state. The state maintains social order by creating what can be theorised as a space of religious neutrality where all religions are equally accepted. But, as is my argument here, this state position does not necessarily conclude only in a neutral space marked by distance between state and religion but may also conclude in abdication. The neutrality which is achieved through simultaneous recognition and abdication, colludes to entrench vulnerabilities already internal to religious communities. And so, what appears to be neutrality and non-entanglement is actually alignment with and legitimation of the centralised religious authority and, by implication, one particular aspect of a religions' various doctrinal orientations at the expense or abandonment of the rights of other doctrinal orientations, namely those of the vulnerable or unrepresented minorities within the same religious community. Guarantees of freedom of religion then do not extend similarly to female and queer worshipers as they do their mainstream religious counterparts, specifically those in the mainstream of religious authority.

---

53. Hurd, "Secularism and International Relations," 71.

Instead, state and religion interact in ways that create constitutional privilege for religious authorities and constitutional marginality for non-normative and minority religious interests within those communities. Without an analysis of the intersectional or assembled systems of power in the lives of religious communities living in constitutional contexts, states cannot realise the constitutional aspirations of religious freedom for minority interests within religious communities.

CONCLUSION

In the current theological-political dynamic, where the state recognizes religious authorities at the expense of the interests of other intersections of power, namely women and people with queer sexualities, the state upholds the power structures of the religious authorities in a manner that suggests that the principle of doctrinal non-entanglement cannot be considered operatively clear. In the recognition of religious authorities, the state also gives legitimacy to one doctrinal affiliation within the religious community over other doctrines. This theological-political intersection results in a dynamic of closeness between the state and mainstream religious authorities, which foregrounds and prioritizes the concerns of the mainstream religious community and reduces or abdicates from the space wherein the concerns of the unrepresented and marginalised minority segments of the religious community may be raised. As religious authorities co-opt the power of the state under constitutional guarantees for religious freedom, the intersectionality of oppressions and the assemblages of discipline and control show that freedom of religion applies only to the normative religious authority and its collective doctrinal affiliations, and at the expense or exclusion of women and queer individuals; the result is a dynamic of constitutional privilege and marginality between religious authorities and non-normative religious minorities.

BIBLIOGRAPHY

Ali, Kecia. *Marriage and Slavery in Early Islam.* Cambridge, MA: Harvard University Press, 2010.

Amien, Waheeda. "Overcoming the Conflict between the Right to Freedom of Religion and Women's Rights to Equality: A South African Case Study of Muslim Marriages." *Human Rights Quarterly* 28 (2006) 729–54.

Asmal, Fatima. "South African Women Push for More Inclusive Eid Prayers: In Durban, Mosques and Communal Eid Prayers Have Traditionally Excluded Women, but That Is Now Beginning to Change." *Al-Jazeera*, July 6, 2016. Online. https://www.aljazeera.com/indepth/features/2016/07/south-african-women-push-inclusive-eid-prayers-160705120351868.html.

Bonthuys, E. "Obtaining a Get in Terms of Section 5A of the Divorce Act: Amar v. Amar." *South African Law Journal* 117.1 (2000) 8–16.

Crenshaw, Kimberle. "Demarginalizing the Intersection of Race and Sex: A Black Feminist Critique of Anti-Discrimination Doctrine, Feminism, and Anti-Racism Politics." *University of Chicago Legal Forum* 1 (1989) 139–67.

Da Costa, Yusuf, and Achmat Davids, eds. *Pages from Cape Muslim History.* Pietermaritzburg: Shuter and Shooter, 1994.

De Freitas, Shaun. "Doctrinal Sanction and the Protection of the Rights of Religious Associations: Ecclesia De Lange v Presiding Bishop of the Methodist Church of Southern Africa (726/13) [2014] ZASCA 151." *PER/PELJ* 19 (2016) 1–21.

Easthorpe, Juanita. "Bruised but Not Broken: De Lange v Presiding Bishop of the Methodist Church of Southern Africa and Another 2016 (2) SA 1 (CC)." *Agenda* 30.3 (2016) 115–23.

Ewi, Martin, and Willem Els. "Is a Terrorist Attack Imminent in South Africa?" *Institute of Security Studies*, September, 18, 2015. Online. https://issafrica.org/iss-today/is-a-terrorist-attack-imminent-in-south-africa

Hurd, Elizabeth Shackman. "Secularism and International Relations Theory." In *Religion and International Relations Theory*, edited by Jack Snyder, 60–90. New York: Columbia University Press, 2011.

Islam Today. "One Ummah—One Eid Gah: Unification And The Durban Eid Gah At The Peoples Park." Online. http://www.islamtoday.co.za/article/1609.

Ismail, Farhana. "The Eid Prayer in South Africa and Muslim Women's Struggle for Sacred Space." *Annual Review of Islam in South Africa* 5 (2002) 36–39. Online. http://www.cci.uct.ac.za/usr/cci/publications/aria/download_issues/2002/2002_M5_farhana.pdf.

———. "Female Musallees 'Insulted' but Insist They Won't Back Down." *Al-Qalam*, June 8, 2018. Online. http://alqalam.co.za/female-musallees-insulted-insist-wont-back.

———. "Struggling to Find God in a Shared Space." *Mail and Guardian*, September 19, 2014. Online. https://mg.co.za/article/2014-09-19-the-prophets-mosque-was-a-space-shared-by-men-and-women.

"Law Reform." *Commonwealth Law Bulletin* 21.1 (1995) 141–88.

Leatt, Annie. "Faithfully Secular: Secularism and South African Political Life." *Journal for the Study of Religion* 20.2 (2007) 29–44.

Mahomed, Ashraf. "The Divorce Amendment Act 95 of 1996: A Case of Doctrinal Entanglement and a Step Closer to the Legitimate Democratization of Religion." *De Rebus* 49 (1997) 495–96.

Moosa, Ebrahim. "Muslim Conservatism in South Africa." *Journal of Theology for Southern Africa* 69 (1989) 73–81.

Omar, Muhammad Ismail. "Nxumalo Hailed as Breath of Fresh Air." *Daily News*, September 5, 2011. Online. https://www.pressreader.com/south-africa/daily-news-south-africa/20110905/281775625871310.

Paur, Jasbir. "I Would Rather Be a Cyborg than a Goddess: Intersectionality, Assemblage, and Affective Politics." *PhiloSOPHIA* 2.1 (2012) 49–66.

Republic of South Africa. "Deputy President Kgalema Motlanthe to Speak at the Graduation Ceremony of the Imams in Cape Town." *Department of Home Affairs*, April 29, 2014. Press Release. Online. http://www.dha.gov.za/index.php/

statements-speeches/456-deputy-president-kgalema-motlanthe-to-speak-at-the-graduation-ceremony-of-the-imams-in-cape-town-30-april-2014-at-10h00.

———. "Maintenance Act 99 of 1998." November 19, 1998. Updated July 30, 2010. Online. http://www.justice.gov.za/legislation/acts/1998-099.pdf.

———. "Minister Gigaba and Deputy Minister Chohan Officiate at Graduation of Imams as Marriage Officers." *Department of Home Affairs*, June 3, 2016. Press Release. Online. http://www.dha.gov.za/index.php/statements-speeches/795-minister-gigaba-and-deputy-minister-chohan-officiate-at-graduation-of-imams-as-marriage-officers.

———. "Muslim Marriages Bill." *Government Gazette Staatskoerant* 547.33946 (2011) 2–27.

Rai, Sasha Claude. "The 'Apartheid' of Spaces, Places, and Voices: A Feminist Challenge to Religious Patriarchy in the Muslim Community—TIP and the Resurrection of the Family Eid Gah." PhD diss., University of Kwazulu-Natal, 2015.

Ripple, Kenneth. "The Entanglement Test of The Religion Clauses—A Ten Year Assessment." *UCLA Law Review* 27.6 (1980) 1195–239.

Singh, Jakeet. "Religious Agency and the Limits of Intersectionality." *Hypatia* 30.4 (2015) 657–74.

South African Law Commission. *Islamic Marriages and Related Matters: Discussion Paper 101.* Pretoria: South African Law Commission, 2001.

———. *Islamic Marriages and Related Matters: Issue Paper 15.* Pretoria: South African Law Commission, 2000.

———. *Islamic Marriages and Related Matters: Report.* Pretoria: South African Law Commission, 2003.

———. *Report on Jewish Divorces.* Pretoria: South African Law Commission, 1994.

Surtee, Safiyyah. "They Don't Have Prayer: The Media and Eid For Muslim Women in South Africa." *Muslim Matters*, October 16, 2010. Online. https://muslimmatters.org/2010/10/16/they-dont-have-prayer-the-media-and-eid-for-muslim-women-in-south-africa.

"Taking Islam to the People." TIP Family Eidgah's Facebook page. Online. https://www.facebook.com/TipFamilyEidgah.

Tayob, Abdulkader. "The One and the Many: Religious Coexistence and Belonging on Postapartheid South Africa." In *The African Renaissance and the Afro-Arab Spring: A Season of Rebirth*, edited by Charles Villa-Vicencio, et al., 121–37. Washington, DC: Georgetown University Press, 2015.

Vahed, Goolam H. "Changing Islamic Traditions and Emerging Identities in South Africa." *Journal of Muslim Minority Affairs* 20.1 (2000) 43–73.

———. "Indian Muslims in South Africa: Continuity, Change, and Disjuncture, 1860–2000." *Alternation* 7.2 (2000) 67–98.

"Women Attending the Eid Gah." *Jamiatul Ulama* (blog), August 15, 2012. Online. http://jamiat.org.za/women-attending-the-eid-gah.

"Women and the Eid Prayer—The Debate Rages On." *Al-Qalam Newspaper*, September 2011.

Court Cases

Amar v. Amar 1999 (2) All SA 376 (W).

———. 1999 (3) SA 604 (W).

Amod v. Multilateral Motor Vehicle Accidents Fund (Commission for Gender Equality Intervening) 1999 (4) SA 1319 (SCA).

Bronn v. Fritz Bronn's Executors and Others 1860 (3) Searle 3.

Daniels v. Campbell NO and Others 2003 (9) BCLR 969 (C).

———. 2004 (5) SA 331 (CC).

De Lange v. Presiding Bishop of the Methodist Church of Southern Africa and Another 2016 (2) SA 1 (CC).

Ebrahim v. Mahomed Essop 1905 T.S. 59.

Faro v. Bingham NO and Others 2013 ZAWCHC 159.

Hassam v. Jacobs NO and Others 2008 (4) All SA 350 (C).

———. 2009 (5) SA 572 (CC).

Ismail v. Ismail 1983 (1) SA 1006.

Kader v. Kader 1972 (3) SA 203 (RAD).

Khan v. Khan 2005 (2) SA 272 (T).

Moosa NO and Others v. Harnakar 2017 (6) SA 425 (WCC).

Rylands v. Edros 1996 (4) ALL SA 557 (C).

———. 1997 (2) SA 690 (C).

Seedat's Executors v. The Master 1917 AD 302.

Walz v. Tax Commission 1970 397 U.S. 664.

Women's Legal Center v. The President of the Republic of South Africa and Others 2018 ZAWCHC 109.

11

Mind the Gap

Freedom of Religion and the "Gay Rights Clause"

CHARLENE VAN DER WALT

A number of disputes have arisen since the inception of the new democratic constitutional dispensation in South Africa. These disputes
highlight the need for a balancing act or a rather skilled hermeneutical engagement when considering, on the one hand, the freedoms and rights protected with regards to churches and religious institutions and on the other
hand the so-called "gay rights clause" protecting the freedom, dignity and
safety of LGBTIQA+[1] people in South Africa.[2] In the Bill of Rights of the
South African Constitution, articles 15 (freedom of religion), 18 (freedom
of association), and 31 (the right to associate with religious communities)
play a very important role in protecting religious institutions and regulating the degree of interference by the state in the internal affairs of these
institutions.

On the other hand, in terms of the so-called "gay rights clause," in
section 9 of the Bill of Rights forbids discrimination on the grounds of
sexual orientation, either from the state or private parties. The Bill of Rights,
according to the Founding Provisions in chapter 1, is the cornerstone of
democracy in South Africa and "any law or conduct inconsistent with it

1. Lesbian, gay, bisexual, transsexual, intersex, queer, asexual, and gender-
nonconforming.

2. Constitution of the Republic of South Africa.

is invalid." This implies that no organ of state of any other institution, including churches, may deny members of the LGBTIQA+ their rights, this includes the right to equality and the right to human dignity.

Probably one of the most prominent examples accentuating the above-mentioned disconnect in the South African context is the embodied reality denoted in the person of Rev. Ecclesia De Lange and the case surrounding her: De Lange vs the Presiding Bishop of the Methodist Church of Southern Africa.[3] Rev. De Lange, whilst being a full time minister of the Methodist Church of Southern Africa, announced to her congregation her intention to marry her same-sex partner. Although the congregation responded positively, Rev. De Lange was soon suspended pending the outcome of a disciplinary hearing. The charge brought against Rev. De Lange was in terms of the "Laws and Discipline of the Church" which stipulated the recognition of only heterosexual marriages, and that "Ministers shall observe and implement the provisions of the Laws and Discipline of the Church and all other policies, decisions, practices and usages of the Church." Rev. De Lange was found guilty of failing to observe the said provisions of the Laws and Discipline of the Church. This initial verdict was challenged and upheld in a number of appeal and arbitration bodies and finally led to the "discontinuation" of Rev. De Lange as a Minister of the Word and Sacrament of the Methodist Church of Southern Africa.[4]

What makes Rev. De Lange's case unfortunate in terms of exploring the poignant disconnect between the constitutional protection of the freedoms and rights of religious institutions and the rights and liberties of LGBTIQA+ people is, as Shaun De Freitas states:

> The appellant was not calling upon "unfair discrimination based on sexual orientation in her claim," but was rather advancing a case based on an entitlement to fair administrative action. For the Court the question was "whether the appellant has shown good cause for avoiding arbitration" and that, according to section 3(2) of the *Arbitration Act,* a court has the discretion to enforce an arbitration agreement. The Court subsequently came to the finding that none of the grounds presented by the Appellant for seeking avoidance of the arbitration was justified.[5]

---

3. De Lange v. Presiding Bishop.

4. For more on the complexity and intricacies of the processes, see Thayer, "Ecclesia De Lange"; De Freitas, "Doctrinal Sanction and the Protection"; Easthorpe, "Bruised but Not Broken"; Kumalo, "Us and Them," 175.

5. De Freitas, "Doctrinal Sanction and the Protection."

Rather than exploring whether the Church discriminated against her in terms of her Sexual Orientation, De Lange's case was focused on administratively just practice and therefore did not create an ideal judicial space to explore the above-mentioned disconnect.

A second example that speaks to this complex point of intersection between freedom of religion and the rights and liberties of LGBTIQA+ people is that of the Dutch Reformed Church in South Africa who in 2015 after much debate became the first church in Africa to make the decision to recognize the status of civil unions between persons of the same gender that is characterised by love and faithfulness and grant permission to ordained ministers to confirm such unions. Moreover, the decision supported the ordination of openly gay clergy. A year later, in 2016, however, in the light of severe conservative backlash and numerous appeals, the decision was overturned, leaving numerous LGBTIQA+ people, family and friends, in a strange impasse after being fully welcomed and affirmed within the vulnerable and diverse communion of the community of faith, only to be "un-welcomed" and "de-valued." The decision and the subsequent overruling has created a jumble within church polity with no current clear disentanglement strategy, being further exasperated by LGBTIQA+ members and allies also threating judicial action against the Synod of the Dutch Reformed Church.

Both of the above-mentioned examples, although perhaps not reaching their full capacity in terms of the legal process, has created often heated and strongly positioned oppositional conversations regarding the complex point of intersection between freedom of religion and the rights and liberties of LGBTIQA+ people within mainline faith communities situated within the South African landscape.

Although both examples warrant further in-depth exploration, I would, however, like to turn my attention to a more recent example and one positioned in the South African Pentecostal faith landscape, by referring to the events that took place at the Grace Bible Church based in Soweto, South Africa, on January 22, 2017. I will use this case study in the first part of the essay as a catalyst to further elaborate and complicate the "gap" that should be 'minded' according to the title of the essay. Besides referring to the gap between the freedom of religion and the rights and liberties of LGBTIQA+ people, as guaranteed by the South African Constitution, this essay will also speak to a number of other gaps that further complicate the discussion— namely the gap between the rule of law and the lived experience of people affected by the law, the gap between our own embodied understanding of personal experiences of exclusion and the capacity to extend that knowledge to the liberation struggle of others, the gap between the letter of the law and the heart of the law, and the gap between the Bible reader and text of the Bible. All these implied gaps call for the development of hermeneutical skills that enable accountability, empathy, and responsibility.

First, I will, however, turn my attention to the events of January 22, 2017 when the Grace Bible Church in Soweto, invited a well-known Ghanaian Pentecostal Bishop and founder of Lighthouse Chapel International, Bishop Dag Heward-Mills, to minister to the congregation.[6] During the sermon, Bishop Heward-Mills made a controversial statement about LGBTIQA+ people in the church, when describing homosexuality as "sinful," "unnatural," and "disgusting."[7]

The sermon resulted in a public outcry,[8] spearheaded by the South African celebrity personality, Somizi Mholongo, who walked out of the sermon of the Ghanaian evangelist and posted a video on social media pleading with churches in general and with Bishop Mosa Sono and the Grace Bible Church in particular to rather "say it out loud, homosexually is not allowed, homosexuality is a sin or gay people must not come to our church. . . . Say it, say it so that we know."[9] The initial incident and the public response it sparked forced Bishop Mosa Sono and the Grace Bible Church to respond publicly.

Bishop Mosa Sono, founder and Senior Pastor of Grace Bible Church, responded on behalf of the leadership of the church in the form of a public statement.[10] Sono affirmed that Grace Bible Church is a "Bible-based institution of faith" functioning in a constitutional dispensation.[11] Sono expressed appreciation for the rights and privileges that the Constitution guarantees for faith communities and institutions of faith but also stated that they "respect and hold in high regard the Constitution and the fact that it prohibits discrimination because of race, gender and amongst other sexual orientation." He confirmed that the Church recognize, respect and fully affirm these rights as championed by the Constitution. He continued by affirming the human dignity of all people because of the fact that every human being is created in the image of God and therefore has intrinsic value and consequently declared that all people are welcome in the church. After confirming the constitutionally respected value, rights and dignity of all people, also those of diverse sexual orientations, he continued by stating

6. Singh, "Grace Bible Church."

7. Live footage of the sermon can be found at eNCA, "'Homophobic' Sermon."

8. Nemakonde, "Somizi Storms Out."

9. Somizi, "Somizi Lashes Out."

10. Grace Bible Church, "Statement to the Congregation."

11. Grace Bible Church, "Statement to the Congregation."

that they also "believe and affirm the constitutional right to choose one's religious affiliation and believes."[12] In this regard, he stated that the Church believes in the Bible as the word of God and that it functions as the superior and ultimate instruction for personal life conduct and the collective life of faith, and that this finds expression in the church's statement of faith.[13]

Sono continued by stating that the church understands that it is within their constitutional rights to determine rules of conduct for life and faith and therefore affirmed the principle regulating intimacy and sexuality in their statement of faith formulated as follows: "With regards to sexual behavior, we believe in heterosexual relationships between a natural man and a natural woman within the confines of lawful matrimony. Adherence to this stated principle of sexual behavior is an inherent requirement of membership of Grace Bible Church."[14] Marriage as the exclusive and ultimate institution sanctioned by God is exclusively possible between one man and one woman and the only form of partnership that is approved by God for sexual relationships. He concludes the argument by stating that the church in no way believes that holding these views are in themselves discriminatory and he implored the church's members to condemn all forms of violence and hate speech targeting especially members of the often stigmatised and vulnerable LGBTIQA+ community.

The initial incident, the responses on social and public media, and the statement by Bishop Mosa Sono and the Grace Bible Church, generated much public reaction and engagement. Following from Sono's response I would like to pick up on a number of gaps that I believe warrant further attention and future collective reflection.

MIND THE GAP: THE CONSTITUTIONAL POSITION IN CONTRAST WITH THE EMBODIED LIVED REALITIES OF THOSE MOST VULNERABLE

The disconnect between the rights and privileges ensured by the South African Constitution and the lived realities of those it aims to protect have often been highlighted and commented upon.[15] In the light of rampant violence

12. Grace Bible Church, "Statement to the Congregation."

13. Grace Bible Church, "Our Statement of Faith."

14. Grace Bible Church, "Our Statement of Faith."

15. The complexity is accentuated by statistics released in a survey conducted by the Other Foundation, which found that "51 percent of all South Africans believe that gay people should have the same human rights as all other citizens, even though 72 percent feel that same-sex sexual activity is 'morally wrong'" (Sutherland et al., *Progressive Prudes*).

and the prevailing rape-culture, questions have often been raised as to how it is possible that South Africa has this remarkably progressive constitution and yet the most vulnerable in society struggle due to stigmatisation, exclusion, and violence. Within South African society this reality is most pertinently experienced by LGBTIQA+ persons. Mark Gevisser remarks regarding the particular vulnerability of LGBTIQA+ people in the South African society:

> Like coal miners used caged canary birds, whose death was a warning sign of toxic gases in the mine tunnels, homosexual women and men, and transgender and intersex people in southern Africa are at the coalface of the multiple dangers in many of our societies today. How our societies treat lesbian, gay, bisexual, transgender an intersex (LGBTI) people is symptomatic of the dangers facing all people who are excluded in some way or another in our societies, by those who have a grip on social, economic and political power.[16]

Considering the high level of stigmatisation and the exceptional vulnerability of LGBTIQA+ people in the South African society amidst the constitutional protection leads one to wonder if the constitutional values and insistence on the dignity of LGBTIQA+ people are indeed owned by the general population of the South African society. If they are not, which is fairly apparent considering the high levels of discrimination and violence, how is it that the so-called "Gay Rights Clause" found its way into the initial draft constitution and successfully maintained this position to make it into the final version of the current constitution?

In an attempt to reflect on the above-mentioned chasm between rights and lived embodied realities I would like to briefly consider the process of reception of LGBTIQA+ rights into the South African Constitution. Jacklyn Cock in her reflection on the strategies employed to ensure the reception of gay rights into the South African Constitution remarks the following:

> There was no single and simple script at work . . . the discourse of diversity, the celebration of difference, and especially the rights to freedom of sexual orientation were defended as part of the challenge of building a diverse, pluralistic society. . . . The 'rainbow' emerged as a strong symbol defining unity among the diverse people of South Africa as a source of national pride.[17]

16. Gevisser, *Canaries in the Coal Mines*, 3.
17. Cock, "Engendering Gay."

Gay rights were thus part of a much broader political project arguing for inclusive social justice and in opposition to all forms of discrimination.[18] The
approach employed echoes something of Audre Lorde's wisdom when she
states: "There is no such thing as a single-issue struggle because we do not
live single-issue lives."[19] Cock comments on the strong focus on coalition
building spearheaded by Peter Thatchall with the ANC in exile in London
and locally by the likes of Simon Nkoli.[20] Nkoli, who went on trial with 19
others for treason in 1987 for mass protest marches organized in the black
townships of the Vaal region, emphasized that the battles against homophobia and racism were inseparable.[21] He is quoted in a speech at the first public
parade in 1990 organized by GLOW:

> I'm fighting for the abolition of apartheid, and I fight for the
> right of freedom of sexual orientation. These are inextricably
> linked with each other. I cannot be free as a black man if I am
> not free as a gay man.[22]

Through effective one-on-one activism and one issue lobbying the clause
became part of the draft constitution and remained in the final version
through a high level and elite legislative process.[23]

The distance between the process for constitutional reception of LG-
BTIQA+ rights and the general attitude of the population probably goes a
long way towards explaining why these progressive rights are not generally
owned by the South African population. Mark Massoud remarks in this
regard:

> The progressive government and constitution, however, did not
> reflect the attitudes of most South Africans, who did not support

---

18. Eric Christiansen argues along the same line when stating that multiple factors
informed the means through which South Africa became the first country in the word
to offer constitutional-level protections to its gay and lesbian citizens. He asserts a tri-
partite explanation: "(1) The uniquely synchronous historical development of the anti-
apartheid liberation movements and the South African gay and lesbian community set
the stage; (2) the radical anti-discrimination ideology of the African National Congress
(ANC) provided the philosophical justification; and (3) the autocratic constitutional
drafting process secured the explicit, favorable content" (Christiansen, "Ending the
Apartheid," 997).

19. Lorde, "Sister Outsider."

20. Cock, "Engendering Gay," 36.

21. Cock, "Engendering Gay," 36.

22. Cock, "Engendering Gay," 36.

23. For more regarding the constitutional drifting process, see Stychin, "Constituting Sexuality."

gay rights. The government created a gap between its tolerant
laws and the conservative social attitudes of its citizens.[24]

The 2016 report by the Other Foundation also offered a sobering reality
check when again affirming that LGBTIQ people are by far the most stigmatised group in South Africa.[25] The report further highlights and discusses
a number of public narratives relating to sexual orientation and gender
identity propagated by the state, the media, religious institutions and other
public actors that inform the stigmatisation and discrimination mentioned
above. These narratives pertaining to homosexuality and gender identity
include: (a) the moral narrative: "It's a sin against God"; (b) the political/
cultural narrative: "It's un-African and a Western neo-colonial imposition!";
(c) the public health narrative: "It's an illness"; (d) the media narrative: "It's
scandalous!"; and (e) the social exclusion narrative: "They don't belong."[26]

The predominant narrative that is strongly informed by combining
the rest of the public narratives, as stated above, is that of social exclusion
informing public and private spaces to maintain and insist on the fact that
LGBTIQA+ people do not belong; not in education, not in the workplace,
not in health spaces, not in tradition, not culture, not in faith nor in family.
In the light of the above, it seems pertinent to work for inclusions and protections beyond rights, and a mere legislative process, labouring for social
tolerance, inclusion and ultimately acceptance and celebration. To address
the disconnect highlighted above a greater emphasis should be placed on the
facilitation of processes that would encourage faith communities to interrogate their commonly held beliefs and practices that inform stigmatisation
and dehumanisation, and to create dynamic spaces to facilitate conversation, discussion and encounter to accelerate the process of constitutional
value reception. Institutions of faith, with their large social footprints in
local communities, seem to be the ideal spaces to have these conversations
and explore the values of human dignity and equality as proposed by the
Constitution, considering how these link to values of radical hospitality,
justice, and love, which are so central to the Christian gospel.

24. Massoud, "Evolution of Gay Rights."

25. Gevisser, *Canaries in the Coal Mines*, 6.

26. Gevisser, *Canaries in the Coal Mines*, 15–29.

MIND THE GAP: EXPLORING THE LACK OF AN
INTERSECTIONAL UNDERSTANDING OF LIBERATION

Maria Frahm-Arp, in an article exploring the complex position of "Pentecostal Evangelical Charismatic" churches in terms of political realities, states:

> During Apartheid, most Pentecostal Charismatic Evangelical style churches were politically neutral and uninvolved in politics. In the new dispensation after 1994, this changed drastically. On Heritage Day (a bank holiday) on 24 September 2002, for example, Grace Bible Church in Soweto offered a programme in which senior members of the African National Congress (ANC) addressed the congregation. In 2009, as President of the ANC, Jacob Zuma invited Pastor Ray McCauley of Rhema Bible Church to head the National Interfaith Leadership Council (NILC) in which the dominant voice is PCE Christianity. Leading up to the 2009 elections McCauley, in turn, invited Zuma to Rhema, thus expressing his political support for him.[27]

Regardless of the complex nature of the relationship between Pentecostal churches and the political landscape it seems apparent that the issue of race discrimination has made it onto the ecclesiastic agenda. From their public statement delivered by Bishop Sono it, however, becomes clear that the link between various liberation struggles, including the fight against racism, sexism, and homophobia, is not easily made.

This is of course not a unique disposition as a similar argument is currently being made about the Uniting Reformed Church in South Africa. The reformed church community who were very active in the struggle against Apartheid and consequently produced the Confession of Belhar, that unequivocally states that God is on the side of the poor and the marginalised and who claimed and confessed this reality in terms of race, has not been able to make the connection between the various systems of oppression. Allan Boesak eloquently states in this regard:

> How could the same church that took such a strong stand against apartheid and racial oppression, gave such inspired leadership from its understanding of the Bible and the radical Reformed tradition; that had, in the middle of the state of emergency of the 1980s with its unprecedented oppression, its desperate violence, and nameless fear given birth to the Belhar Confession that spoke of reconciliation, justice, unity, and the Lordship of Jesus

27. Frahm-Arp, "Political Rhetoric."

Christ, now display such blatant hatred and bigotry, deny so vehemently for God's LGBTI children the solidarity we craved for
ourselves in our struggle for racial justice, bow down so easily at
the altar of prejudice and homophobic hypocrisy? We who had
rescued the Reformed tradition from the heresy and blasphemy
of the theology of apartheid and forged a new identity for that
tradition in struggles for justice and compassion were now the
ones embracing that heresy in our howling condemnation of
our own flesh because of their different sexual orientation.[28]

As argued elsewhere, African Christianities, even those with Evangelical
leanings, have been able to reject slavery because they were rejecting an
evil system. In the South African context, the mobilisation of faith communities and the theological imperative of Black and Liberation theology
were instrumental in the fight against Apartheid. But all forms of African
Christianity, including Africa's liberation theologies, have found it difficult,
theologically, to develop a theology of hospitality and radical inclusion that
would include LGBTIQA+ people.[29]

In light of the above, it seems important to reflect on the systemic nature of oppression and to move beyond the personal or individual dimensions of faith and salvation. It would be important to recognize the affinities
between systems of slavery, systems of racism and systems of homophobia
and to develop an understanding, for example, that all of the above are constructed on the desire to control the bodies of the denigrated.

In order to unmask the systemic and embodied nature of systems of
oppression the importance of the concept of intersectionality cannot be
denied in the sense that it maintains that in order to comprehensively deal
with embodied experiences of oppression, domination, and marginalisation
one has to take into consideration how multiple social forces such as race,
class, gender, sexual orientation, religion, and culture converge in order to
bring into being a certain phenomenon, position or situatedness.[30] An intersectional analysis assists in the process of reflecting on the strategic and
systemic ways in which systems of oppression operate, exploring the realities
of multiple intersecting axes of oppression. Otherwise, as illustrated above,
we will indeed discover faith communities who are champions for justice in
one arena of oppression but the perpetrators of injustice in another.

28. Boesak, *Kairos, Crisis, and Global Apartheid*, 93–117.

29. West et al., "When Faith Does Violence."

30. For more regarding intersectionality, please see Crenshaw, "Mapping the Margins"; Cho et al., "Toward a Field of Intersectionality."

Central to any intersectional approach is the insistence on the significant centrality of the body in any analysis and engagement with systems of oppression. In taking the cue from James B. Nelson it is important to reclaim the body in the process of doing theology, and to privilege the appropriation of the body as a site of revelation.[31] Elisabeth Gerle poignantly remarks in this regard:

> Feminist and eros theologians have also foregrounded the body as a meeting-point for sexual desire and the divine. Today this in-between space is emphasized as the place where God, relationship, exists.[32]

In terms of LGBTIQA+ persons, the church context has often been a painfully reductionist reality as one-directional discussions around sexual practice and conduct have often dominated conversations engaging the interface between faith and sexual diversity. Church appropriated 'theologies of sexuality' dictate, in a normative way, what a body "should do" by means of employing understandings of scripture and tradition as the starting points of doing Theology. A 'sexual theology' in turn takes a contrasting position by starting theological reflection from the reality of the body inescapable and asking the performative question of what a body "can do"?[33] As argued elsewhere, by shifting the emphasis from normative to performative, we make space for more bodies to matter and for the inclusion of the embodied lived experience of LGBTIQA+ bodies.[34]

In order to access these new, often excluded or silenced, embodied understandings and experiences as a starting place of doing theology it is important to develop the vocabulary to name authentic embodied experiences but also to unmask often unquestionable systems of domination. "Finding language," according to Elize Morkel is also a way of undoing the destructive discourses that violate people and lead to silencing practices.[35] When risking the endeavour of finding a vocabulary to give voice to our embodied experience and name our vulnerabilities new imaginings of solidarity and community are made possible. This, to my mind, might be one of the greatest gifts of the LGBTIQA+ community brings to the life of the church in general as space is opened up for all to reflect on their embodiment, desire, longing, and vulnerability. After all, these are experiences that are central to

---

31. Nelson, *Body Theology*.

32. Gerle, *Passionate Embrace*, 277.

33. From more in this regard, see Gerle, *Passionate Embrace*, 277; Isherwood and Stuart, *Introducing Body Theology*.

34. West et al., "When Faith Does Violence," 6.

35. Morkel, "Responses to Gender Injustice."

the human condition and so foundational to the mystery of our relational encounter with God and others in vulnerable communion.

MIND THE GAP: HOLDING AN EXCLUSIVIST POSITION AND RESULTING DISCRIMINATION, EXCLUSION, AND VIOLENCE

Bishop Mosa Sono concludes the statement of the Grace Bible Church concerning the status of LGBTIQA+ people within the faith community by stating that the church leadership does not believe that holding a Bible-based normative position that marriage between one "normal" man and one "normal" woman as the only, exclusive and ultimate institution sanctioned by God for sexual relations as in itself discriminatory.[36]

The statement, however, warrants further interrogation especially considering the often discussed link between faith and violence.[37] Much of what underlies the position statement of the church is the often unquestionable reality of Bible-based patriarchy infused heteronormativity. Gust A. Yep describes Heteronormativity as follows:

> The process of normalization of heterosexuality in our social system actively and methodically subordinates, disempowers, denies and rejects individuals who do not conform to the heterosexual mandate by criminalizing them, denying them protection against discrimination, refusing them basic rights and recognition, or all of the above.[38]

Heteronormative discourse describes reality primarily and exclusively from the position of the heterosexual.

> This is the idea, dominant in most societies, that heterosexuality is the only 'normal' sexual orientation, only sexual or marital relations between women and men are acceptable and each sex has certain natural roles in life, so-called gender roles.[39]

Within the heteronormative there is thus only space for heterosexual experiences, constructions and realities, and no other alternatives are tolerated. By employing the discourse of 'normalcy', any other reality that does not confirm or live up to this gold standard is constructed to be abnormal,

---

36. Grace Bible Church, "Statement to the Congregation."
37. West et al., "When Faith Does Violence," 6.
38. Yep, "Violence of Heteronormativity," 24.
39. Martin et al., *Hate Crimes*, 1.

inferior, disgusting and consequently informs stigmatizing homophobic attitudes and hate crimes.

Besides referring to 'normal' men and 'normal' women the statement also defines marriage in line with heteronormative ideology as the only and exclusive institution to celebrate the embodied gift of sexuality.[40] Although heteronormative discourse would like to insist on the stability and unquestionability of the institution of marriage informed by an apparent monophonic voice from scripture it is important to take note of alternative viewpoints.[41] The stability of a so-called Biblical model of marriage is interrogated by highlighting the Bible as an internal site of struggle that speaks with many contested voices and that offers numerous alternative and even contradictory constructions, understandings, ideas and models of "marriage."[42] Beyond not having one single and stable construction of marriage that can be deduced from the Bible, the precarity of the institution in its contemporary form also warrants further exploration as it has been argued to be unsafe for many women and a loveless trap for LGBTIQA+ people desperately trying to conform to the heteronormative ideal.[43]

Although I am not trying to argue that all manifestations of marriage are problematic, or that people should not pursue fulfilment in this dimension of life by pledging the commitment of lifelong union and getting married, I am arguing for a critical systematic engagement with the institution of marriage as it functions as a dominant regulating practice within heteropatriarchy. The importance of an understating of marriage as it is imbedded in a patriarchal society, and as it functions as an incubator for heteronormative standards and ideals, seem essential to the task of "unmaking"[44] the discrimination, stigmatisation and dehumanisation that informs homophobia and hate crimes against LGBTIQA+ people.

Within the African context, heteronormativity is reinforced by describing homosexuality as un-African, un-Christian and counter the Biblical norm. Motsau Motsau and Mbuyiselo Botha argue along the same lines when stating:

> When faith communities exclude and discriminate against anyone based on their genderedness, they create a hierarchy of

---

40. Grace Bible Church, "Statement to the Congregation."

41. Thatcher, *Marriage after Modernity*.

42. For more on the Bible as a site of struggle, please see West, *Stolen Bible*.

43. Phiri, "Why Does God Allow," 19.

44. Thatcher, *Liberating Sex*.

what is normal and acceptable and what is not. This is often supported by readings of their sacred texts as justification.[45]

MIND THE GAP: THE TEXT AND THE READER

The centrality of the Bible in much that has been discussed above is undeniable and it could be argued that it is the central issue when engaging the LGBTIQA+ realities within faith communities.

In order to counter fundamentalist, exclusivist, uncritical and non-contextual readings of the Bible, that often result from patriarchal and heteronormative communities as mentioned above, it is important to strive towards and seek for life-affirming inclusive alternative approaches and strategies.

Rather than appropriating the Bible as a simple conversation terminator in the fashion of the often quoted dictum: *The Bible says it, I believe it, and that settles it,* and that seems simple and clear in phrases like Sono's affirmation that Grace Bible Church is a "Bible-based institution of faith,"[46] in the conclusion, I would like to argue for a responsible contextual and intercultural Bible reading process to inform moral reflection on the issue.[47]

Responsible Bible readers should be encouraged to resist simple 'applications' of so-called Biblical principles in the process of ethical reflection and should be encouraged to commit to the hard work of engaging with the rich complexity of Biblical literature by taking amongst other things the following dimensions seriously in the process of Bible interpretation: a) The so-called world-behind-the-text that takes into consideration the realities of the process of the text in a socio-cultural reality removed from our contemporary landscape; b) The world-of-the-text that takes seriously the fact that the Bible is a literary document that consists of the contribution of many writers who wrote in a number of different styles and c) The world-in-front-of-the-text, in which the role of the reader is taken seriously in the interpretation process. Within a responsible approach to Bible interpretation, it is thus important to become aware of one's own interpretative context and the biases that one brings to the process.

In order to open up new and dynamic spaces in the often-beleaguered landscape of Bible engagement when considering ethical realities, tools and insights developed within related fields of Contextual Bible study and Intercultural Bible reading seem helpful. In terms of Contextual Bible Study, a

---

45. Motsau and Botha, "Faith Can Promote Rape Culture."

46. Grace Bible Church, "Statement to the Congregation."

47. For more regarding this process, please see Van der Walt, "Is 'Being Right.'"

rich legacy of work that has been done and developed by the Ujamaa Center for Community Development and Research under the leadership of Professor Gerald O. West based at the University of KwaZulu-Natal.

Contextual reflections by "ordinary readers" and insisting on the epistemological privilege of the poor as described by Gerald West and others have a long and powerful history.[48] Readers always bring their context to the text through the questions and concerns that inform their interpretation. Our contexts, therefore "always shape our reading practice."[49]

Contextual Bible Study provides readers "access to unfamiliar texts" that are historically "suppressed by their church traditions" but have to remain part of the reading and interpretive world of biblical scholars. It also provides access to "unfamiliar literary units" in texts that are otherwise familiar. Finally, it "provides ways of reading familiar texts in unfamiliar ways."[50]

Beyond the important first step of a contextual Bible reading, I would like to argue in favor of the endeavour of risking the encounter with the "other" by incorporating insights as developed within the praxis of Intercultural Bible reading. Intercultural Bible reading is an important space for dialogue to take place and for people to find new ways of talking about ethical issues.[51] The method encourages interpreters to enter into the process of reading and reflecting on Bible stories with others, also those ideologically removed from them, and has proven to create space for alternative understandings, positions, and insights to develop. Rather than remaining closed, exclusivist and isolated in the engagement with the Biblical text the Intercultural Bible reading process imagines an alternative. An alternative where we no longer refuse to listen to those most affected, most marginalised and most silenced, but where we dare to risk the possibility the recognition of

---

48. Gerald West remarks concerning so-called ordinary readers: "Part of the substantive claim I am making in differentiating between the scholar and nonscholar/ordinary reader is that there is a difference in the way each of these sectors read biblical texts. This difference is significant, and recognition of this difference can lead to creative and socially transformative collaboration between different sets of interpretive resources these different sectors bring to a collaborative reading project. So, in the general sense, I am focusing on the kind of interpretive training different sectors have received. The ordinary reader has been 'trained' by his or her primary (for example, the family) and secondary (for example, the church, and school) communities, whereas the scholarly reader has been trained by a tertiary community, the academy" (West, *Reading Other-Wise*, 2). See also West, *Biblical Hermeneutics*.

49. West, "Contextual Bible Reading."

50. West, "Contextual Bible Reading," 145.

51. Van der Walt, "Is 'Being Right,'" 132.

the humanity of the other and in the process restore the mystery of life in the rich diversity of vulnerable communion.

For an Intercultural Bible reading process to be authentic the starting point has to be an in-depth embodied contextual engagement with the Biblical text in order to bring to the encounter with "the other" a unique reading of the text in the specificity of the local. On the other hand, the Intercultural dimension encourages local contextual readers to consider the possibility of a diversity of interpretations and the imperative for critical self-reflection and the possibility for a change in interpretation, understanding or position.

At the outset of this contribution a number of examples were highlighted that spoke to the complex process of the balancing of rights when rights protecting the freedom of religion on the one hand is brought into conversation with rights protecting personal liberty pertaining to issues such as race, class, gender and particular to this contribution, sexual orientation. Although none of these sited examples has driven this complex conversation to a climax within the South African context, forcing the hand of the judicial system in making final rulings pertaining to what rights might or might not trump others, it is clear that the drive of these competing rights necessitates robust conversations within a maturing constitutional dispensation. Central to much of the argument driving this contribution is the instance on the development and maturation of hermeneutical skills that will enable us collectively to negotiate the process of navigating conflicting or oppositional rights protected within the South African constitutional dispensation. Beyond, however, arguing for an objective or impersonal hermeneutical balancing act, the contribution, aimed at highlighting the embodied reality of those most affected and an instance of starting the process of reflection from the embodied position of those most vulnerable and disenfranchised. Although not making any concrete or directive suggestions as to how this process of the balancing of rights should develop in the South African society, a pertinent question that we need to reflect on as faith communities, embedded within the constitutional dispensation, is if we really want to leave the final word on the determination of what is considered just, in service of love and affirming of human dignity to the judicial system? Maybe at the heart of these test cases lives the question of who we are as faith communities in the South African society and how free our religion truly is if those most vulnerable in our society finds no shelter or affirmation of dignity in our midst.

BIBLIOGRAPHY

Boesak, Allan Aubrey. *Kairos, Crisis, and Global Apartheid: The Challenge to Prophetic Resistance*. New York: Palgrave Macmillan, 2015.

Cho, Sumi, et al. "Toward a Field of Intersectionality Studies: Theory, Applications, and Praxis." *Signs: Journal of Women in Culture and Society* 38.4 (2013) 785–810.

Christiansen, Eric C. "Ending the Apartheid of the Closet: Sexual Orientation in the South African Constitutional Process." *NYUJ Int'l L & Pol* 32 (1999) 997–1058.

Cock, Jacklyn. "Engendering Gay and Lesbian Rights: The Equality Clause in the South African Constitution." *Women's Studies International Forum* 26.1 (2003) 35–45.

Crenshaw, Kimberle W. "Mapping the Margins: Intersectionality, Identity Politics, and Violence against Women of Color." *Stanford Law Review* 43.6 (1991) 1241–99.

De Freitas, Shaun. "Doctrinal Sanction and the Protection of the Rights of Religious Associations: Ecclesia De Lange v the Presiding Bishop of the Methodist Church of Southern Africa (726/13) [2014] ZASCA 151." *PER: Potchefstroomse Elektroniese Regsblad* 19.1 (2016) 1–22.

Easthorpe, Juanita. "Bruised but Not Broken: De Lange v. the Presiding Bishop of the Methodist Church of Southern Africa and Another 2016 (2) SA 1 (CC)." *Agenda* 30.3 (2016) 115–23.

eNCA. "'Homophobic' Sermon at Grace Bible Church." *YouTube* video, 1:21. January 23, 2017. Online. https://www.youtube.com/watch?v=ez31LhDt8Nk.

Frahm-Arp, Maria. "The Political Rhetoric in Sermons and Select Social Media in Three Pentecostal Charismatic Evangelical Churches Leading up to the 2014 South African Election." *Journal for the Study of Religion* 28.1 (2015) 114–41.

Gerle, Elisabeth. *Passionate Embrace: Luther on Love, Body, and Sensual Presence*. Eugene, OR: Cascade, 2017.

Gevisser, Mark. *Canaries in the Coal Mines: An Analysis of Spaces for LGBTI Activism in Southern Africa*. Johannesburg: Other Foundation, 2017.

Grace Bible Church. "Statement to the Congregation & Members of the Church." *YouTube* video, 5:04. January 29, 2017. Online. https://www.youtube.com/watch?v=fhoCqlvZDVw.

———. "Our Statement of Faith." Online. http://gracebiblechurch.org.za/about-grace/our-statement-of-faith.

Isherwood, Lisa, and Elizabeth Stuart. *Introducing Body Theology*. Sheffield: Sheffield Academic, 1998.

Lorde, Audre. *Sister Outsider: Essays and Speeches*. Freedom, CA: Crossing, 1984.

Kumalo, Raymond Simangaliso. "'Us and Them' in the One and Undivided Church: The Methodist Church and the Same-Sex Sexuality Debate." *Journal of Gender and Religion in Africa* 17.2 (2011) 175–91.

Martin, Andrew, et al. *Hate Crimes: The Rise of Corrective Rape in South Africa*. London: Action Aid, 2009.

Massoud, Mark F. "The Evolution of Gay Rights in South Africa." *Peace Review* 15.3 (2003) 301–7.

Mhlongo, Somizi. "Somizi Lashes out at Grace Bible Church for Homophobic Sermon." *YouTube* video, 2:59. January 23, 2017. Online. https://www.youtube.com/watch?v=w8shU9ogLAQ.

Morkel, Elize. "Responses to Gender Injustice." In *Living with Dignity: African Perspectives on Gender Equality*, edited by Elna Mouton, et al., 125–46. Stellenbosch: African Sun, 2015.

Motsau, Motsau, and Mbuyiselo Botha. "Faith Can Promote Rape Culture." *Mail and Guardian*, December 25, 2017. Online. https://mg.co.za/article/2017-12-15-00-faith-can-promote-rape-culture.

Nelson, James B. *Body Theology*. Louisville: Westminster John Knox, 1992.

Nemakonde, Vhahangwele. "Somizi Storms Out of Grace Bible Church over Homosexuality Remarks." *Citizen*, January 22, 2017. Online. https://citizen.co.za/lifestyle/1404845/somizi-storms-out-of-grace-bible-church-over-homosexuality-remarks.

Phiri, Isabel Apawo. "'Why Does God Allow our Husbands to Hurt Us?' Overcoming Violence against Women." *Journal of Theology for Southern Africa* 114 (2002) 19–30.

Singh, Kaveel. "Grace Bible Church Trends after Homophobic Comments." *News24*, January 22, 2017. Online. https://www.news24.com/SouthAfrica/News/grace-bible-church-trends-after-homophobic-comments-20170122.

Stychin, Carl F. "Constituting Sexuality: The Struggle for Sexual Orientation in the South African Bill of Rights." *Journal of Law and Society* 23.4 (1996) 455–83.

Sutherland, Carla, et al. *Progressive Prudes: A Survey of Attitudes Towards Homosexuality & Gender Non-Conformity in South Africa*. Johannesburg: Other Foundation, 2016.

Thatcher, Adrian. *Liberating Sex: A Christian Sexual Theology*. London: SPCK, 1993.

———. *Marriage after Modernity. Christian Marriage in Postmodern Times*. Sheffield: A & C Black, 1999.

Thayer, Donlu. "Ecclesia De Lange v. the Presiding Bishop of the Methodist Church of Southern Africa for the Time Being: (726/13) [2014] ZASCA 151: The Supreme Court of Appeal of South Africa: Ponnan, Wallis, Pillay JJA and Fourie, and Mathopo AJJA: 29 September 2014." *Oxford Journal of Law and Religion* 4.2 (2015) 320–22.

Van der Walt, Charlene. "Is 'Being Right' more Important than 'Being Together'? Intercultural Bible Reading in the Dutch Reformed Church, South Africa." In *Christianity and Controversies over Homosexuality in Contemporary Africa*, edited by Ezra Chitando and Adriaan van Klinken, 125–37. New York: Routledge, 2016.

West, Gerald. *The Stolen Bible: From Tool of Imperialism to African Icon*. Leiden: Brill, 2016.

West, Gerald, et al. "When Faith Does Violence: Reimagining Engagement between Churches and LGBTI Groups on Homophobia in Africa." *HTS Teologiese Studies* 72.1 (2016) 1–8.

Yep, Gust A. "The Violence of Heteronormativity in Communication Studies: Notes on Injury, Healing, and Queer World-Making." *Journal of Homosexuality* 45.2–4 (2003) 11–59.

Court Cases

De Lange v. Presiding Bishop of the Methodist Church of Southern Africa for the time being and Another (CCT223/14) 2015 ZACC 35; 2016 (1) BCLR 1 (CC); 2016 (2) SA 1 (CC) (24 November 2015).

Part IV

Freedom of Religion:
Perspectives from Europe

12

Freedom of Religion as Perceived
by the States

A European Perspective

Göran Gunner

The World Conference on Human Rights, held in Vienna 1993, states that "all human rights are universal, indivisible and interdependent and interrelated."[1] Still, in a pluralistic Europe—and a pluralistic world—human rights, which include freedom of religion or belief, are interpreted and implemented differently in national settings. Obviously, there is a tension between a universalist and a particularist approach. Is it the same rights for all? Or, is there a need for considering the particular specificities of each country?

Freedom of religion or belief extends further than being of concern for each individual since it is provided that the right can be manifested together with others. Can all organizations based on religion or belief be treated the same way or should traditional and numerical majority faith-communities have a priority in the interpretation? Is there a specific national interest to preserve or an interest to give numerical minorities their rights?

This chapter will deal with freedom of religion or belief on a European level and the intention is to high-light a trend in European decision-making. The discussion will relate to regulations as well as implementations

---

1. UN, "Vienna Declaration" art. 5.

in practice concerning freedom of religion or belief on both the general European level and the European Union (EU) level. In this study, I am especially interested in how the European Union, still with 28 members, and the Council of Europe with 47 members, including the ones in the European Union regulate, protect and implement the freedom of religion for the right-holders in the different member-states.[2]

Even if Europe can be described as a union or as united in a council, each European state has its special constitutional and legal approaches. This creates a kind of common heritage and common values but at the same time tensions through national and regional diversity. It raises questions about equal rights for every person in Europe. However, it also pin-points violations going on and possibilities as well as limits for practitioners of religions, beliefs and confessions.

During the years, a huge number of books and articles have been published about freedom of religion or belief as such, discussing the scope of freedom of religion or belief. Another instrument for catching the scope is the European case law as well as case law depending on decisions in different state courts. Just to mention a few of the books published: *The Changing Nature of Religious Rights under International Law* (2015); *Religion, Rights and Secular Society: European Perspectives* (2012); *Religious Liberty and International Law in Europe* (2005); and *Freedom of Religion: UN and European Human Rights Law and Practice* (2005).[3] I will also mention three articles of importance: "Managing Religion and the Judicialization of Religious Freedom" (2015); "Normative fault-lines of trans-national human rights jurisprudence" (2013); "The Complexity of Religion and the Definition of 'Religion' in International Law" (2003).[4] In a recently published book, *Freedom of Religion or Belief. An International Law Commentary* (2016), the authors give both the underlying principles and an overview of international human rights mechanisms in relation to freedom of religion or belief. They also deal in depth with issues of discrimination, vulnerable groups and the relation between freedom of religion and other human rights.[5]

---

2. For the Council of Europe, see CoE, "Who We Are." For the EU, see EU, "Official Website."

3. Evans et al., *Changing Nature of Religious Rights*; Cumper and Lewis, *Religion, Rights, and Secular Society*; Evans, *Religious Liberty*; Taylor, *Freedom of Religion*.

4. Richardsson, "Managing Religion"; Augenstein, "Normative Fault-Lines"; Gunn, "Complexity of Religion."

5. Bielefeldt et al., *Freedom of Religion or Belief*.

FREEDOM OF RELIGION OR BELIEF

Freedom of religion or belief is one of the human rights intending to protect the rights of each individual in relation to the state. This right is included in the Universal Declaration on Human Rights (article 18) and basic conventions on human rights such as in the International Covenant on Civil and Political Rights (article 18); the Convention on the Rights of the Child (article 14); and the European Convention for the Protection of Human Rights and Fundamental Freedoms (article 9).

Let's give some general remarks on freedom of religion or belief. Freedom of religion or belief includes the faith or belief for each and every person—the thought, the ideas, the reflections a religious, philosophical, or confessional believer may have. In the Universal Declaration from 1948, article 18 states: "The right to freedom of thought, conscience and religion."[6] It also includes manifestations of religion or belief, private and in public, as well as the use of special items essential in rituals and practice in different religious traditions. It is also about the right to join together through establishing faith-based or confessional organizations as well as in manifesting the faith or belief in teaching, practice, worship, and observance and to use special buildings and facilities. This freedom includes the right to adopt a religion or belief by choice or being without any religious affiliation at all.

Article 9 in the European Convention states:

1. Everyone has the right to freedom of thought, conscience and religion; this right includes freedom to change his religion or belief and freedom, either alone or in community with others and in public or private, to manifest his religion or belief, in worship, teaching, practice and observance.

2. Freedom to manifest one's religion or beliefs shall be subject only to such limitations as are prescribed by law and are necessary in a democratic society in the interests of public safety, for the protection of public order, health or morals, or for the protection of the rights and freedoms of others.

We shall return to the European Convention later in the chapter.

On the UN level, the United Nations Human Rights Committee is a body of independent experts monitoring the states implementation of the International Covenant on Civil and Political Rights. In a General Comment No. 22, the Committee explains the far-reaching and profound rights laid down in article 18 and concludes that freedom of religion or belief

---

6. United Nations, "Universal Declaration of Human Rights."

encompasses a broad range of acts and what the observance and practice of religion may include, for example the observance of dietary regulations, the wearing of head coverings, the building of places of worship, the use of ritual formulae and objects, the display of symbols, and the observance of holidays and days of rest. The General Comment continues that the observance and practice of religion or belief may include "such customs as the observance of dietary regulations, the wearing of distinctive clothing or head-coverings, participation in rituals associated with certain stages of life, and the use of a particular language customarily spoken by a group." The General Comment also clarifies that the terms "religion" and "belief" are broadly constructed to "protect theistic, non-theistic and atheistic beliefs, as well as the right not to profess any religion or belief."[7]

RELIGIOUS BODIES AND FREEDOM OF RELIGION OR BELIEF

Freedom of religion or belief is, of course, of special concern for persons belonging to different religious communities, or faith-based and confessional organizations. On an individual as well as on an organizational level work is being done with the aim of understanding, securing, and protecting the scope of freedom of religion of belief. One example of a religious body entering into the issue of freedom or religion is the Swedish Mission Council, consisting of 35 member-organizations with different church traditions. One of the main objects is to look into how freedom of religion or belief is included in Swedish foreign policy and development cooperation.

When the Swedish Mission Council summarized the important aspects of freedom of religion or belief, the claim was that the state has a responsibility to respect, protect, and promote seven dimensions of the freedom of religion or belief. The freedom comprises of:

1. the freedom to have, choose, change, or leave a religion or belief;

2. freedom to manifest a religion or belief;

3. freedom from coercion;

4. freedom from discrimination;

5. the right to conscientious objection;

6. parents rights, children's rights;

7. employers and employees.[8]

7. Human Rights Committee, "General Comment 22."

8. For a detailed explanation on each of the aspects, see *What Freedom of Religion*

The rights included in point one may never be limited while the rights described in point two may in some circumstances be limited. The council declared that among internationally recognized manifestations, European states need to relate to these freedoms:

- to worship or assemble in connection with a religion or belief, and to establish and maintain premises for these purposes;
- to establish religious, humanitarian, and charitable institutions;
- to make, acquire, and use articles and materials related to the rites or customs of a religion or belief, including to follow a particular diet;
- to write, issue, and disseminate relevant publications;
- to teach a religion or belief in places suitable for the purposes and to establish theological seminaries or schools;
- to solicit and receive voluntary financial and other contributions;
- to train, appoint, or elect leaders, priests, and teachers;
- to celebrate religious festivals and observe days of rest;
- to communicate with individuals and communities on faith issues at national and international level;
- to display religious symbols including the wearing of religious clothing.[9]

A NEW EUROPE WHEN IT COMES TO RELIGION AND FREEDOM OF RELIGION

With regards to human rights in general, the states in Europe are obliged to follow human rights regulations and agreements. Naturally this also relates to freedom of religion or belief. At the same time, it seems that something else is happening when religion is involved. This may apply to states with only one dominant religion, but it also relates to states with a more plural distribution of faith communities, as well as in states with a more secularised population. Adding to this is that the diversity of religions and belief-systems in the European societies have increased dramatically over the last decades, not least due to migration. This migration is not only internally between European states but increasingly from other parts of the world as the flow of asylum-seekers, refugees, and those seeking for work-opportunities arrive in Europe from both Asia and Africa. These non-European

---

Involves, 6–10.

9. *What Freedom of Religion Involves*, 7–8.

immigrants bring their traditional religions and belief-systems into the religious pattern of Europe.

Another significant change is the rapid development of new religions and beliefs. A comprehensive term is "New religious movements" identifying belief communities with rather modern origins. This can be exemplified with Raëlism described as a UFO religion or the different movements with background in religions or beliefs in Eastern Asia. Another example is The Missionary Church of Kopimism,[10] recently (2012) established as a completely new religion in Sweden with branches in several other countries. Copying is considered a sacrament, and the creeds assert, "copy and paste" and "knowledge for all." They have published their Gospel—"the real good news"—which is a confession to Science. In Sweden, the Church of Kopimism fulfils the formal criteria for establishing a religious community—and thus was registered by the authorities. Still the question arises whether they are a religion, a belief or merely a group testing the limits of copy-right issues, or perhaps something else?

This new Europe creates a certain question facing multi-religious societies. Are the European institutions as well as individual states ready to encounter this new situation through accepting religious manifestations according to the concept of freedom of religion or belief? Or, what is happening with the right to freedom of religion or belief when it comes to the implementation in the European setting?

When studying basic human rights, there are few questions concerning the rules and regulations governing such a study, but when it comes to freedom of religion, the rules and regulations seem to be open for discussion. In the media, in the parliament, and among neighbours it is open for discussion. What to do with religion? Can a society simply allow everything? Will they not over-rule our religious and cultural heritage? Some faith-based communities question the rights of existence for other faith communities, or at least find it threatening when new religious groups enter the arena. In the classroom discussions on freedom of religion or belief, are performed as a matter of personal opinion—of course influenced by debates in media. Such a take on freedom of religion is given priority and shapes the discussion. Should circumcision of boys be allowed? Should a school allow head coverings such as head scarfs, niqab, or burqa? What about state registration of faith communities? Should the state allow halal and kosher slaughter of animals? What about the ringing of church-bells on Sunday morning, or the call to prayer from the minaret? Or even building a minaret as such? The

10. In Swedish, "Det missionerande kopimistsamfundet."

result is that voices are questioning new manifestations as well as traditional serious manifestations being at the heart of individual faithful persons.

The Pew Research Center conducts an annual study on global restrictions on freedom of religion. This includes both government restrictions and social hostilities involving religion. In a Government restrictions index, three of the member-states in the Council of Europe (Azerbaijan, Russia, and Turkey) are categorized as with "very high" restrictions, three with "high" restrictions (France, Bulgaria, Moldova as well as Belarus, not being a member), and fourteen as having "moderate" restrictions.[11] When it comes to social hostilities involving religion, it is "very high" in one member-state (Russia), "high" in thirteen states (Armenia, Bosnia-Herzegovina, Denmark, France, Georgia, Germany, Italy, Kosovo, Moldova, Slovakia, Switzerland, Turkey, Ukraine), and "moderate" in ten more states.[12]

In the following section I will deal with the question: what is happening with freedom of religion or belief at the European level? The question is if freedom of religion or belief belongs to the realm of universal rights (as obviously stated by the regulations) or whether it belongs to the field of particularity (each country decides upon the issue). First I will describe the issue of religious minority rights.

RELIGIOUS MINORITIES

Religious Minorities may be a numerical designation in the relationship between majorities and minorities in numerical terms. There seems to be a difference in Europe. The term is more commonly used in the Eastern and Central part of Europe while expressions like faith communities seem to be preferred in, for example, the Nordic context. One of my students, when discussing the issue, claimed:

> I do not want to be named a minority. Sure, my parents are from Ethiopia but I'm born in Sweden, Swedish is my language, I'm like all others but my faith is Islam. I'm a Swedish Muslim. Why should that make me a minority? The concept minority only indicates I'm not belonging and being look upon as a foreigner.

However, for a Central-European person living in Slovenia with Hungarian ethnic belonging, speaking the Hungarian language, and being member of a Hungarian speaking church, it is important to be named a minority. It is then a combination indicating belonging to a non-dominant group of individuals who share certain national, ethnic, religious, or linguistic

11. "Trends in Global Restrictions," 50.
12. "Trends in Global Restrictions," 53.

characteristics. With a combination like that you may be eligible for protection but when isolating the religious dimension in relation to minority it is possible to conclude with Nazila Ghanea, writing in *Oxford Journal of Law and Religion* 2012:

> Though religious minorities have been one of the three most explicitly recognized categories of minorities in the minority rights regime, they have largely been excluded from consideration under the umbrella of minority rights.[13]

Hence, in the European setting, the concept of minority rights has not been used in any higher degree as protection of religious groups and we are basically ending up with using the concept freedom of religion or belief.

THE EUROPEAN UNION

In 2013, the European Union set out *EU Guidelines on the promotion and protection of freedom of religion or belief* with the clear aim of integrating freedom of religion or belief into EU foreign policy. The guidelines proclaim that the EU and its member States are committed to respecting, protecting, and promoting freedom of religion or belief within their borders. But it is to be observed, the guidelines are for the external policy, stressing freedom of religion or belief as a right to be exercised by everyone everywhere, based on the principles of equality, non-discrimination, and universality. The guidelines stress the universal character of freedom of religion or belief, that freedom of religion or belief is an individual right which can be exercised in community with others, and that it is the primary role of States to ensure freedom of religion or belief.

This may give the idea that at least the states belonging to the EU do have a codified united approach to freedom of religion or belief enabling each and every EU-citizen the same protections and the same rights. But the situation varies from state to state and the policies are very different just comparing different countries (like Germany, the United Kingdom (still a member), France or Romania).

Of course, issues related to freedom of religion or belief are discussed in different EU agencies. For example, the European Union Agency for Fundamental Rights, even if they do not have freedom of religion as a theme. Still, freedom of religion or belief may be dealt with when focusing on issues like discriminatory procedures, combating intolerance and hate, and promoting respect and diversity.

---

13. Ghanea, "Are Religious Minorities Really Minorities?," 60.

By comparing two fundamental documents from the European Union (EU), I will show that there seems to be a special intention from the side of the member states in relation to freedom of religion or belief. The first document was rejected and the second one was approved. The treaty establishing a Constitution for Europe intended to create a consolidated Constitution for the European Union. 25 member-states signed the treaty on October 29, 2004, and then the treaty was ratified by 18 member states. Referendums by French and Dutch voters ended up in a complete rejection of the Constitution in June 2005. In order to replace the Constitution, a new process took place ending up in the Treaty of Lisbon signed in December 2007, entering into force on December 1, 2009. What is said about freedom of religion or belief when looking for corresponding articles in the two documents? When comparing the texts in relation to religion it is easy to see a difference. But what is the intention behind the changes?

Let's first go to the rejected Constitution for Europe and look for freedom of religion or belief. The Constitution states in article II-70:

> 1. Everyone has the right to freedom of thought, conscience and religion. This right includes freedom to change religion or belief and freedom, either alone or in community with others and in public or in private, to manifest religion or belief, in worship, teaching, practice and observance.

> 2. The right to conscientious objection is recognized, in accordance with the national laws governing the exercise of this right.

This basic text resembles very closely both the Universal Declaration on Human Rights and the European Convention for the Protection of Human Rights and Fundamental Freedoms. The article is also included as article 10 in the "Charter of Fundamental Rights" of the European Union. But when going to the approved main text of the Treaty of Lisbon for a corresponding text you will read a quite different text in article II-17:

1. The Union respects and does not prejudice the status under national law of churches and religious associations or communities in the Member States.

2. The Union equally respects the status under national law of philosophical and confessional organizations.

3. Recognizing their identity and their specific contribution, the Union shall maintain an open, transparent and regular dialogue with these churches and organizations.

Although the EU is fully aware of the conventions on freedom of religion as well as the fact that freedom of religion or belief is included in its own Charter, something seems to happen. The Union respects the national law for religious associations as well as for philosophical and confessional organizations. Either they believe that the national laws correspond with freedom of religion or belief or they leave the issue completely up to each state. In addition, the European Union shall have dialogue with churches and organizations. But here is no mentioning of for example Jewish and Muslim communities unless they are considered by the EU to be organizations. It may be possible to interpret the discrepancy as an issue the member-states are unable to agree upon even if there are clear regulations at hand in the conventions. The EU simply claims that religion is not its business even if there should be an ongoing dialogue. So, in reality the EU wants to hand over the issue of freedom of religion or belief to each state to be independently responsible for its regulation and enforcement. There appears to be a conflict between the universal scope of freedom of religion and specific national interests. At the same time, there is a shift going on from the freedom of religion for each and every person to respecting the religious denominations and organizations. Hence there is a shift from attention to the individual's freedoms and rights to the organizational level.

It is possible to compare a few other articles, with themes that are closely connected with religion. The rejected Constitution declares in article II-82:

> The Union shall respect cultural, religious and linguistic diversity.

On the other hand, the Treaty of Lisbon states in article XIII-167.1:

> The Union shall contribute to the flowering of the cultures of the Member States, while respecting their national and regional diversity and at the same time bringing the common cultural heritage to the fore.

The Constitution states clearly that the member states should respect cultural diversity while the Treaty talks about respecting national and regional diversity. Is it, once again, up to each state to decide and to keep the existing regional and national diversity instead of giving room for a general respect and space for cultural, religious and, linguistic diversity?

Let me show one more example that relates to articles concerning the central issue on the grounds for non-discrimination. The rejected Constitution declares in article II-81.1:

> Any discrimination based on any ground such as sex, race, color, ethnic or social origin, genetic features, language, religion or belief, political or any other opinion, membership of a national minority, property, birth, disability, age or sexual orientation shall be prohibited.

The Treaty of Lisbon has a different reading in article II-10

> In defining and implementing its policies and activities, the Union shall aim to combat discrimination based on sex, racial or ethnic origin, religion or belief, disability, age or sexual orientation.

Once again it is easy to see a big difference just in the one sentence-long text. In the rejected Constitution, the discrimination based on religion etc. shall be prohibited. This seems to be a very strong commitment for a state to fulfil. On the other hand, in the approved Treaty, there shall be an aim to combat discrimination based on religion etc. Is the EU leaving it up to each state to keep on "aiming at"? Is it a way to give in for a majority population considering this to be the best in a national or a regional setting? Or is it really in protection of individuals belonging to different religious faith communities based on her/his human rights?

In analyzing this change it seems to be as a signal to the member countries that religion is basically a matter for each country to take care of. The EU seems to leave it up to each state to decide on freedom of religion or belief and does not want to interfere in the existing laws and regulations in the member states concerning freedom of religion or belief. But isn't the European Union thereby weakening the universal conventions on freedom of religion or belief? So, in one way the European Union talks about the importance of the same rights for everyone as well as the value of religious diversity. In relation to the EU's external affairs it is much clearer—and in the foreign policy it should be clear, it is the primary role of states to ensure freedom of religion or belief. But at the same time, internally, the EU opens up for a kind of national majority model when it comes to social cohesion. It is acceptable when it comes to religious freedom to be without internal European consensus, giving space for different national regulations and traditions. As a result of this we can currently see in different EU member states that religious diversity and pluralism is threatened.

COUNCIL OF EUROPE—COURT OF HUMAN RIGHTS

The European Convention for the Protection of Human Rights and Fundamental Freedoms is fundamental to the member states in the Council of

Europe. Here, I am coming back to an article quoted in the beginning of this chapter. Article 9 is about freedom of thought, conscience, and religion:

> 1. Everyone has the right to freedom of thought, conscience and religion; this right includes freedom to change his religion or belief and freedom, either alone or in community with others and in public or private, to manifest his religion or belief, in worship, teaching, practice and observance.
>
> 2. Freedom to manifest one's religion or beliefs shall be subject only to such limitations as are prescribed by law and are necessary in a democratic society in the interests of public safety, for the protection of public order, health or morals, or for the protection of the rights and freedoms of others.

Violations of the rights set out in the European Convention on Human Rights can be taken to the European Court of Human Rights and be brought to the Court after domestic remedies have been exhausted. The court rules on state or individual applications alleging violations. Judgments taken by the court are binding on the country concerned. Decisions taken have led to governments altering the legislation and administrative practice. Below I will briefly look into some of the decisions related to religion at the European Court of Human Rights.

In order to deal with religion, the European Court has used several possibilities. The first is a differentiation between *forum internum* and *forum externum*. The forum internum is always protected as a kind of inner freedom of religion or belief referring to faith in a narrow sense like holding a conviction, such as a religion or philosophical conviction, as well as not to have one. Included is also the right to change religion. The forum internum cannot be limited by the state. The forum externum is the manifestations of religion or belief and can be limited under certain circumstances. Interference with the exercise of freedom to manifest one's religion or beliefs can be justified if: (1) the interference must be prescribed by law; (2) the interference must have a legitimate aim: public safety, protection of public order, health or morals, protection of rights and freedoms of others; (3) the interference is necessary in a democratic society.

A second possibility is given with the concept "margin of appreciation." This is the concept used by the court for giving the national authorities space for arguing based on the cultural and legal traditions embraced in the member state when fulfilling their obligations. At the same time, this indicates that it has been difficult to identify a uniform European standard of human rights. So, it is fair to say, there is non-existence of a European consensus based on case-law from the European Court in matters concerning freedom of religion or belief. Concerning margin of appreciation, the Court held in the case of *Kokkinakis v. Greece* that

> a certain margin of appreciation is to be left to the Contracting States in assessing the existence and extent of the necessity of an interference, but this margin is subject to European supervision. ... The Court's task is to determine whether the measures taken at national level were justified in principle and proportionate.[14]

The same argument is used in the case of *Leyla Şahin v. Turkey*. Later, the Court more or less repeated the same in the case of *Dogru v. France* as well as in the case of *Kervanci v. France*.[15]

> Where questions concerning the relationship between State and religions are at stake, on which opinion in a democratic society may reasonably differ widely, the role of the national decision-making body must be given special importance. This will notably be the case when it comes to regulating the wearing of religious symbols in educational institutions, especially in view of the diversity of the approaches taken by national authorities on the issue. It is not possible to discern throughout Europe a uniform conception of the significance of religion in society and the meaning or impact of the public expression of a religious belief will differ according to time and context. Rules in this sphere will consequently vary from one country to another according to national traditions and the requirements imposed by the need to protect the rights and freedoms of others and to maintain public order. Accordingly, the choice of the extent and form such regulations must take must inevitably be left up to a point to the State concerned, as it will depend on the domestic context concerned.

So, even the European Court expresses the view that there is no European (universal) view in relation to freedom of religion or belief but very much up to each state.

Obviously, there are today, limits for the states even if we do have the *margin of appreciation*. Forty years after the European Convention of Human Rights entered into force, the first case of a violation of article 9—about freedom of religion or belief—took place. Before that, the original member states were granted a considerable freedom. But in the 1990s a new development took place following, not least, the breakdown of the Soviet block and

---

14. Kokkinakis v. Greece.

15. Leyla Şahin v. Turkey (references to other cases are excluded from the quotation); Dogru v. France; Kervanci v. France.

the appearance of a considerable amount of new states in Europe. James T. Richardson and others talk about "judicialization of religious freedom." And it seems to go partly in the same direction as the Lisbon Treaty from protecting the individual religious freedom to protection of religious organizations but also other than the traditional one's. The Court of Human Rights takes decisions in individual cases but at the same time protects a group like Jehovah's Witnesses.

> It should be noted that the recent spate of article 9 decisions seem to be based not so much on protecting individual religious freedom, as on preserving the right of religious organizations to exist.[16]

Several of the cases have dealt with the refusal of different states to register or re-register religious organizations and thereby harming the freedom of religion or belief for individuals. The court have given organizations the right to complain to the Court on behalf of their members. At the same time, the Court takes into account minority religions in problematic situations in the states. For example, you will find cases concerning the Metropolitan Church of Bessarabia, the Moscow Branch of The Salvation Army, the Biblical Center of the Chuvash Republic, and the Lupeni Greek Catholic Parish.[17]

Still there are complaints originating from persons accusing a state of violating their freedom of religion or belief. In the section below, I will briefly describe a few examples of court decisions concerning individual complaints to the European Court—all of them dealing with religious symbols.

The schoolteacher Lucia Dahlab, a Swiss national, complained about the measure prohibiting her to wear a head scarf at school while teaching. The Court argued that the authorities did not exceed their margin of appreciation. Prohibiting the wearing of the head scarf in the context of being a teacher was reasonable. It was considered a potential interference with the religious beliefs of her pupils, other pupils and the parents.

> The Court observed that in democratic societies, in which several religions coexist within one and the same population, it may be necessary to place restrictions on this freedom in order to reconcile the interests of the various groups and ensure that everyone's beliefs are respected. . . .

16. Richardsson, "Managing Religion," 7.

17. See Metropolitan Church of Bessarabia and Others v. Moldova; Moscow Branch of The Salvation Army v. Russia; Biblical Center of the Chuvash Republic v. Russia; Lupeni Greek Catholic Parish and Others v. Romania.

> The Court accepts that it is very difficult to assess the impact that a powerful external symbol such as the wearing of a headscarf may have on the freedom of conscience and religion of very young children.[18]

The university student Leyla Şahin complained that the prohibition at Istanbul University for students to wear a head scarf at class or during exams was violating article 9. At the European Court, the margin of appreciation—on regulating the wearing of religious symbols in educational institutions—gave the state rights:

> It is the principle of secularism . . . which is the paramount consideration underlying the ban on the wearing of religious symbols in universities. . . . The relevant authorities should wish to preserve the secular nature of the institution concerned and so consider it contrary to such values to allow religious attire, including, as in the present case, the Islamic headscarf, to be worn.[19]

The third case is the schoolgirl Belgin Dogru in France. The applicant was excluded from school after refusing to remove her head scarf during physical education and sports classes. The Court considered that the national authorities' conclusion that the wearing of head scarf was incompatible with sports classes for reasons of health or safety was not unreasonable. The interference in question had been justified as a matter of principle and had been proportionate to the aim pursued. But the court also entered into a long discussion about necessity in a democratic society, stressing that

> the "powerful external symbol" represented by wearing the headscarf and also considered the proselytizing effect that it might have seeing that it appeared to be imposed on women by a religious precept which was hard to square with the principle of gender equality.[20]

The Court also noted:

> It was for the national authorities, in the exercise of their margin of appreciation, to take great care to ensure that, in keeping with the principle of respect for pluralism and the freedom of others, the manifestation by pupils of their religious beliefs on school

18. Dahlab v. Switzerland.
19. Leyla Şahin v. Turkey.
20. Dogru v. France.

premises did not take on the nature of an ostentatious act that would constitute a source of pressure and exclusion.[21]

So, in these three cases the margin of appreciation has been used with quite different arguments depending on the state concerned. According to the Court, it was no interference in the freedom of religion when states prohibited the head scarf. Part of the argument was that in respect of pluralism it was not allowed to wear a head-scarf since it was considered as a "powerful external symbol." Referring to this case, Daniel Augenstein, concludes that "the religious clothing of an eleven-year-old girl endangers the pluralistic nature of the French secular-republican education system that its teaching staff is called to uphold."[22]

Now, the case of Lautsi and others versus Italy. In Italy, crucifixes are mandatory in public schools, since they are considered to represent an expression of Christian civilisation and culture. The applicants Soile Lautsi and her sons Dataico and Sami Albertin questioned the presence of religious symbols in the classrooms. The Second section of the Court decided in favor of the applicants but a lot of protests from different parties resulted in a new decision. The Grand Chamber of the Court gave Italy the right to use the religious symbol of a crucifix and held that "a crucifix on a wall is an essentially passive symbol."[23] Furthermore, the Court declared "there was nothing to suggest that the authorities were intolerant of pupils who believed in other religions, were non-believers or who held non-religious philosophical convictions."[24]

A conclusion from the court-decisions may be that a head-scarf on the head of a school-girl is considered to be a powerful external symbol but a crucifix in a class-room is a passive symbol. But, in the end, it is may be about the authority of each state to decide according to their national traditions and interests.

The 2013 case of Eweida and others versus United Kingdom is also about external symbols. However, in this case, it was about a cross. There were four applications in one case but I will only relate to Eweida here. She was a Coptic Christian working at a private company—the British Airways. Her wearing of a cross openly around her neck did not comply with the uniform code of the company. In the decision it is stated:

> The Court considers that Ms Eweida's behavior was a manifestation of her religious belief, in the form of worship, practice and observance, and as such attracted the protection of article 9. . . .

21. Dogru v. France.
22. Augenstein, "Normative Fault-Lines," 486.
23. Lautsi and Others v. Italy.
24. Lautsi and Others v. Italy.

There is no evidence of any real encroachment on the interests of others, the domestic authorities failed sufficiently to protect the first applicant's right to manifest her religion.[25]

It would be easy to draw the conclusion that at stake is how and when manifestations of religion in different European settings may be restricted. In the end, the decisions are left with each state to decide according to the margin of appreciation. When looking into both the European Union and the Council of Europe, the question must be raised if this is a trend moving away from the universal aspect of human rights in favor of the particular? And at the same time if this trend focuses more on the majority situations than protecting persons belonging to different minority faith communities? Is it a trend and time for strengthening the majority national approach rather than protecting pluralistic and diverse societies?

BIBLIOGRAPHY

Augenstein, Daniel. "Normative Fault-Lines of Trans-National Human Rights Jurisprudence: National Pride and Religious Prejudice in the European Legal Space." *Global Constitutionalism* 2.3 (2013) 469–97.

Bielefeldt, Heiner, et al. *Freedom of Religion or Belief: An International Law Commentary.* Oxford: Oxford University Press, 2016.

Council of Europe (CoE). "Who We Are." Online. https://www.coe.int/en/web/about-us/who-we-are.

Cumper, Peter, and Tom Lewis. *Religion, Rights, and Secular Society: European Perspectives.* Cheltenham: Edward Elgar, 2012.

European Court of Human Rights (ECHR). "European Convention for the Protection of Human Rights and Fundamental Freedoms." June 1, 2010. Online. http://www.echr.coe.int/Documents/Convention_ENG.pdf.

———. "HUDOC." Online. https://hudoc.echr.coe.int/eng.

European Union. "EU Guidelines on the Promotion and Protection of Freedom of Religion or Belief." June 24, 2013. Online. http://www.consilium.europa.eu/uedocs/cms_data/docs/pressdata/EN/foraff/137585.pdf.

———. "Official Website." Online. https://europa.eu/european-union/index_en.

———. "Treaty Establishing a Constitution for Europe." *Official Journal of the European Union* 47 (2004) 1–474. Online. http://eur-lex.europa.eu/legal-content/EN/TXT/PDF/?uri=OJ:C:2004:310:FULL&from=EN.

Evans, Malcolm D. *Religious Liberty and International Law in Europe.* Cambridge Studies in International and Comparative Law. Cambridge: Cambridge University Press, 2005.

Evans, Malcolm D., et al., eds. *The Changing Nature of Religious Rights under International Law.* Oxford: Oxford University Press, 2015.

Ghanea, Nazila. "Are Religious Minorities Really Minorities?" *Oxford Journal of Law and Religion* 1.1 (2012) 57–79.

Gunn, T. Jeremy. "The Complexity of Religion and the Definition of 'Religion' in International Law." *Harvard Human Rights Journal* 16 (2003) 189–216.

25. Eweida and Others v. United Kingdom.

Human Rights Committee. "General Comment 22, Article 18 (Forty-eighth session, 1993). Compilation of General Comments and General Recommendations Adopted by Human Rights Treaty Bodies, UN Doc. HRI/GEN/1/Rev.1 at 35 (1994)." Human Rights Library, University of Minnesota. Online. http://hrlibrary.umn.edu/gencomm/hrcom22.htm.

"The Lisbon Treaty." Online. http://www.lisbon-treaty.org/wcm.

Pew Research Center. "Trends in Global Restrictions on Religion." *Religion and Public Life*, June 23, 2016. Online. http://www.pewforum.org/2016/06/23/trends-in-global-restrictions-on-religion.

Richardson, James T. "Managing Religion and the Judicialization of Religious Freedom." *Journal for the Scientific Study of Religion* 54.1 (2015) 1–19.

Swedish Mission Council. *What Freedom of Religion Involves and When It Can Be Limited: A Quick Guide to Religious Freedom*. Stockholm: Swedish Mission Council, 2010. Online. http://www.missioncouncil.se/wp/wp-content/uploads/downloads/2013/03/lathund_religionsfrihet_engelsk.pdf.

Taylor, Paul M. *Freedom of Religion: UN and European Human Rights Law and Practice*. Cambridge: Cambridge University Press, 2005.

United Nations. "The Convention on the Rights of the Child." November 20, 1989. Online. http://www.ohchr.org/EN/ProfessionalInterest/Pages/CRC.aspx.

———. "International Covenant on Civil and Political Rights." December 16, 1966. Online. http://www.ohchr.org/EN/ProfessionalInterest/Pages/CCPR.aspx.

———. "The Universal Declaration of Human Rights." December 10, 1948. Online. http://www.un.org/en/universal-declaration-human-rights/index.html.

———. "Vienna Declaration and Programme of Action." June 25, 1993. Online. https://www.ohchr.org/EN/ProfessionalInterest/Pages/Vienna.aspx.

Court Cases

Biblical Center of the Chuvash Republic v. Russia (33203/08), European Court of Human Rights, October 13, 2014.[26]

Dahlab v. Switzerland (42393/98), European Court of Human Rights, February 15, 2001.

Dogru v. France (27058/05), European Court of Human Rights, March 3, 2009.

Eweida and Others v. United Kingdom (48420/10, 59842/10, 51671/10, 36516/10), European Court of Human Rights, May 27, 2013.

Kervanci v. France (31645/04), European Court of Human Rights, March 3, 2009.

Kokkinakis v. Greece (14307/88), European Court of Human Rights, May 25, 1993.

Lautsi and Others v. Italy (30814/06), European Court of Human Rights (Grand Chamber), March 18, 2011.

Leyla Şahin v. Turkey (44774/98), European Court of Human Rights, November 10, 2005.

Lupeni Greek Catholic Parish and Others v. Romania (76943/11), European Court of Human Rights, November 29, 2016.

Metropolitan Church of Bessarabia and Others v. Moldova (45701/99), European Court of Human Rights, March 27, 2002.

Moscow Branch of the Salvation Army v. Russia (72881/01), European Court of Human Rights, January 5, 2007.

26. All the Court Decisions in the European Court of Human Rights may be found online at ECHR, "HUDOC."

13

Freedom of Religion, of Belief, Universality, and Subsidiarity in the Jurisprudence of the European Court of Human Rights[1]

PETER PETKOFF

One of the central features of "European Convention on Human Rights" (ECHR) and its article 9 jurisprudence which often remains hidden is the tension between universality and subsidiarity, between liberal internationalism and constitutional politics, between neutrality and accommodation, between right and good, between neutrality and political perfectionism.[2] This is an emerging public discourse which shapes for better or worse the understanding of the scope of freedom of religion or belief within and beyond the Council of Europe and which defines the patterns though which international human rights continue (despite some emerging

1. The present text is based on and substantially modified from a chapter I have written with Malcolm Evans. See Evans and Petkoff, "Marginal Neutrality."

2. "Everyone has the right to freedom of thought, conscience and religion; this right includes freedom to change his religion or belief and freedom, either alone or in community with others and in public or private, to manifest his religion or belief, in worship, teaching, practice and observance. . . . Freedom to manifest one's religion or beliefs shall be subject only to such limitations as are prescribed by law and are necessary in a democratic society in the interests of public safety, for the protection of public order, health or morals, or for the protection of the rights and freedoms of others" ("ECHR" art. 9)

challenges) to dominate the grammar of consent in the field. Developing more sophisticated strategies for a contextual application of freedom of religion or belief through the lens of universality and subsidiarity is gradually becoming an important measure about the complex interplay and dynamics between international vision and aspiration and particular application of international human rights.

In the age of Trump and Brexit, and at least a rhetorical withdrawal from liberal internationalism's commitments,[3] the Council of Europe no longer looks like the icon of liberalism which was once presented as the framework which will end totalitarianism and lead emerging democracies through the purgatory of their transition. It faces a Tory electoral platform proposing a further withdrawal from the Convention, a wave of right wing conservative revolutions across Europe which close universities, perform "sausage-slicing" of democratic institutions and of central freedoms such as freedom of speech,[4] the emergence of convincing far right voices in the European political space, sovereignty driven religious exceptionalism in Turkey and Russia, and a constitutional transformation of the tectonic plates of Europe driven by the fear of immigration.

Revisiting the *modus operandi* of the Convention has become particularly urgent now and the particular focus that seems to emerge is centerd on the interplay between neutrality and the margin of appreciation in balancing the frictions between universality and subsidiarity. Neutrality and a margin of appreciation in relation to articles 9 and 10 have been used to protect the core of Convention rights in the context of functioning democracies as a one-directional legal and political perfectionism. Increasingly however articles 9 and 10 are being interpreted through the lens of a margin of appreciation to be the means of protecting 'culture,' and this protection is not dissimilar from Bismark's *Kulturkampf*, Putin's Russian Commonwealth (*Ruskij Mir*) and the emerging center-right nationalist ideologies from France, through Hungary, Poland to Bulgaria and Turkey. This is a trend which emerged steadily with cases like *Lautsi v. Italy* and *SAS v. France* but had its contours in cases like *Whitehouse v. UK*; *Otto Preminger v. Austria*; *Wingrove v. UK*; *Sahin v. Turkey*; and *Refah v. Turkey*.

The margin of appreciation in all these cases reflects a sense that under certain circumstances the articles 9 and 10 right may undermine 'the good'

---

3. Conservatives, "Protecting Human Rights." In May 2017 Theresa May said the UK will remain signatories to the European Convention of Human Rights for the next Parliament. The Prime Minister was reportedly planning to make the case to leave the ECHR a central aspect of her 2020 election campaign before she called for an early election.

4. Garton Ash, "We Know the Price."

which a particular majority culture represents—'the good' ranges from constitutional secularism or its opposite—established religion to a cultural makeup which might be undermined, mis-calibrated by obscene speech. As far as article 9 is concerned there are two sides in the debate—right v good often presented through the Rawlsian prism of neutrality which implies that the state must not take sides in theological debates and religious divisions. We know only too well that this is an oversimplified version of Rawls and that Rawlsian good intentions are not sufficient. The state in fact has to deal with two coexisting paradigms of a separation between religion and the state (with or without the existence of an established religion in Europe) and the accommodation rules regarding freedom of religion or belief. The coexistence of these two paradigms gives very little scope for the state to be neutral since it implies both a substantial detachment from religious matters (separation of religion and state) and at the same time deep interest in religious matters (through the protection of freedom of religion or belief, reasonable accommodation etc.).

Implicitly the tension, among other things, foreshadows an emerging challenge of the complex balancing of state neutrality with the existence of established or quasi-established religions in a number of Council of Europe (CoE) member states and the recognized complexities of secular and religious constitutional architectures in *travaux preparatoire*[5] and the reservations of a number of member states.

This approach proposes that when one deals with matters arising from article 9 maintaining the *status quo* is often seen as a *conditio sine qua non* for the fulfilment of state duties under existing international treaties. Article 9 rights go hand in hand with limitations in *forum externum* which are generally aimed at maintaining the good of the social makeup, the communitarian status quo and, in cases like the United Kingdom (UK) and Greece, the constitutional status of the majority faith. Undermining this faith is often conceived as an attack on the constitutional makeup of society and even borderline treason (an argument made in *Lemon v. UK* following a long line of Victorian blasphemy cases which viewed blasphemy as a form of high treason).

This tension already apparent in the *travaux preparatoire* of the Convention highlights an ongoing challenge of the contextual application of international human rights' norms.[6] It flags that a broader margin of appreciation[7] in relation to article 9 highlights the lack of a Europe wide con-

5. An official record of the negotiation of an international treaty.

6. See Evans, *Freedom of Religion*.

7. The term "margin of appreciation" refers to the space for manoeuvre that the

sensus on the scope of freedom of religion or belief. This lack of consensus merits a broader range of solutions in relation to contextual application of freedom of religion or belief taking into account constitutional traditions and the possibility of diversity in the constitutional grammar through which freedom of religion or belief might be articulated. Having said that such a broad margin of appreciation because of a lack of consensus, is contrasted with other areas where margin of appreciation is narrower because there is apparently a broad-based consensus about the scope of these rights such as freedom of expression or torture and inhuman and degrading treatment. We do not agree on the broad scope of freedom of religion or belief in the way we agree on torture or the inhuman and degrading treatment of persons, or on issues related to freedom of speech. It is time to acknowledge that the tension between cosmopolitan liberal internationalism and sovereignty driven skeptical approaches to human rights has always dominated, and will continue to dominate, the application of Convention rights. We have largely ignored this tension and we will have to engage with it seriously if the international human rights system is to survive.

BALANCING BETWEEN SOVEREIGNTY AND INTERNATIONAL HUMAN RIGHTS COMMITMENTS

In this text I propose that the tension between international commitments and states' duties, and a contextualisation of these states duties through a complex balancing of state sovereignty and rights, between right and good, has been a central feature in political theory as well as article 9 jurisprudence and developing more sophisticated approaches, particularly regarding neutrality and margin of appreciation, is critical to the recalibration of the ECHR jurisprudence and in particular its article 9 and 10 jurisprudence. Instead of offering a complex balance between universality and subsidiarity, which is at the center of the application of convention rights, and rather than engaging with the challenges of their interplay and interdependence, these recent cases have effectively used a margin of appreciation—an European Court of Human Rights (ECtHR) technical tool for applying a concept of subsidiarity—to substitute universality with subsidiarity and right with good.

A moderate obsession with a few remaining state churches and their compatibility with democracy has somehow served as a distraction. While these state churches (the Church of England in particular) represent an

---

Strasbourg organs are willing to grant national authorities, in fulfilling their obligations under the European Convention on Human Rights (the Convention). See Council of Europe, "Margin of Appreciation."

anomalous legal framework from the point of view of the prevailing systems based on disestablishment, their relationship with the state is more of an example of good practice of coexistence of state religion and a secular state and society rather than a clear justification that this model has to go. In some way the focus on established churches and the question to what extent their existence has a disproportionate impact on freedom of religion or belief in a secular state and the principled justification for their *raison d'etre* in a modern secular state has taken the focus away from a discussion we should actually be having—what happens when a secular state places a disproportionate emphasis on a particular religion or belief (including non-belief such as constitutional secularism) from the point of view of Convention rights and reverses the Kantian-Rawlsian paradigm to a priority of good over right? In a deeply disturbing way both *Lautsi v. Italy* and *SAS v. France* achieve exactly that result.

One of the most remarkable developments in terms of recasting the concept of neutrality in the ECtHR's jurisprudence is unabatedly *Lautsi v. Italy*. In this case the overarching tension between universality and subsidiarity in the Court's approach has been described elsewhere as

> oscillating between focusing upon the potential impact which the presence of religious symbols within an educational environment might have on perceptions of the impartiality of the State in matters of religion or belief, and focusing on the substantive aspects of the overall education experience provided within the educational environment.[8]

In some way this judgment marks a significant departure from a plethora of "established religion" cases by attempting to reconcile state neutrality with the protection of a majority culture. The Grand Chamber implicitly endorsed the view that the principle of neutrality does not demand the absence of religious symbolism in the educational setting and no longer maintains the view that the "public realm" need be a "religiously neutral space" in order for a state to fulfil "a duty of neutrality and impartiality."[9]

This form of neutrality is articulated very differently earlier ECtHR cases. In *Lautsi* neutrality resembles an appeal to a form of sovereignty-driven political exceptionalism projected by the court both as an accomplishment of a subsidiarity principle and as a positive state duty.

In many ways the recasting of neutrality in *Lautsi v. Italy* prepared the ground for *SAS v. France* where the state duty to perpetuate respect for the majority culture articulated in Lautsi acquired a new traction in the context

---

8. Evans, "Lautsi v. Italy." See also Evans, "From Cartoons to Crucifixes"; "Neutrality."

9. Lautsi v. Italy para. 60.

of the projection of a similar state duty to protect a more secular version of the majority culture in France which tackles, more broadly, the delicate relationship between minority religious claims and majority consensus. In a leap similar to the one the Court took in *Lautsi* the *SAS* judgment of ECtHR took the view that the state has a margin of appreciation to treat the full-face veil through a lens of a state-driven political perfectionism and prohibit it because of the importance in today's societies of facial communication. And with such a leap of jurisprudence a sociological justification feeds into the broader notion of "living together" and human rights law is reduced to simply reflecting social norms.[10] In the *SAS* judgment something which is perceived sociologically as common values acquires an independent normative status when it confronts a minority practice which is perceived as non-compliant with these common values to justify a form of state neutrality which propels a withdrawal from, rather than an engagement with, its international commitments. In a similar way this is done in the *Lautsi* decision, *SAS* transforms culture into dominant normative viewpoints and blurs the distinction between social and legal norms.

EMERGING CHALLENGES OF SOVEREIGNTY DRIVEN CLAIMS

Our initial "post-Refah" approaches somehow took for granted that the Court's overarching intellectual strategies are aimed to protect convention values and in particular functioning democracy which is a *conditio sine qua non* for the life of the Convention. This meant that political and religious ideas which may have been perceived as undermining the constitutional order of a member state might not be protected by the Convention. Such an approach naturally shifted the understanding of neutrality from something which depicts the state as sitting on the fence and arbitrating the articulation of public reason in a free and open market of ideas (one of many plausible forms of the exercise of neutrality) is nevertheless potentially biased when it comes to defending political beliefs which are rightly OR wrongly conceived as foundational for their constitutional order and confronts beliefs which are again rightly OR wrongly considered a threat to this constitutional order. Seen through such a lens neutrality may become a device for defending something which is rightly or wrongly conceived as an existential cultural or civilisational frontier (a good) rather than as a contextual and unbiased adjudication of a particular rights-driven legal problem (using the Kantian formula of a priority of right over good). This is particularly tempting when neutrality is used as a way to consider a dispute beyond its specific scope as

10. Hunter-Henin, "Living Together."

in the case of the perceived cosmic battle between religion and the secular (whatever secular might be designated to mean). Seen through such a lens secular is often perceived as part and parcel of constitutional democracy (essential for the existence of convention rights) and the religious is not (even if in theory a society with an established religion like the UK may be more liberal and accommodating to different voices in the public sphere than societies like Russia, France, and Turkey which at least in theory operate within the framework of constitutions which are supposed to defend political secularism). The reason neutrality has the potential to be very biased and protectionist is partly related to the way neutrality and margin of appreciation interact. The Court is prepared to allow a broader margin of appreciation and give member states the benefit of the doubt when it comes to article 9 and possibly article 10. The limits it has set historically have been related to something which is considered an outright state interference into internal religious autonomy and potentially secessionist projects.[11] What the court has paid less attention to is an exercise of state neutrality which demonstrates a disproportionate concern for the protection of secular or cultural paradigms of self-perception to the detriment of the exercise of conventional rights, of established and credible political projects to the detriment of civil society or private concerns or political projects which are considered less credible (potentially secessionist projects or projects which are considered defective because they emerge from within fragile democracies). In cases like *Sahin, Lautsi* and *SAS* we deal with challenges of secularism which are perceived as shifting the techtonic plates of the secular state. The *Moscow Branch of the Salvation Army* flashpoints a concern which makes foreign forms of spirituality a threat to national security.[12] In a similar way cases like *Lemon v. UK* explored in what way blasphemy may be considered a threat to the constitutional order.[13] In all these cases the Court has considered whether the state has acted neutrally and whether a wider margin of appreciation may be considered appropriate. Increasingly the ECHR has been very generous with its margin of appreciation in order to counterbalance certain member states' contemptuous dissent and an emerging scepticism about the role of the Court in relation to what some have perceived as its interventionist jurisprudence. The most recent cases are in this respect

11. Communist Party (KPD) v. the Federal Republic of Germany; Kalaç v. Turkey; Yanasik v. Turkey; Karaduman v. Turkey; Dahlab v. Switzerland; X. v. Italy; United Communist Party v. Turkey; Herri Batasuna v. Spain; Vatan v. Russia; Artyomov v. Russia.

12. Several National Security doctrines of the Russian Federation engage with the notion of foreign spiritualties representing a threat to national security.

13. See Robertson, "Legal Protection," 175–78.

reason to query how to relate neutrality with margin of appreciation in cases where a state (becomes potentially self-destructing) attempts to protect its secular constitutional order by applying disproportional restrictions of convention rights. The Court has dealt in a fairly swift manner with cases of potential political insurgency when it comes to religious movements and political movements and has given the appropriate margin of appreciation to deal with such threats.[14] But how do we deal with an insurgent state which suddenly considers disproportionate measures to protect what is clearly not a very neutral, or at least not necessarily liberal perception of its own secular identity?

ABSTRACTIONS, ASPIRATIONS, APPLICATIONS

In the past the court has been quite radical in intervening in article 9 cases coming from an emerging new Europe (where in fact majority of the article 9 cases originated after almost fifty years of non-existent article 9 jurisprudence) taking the view that these interventions facilitated the appropriate calibration of state politics in relation to religion.[15] Today, with nationalist movements effectively ruling a substantial part of New and Old Europe, new religious policies quickly eradicate the achievements of the past 20 years, aligning these religious policies to a greater extent with Moscow and with Ankara rather than with Brussels or Strasbourg. It seems that the ways ECHR reflects this paradigm shift is to tacitly endorse rather than challenge such policies. *SAS* effectively endorses a form of a communitarian French laicite which is not much different from the status of the Church of Greece in the Hellenic Constitution, Putin's Russian Kulturkampf or Orban's Hungary, or Cameron's and May's idea of a British Bill of Rights as a departure from the ECHR obligations.[16] It is a jurisprudence which uses the interdependence between neutrality and margin of appreciation to develop multiple forms of Council of Europe exceptionalism. This emerging exceptionalism exploits the perennial tension between universality and subsidiarity which has been embedded in the Convention from the very start but does not attempt to engage with this tension as something central for any interpretation and adjudication of Convention rights. Lord Hoffmann has described the core of this tension by arguing that human rights are universal in abstraction, but national in application and regretted that the Strasbourg court has

14. This is perhaps the last case in the history of English jurisprudence which—like many Victorian cases—links blasphemy with high treason as an attack against the established religion and the Crown.

15. Bos, "Book Review."

16. See Christoffersen and Rask Madsen, *European Court of Human Rights.*

recognized to a limited extent the importance of the doctrine of the "margin of appreciation" which the court has not taken nearly far enough.[17]

UNIVERSALITY, SUBSIDIARITY, AND EXCEPTIONALISM

One of the ways of recognizing and increasing the importance of the margin of appreciation could be delivered by the ECtHR through a recognition of a comprehensive US style political exceptionalism at the level of CoE. States with functioning democracies and rule of law and independent courts are perceived as being entitled to exercise an American style political exceptionalism because their independent institutions have the ability to protect human rights via their existing domestic institutional frameworks. This can only be achieved by developing comprehensive safeguards and transparent forms of application of a taxonomy which would recognize the justification of such political exceptionalism. But the world we live in, at least the world of the Council of Europe does not look like a family of states capable of exercising political exceptionalism in adjudicating human rights at a municipal level. And an arbitrary application of a margin of appreciation without balancing such exercise comprehensively against the universal norm it departs from may only strengthen the trend towards souvereigntism. A number of major players within the Council of Europe (Russia, Turkey, France, and even the UK) choose to articulate more skeptical perspectives about the international legal order and to shift the focus on human rights protection to the protection of state sovereignty. A number of CoE minor players enthusiastically follow this complex example which is not often easy to reconcile in terms of political objectives. In these situations, the Court has to act as an arbiter to make sure that the state acts in such a way that it does not self-destruct the democracy which it is supposed to protect and which is needed for the Convention to operate. This could only be achieved through developing a rich legal culture of neutrality which engages on every possible level: in which public reason is articulated keeping a balance between universality and margin of appreciation in the crafting of a comprehensive rights-driven political exceptionalism.

NEUTRALITY, ADJUDICATION, AND LEGISLATIVE IMAGINATION

There is a challenge which the Strasbourg jurisprudence presents. On the one hand it does what it promises to do—to provide a treaty-based means for human rights dispute resolution when domestic remedies have been

17. Hoffmann, "Universality of Human Rights."

exhausted. Resolving any such dispute does not create a law of precedent and the ECHR jurisprudence cannot be viewed as judicial review which re-aligns the tectonic plates of a Constitution. And yet in a colloquial fashion the Convention and the jurisprudence of the ECHR are often perceived as *constitutional calibration.* Instead of perceiving a particular case as an evolving process which may have a greater or a lesser impact on the greater evolution of the Convention as a living document reported cases are seen more as a project of a constitutional alignment rather than as cases which address a specific dispute and cannot be used as a precedent in deciding a similar dispute in the future. This view of the in perception of the Convention has been shared by a number of judges within and beyond the Court:

> The human rights system established by the [ECHR] has been in existence for more than thirty years. . . . The treaty, once perceived as a daring experiment of limited significance, has become a veritable Magna Carta of Western Europe. The institutions established to enforce the rights it guarantees . . . have also undergone a significant change. Conceived as regional international organs with limited jurisdiction and even more limited powers, they have gradually acquired the status and authority of constitutional tribunals. This transformation of the Convention and its institutions, a process that has by no means reached its final stage, marks a fascinating chapter in the evolution of modern international law.[18]

In a similar vein Ryssdal asserts:

> It is my firm conviction that if the Court continues in the course that it has followed since its early days it will consolidate more and more its emergent role as a European constitutional court.[19]

It is indeed the case that a great deal of Art 9 cases in particular have seen as a means of propelling a freedom of religion or belief constitutional revolution within the Council in Europe after the fall of the Berlin Wall.[20] A fifty-year silence of Art 9 was broken by the abrupt end of Communism and produced the complex cases for religious associations and individual believers. And while these cases clearly addressed often multiple disputes between religious associations and religious associations[21] and the state there was an

---

18. Buergenthal, "Book Review," 280.

19. Ryssdal, "Future of the European Court."

20. Martínez-Torrón, "Perspectives from Europe," 99–127.

21. Holy Synod of the Bulgarian Orthodox Church v. Bulgaria; Supreme Holy Council of the Muslim Community v. Bulgaria; Metropolitan Church of Bessarabia v.

implied theme that the Court's judgment, interpretation of neutrality and margin of appreciation in many of these early article 9 cases was pushing not only for a resolution of a particular dispute but also for the evolving of an environment where Convention rights may thrive. One could argue that this is something the Court does anyway and each case implies an exercise of ECHR *soft power* through the development of societies driven by respect for Convention rights. But these early cases were also different in the way they engaged with article 9 rights. The way we could reconcile some of the article 9 cases of old democracies and those of the emerging democracies in the nineties is by understanding the court jurisprudence as a *soft power* for building legal cultures based on democracy, rule of law and human rights. And the early article 9 jurisprudence does imply that there is greater mileage in exercising soft power in emerging democracies than in old democracies.[22] The difficulty with this incidental result is that it has concocted a misguided perception regarding the nature of the ECHR jurisprudence and the member states' commitments to comply with their duties as signatories to an international treaty. By developing a notion of interdependence of convention rights and constitutions it has in some way generated a perception that the ECHR is emerging as the Council of Europe's constitutional Court and its role is to scrutinise the constitutions of the Council of Europe.

So how did we end up where we are now—at a junction where the legacy of the Convention is that the jurisdiction of the court is undermined more than ever before?

GETTING SERIOUS ABOUT SOMETHING WHICH WAS NOT MEANT TO BE THAT SERIOUS

Article 9 cases as late arrivals did not share the clear cut approaches adopted in connection with cases relating to other articles of the Convention. It could be argued that the court fairly early in the day took the view that Convention rights can only be operational in the context of an operational democracy.[23] This was never articulated explicitly in the early article 9 cases even if in reality the interdependence between articles 9 and 10, often seen through the lens of *travaux preparatoire* of the Convention effectively, achieved a similar effect (*Whitehouse v. UK, Wingrove v. United Kingdom, Otto-Preminger-Institut v. Austria, Sahin v. Turkey, Refah v. Turkey*). The perennial confusion about the interdependence between Art 9 and 10 appears

---

Moldova; Hasan v. Bulgaria; Dogan v. Turkey.

22. Gross, "Reinforcing the New Democracies"; Harmsen, "European Convention on Human Rights."

23. "ECHR" art. 17.

to have contributed to the erosion of article 9 jurisprudence by associating the rationale of article 9 cases too closely with the "secessionist" cases which have been perceived as undermining the constitutional (and democratic) order of the state. And once this is done it is a matter of time before article 9 cases are dealt with as a way of addressing constitutional secessionist threats. This small leap effectively places article 9 cases at the center of a problematic discussion about the circumstances under which religion or belief could undermine *disproportionately* constitutional democracies.

We have seen this approach creeping in the 'religious symbols' cases as well as the 'blasphemy' cases but earlier cases never achieved the extreme obsession with the defense of the cultural (and religious) frontier in the way seen in cases like *Lautsi* and *SAS* have. These most recent cases have effectively adopted an approach in relation to article 9 disputes which treats article 9 adjudication as a frontier which determines constitutional legitimacy balanced against the right to freedom of religion or belief. This is not unproblematic. After all, even if it influences indirectly political speech freedom of religion or belief is not a political speech. Viewing article 9 rights as undermining of constitutional orders is a step which could effectively be applied in relation to virtually any form of religious expression (which is sometimes easier to decontextualise than political speech). This is already demonstrated by Russia's National Security Doctrine which has labelled all forms of foreign spirituality as a threat to national security and by *Moscow Branch of the Salvation Army v Russia* in which the rationale of the Russian government follows the same argument.[24] While regime change in the context of political speech could be easily examined in the context of article 10 adjudication the threat of virtually any religious message which challenges the *status quo* even by spiritual means and without political action (partly because such distinction is very hard to make with reliable means) is seriously problematic. Apart from offering a completely misguided approach to article 9 jurisprudence, which is meant to address specific disputes (without transforming this dispute into a precedent) rather than major constitutional questions, such approaches are often used as a green light to introduce restrictions of religious autonomy and registration of religious associations which are perceived as "the Other."[25]

Being nice to member states by way of ECHR adjudication and granting them a broad margin of appreciation by default in all the most recent cases has probably resulted in resetting cultural wars and effectively

---

24. See also Ministry of Foreign Affairs, "National Security Concept," 8

25. There are presently several bills within the CoE and OSCE region which propose once again restrictive regimes of registration of religious associations—Hungary, Bulgaria, and Russia, to name a few.

undermining article 9 convention rights in favor of the building of new cultural spaces through a misguided political perfectionism, often detrimental to the protection of convention rights. State neutrality may appear to be compatible with particular forms of state perfectionism where the state can choose social goals worth pursuing and the context in which citizens could exercise their autonomy including autonomy based on freedom of religion or belief.

Legal and political theory have already identified the shortcomings of discourses which develop assimilationist projects of political perfectionism where the state decides on the scope of meaning of the good life by limiting directly or indirectly the pursuits of alternative choices. In both *Lautsi* and *SAS* the protection of dominant culture does indeed imply such a project of political perfectionism. The fact that the Court in *SAS* follows obediently the CoE policy paper to construct a "living together" environment[26] does not change the fact that the judgment displays the shortcomings which have already emerged in a number of earlier article 9 cases—the inability to acknowledge that every political theory, including the full range of liberal legal and political theories, is based on a set of values and cannot give a neutral justification of specific state policies.

PREVENTATIVE APPROACHES AT THE CENTER OF THE DEVELOPING OF EFFECTIVE TOOLS TO INTERPRET THE BALANCE BETWEEN UNIVERSALITY AND SUBSIDIARITY

In this piece I have argued that the interplay between neutrality and margin of appreciation has downplayed a significant tension between international perspectives on human rights and implementation. I argue that this tension which is at the center of the perception of the Convention as a living document is inevitable and often overlooked. Instead I therefore propose that this tension could be better served if it is approached through the lens of prevention. In that way margin of appreciation will no longer disguise the complexities of municipal constitutional politics, but will allow a fluidity of approaches to factor in ECHR jurisprudence as a way of shaping evolving rights based approaches measured against a wide range of ECHR jurisprudence without having to make margin of appreciation compliant at the level of "constitutional architecture." In that context state neutrality will have to serve such preventative strategies rather than maintain a constitutional *status quo* which has been one of the key problems of translating across ECHR jurisprudence. This approach centerd around prevention

26. *Living Together.*

also mirrors concepts such as multi-centerd perfectionism in the work of Joseph Chan and the concept of three centers of sociality in the works of Simeon Frank.[27] In this form of multi-centerd perfectionism the liberal state cannot decide independently and without an agreement with civil society which social practices are of value and need state support. Multi-centerd perfectionism may reset relationships between international organizations and their courts, national constitutional courts (who can be part of the conversation rather than an alternative to ECHR[28]) and ultimately "the minimal state" represented at a subsidiarity level even by the smallest group capable of exercising the role of the state. Civil society needs the state to remedy its defects, and the state in turn requires a strong civil society to counterbalance and contain its enormous power. There is no deep distinction between the state and the civil society so far as their vulnerability and their impact on people's lives are concerned. And in fact, those two require each another in the pursuit of perfectionist goals.[29] A prevention driven approach is more likely to develop actionable policy points which could develop a fairly robust test for the Court in determining whether margin of appreciation is granted for deliberation of political reasoning in cases where this reasoning can demonstrate an inclusive perfectionism—a political deliberation where the state has involved all actors. In such a context subsidiarity approach cannot simply be considered to be a privilege of a member state and can only be justified as a legitimate approach in cases where subsidiarity extends to the 'minimal state' to the smallest group capable to articulate public reason in a particular society.

This democratic state perfectionism provides opportunities that most, if not all, major reasonable specific conceptions of goods would have a fair chance to be heard and supported. While this is still a state-driven perfectionism, it is civil society, and not the state that decides which options are (or are not) of value. Approached through that lens a wider margin of appreciation and state exceptionalism become justified only if they provide safe dialogical spaces to develop comprehensive rule of law and rights-driven cultures and neutrality will serve to safeguard these dialogical spaces rather

---

27. Chan, "Legitimacy, Unanimity, and Perfectionism"; Франк, *Дукховние основий обштества*. Frank argues that societies operate at three levels—universality which represents forms of universal shared humanity, sociality, which represents conventional social structures and sobornost (solidarity, council) which represents the 'I-Thou' social level of deep dialogical social penetration of the Other. These three levels are interdependent and can only operate fully if this interdependence works.

28. A trend which has certainly been emerging in countries like Turkey, Hungary, and Russia.

29. Chan, "Legitimacy, Unanimity, and Perfectionism," 30–31.

than assert, amplify or impose dominant social normative paradigms. In this environment the focus will not be so much on balancing between the liberal international order and the inherently communitarian constitutional politics but on making human rights part of any form of articulation of these two extreme ends of the spectrum of articulation of public reason.

Decades of article 9 resemble the cavern story from Plato's Republic, presenting article 9 interpretations as if there is not a real world out there and that the Convention has to protect not simply democracy but an idealised model of democracy and a liberal world without internal philosophical tensions. Affirmation of particular cultures and flirting with artificial and largely content-empty conceptual models such as multiculturalism, inter-culturalism, integration and absorption clearly driven by the fear of "Muslim Europe" or simply "Religious Europe" and the desperate attempt to save what is described as a 'museum piece Christian civilization' clearly indicates that the Court's jurisprudence has been moving beyond the objectives of the court and has been engaging with questions of crucifixes, minarets and headscarves in ways which make these questions sound like constitutional questions rather than specific human rights challenges in specific cases in very specific constitutional contexts.

The illusion that human rights-driven cultures have almost undergone constitutional transformations is apparent in the remarkably rapid derogation of Turkey,[30] Ukraine,[31] France[32] in 2016 and 2017 and by the UK's "rhetorical" intention to derogate[33] from their obligations under the European Convention of Human Rights. Once again human rights universal in abstraction and national in application display the inherent dormant challenge of the interplay between universality and subsidiarity. And the way this challenge appears to be faced by governments is through the assertion of state sovereignty at all costs, through blanket derogations from the Convention rather than through the development of human rights-driven multi-centerd spaces of debate, dialogue and articulation of public reason in

---

30. In the aftermath of the failed July 15 coup, Turkey's government declared a state of emergency and subsequently notified the Council of Europe, on July 21, that it "may" derogate from the European Convention on Human Rights (ECHR). So far there is no information of a possible notification to the United Nations concerning derogations from the International Covenant on Civil and Political Rights (ICCPR).

31. In June this year, Ukraine formally derogated from the International Covenant on Civil and Political Rights and the European Convention on Human Rights.

32. On November 24, 2017, France filed a formal notice of derogation from the European Convention on Human Rights with the Secretary-General of the Council of Europe.

33. "Government's Proposed Derogation."

order to strengthen engaging sovereignty driven approaches with the complex challenges of implementation of universal commitments.

The complex interdependence between universality and subsidiarity is embedded in the very grammar of the Convention—on the one hand it is a living document which thrives on and depends on liberal democracy, on the other it is a document which protects and highlight a number of conservative values.

The late Lord Bingham often highlighted the British conservative values built into the grammar of the European Convention through the remarkable contribution by Conservative lawyers and politicians such as Sir David Maxwell-Fyfe. If we are to relate to this as one of the blindspots of article 9 adjudication we will have to accept that it is inherently built around conservative and liberal values, containing the pressures and mechanisms for maintaining and at the same time for changing the *status quo* (which is perceived as a way of balancing between liberal and conservative values in a liberal democracy). This dual aspect has been long overlooked and the Convention has often been presented as a beacon of liberalism where liberal choices trump conservative ones. A quick glance through the *travaux preparatoire* indicates that this is certainly not the case—the Convention drafted by conservative thinkers envisaged the protection of liberal democracy through balancing between liberal and conservative socio-political concepts and provided spaces for the protection of established religion, the right to family life and constitutional secularism (to name a few) which do not always represent liberal values but rather reflect a context in which a particular status quo is to be maintained for the functioning of a liberal democracy. And while this did not in any way serve as a blueprint for the ways in which the ECHR was to become a beacon of liberation for the countries behind the Iron Curtain in the first decades after the end of the Cold War it has certainly affected a variety of complex trends associated with article 9. We have taken for granted the transformative nature of ECHR and have completely misjudged the resilience of political authoritarianism in its various forms (from the left as well as from the right) when it comes to balancing strong sovereignty driven claims and rights driven claims. And rather than engaging with the complex balancing between right and good in the universality-subsidiarity interdependence the Strasbourg system has simply proposed a simplified and decontextualised Kantian-Rawlsian proposal that right trumps good. In reality this is far from the Rawlsian paradigm. Rawls is as much concerned with priority of right over good as he is about the complexity of the reality on the ground—in particular the complexity in the interaction between sovereignty and internationalism which invites a more nuanced and contextual right versus good balancing.

In *The Law of Peoples*, Rawls argues that international peace and justice can only be advanced through well-governed societies.[34] Rawls and other legal and political theorists tend to come to the conclusion that the foundation of a humane global order is the stability provided by nations that take care of their own people and respect the sovereignty of other nations. In a similar vein Michael Ignatieff argues:

> If we want human rights to be anchored in the world, we cannot want their enforcement to depend on international institutions and NGOs. We want them anchored in the actual practice of sovereign states.[35]

The proposal that strong nation-states are crucial for the development of rights-driven legal cultures is not merely an easily recognisable communitarian platform. John Tasioulas argues that such trends towards "sovereigntism" projected through the lens of political exceptionalism[36] and providing that such exceptionalism is compliant as far as commitments to democracy and the rule of law are concerned may strengthen rather than weaken the interdependence between universality and subsidiarity. Such a project departs from a communitarian proposal which concedes that there are bound to be injustices in a sovereignty driven political project where some countries will accord more respect for human rights than others. Instead an exceptionalism driven sovereignty has to be rule of law and human rights compliant in order to be justified and the only way such compliance may be measured is through its interdependence with international commitments and a commitment to multi-centerd perfectionism. In that way the realisation that without well-governed sovereign nations—strong national communities—the global system will decay into far worse disorder, and the rule of law will weaken within countries will not be simply a concession, but a realisation of the interdependence between universality and subsidiarity. The communitarian proposal that only national communities have the power consistently to protect rights and enforce laws is thus taken to a new level. Strong nation-states that are solicitous of the well-being of their citizens and respectful of the sovereignty of other states may advance human dignity and prosperity in the world even if the cost is an exercise of political exceptionalism provided that this exceptionalism is not at the cost of surrendering of their international commitments.[37] Such a contextual ap-

---

34. Rawls, *Law of Peoples*, 6–7.

35. Ignatieff, "Return of Sovereignty."

36. See Tasioulas, "Human Rights, Legitimacy."

37. Petkoff, "Religious Exceptionalism." See also Tasioulas, "Human Rights, Legitimacy."

plication of their international commitments may paradoxically strengthen the international system, especially if such rule of law exceptionally could be exercised by a greater number of sovereign states—not in contempt but in compliance.

The above accounts remind us that in practice international human rights as we know them within the wider body of international law do not simply represent a constitutional liberal paradigm but play a central balancing role between communitarian and liberal claims, and moderate these claims particularly, when they reach spectrums of the extreme. Article 9 in the context of ECtHR adjudication is not an exception and deals with particularly complex and often delicate concepts of rights within the language of the Convention. The paradox is that such jurisprudence may potentially undermine the purpose of the Convention and of the European Court of Human Rights by creating a perception of double standards in relation to the assessment of the exercise of neutrality and margin of appreciation. At the same time any attempt at a systematic approach to neutrality will be inappropriate and will not engage with the key challenge presented before the Court which makes doomed any quest for conceptual coherence with regards to neutrality and margin of appreciation—that on the one hand as an international tribunal ECHR issues judgments addressing a specific dispute and which in no way act as a precedent or a measure for future disputes, on the other—the fact that after Protocol 11 ECHR has acquired a status of a quasi-constitutional court in the CoE hemisphere and the perceptions and the expectations with regards to its jurisprudence seem to shift in the direction of what we expect the jurisprudence of constitutional courts to do. This presents ample challenges in terms of how to apply margin of appreciation in order to define the scope of state neutrality in relation to article 9 jurisprudence. The present text proposes approaching neutrality and margin of appreciation as multi-centerd and multi-vectored through the lens of prevention which is a model which has a greater chance to maintain open channels and invites all persons and groups to become co-participants in the articulation of public reason.

The Court has emerged as both a political body and a judicial tribunal and its emerging tools play different roles in these two contexts.

As a policy driven approach, the court may use margin of appreciation and neutrality as a discretionary way of dealing with complex cases. And then there is the use of margin of appreciation as a legal tool which enables the court to consider subsidiarity driven claims in the application of universal human rights. In this context margin of appreciation is a subsidiarity principle which has to be considered against a universal claim that rules of higher order trump the municipal rules. But in order to do this, judges will have to consider a subsidiarity claim all the way down to the bottom to the minimal state to use Nozick's term (the smallest group), in order to assess properly the subsidiarity claim. This is terribly important because in order to properly assess any claim for a margin of appreciation one has to consider the complex multi-centerd state perfectionism any subsidiarity driven state interference may entail. Such a claim cannot be properly considered juridically (but it could perhaps be as a policy) unless it takes into account the multi-centerd, multi-vectored set of relations and a bottom—up application to the subsidiarity principle for the justification of any specific state responses. We are reminded of an inherent tension between a universal vision and a national context in ECHR adjudication and about the centrality of the concept of neutrality in the shaping of a jurisprudence which is driven by the overarching tension and interdependence between universality and subsidiarity. It also reminds us that any coherence in the ECHR jurisprudence would derive, not from the emergence of consistent precedents but from a consistent application of the principle of neutrality as dynamic hermeneutic tool which maintains the complex interdependence between an international vision and contextual implementation. We are also reminded that the tension between universality and subsidiarity in human rights adjudication should be seen as a gift which renews our engagement with the Convention rights, rather than as a problem which has to be eliminated.

BIBLIOGRAPHY

Bos, Nienke. "Book Review: *Militant Democracy: Undemocratic Political Parties and Beyond*, by Svetlana Tyulkina, Routledge, Abingdon, Oxon and New York, 2015." *Acta Politica* 52.2 (2017) 261–63.

Buergenthal, Thomas "Book Review: *Europäische MenschenRechtsKonvention: EMRK Kommentar* by Jochen Abr. Frowein and Wolfgang Peukert. Kehl am Rhein, Strasbourg and Arlington: N. P. Engel Verlag, 1985. Pp. 604. DM 188." *AJIL* 81 (1987) 280–82.

Chan, Joseph. "Legitimacy, Unanimity, and Perfectionism." *Philosophy & Public Affairs* 29.1 (2000) 5–42.

Christoffersen, Jonas, and Mikael Rask Madsen, eds. *The European Court of Human Rights between Law and Politics*. Oxford: Oxford University Press, 2011.

Conservatives. "Protecting Human Rights in the UK the Conservatives' Proposals for Changing Britain's Human Rights Laws." Online. https://www.conservatives.com/~/media/files/ . . . /human_rights.pdf

Council of Europe. "Living Together: Combining Diversity and Freedom in Twenty-First-Century Europe." Report of the Group of Eminent Persons of the Council of Europe. May 12, 2011. Online. https://www.coe.int/t/dg4/highereducation/2011/KYIV%20WEBSITE/Report%20on%20diversity.pdf.

Council of Europe. "Margin of Appreciation." Online. https://www.coe.int/t/dghl/cooperation/lisbonnetwork/themis/echr/paper2_en.asp

Evans, Carolyn. *Freedom of Religion under the European Convention on Human Rights.* Vol. 1. Oxford: Oxford University Press, 2001.

Evans, Malcolm D. "From Cartoons to Crucifixes: Current Controversies Concerning the Freedom of Religion and the Freedom of Expression before the European Court of Human Rights." *Journal of Law and Religion* 26.1 (2010) 345–70.

———. "Lautsi v. Italy: An Initial Appraisal." *Religion & Human Rights* 6.3 (2011) 237–44.

———. "Neutrality In and After Lautsi v. Italy." In *The Lautsi Papers: Multidisciplinary Reflections on Religious Symbols in the Public School Classroom*, edited by Jeroen Temperman, 329–54. Leiden: Brill, 2012.

Evans, Malcolm, and Peter Petkoff. "Marginal Neutrality—Neutrality and the Margin of Appreciation in the Jurisprudence of the European Court of Human Rights." In *The European Court of Human Rights and the Freedom of Religion or Belief: The 25 Years since Kokkinakis*, edited by Jeroen Temperman, et al., 128–53. Leiden: Brill, 2019.

Франк, Семён. *Духовные основы общества, Вединие в социальную философию.* Мосцов: Республика,, 1992.

Garton Ash, Timothy. "We Know the Price of Appeasement. That's Why We Must Stand up to Viktor Orbán." *Guardian*, April 12, 2017. Online. https://www.theguardian.com/commentisfree/2017/apr/12/viktor-orban-appeasement-merkel-center-right-hungary.

Gross, Aeyal M. "Reinforcing the New Democracies: The European Convention on Human Rights and the Former Communist Countries—A Study of the Case Law." *Eur. J. Int'l L* 7 (1996) 89–102.

Harmsen, Robert. "The European Convention on Human Rights after Enlargement." *International Journal of Human Rights* 5.4 (2001) 18–43.

Hoffmann, Leonard. "The Universality of Human Rights." Judicial Studies Board Annual Lecture. March 19, 2009. Online. https://www.judiciary.gov.uk/wp-content/uploads/2014/12/Hoffmann_2009_JSB_Annual_Lecture_Universality_of_Human_Rights.pdf.

Hunter-Henin, Myriam. "Living Together in an Age of Religious Diversity: Lessons from Baby Loup and SAS." *Oxford Journal of Law and Religion* 4.1 (2015) 98–101.

Ignatieff, Michael. "The Return of Sovereignty." *New Republic* 243 (2012) 4–917.

Joint Committee on Human Rights. "The Government's Proposed Derogation from the ECHR Inquiry." *Parliament.uk*, June 8, 2017. Online. https://www.parliament.uk/business/committees/committees-a-z/joint-select/human-rights-committee/inquiries/parliament-2015/government-proposed-echr-derogation-16-17.

Martínez-Torrón, Javier. "Perspectives from Europe." In *Religious Liberty and Human Rights*, edited by Mark Hill, 99–127. Cardiff: University of Wales Press, 2002.

Ministry of Foreign Affairs of the Russian Federation. "National Security Concept of the Russian Federation." January 10, 2000. Online. http://www.mid.ru/en/foreign_policy/official_documents/-/asset_publisher/CptICkB6BZ29/content/id/589768.

Petkoff, Peter. "Religious Exceptionalism, Religious Rights, and Public International Law." In *The Changing Nature of Religious Rights Under International Law*, edited by Malcolm Evans, et al., 211–34. Oxford: Oxford University Press, 2015.

Rawls, John. *The Law of Peoples: With, The Idea of Public Reason Revisited.* Cambridge, MA: Harvard University Press, 2001.

Robertson, David. "The Legal Protection of Religious Values in Europe." In *Secularism and Religious Liberty*, edited by Jorge Rodriguez, 185. Vatican City: Vatican, 1998.

Ryssdal, Rolv. "The Future of the European Court of Human Rights." Lecture delivered at King's College London, March 22, 1990.

Tasioulas, John. "Human Rights, Legitimacy, and International Law." *The American Journal of Jurisprudence* 58.1 (2013) 1–25.

Court Cases

Artyomov v. Russia (14146/02), European Court of Human Rights, 27 May 2010.

Communist Party (KPD) v. the Federal Republic of Germany, (250/57), European Commission on Human Rights, 20 July 1957, Yearbook 1.

Dahlab v. Switzerland (42393/98), European Court of Human Rights, 2001-V.

Dogan v. Turkey (62649/10), European Court of Human Rights, 26 April 2016 (2017) 64 EHRR. 5.

Hasan v. Bulgaria (30985/96), European Court of Human Rights, 26 October 2000 (2002) 34 EHRR 55; 10 BHRC 646.

Herri Batasuna v. Spain (25803/04 & 25817/04), European Court of Human Rights, 30 June 2009.

Holy Synod of the Bulgarian Orthodox Church (Metropolitan Inokentiy) and Others v. Bulgaria (412/03 35677/04), European Court of Human Rights, 22 January 2009.

Kalaç v. Turkey (20704/92), European Court of Human Rights, 23 June, 1997, Reports 1997-IV; (1997) 27 EHRR 552.

Karaduman v. Turkey (16278/90), European Commission on Human Rights, 3 May 1993, DR 74.

Lautsi v. Italy (30814/06), European Court of Human Rights (Grand Chamber), 18 March 2011 (2012) 54 EHRR 3; 30 BHRC 429; [2011] Eq. LR 633; [2011] ELR 176.

Metropolitan Church of Bessarabia v. Moldova (45701/99), European Court of Human Rights, 14 December 2001 (2002) 35 EHRR 13.

Otto-Preminger-Institut v. Austria (13470/87), European Court of Human Rights, 20 September 1994 (1994) 19 EHRR 34, [1994] ECHR 26.

Refah Partisi (Welfare Party) v. Turkey (41340/98) (No.1), European Court of Human Rights, 31 July 2001 (2002) 35 EHRR 3.

Sahin v. Turkey (44774/98), European Court of Human Rights (Grand Chamber), 10 November 2005 (2007) 44 EHRR 5; 19 BHRC 590; [2006] ELR 73.

SAS v. France (43835/11), European Court of Human Rights (Grand Chamber), 1 July 2014: (2015) 60 EHRR 11; 36 BHRC 617; [2014] Eq. LR 590.

Supreme Holy Council of the Muslim Community v. Bulgaria (39023/97), European Court of Human Rights, 16 December 2004 (2005) 41 EHRR 3.

United Communist Party v. Turkey (19392/92), European Court of Human Rights [ECHR]; Grand Chamber 30 January 1998, ECHR 1998-I, [1998] ECHR 1, (1998) 26 EHRR 121, IHRL 3346 (ECHR 1998)

Vatan v. Russia (47978/99) European Court of Human Rights, 7 October 2004.

Whitehouse v. Lemon (8710/79), [1979] 2 WLR 281; *Whitehouse v. Gay News Ltd* [1979] AC 617, HL; *Gay News Ltd. and Lemon v. United Kingdom* [Eur Comm HR] 5 EHRR 123 (1982).

Wingrove v. UK (19/1995), European Court of Human Rights, 25 November 1996. European Court of Human Rights Times 05-Dec-1996, Case, [1997] 24 EHRR 1, 17419/90, [1996] ECHR 60, [1996] ECHR 60.

X. v. Italy (6741/74), European Commission on Human Rights 5 Eur. Comm'n H.R. Dec. & Rep. 83–85 (1976).

Yanasik v. Turkey (14254/89), European Commission on Human Rights, 6 January 1993, DR 74.

14

Religious Freedom in Europe and Work of the Conference of European Churches on This Matter

Elizabeta Kitanovic

The Conference of European Churches (CEC) was created in 1959 and has 115 members who belong to Orthodox, Protestant, Anglican, and Old Catholic Churches around Europe and more than 40 National Councils of Churches and Organizations in Partnership. The CEC has members coming from around 40 European countries. Therefore, it has offices in Brussels to relate to the European Union's institutions (EU 28—member states) and Strasbourg to relate to the context of broader Europe via Council of Europe (CoE 47—member states). In the area of human rights, the CEC also relates to the Organization of Security and Cooperation in Europe (OSCE 57—member states) as well as to the United Nations (UN—193 member states). In terms of human rights, the CEC's main work is focused on religious freedom or belief.

Why is this necessary? The members of the CEC face different challenges in the field of human rights: the majority of the CEC membership are from minority churches and they have their specific challenges in terms of legal recognition.[1] In some cases, their members are often discriminated

---

1. According to a definition offered in 1977 by Francesco Capotorti, Special

against and excluded by state and society, or dominant religious community. They experience difficulties in gaining licenses to build places of worship etc. Many challenges arise from the complex relationships between church and state which have the potential to change with every new government. Some of the CEC members are state churches, others had the status of the state churches and then they became independent, some due to the disintegration of states, change from majority to minority churches overnight etc. In some countries there is strong secularism such as in France as well as in Turkey, a country split between the inherited secular ideals from Ataturk and a strong presence of Islam in the ruling party. In some predominantly Orthodox countries, the relations between church and state are still relatively strong which is related to the history of the country. After a communist past or any other sort of dictatorship, numerous challenges are still linked with the depravation of church property by state authorities. Even so, one needs to admit that in general the situation on religious freedom and awareness in Europe is much wider than it was a few decades ago.

WHY ARE CEC MEMBER CHURCHES DEALING WITH FREEDOM OF RELIGION OR BELIEF?

Let us look at some of the challenges that we find in Europe with which the CEC Member Churches are faced and see what is happening in some European countries, which are members of the EU, or not.

One of the most visible violations of religious freedom is still in the Northern part of Cyprus. While the Southern part of Cyprus became a member of the European Union in 2004, the North is still occupied by Turkey and not a member of the EU. In the South people are still struggling to gain access to their places of worship, shrines, churches, and monuments which are collapsing under Turkish control since 1974.[2] The issue of the return of property, as well as what happened to missing persons, are important questions. After the invasion by the Turkish military in 1974 there was deliberate destruction of Greek cultural heritage which was in line with the process of ethnic cleansing of Greek Cypriots who were living in the Northern part of the island. This destruction includes:

Rapporteur of the United Nations Sub-Commission on Prevention of Discrimination and Protection of Minorities, a minority is "a group numerically inferior to the rest of the population of a State, in a non-dominant position, whose members—being nationals of the State—possess ethnic, religious, or linguistic characteristics differing from those of the rest of the population and show, if only implicitly, a sense of solidarity, directed towards preserving their culture, traditions, religion or language" (United Nations, "Minorities under International Law").

2. Demosthenous, *Occupied Church of Cyprus*, 1.

- The destruction of ancient historic sites and monuments.
- The looting of museums and other private collections.
- The destruction and desecrations of important religious sites to Orthodox, Maronite and Armenian Cypriots.

Known as the "island of saints," Cyprus has played an important role in the evolution and spread Christianity in the West.[3] After the Turkish invasion, the fate of Christian churches and monasteries is the following:

> 125 churches have been turned into the mosques, an old Islamic tradition in occupied territories, 67 have been turned into stables or hay warehouses, 57 have become museums, cultural centers or hotels, 17 have become hostels, restaurants or military warehouses, 25 have been demolished, 229 have been totally desecrated.[4]

The Church of Cyprus has opened an office in Brussels in order to continue their struggle for human rights in this regard and they work very closely with the CEC to reach their goals.

On the other hand, for the churches and other religious communities in Turkey, religious freedom according to international standards are still not being fully implemented. As stated by Dr Mine Yildirim from the Norwegian Helsinki Committee, in Turkey:

> Alevis worship are not considered as places of worship, the Baha'i faith and Jehovah's Witnesses are not religions, and conscientious objection to military service is not accepted as manifestation of a religion or philosophical belief.[5]

This means that religious pluralism is carried out in a very selective way. Also, on June 21, 2017, "the president of the Presidency of Religious Affairs of Turkey, Mehmet Görmez, took part in Islamic prayers at Hagia Sophia in Istanbul, which was also broadcast on state television. Hagia Sophia is built as a Christian church, then later converted to a mosque, and Hagia Sophia was opened as a museum in 1935 following orders from Mustafa Kemal Atatürk, the founder of the Turkish Republic. As a museum, no prayers in any tradition have been held there since 1935. The Conference of European Churches urged the Turkish authorities to assure the continuation of this

3. Miltiadou, *Windows on Cyprus*, 70.
4. Miltiadou, *Windows on Cyprus*, 70.
5. Yildirim, "Freedom of Religion," 85.

historic and unique role of Hagia Sophia and to ensure a positive climate for open and transparent dialogue among religions in Turkey.[6]

In the Ukraine on May 18, 2017, the Verkhovna Rada of Ukraine was scheduled to vote on bills number 4128 and 4511. The first one—On Amendments to the Law of Ukraine on Freedom of Conscience and Religious Organizations—had as an aim

> to introduce into the religious legislation a vague notion of 'a person's belonging to a religious community' on the basis of some 'self-identification.' Those who 'belong to a religious community,' whoever may claim this title, are to be granted a right to change the statute of a community by simple majority vote. The new bill in fact proposes to legalize the practice of fictitious 'referendums' with participation of all the inhabitants of a settlement (and possibly that of visitors as well) who claim to belong to this religious community.[7]

The second one—On the Special Status of Religious Organizations Whose Governing Centers Are Located in the State Recognized by the Verkhovna Rada as Aggressor-State—proposes

> to impose on all communities whose centers of canonical subordination are located in Russia (that is, primarily, the communities of the Ukrainian Orthodox Church) a certain 'special status' involving the essential deprivation of rights.[8]

If these bills were to be implemented it would mean that the Russian Orthodox Church could start losing their parishes and also their proprieties.

Even for Jehovah's Witnesses, who are not a member of the CEC, there is general concern that just before this political Ukrainian action, on April 20, 2017, the Russian Federation's Supreme Court banned the activities of the Administrative Center of Jehovah's Witnesses, active in Russia since 1991. This ban is based on "extremism" and in practice it means that if there is an act of worship by Jehovah's Witnesses it is possible to launch criminal proceedings against them. This means that about 395 of its local communities across Russia will be closed and that about 175 000 of their believers will be affected.

> On 4 April the Special Rapporteur on Freedom of Opinion and Expression David Kaye, then—Special Rapporteur on Freedoms of Peaceful Assembly and Association Kiai, and Special

---

6. Conference of European Churches, "Islamic Prayers Take Place."
7. "His Holiness Patriarch Kirill."
8. "His Holiness Patriarch Kirill."

Rapporteur on Freedom of Religion and Belief Ahmed Shaheed stated that the use of counter-extremism legislation in this way to confine freedom of opinion, including religious belief, expression and association to that which is state-approved is unlawful and dangerous, and signals a dark future for all religious freedom in Russia.[9]

In Kosovo and Metohija,[10] a pogrom took place March 17, 2004:

This pogrom of the Albanian terrorists drove out new more than four thousand Serbs from their ages-long hearts, destroyed hundreds of homes, demolished new over thirty churches, and because of it also new innocent victims were fallen. All this happened in the presence of international civilian and military forces, the UNMIK and the KFOR. Until today no one has been accused for this violence and public crime.[11]

The situation today still doesn't provide the conditions for peaceful co-existence among Serbian and Albanian people. The last disturbing incident took place on Orthodox Easter, April 20, 2017 when "a group of vandals attacked the church of St. Peter and Paul in Talinovec and smashed windows. The UNMIK team visited the church and made a report."[12]

These were just few examples coming from the European context and there are many more similar events and instances.

RAISING AWARENESS AND ADVOCATING ON FREEDOM OF RELIGION OR BELIEF

The CEC has been working for the past ten years in the area of human rights education. The book *European Churches Engaging in Human Rights—Present challenges and training material*[13] is one of the materials developed, and transposed, into the project of the CEC's Summer School on Human Rights. Every year, for the last 5 years, the CEC and its Thematic Reference Group on human rights organized the programme for theologians tackling different human rights topics from the theological and legal points of view. The first summer school was organized with the academic support of KU Leuven, Belgium and discussed religious freedom or belief. The second

9. "Russia: Jehovah's Witnesses Banned."

10. Understood in accordance with the United Nations Security Council Resolution 1244.

11. Serbian Orthodox Church, "Communique Regarding the Pogrom."

12. Serbian Orthodox Diocese of Raska-Prizren and Kosovo-Metohija.

13. Kitanovic, *European Churches*.

one related to the issue of anti-discrimination and it took place in Sweden. The third one was organized with the academic support of the Theological School of Thessaloniki, Greece and the fourth one took place in Palermo, Italy and discussed the issue of migration. The last one in 2018 will discuss the religious freedom or belief and the new developments in this area and will take place in Malaga, Spain. One of the reasons for all those discussions and strategies is to enable pastors and churches to help their members in protecting their human dignity.

One of the most important duties of the CEC is to support and put pressure on European institutions in advocating for, and securing, freedom of religion or belief. At the same time this is an opportunity to show the member churches how to relate to issues such as freedom of religion or belief. The developing position of the CEC can be seen through different statements originating in seminars and conferences.[14]

In 2013 the European Union adopted the "EU Guidelines on the promotion and protection of freedom of religion or belief."[15] The document gave the CEC a reason to raise the issue among the European churches, not only in relation to the external contexts (outside of the EU) but also to stress how freedom of religion or belief is handled within the EU and the broader European context. In a conference "Advancing Religious Freedom or Belief for all" there was a focus upon what to address to the EU institutions:

> We also want the EU itself to pay fuller attention to the internal and external coherence of the application of its human rights policies. The EU has adopted the Guidelines on freedom of religion and belief. The European institutions can do great service to the cause of Human Rights, including the fundamental human right to belief and the practice of religion, by such unbiased reporting such as the one we request.

Therefore, we suggest that European institutions should:

- Report on the state of fundamental religious freedoms of beliefs within the countries of the EU relating to the discrimination based on religion or belief, hate speech, discriminatory legislation, Islamophobia, anti-Semitism, and so forth.
- Publish a separate report on the situation on religious freedom or belief outside the EU. 184 Advancing Freedom of Religion or Belief for All

14. For more CEC advocacy papers, see CEC, "Human Rights."
15. Council of the European Union, "EU Guidelines."

- Encourage high standards and implementation of human rights in respect of the treatment of migrants and asylum seekers.[16]

In another conference, the focus was put on religious minorities living in European societies, specifically those characterised by being culturally and religiously diversified societies. The conclusions from the conference included:

> Minorities can often be subject to unequal treatment in European states and societies. This applies particularly to minorities of an ethnic, national, linguistic or religious character, being in a non-dominant position in society and state. . . . Aware of the part religion has played and still plays in situations of conflict, and conscious of our responsibility as churches towards peaceful coexistence of different communities in our societies, this consultation of the Conference of European Churches and partners asks the European institutions and their members/participating states to assume, in accordance with their obligations under law, the responsibility for:
>
> - preventing and punishing hate crimes and breaking the cycle of violence, also seeking cooperation with civil society, churches, and religious communities
> - producing a report about the state of rights of minorities
> - implementing all pertinent legislation protecting the status and rights of minorities
> - ensuring conditions that enable individuals and groups to co-exist in diversity, and creating a positive climate for the expression of pluralism, tolerance, and respect as corner stones of democratic societies promoting ongoing dialogue between majorities and minorities, so as to form a common basis of ideals and values for convenience in our pluralistic and diverse societies"[17]

The year 2018 was a "European Year of Cultural Heritage" and celebrated on local, regional, and national level as well as by the EU and the rest of Europe. This gave the CEC an opportunity to organize a conference in order to discuss crucial topics related to holy sites and places of worship. In focus were Europe and the Middle East, not least among the issues under consideration was the destruction of holy sites and the prevention for worshipers from celebrating in their traditional settings. The final communique of the

16. CEC, "Final Statement."
17. CEC, "Communique of the Consultation."

conference was endorsed by the CEC Governing Board calling all members, as well as other churches and religious or belief communities in Europe and the Middle East, to:

- seek the spirit of peace and understanding, and a common understanding in particular, on the handling of such sites that are of religious or spiritual significance to more than one denomination. This applies to religious engagement as well;

- engage in dialogue on how religious actors can raise political awareness together about the importance of these sites, while forestalling a politicisation of religious sites in conflicts;

- join in common action to defend each other's rights. This includes taking a stand on minority concerns.[18]

This was followed by directly urging both the EU member states and the European institutions to co-operate with other international actors in order to:

- use the upcoming European Year of Cultural Heritage 2018 to increase their efforts to ensure respect and protection for places of worship and holy sites. This should be reflected both in EU law, its Common Foreign and Security Policy; and in the law of other countries in Europe and the Middle East;

- work towards a comprehensive international framework of legal protection, building on a better understanding of the fundamental right to Freedom of Religion or Belief, including a common definition of such places and sites, as well as legal solutions to ensure proper implementation. In particular, religious communities must be able to acquire or build, own and administer, maintain or restore, and access and use such places.[19]

In May 2017, the Council of Europe issued a Convention on Offences Relating to Cultural Property. The CEC considered the convention so important that it urged the member states of the Council of Europe to sign the convention. But it went further in relation to other countries:

> It also urges non-member-states who participated in its elaboration, and any other country who wants to fight against illicit trafficking and the destruction of cultural property, as an

---

18. CEC, "Governing Board Meeting."
19. CEC, "Governing Board Meeting."

integral part of the fight against terrorism and organized crime to do the same.[20]

CEC RESPONSE TO THE SITUATIONS ON FREEDOM OF RELIGION OF RELIEF

After receiving a request from the CEC member churches, the CEC developed a strategy on how to help churches to handle violations against human rights, including freedom of religion or belief, in order to find justice.

One of the latest cases where the CEC has been involved has to do with Mr. Peter Steudtner, a Lutheran peace activist from the Berlin-Brandenburg Church in the the Evangelical Church in Germany (EKD). He was arrested in Turkey on July 2, 2017 while attending a Human Rights Training with Amnesty International, in which he participated in his professional capacity as an IT expert. Mr. Steudtner is an active member of the Berlin-Brandenburg Church in the EKD, and he has a longstanding reputation as an expert on peace issues, having committed all his life to non-violent conflict resolution, on which he has also given a lot of training. Moreover, he is an expert on peace issues working with the Church, with Bread for the World and the INformation, KOordination, TAgungen (INKOTA)[21] network (which was founded by the Protestant church in the former socialist republic in Eastern Germany). He is not an expert on Turkey and has not had any relations to the Turkish Human Rights movement prior to the meeting during which he was arrested together with the head of the Turkish section of Amnesty International and several other human rights experts. Hence, it is remarkable that he is being charged with supporting terrorism in Turkey.[22] What we can see is that these states are using the excuse of "terrorism" and "extremism" to limit religious freedom.

Another case relates to Pastor Rev. Francisco Manzanas Martin, a Spanish citizen (born in 1926), who lives and works in Barcelona. On March 26, 2010, he submitted an application to the European Human Rights Court in Strasbourg. He complained to the ECHR that the Spanish state refused "to pay him a retirement pension" which "was in breach of the principle of non-discrimination enshrined in article 14 of the Convention in conjunction with article 9 of the Convention and article 1 of protocol no. 1" according to which it was assumed that the "Spanish law treated evangelical ministers in a different and discriminatory manner compared to Catholic

---

20. Conference of European Churches, "Governing Board Meeting."
21. INKOTA, "Together for a Just World."
22. Rev. Dr. Patrick Roger Schnabel mail correspondence on the case.

priests in respect of pensions."[23] During his ministry he received a salary from the Evangelical Church.[24] The Conference of European churches was engaged in this case via channels of the Council of Europe and bringing this case to the Member Churches of the CEC in order to create solidarity for remaining pastors who are in the same, or a similar, situation in Spain. The European Human Rights Court concluded that there is different treatment of the applicant based on religious freedom or belief in the cases of protestant pastors as related to the treatment received by catholic priests: "in so far as the applicant has no means of having his years of pastoral service as an Evangelical minister before such ministers were included in the Social Security scheme taken into account for the purpose of a retirement pension."[25]

Another example is that in order to help communities coming together after the war in the Western Balkans region, the Conference of European Churches during Holy Week (April 2017) invited 20 young adults of the Serbian minority in Croatia and of the Croatian minority in Serbia to visit the European institutions. The programme included several mediation sessions which were facilitated by the Quaker Council for European Affairs. The youth from Serbia and Croatia sent a very strong message that they get along very well together, but many difficulties arose from the political authorities in both countries as a result of this engagement. During the war in the Western Balkans ethnicity and religion were mixed. In practice it means that one had 3 options: being Serbian Orthodox, Croatian Catholic, Bosnian Muslim-Bosniak. The young people saw the reasons for this backlash as the inability of the political elite to create positive and strong economic ties in the South-Eastern European region and better possibilities for foreign investments in both countries.[26]

CONCLUSION

Work on human rights, including freedom of religion or belief, is needed in Europe since the region faces growing tensions including nationalistic intolerance and extremism. Such work concerns the protection of the human dignity of all people throughout Europe. A focus on freedom of religion or belief is an important component in the human rights bill. This focus is increasing among European institutions. This gives strength to the European churches and the CEC in collaboration with other actors to let their voices

23. Manzanas Martín v. Spain.

24. Heras, "Spain."

25. Heras, "Spain."

26. CEC, "Young Serbs and Croats." If you would like to learn more about this case, see CEC, "Standing up for Minority Rights."

be heard in the public sphere in order to promote, and protect, the human rights. Yet these challenges persist in Europe and more research and work is needed. It could be claimed that European churches are committed to work on these issues and help those who are the most vulnerable to find justice and peace.

BIBLIOGRAPHY

Arnold, Victoria. "Jehovah's Witnesses Banned, Property Confiscated." *Forum 18*, April 20, 2017. Online. http://www.forum18.org/archive.php?article_id=2274.

Council of European Union. "EU Guidelines on the Promotion and Protection of Freedom of Religion or Belief." June 24, 2013. Online. https://eeas.europa.eu/sites/eeas/files/137585.pdf.

Conference of European Churches (CEC). "Final Statement: Theological School of Halki, Hebeyliada Island, Turkey." September 9, 2015. Online. http://www.ceceurope.org/wp-content/uploads/2015/09/Statement_Halki_9_Sept_15.pdf.

————. "Governing Board Meeting." Press Release 17/43. November 27, 2017. Online. https://www.ceceurope.org/5352-2.

————. "Human Rights." Online. https://www.ceceurope.org/human-rights.

————. "Islamic Prayers Take Place at Historic Hagia Sophia." Press Release 17/24. June 22, 2017. Online. https://www.ceceurope.org/islamic-prayers-take-place-at-historic-hagia-sophia.

————. "Religious Minorities as Part of Culturally Diverse Societies." October 2016. Online. http://www.ceceurope.org/wp-content/uploads/2016/10/Statement-Final-Religious-Minorities-2016.pdf.

————. "Standing up for Minority Rights." October 23, 2017. Online. http://www.ceceurope.org/standing-up-for-minority-rights.

————. "Young Serbs and Croats in Brussels: 'We Had Enough.'" Press Release 17/15. April 18, 2017. Online. https://www.ceceurope.org/young-serbs-and-croats-in-brussels-said-we-had-enough.

Demosthenous, D. *The Occupied Church of Cyprus*. Nicosia: Byzantine Academy, 2001.

Heras, Alfredo Abad, et al. "Spain: Discrimination against Evangelical Pastors in the State Pension Scheme." In *Religious Diversity in Europe and the Rights of Religious Minorities*, edited by Elizabeta Kitanovic and Patrick Roger Schnabel, 73–86. Geneva: Globethics.net, 2019.

"His Holiness Patriarch Kirill Sends Letters to Heads of Normandy Four States, Primates of Local Orthodox Churches, Pope Francis, UN Secretary-General, and WCC General Secretary Concerning Anti-Church Bills Due to Be Adopted by Verkhovna Rada of Ukraine." *Reor Strasbourg*, May 17, 2017. Online. http://strasbourg-reor.org/?topicid=1259.

INKOTA. "Together for a Just World." Online. https://www.inkota.de/english/#c9717.

Kitanovic, Elizabeta, ed. *European Churches Engaging in Human Rights*. Brussels: Church and Society Commission of CEC, 2012.

Miltiadou, Miltos, et al., eds. *Windows on Cyprus*. Nicosia: Press and Information Office, 2010.

Serbian Orthodox Church. "Communique Regarding the Pogrom in Kosovo and Metohija on March 17, 2004 and 10-years of the NATO Bombing." *Office of the Holy Synod of*

Bishops, March 16, 2009. Online. http://www.spc.rs/eng/communique_regarding_pogrom_kosovo_and_metohija_march_17_2004_and_10years_nato_bombing.

Serbian Orthodox Diocese of Raska-Prizren and Kosovo-Metohija. http://www.eparhija-prizren.com/sr/vesti/u-vreme-vaskrsnjih-praznika-nepoznati-napadaci-porazbijali-stakla-na-hramu-sv-petra-i-pavla-u.

United Nations. "Minorities under International Law." Online. https://www.ohchr.org/EN/Issues/Minorities/Pages/internationallaw.aspx.

Yildirim, Mine. "Freedom of Religion or Belief in Turkey—Need for a Principled Approach." In *Advancing Freedom of Religion or Belief for All: Contributions from the Conference 6–9 September 2015, Halki, Istanbul, Turkey*, edited by Elizabeta Kitanovic and Aimilianos Bogiannou, 81–88. Geneva: Globethics.net, 2016.

Court Cases

Case of Manzanas Martín v. Spain. (17966/10), European Court of Human Rights. April 3, 2012.

15

Freedom of Religion in Swedish Schools?

MARIA KLASSON SUNDIN

In early June, on the last day of the school year, when the lilacs are in full bloom in most of the country, many Swedish schools gather their pupils and teachers in the local church building for the graduation ceremony. The headmaster or headmistress of the school or the local parish priest will give a speech, one or two traditional hymns and some summer songs will be sung, maybe some of the classes will perform a song or recite a poem. After the final hymn, *Den blomstertid nu kommer* [*The Time of Blossoming Is Coming*], the summer vacation begins.

This tradition goes back to the time when the local Church board was responsible for primary education and social care in the local community. In 1842, when primary school was made compulsory for Swedish children, the Church of Sweden was a state church and confessional instruction in the Christian faith a central part of the curriculum.[1] There was no clear separation between civil and church authorities when it came to school matters. When the local parish priest led the ceremony, he was there both as pastor of the local parish and as chairperson of the school board. Today, when the Church of Sweden no longer is a state church[2] and the Swedish society

1. Algotsson, *Från katekestvång*, 29.
2. In the year 2000, the relations between Church and state went through a major change. The Church of Sweden is no longer a state church, but still has a special position among the religious communities, since it is by law obliged to cover the whole country

is more multicultural, this traditional setting for the graduation ceremony is questioned. Every year, the local and national newspapers print opinion pieces on whether or not schools should hold their graduation ceremonies in church. Is the ceremony to be seen as a valuable or at least harmless part of the Swedish cultural heritage or as religious indoctrination and forced religious practice? The intense debate has led the Swedish National Agency for Education to issue guidelines, which state that the ceremony, if held in a church, should "focus on traditions, solemn atmosphere and fellow-ship." Traditional hymns may be sung, but the ceremony must not include prayers, preaching or any blessing, but should be strictly non-confessional.[3] This non-confessionality is also demanded from the so-called religious free schools (faith-based schools). These schools are often run by religious de-nominations or groups associated with a specific religious tradition. In 1991, a law was passed, making it possible for schools run by private enterprises or groups to be approved for funding through the tax system.[4] Since then the number of "free schools" has increased. These schools are, however, not allowed to give religious instruction in their teaching, but have to adhere to the same regulations as the municipal schools in their teaching. They may—outside of the lessons—hold a morning prayer or something similar, but the school children must be free to choose whether or not to participate.[5] In the public debate on the graduation ceremony in church and on religious free schools, the concept of religious freedom is under discussion: How is the graduation ceremony to be evaluated in relation to children's freedom of religion? Are religious free schools protecting or violating the right of children to freedom of religion?

In this chapter, I want to set the Swedish debate on religion in schools in relation to the United Nation's *Convention of the Rights of the Child* (CRC)[6] and different ways of interpreting its article 14 on religious free-dom. I will start by giving a few examples of arguments from the public debate for and against religious free schools and having the graduation ceremony in a church building with or without contributions from a priest. Then I will take a look at the article on religious freedom in the CRC and what space there may be for the different arguments. After that, I will pres-ent three models for thinking about children's freedom of religion and relate

---

with its work. See Karnov Group. "Kyrkolagen."

3. *Skol- och förskoleverksamhet.*

4. *Förordning om statsbidrag.*

5. Karnov Group, "Skollagen" 1.6–7.

6. United Nations, "Convention on the Rights of the Child."

them to the debate. My hope is that these models will contribute to a better understanding of the different positions in the debate.

THE PUBLIC DEBATE ON RELIGIOUS FREEDOM IN SWEDISH SCHOOLS

There are many arguments in the debate on religious free schools. Many of them deal with the fact that some of these free schools are run by religious minority groups with cultural values that differ from the majority culture in Sweden. Issues of segregation and integration, equality or discrimination for girls etc. are frequent. In this chapter I will leave most of these aspects aside and just bring up a few examples from the debate with explicit relevance for views on freedom of religion for children.

Among those who are *negative* towards free schools, these schools are often seen as places for religious indoctrination.[7] Religious free schools are also seen as places where children are isolated from encountering people with other religious traditions and world views than their own, which is problematic in a multicultural society.[8] Another line of argument claims that religion is a private matter, which should be kept from the common public space that a school is. For some, religion is in itself seen as contradicting a democratic society, which must be secular in its basic structure:

> Religion is a private matter and everyone may believe in whatever they like and practice their religion as they choose. But religious indoctrination must not exist in public places like the schools of the country. Here we must have strict rules such as phasing out of free schools with a religious message and to stop mandatory graduation ceremonies in the Church of Sweden.[9]

Some see a direct conflict between children's right to freedom of religion and the right of the parents to make choices about their education:

> The Swedish state is accepting that children are forced to live their whole childhood according to religious codes decided by parents and religious community. The child's right to development and knowledge, to have its own opinions and values are destroyed when they are forced to education strongly shaped by religion, in the home or at religious free schools. . . . It is high time that society unconditionally side with the children

7. The translation of the quotes from the debate is my own. See Ulvaeus, "Gud finns inte"; Fjelkner, "Förbjud friskolor"; Melki et al., "Religiös friskola ett svek."

8. See Avci and Svensson, "Vi behöver förbud."

9. Holtzer et al., "Valet borde trots allt vara lätt."

and stand up for a school and education founded on secular principles. Children should not . . . have to submit to the faith of their parents. Children's rights have to be more important than religion. That is freedom of religion—for the children.[10]

As religious belonging should build on an active choice of religion by the individual, this means that a child should be assured of freedom from religion in mandatory contexts outside of the home, i.e., in school. There is a conflict of aims in the conventions, where the right of parents stands against the right of the children. Since the UNCRC is a part of international law, but cannot be brought to an international court, it is of extra importance that it is interpreted in a way that guarantees freedom from religious and political indoctrination.[11]

Those who argue in favor of religious free schools do not see a conflict between the right of parents to choose education and the religious freedom of their children. Rather, they see religious free schools as a natural thing in a society with freedom of religion:

We need to see religion as an asset in our important integration work, and help people to be a part of the western free society, with their faith. A good dialogue and cooperation with confessional free schools may be a forceful tool against exclusion and segregation. Religion is also one of the strongest forces in the transmission of sound values. It is about time that we see it as an asset and not as a threat. A freedom worth defending.[12]

They are also critical against the talk of indoctrination and say that this is a part of the prejudice against religion that the debate on religious free schools is full of.[13] Instead of seeing religion as something that children should have freedom from, they claim the right of children to have access to religion:

Existential questions do not . . . turn up when someone becomes an adult. They are a part of the natural horizon of humans all through life, not least when they are children. These questions cannot be silenced. The child needs to see itself through the views of different people, also the religious, and focus lies

---

10. Qaraee, "Strikt religiös tro."
11. Fjelkner, "Förbjud friskolor."
12. Olofsgård and Ekström, "Religiösa skolor."
13. Sandlund, "De som vill förbjuda."

rather on maturity, empathy and integrity than on what faith you have—or don't have.[14]

Some of the arguments for and against graduation ceremonies in church are similar. They focus on the role of the state in a multicultural society and on the role of religion in the public space. The Minister for Education, Anna Ekström, wants school to be a neutral place in regard to religion. At the same time, it can still use traditions with their roots in religion as long as there is no explicitly confessional part that pupils are forced to take part in:

> We social democrats want the pupils' freedom to form their own convictions and future to be a priority. No pupil should ever have to be exposed to religious indoctrination by the head master, teachers or other school personnel. The Swedish school should be a place for openness, democracy and knowledge, where different opinions—whether they be political or religious—will be seen from different angles, questioned and challenged. We have no problems when pupils of their own free will pray, confess their faith or in other ways practice their religion in schools. But we don't think that school should arrange confessions of faith or religious practice for the pupils. . . . School should be a neutral place and not opt for any particular religion or faith. This doesn't mean that solemn ceremonies, that have been an important part of the Swedish school for a long time, suddenly shall be turned away. On the contrary, it is important that school cherishes traditions, even those that used to have religious connotations but today are a part of our common cultural heritage.[15]

Others say that the graduation ceremony should not be held in church, and especially not contain any "confessional elements." Some argue that religion has no place in school, others that the graduation ceremony needs to be accessible to all pupils:

> Nylander says that participation in the graduation ceremony should be "voluntary." This is deeply cynical. The problem is not whether half of the school wants something else, but if there are a few pupils, Jews, Muslims, secular humanists or others, who do not want to participate in a Christian confessional ceremony. Will those children have to stand up and say that they are not comfortable with the planned graduation ceremony? Will they not be able to participate in one of the few celebrations that the school has together? And this in a time of growing

14. Brandström and Nyberg, "Ulvaeus strider mot religionsfriheten."
15. Ekström, "Eleverna får visst."

anti-Semitism and islamophobia? Talking about "voluntary" is lacking in respect for the multicultural Sweden.[16]

In the debate, there are different views of how the freedom of religion of children is to be expressed in school. Now we turn to the international conventions and what guidance they can give in the matter.

THE RIGHTS OF THE CHILD—AND OF ITS PARENTS

The *Convention of the Rights of the Child* (CRC) is a game changer in the way it views children's rights. In the 1924 *Geneva Declaration of the League of Nations*, the child is mainly seen as a recipient of protection and social welfare and the focus of the declaration lies on the responsibilities of adults to protect and provide for children in order to fulfil their basic needs and possibilities for development.[17] This is repeated in the *UN Declaration on the Rights of the Child* from 1959.

In the CRC, the child, defined as "every human being under the age of eighteen years unless under the law applicable to the child, majority is attained earlier"[18] is not only a passive recipient but an active subject in exercising its own rights and a participant in decision-making regarding its life. It is the responsibility of adults to protect and respect the child's own rights and (partial) autonomy. There are four agents with different roles in relation to the rights of the child. The child itself is the first agent. As a member of the human family, it has inherent dignity and equal and inalienable rights.[19] These rights are not only received, they are exercised by the child, even though it may need guidance and support to do this.[20]

The parents are the next agent. Article 5 states that they have the rights and duties to

> provide, in a manner consistent with the evolving capacities of the child, appropriate direction and guidance in the exercise by the child of the rights recognized in the present Convention.

As we can see in this article, the right to give guidance and direction is not unrestricted: it has to be "appropriate" and it needs to take into account the "evolving capacities" of the child. The child is growing and maturing and

16. Sturmark, "Fel att blanda in präster."
17. Marshall, "Construction of Children," 137.
18. UN, "Declaration of the Rights of the Child" art. 1.
19. UN, "Declaration of the Rights of the Child" preamble.
20. UN, "Declaration of the Rights of the Child" art. 5.

will be able to take more responsibility for its life and decisions the older it gets.[21]

The third agent is the cultural group the child belongs to. In article 30, the convention explicitly mentions minority groups based on ethnicity, religion or language:

> In those States in which ethnic, religious or linguistic minorities or persons of indigenous origin exist, a child belonging to such a minority or who is indigenous shall not be denied the right, in community with other members of his or her group, to enjoy his or her own culture, to profess and practice his or her own religion, or to use his or her own language.

The group is not described as active in relation to the rights of the child in the same way as the parents. They are bearers of culture and important for the child's identity and sense of belonging. The child professes and practices "in community with" other members of the group, but the professing and practice is the child's own.

So, we have the child with rights of its own, exercising them in accordance with its evolving capacities, the parents who raise, protect, guide and love the child and the (minority) group that offers an environment of language, cultural practices and traditions. The fourth agent is the state, which through ratifying the convention has taken on the task to guarantee, protect, acknowledge, safeguard and respect the rights of the child. This is to be undertaken through legal and administrative means and by building systems of social welfare and education. In all decisions and actions concerning children, the "best interest" of the child should be a primary consideration.[22] What this means in practice is a matter of interpretation and many conflicts in the area of children's rights come down to different views on what is good for children. With four different agents, we may have four different views. There may also be cultural differences that influence different interpretations. In the World Values Survey, which researches value changes over time in countries all over the globe, Sweden scores high on individualistic and secularised approaches and there is less appreciation for traditional values and authorities.[23] This may be one component in the different views on religion in school.

---

21. Lansdown, *Evolving Capacities*.
22. UN "Convention on the Rights of the Child" art. 3.
23. World Values Survey, "Findings and Insights."

CHILDREN AND FREEDOM OF RELIGION

Article 14 in the CRC, on freedom of thought, conscience and religion has been controversial from the beginning. It has the highest number of reservations and comments by states that have ratified the convention and its legislative history reveals that it almost made some countries leave the negotiations leading up to the present wording of the convention.[24]

Before the CRC, the freedom of religion of children was mainly defined as a right of the parents. In the "International Covenant on Economic, Social, and Cultural Rights," parents are given the right to choose the education of their children:

> The States Parties to the present Covenant undertake to have respect for the liberty of parents and, when applicable, legal guardians to choose for their children schools, other than those established by the public authorities, which conform to such minimum educational standards as may be laid down or approved by the State and to ensure the religious and moral education of their children in conformity with their own convictions.[25]

This should, however, not primarily be understood as the right of the parents as opposed to the right of the child. Rather, it is the right of the parents against state indoctrination of children.[26] Even so, there is no mentioning of the child as subject of the right in question.

On this point, the CRC is more explicit. Article 14 states:

1. States Parties shall respect the right of the child to freedom of thought, conscience and religion.

2. States Parties shall respect the rights and duties of the parents and, when applicable, legal guardians, to provide direction to the child in the exercise of his or her right in a manner consistent with the evolving capacities of the child.

3. Freedom to manifest one's religion or beliefs may be subject only to such limitations as are prescribed by law and are necessary to protect public safety, order, health or morals, or the fundamental rights and freedoms of others.

In the wording of this article, the right is the child's own and it is to be exercised with support and direction from its parents "in a manner consistent

---

24. Van Bueren, *International Law*, 155.

25. UN, "International Covenant (Economical)" art. 3:3.

26. Van Bueren, *International Law*, 159.

with the evolving capacities of the child" in the same way that was stated in article 5.

"PROFESS AND PRACTICE"

The CRC, unlike earlier conventions, does not define freedom of religion. The UN committee on the rights of the child uses the definition in the International Covenant on Civil and Political Rights (ICCPR), when it assesses the way the state parties fulfil their responsibilities in the CRC. This definition includes

> freedom to have or to adopt a religion or belief of his choice, and freedom, either individually or in community with others and in public or private, to manifest his religion or belief in worship, observance, practice and teaching.[27]

The ICCPR also states that "no one shall be subject to coercion which would impair his freedom to have or to adopt a religion or belief of his choice."[28]

In the legal applications of this right, a distinction is made between *forum internum*: the right to have or change religion or belief and *forum externum*: the right to manifest your religion or belief through outer actions, individually as well as collectively. *Forum internum* is thus seen as an inner freedom with focus on beliefs and religious affiliation. It is non-negotiable, while *forum externum* may be limited under certain specific circumstances, stated in article 18:3.[29] Even if freedom of religion is defined in a way that makes it both about inner convictions and outer practices, there is still a lot of room for interpretation. A major factor in this interpretation is the conception of religion. What is it that this freedom is supposed to protect?

RELIGION AS BELIEF, PRAXIS, AND IDENTITY

There are many ways to define and understand what religion is.[30] Different conceptualisations will have different consequences for how the child's exercising of its freedom of religion will be understood and what capacities that need to evolve for the child to be able to take over responsibility for this exercising from the parents.[31] Here, I will use a categorization by T. Jeremy

---

27. UN, "International Covenant (Civil)" art. 18:1.

28. UN, "International Covenant (Civil)" art. 18:2.

29. Taylor, *Freedom of Religion*, 24–114.

30. See, e.g., Smith, *Meaning and End*; Schilbrack, *Philosophy*.

31. I have previously discussed these issues in Klasson Sundin, "Barnets religionsfrihet"; *Barnets religionsfrihet*.

Gunn, who has studied how the concept of religion is used in international law.[32]

The first dimension is *religion as faith or belief*. Some definitions of religion focus on the theoretical, cognitive aspects of the individual's belief and convictions. Religion is mainly seen as the intellectual affirmation of certain confessional statements. This means that religion will be seen as something close to a philosophy or ideology, composed of thoughts and ideas. To exercise your freedom of religion according to this dimension is to be able to think and believe what you want and to be able to make choices between different religious convictions or world views. The ability to make these choices is dependent on the cognitive capacity and maturity of the individual, which makes children less competent in this dimension until this capacity has evolved to a level where they can make autonomous and well-founded choices.

The next of Gunn's dimensions is *religion as way of life*. It includes actions of different kinds: traditions, rites and observance as well as ethical and lifestyle choices. Here, religion is more about what you do than what you think. It is possible to practice religion without having accepted any beliefs in the form of truth claims. Freedom of religion becomes more focused on making it possible for the individual to perform actions and live their lives in certain ways. This makes it possible for children to exercise their freedom of religion without having to wait until their intellectual capacities are fully grown. They can participate in communal rites and make choices about how and if they want to participate.

The third dimension is *religion as identity*. This dimension focuses on the problem-solving and meaning-making aspects of religion, which are identity building. Religion in this dimension has to do with the interpretation of the big existential questions of life, as well as with the affective aspects relating to experience. This dimension of religion gives children of all ages the possibility of being seen as subjects in exercising their freedom of religion, as long as the problem-solving is not purely abstract and theoretical, but centerd round the possibility and encouragement to ask and engage with questions in a way that contributes to meaning-making. The understanding of the child's right to freedom of religion also includes assessing the child's "evolving capacities" in relation to the issue of autonomy and the right of the parents to guide the child and an understanding of the responsibilities of state and family in protecting the rights of the child.[33]

32. Gunn, "Complexity of Religion."

33. I will not go deeper into these issues here, but refer to my doctoral thesis, where I have dealt with them. See Klasson Sundin, "Barnets religionsfrihet." It includes a summary in English.

THREE MODELS FOR THE RELIGIOUS
FREEDOM OF THE CHILD

In order to understand the debate on children's religious freedom better, I have developed three different models of thought that conceptualise the freedom of religion of the child in quite different ways. The models are based on different understandings of religion, the responsibility of the state and the parents respectively and the balance between the child's autonomy and the parents' right to guide the child. They are not to be seen as the only possible ways of conceptualizing freedom of religion for children, but it is my hope that they can bring some clarity to the understanding of the differences in viewing these issues.

The first model is the *Tradition-model.* According to this model, the freedom of religion of the child is first of all the right to take part in the religious and cultural traditions of the parents. This model conceptualizes religion as praxis. Freedom of religion is about things like prayer, going to the place of worship, fasting, wearing certain kinds of clothes, celebrating feasts and holidays and other kinds of observance and actions. This model focuses on the parental right to raise their child in their own tradition and claims that the state shall not limit this right without very good reasons. This understanding of the child's freedom of religion stresses belonging to a community more than being an independent individual. It sees the evolving autonomy of the child as a matter of growing in responsibilities in continuity with the tradition to which the child belongs.

The second model, the *Liberty-of-thought-model,* sees the freedom of religion of the child as the right of the individual to choose a worldview. Religion is conceptualised in terms of belief, as different systems of ideas. Freedom of religion is seen as freedom of thought in religious matters and stresses the right to make decisions on what to believe and how to practice. Since the right is the right of the individual child, both parents and state need to be neutral and not actively influence the child. Children are to be protected from coercion and indoctrination. There is more focus on the individual than on the community and the evolving autonomy of the child is thought of in terms of growing independence and individual decision-making.

The third model, the *Life-interpretation-model* sees children's freedom of religion as their right to search for meaning in relation to existential issues in life. Religion is conceptualised as identity and meaning-making. In order for the child to have access to forms and arenas for this problem-solving, both parents and state should promote and facilitate the exercising of the right. This means an interplay between the individual and the community.

The child's evolving autonomy mainly consists in being recognized as a subject in interaction with its environment. Now it is time to see whether these models can shed some light on the debate.

APPLYING THE THREE MODELS TO THE DEBATE ON RELIGION IN SCHOOLS

Many of the arguments *for* religious free schools belong in the Tradition-model. They see these schools as a help for the parents in raising their children in their own tradition and stress belonging to a religious (or non-religious) community more than the individual's right to make choices. According to this model, religion is more like a language that you start to learn early, and school is a natural place for that learning. Some of the arguments for religious free schools also belong in the Life-interpretation model, where both parents and school need to support children with the tools and arenas that they need to grapple with existential questions.

Most of the arguments *against* religious free schools belong in the Freedom-of-thought-model. Here, putting children in religious free schools is seen as coercion and indoctrination preventing them from making their own choices in religious matters. Schools should be neutral, which is often understood as actively non-religious, and parents should refrain from restricting their children's abilities to make choices. In the debate on holding graduation ceremonies in church buildings, the arguments against this often belong in the Freedom-of-thought-model. Most of the arguments pro ceremonies in church also belong in this model, since they claim that these ceremonies are not religious practice or proclamation. Instead, the ceremony is seen as a part of the Swedish cultural heritage that is no longer religious. The definition of religion they have in mind is not based on practice, but on intellectual acceptance of religious truth claims.[34] Most likely, the Freedom-of-thought-model is the most common in Sweden, where the World Values Survey has shown Sweden to be more shaped by individualistic and secular-rational values than every other country in the world.[35]

FINAL REFLECTIONS

The European Court on Human Rights gives the signatory countries of the European Convention on Human Rights a certain *margin of appreciation* when applying the convention to their own national context.[36] In this

34. See Elisabeth Gerle's chapter in this book.

35. World Values Survey, "Findings and Insights."

36. Brems, "Article 14"; "Reconciling Universality." See also Göran Gunner's chapter

margin of appreciation, it is accepted that cultural views and practices are allowed to influence the interpretation of the rights in question.

In the field of freedom of religion, there is a risk that this interpretation will not be religiously neutral. We know that different religious traditions stress different aspects of religious faith and practice. The protestant Lutheran tradition that has shaped Swedish tradition has had a strong focus on faith, often conceived as propositional truths, where, e.g., memorizing the Catechism word by word was the main focus of religious instruction both in schools and in church. This tradition is also suspicious against religious practices that may be seen as not relying on God's grace, but instead wanting to gain merits to achieve salvation. A cultural tradition shaped by these confessional aspects will have difficulties in understanding the importance and function of praxis in, e.g., Judaism, Islam, and the Catholic and Orthodox Churches.[37] This tradition also shapes a secular understanding of religion that guides the actions of state authorities such as the Swedish National Agency of Education. There is a strong risk that children and parents from other religious traditions than Protestant Christianity will have difficulties in getting the understanding and recognition that the CRC presupposes.

In Sweden, many who are strong supporters of human rights have an understanding of religion as undemocratic and dangerous to children, as we have seen in the debate. The struggle for religious freedom in this country was a struggle against the State Church and for the religious choices of the individual, which has shaped the discourse on religion. So these human rights activists may not have freedom of religion for children high on their agenda. Others, who belong to minority groups that would benefit from a strong standing for the freedom of religion in society are not comfortable with "human rights language," especially in relation to children, since they find it too individualistic. This means that they may not speak up for themselves and their children in the debate on religious freedom. In this situation, we need to go deeper in our discussions on religion in schools to be able to agree on fair and reasonable ways of putting children's right to freedom of religion into practice.

---

in this book.

37. See Elisabeth Gerle's chapter in this book.

BIBLIOGRAPHY

Algotsson, Karl-Göran. *Från katekestvång till religionsfrihet: Debatten om religionsundervisningen i skolan under 1900-talet.* Stockholm: Rabén & Sjögren, 1975.

Avci, Gulan, and Frida Svensson. "Vi behöver förbud mot alla religiösa friskolor." *Aftonbladet,* November 17, 2017. Online. https://www.aftonbladet.se/debatt/a/dgoMz/vi-behover-forbud-mot-alla-religiosa-friskolor.

Brandström, Lars, and Bo Nyberg. "Ulvaeus strider mot religionsfriheten." *Svenska Dagbladet,* November 14, 2009. Online. https://www.svd.se/ulvaeus-strider-mot-religionsfriheten.

Brems, Eva. *Article 14: The Right to Freedom of Thought, Conscience, and Religion.* Vol. 14 of *A Commentary on the United Nations Convention on the Rights of the Child.* Edited by André Alen, et al. Leiden: Martinus Nijhoff, 2006.

———. "Reconciling Universality and Diversity in International Human Rights: A Theoretical and Methodological Framework and Its Application in the Context of Islam." *Human Rights Review* 3.1 (2004) 5–21.

Ekström, Anna. "Eleverna får visst fira sommarlov i kyrkan." *Aftonbladet,* June 26, 2017. Online. https://www.aftonbladet.se/debatt/a/lq3LL/eleverna-far-visst-fira-sommarlov-i-kyrkan.

Fjelkner, Metta "Förbjud friskolor som står på religiös grund." *Dagens Nyheter,* April 16, 2006. Online. https://www.dn.se/debatt/forbjud-friskolor-som-star-pa-religios-grund.

Förordning om statsbidrag m.m. till fristående skolor. SFS 1991:1079. Online. https://www.riksdagen.se/sv/dokument-lagar/dokument/svensk-forfattningssamling/forordning-19911079-om-statsbidrag-m-m-till_sfs-1991-1079.

Gunn, T. Jeremy. "The Complexity of Religion and the Definition of 'Religion' in International Law." *Harvard Human Rights Journal* 16 (2003) 189–215.

Holtzer, Gerhard, et al. "Valet borde trots allt vara lätt." *Västerbottens-Kuriren,* April 22, 2006.

Karnov Group. "Kyrkolagen." *Lag (1998:1591) om Svenska kyrkan,* November 26, 1998. Online. https://open.karnovgroup.se/kyrkoratt/SFS1998-1591.

———. "Skollagen." *Skollag (2010:800),* July 6, 2010. Online. https://open.karnovgroup.se/utbildning/skollagen.

Klasson Sundin, Maria. "Barnets religionsfrihet—eller föräldrarnas?" In *Frihet och gränser: Filosofiska perspektiv på religionsfrihet och tolerans,* edited by Johan Modée and Hugo Strandberg, 115–38. Stockholm/Stehag: Symposion, 2006.

———. *Barnets religionsfrihet—en villkorad rättighet?: En filosofisk undersökning utifrån FN:s barnkonvention.* Uppsala Studies in Philosophy of Religion. Uppsala: Acta Universitatis Upsaliensis, 2016.

Lansdown, Gerison. *The Evolving Capacities of the Child.* Florence: UNICEF, 2005.

League of Nations. "Geneva Declaration of the Rights of the Child." September 26, 1924. Online. http://cpd.org.rs/wp-content/uploads/2017/11/01_-_Declaration_of_Geneva_1924.pdf.

Marshall, Dominique. "The Construction of Children as an Object of International Relations: The Declaration of Children's Rights and the Child Welfare Committee of League of Nations, 1900–1924." *International Journal of Children's Rights* 7 (1999) 103–147.

Melki, Aphram, et al. "Religiös friskola ett svek." *Dagens Nyheter*, June 3, 2009. Online. https://www.dn.se/debatt/religios-friskola-ett-svek.

Olofsgård, Jakob, and Anna Ekström. "Religiösa skolor är en tillgång—inte ett hot." *Svenska Dagbladet*, March 21, 2017. Online. https://www.svd.se/religiosa-skolor-ar-en-tillgang--inte-ett-hot.

Qaraee, Leila. "Strikt religiös tro ska inte påverka barnen." *Svenska Dagbladet*, November 11, 2012. Online. https://www.svd.se/strikt-religios-tro-ska-inte-paverka-barnen.

Sandlund, Elisabeth. "De som vill förbjuda religiösa friskolor har uppförsbacke." *Dagen*, April 4, 2017. Online. https://www.dagen.se/ledare/elisabeth-sandlund-de-som-vill-forbjuda-religiosa-friskolor-har-uppforsbacke-1.950023.

Schilbrack, Kevin. *Philosophy and the Study of Religions: A Manifesto*. Wiley Blackwell Manifestos. Chichester: Wiley Blackwell, 2014.

"Skol- och förskoleverksamhet i kyrkan eller annan religiös lokal." *Skolverket*, October 18, 2012. Online. https://www.skolverket.se/download/18.6011fe5 01629fd150a27845/1529062314683/Skolan%20och%20kyrkan%20121016_ granskad121018.pdf.

Smith, Wilfred Cantwell. *The Meaning and End of Religion: A New Approach to the Religious Traditions of Mankind*. New York: Macmillan, 1963.

Sturmark, Christer. "Fel att blanda in präster i skolavslutningar." *Svenska Dagbladet*, February 5, 2015. Online. https://www.svd.se/fel-att-blanda-in-praster-i-skolavslutningar.

Taylor, Paul M. *Freedom of Religion: UN and European Human Rights Law and Practice*. Cambridge: Cambridge University Press, 2005.

Ulvaeus, Björn. "Gud finns inte—njut av livet." *Svenska Dagbladet*, January 13, 2009. Online. https://www.svd.se/gud-finns-inte--njut-av-livet.

United Nations. "The Convention on the Rights of the Child." November 20, 1989. Online. http://www.ohchr.org/EN/ProfessionalInterest/Pages/CRC.aspx.

———. "Declaration of the Rights of the Child." November 20, 1959. Online. https://www.ohchr.org/EN/Issues/Education/Training/Compilation/Pages/1Declaration oftheRightsoftheChild(1959).aspx.

———. "International Covenant on Civil and Political Rights." December 16, 1966. Online. http://www.ohchr.org/EN/ProfessionalInterest/Pages/CCPR.aspx.

———. "International Covenant on Economical, Social, and Cultural Rights." December 16, 1966. Online. https://www.ohchr.org/en/professionalinterest/ pages/cescr.aspx.

Van Bueren, Geraldine. *The International Law on the Rights of the Child*. Dortrecht: Nijhoff, 1998.

World Values Survey. "Findings and Insights." Online. http://www.worldvaluessurvey. org/WVSContents.jsp.